בס"ד

BOOK 1

יהדות Yahadus

BOOK 1

The Sarah Rohr
YAHADUS CURRICULUM
Book One

Published by
LIVING LESSONS
1375 Coney Island Avenue #207
Brooklyn, New York 11230
347-709-8660
www.livinglessons.com

Information & Orders:
347-709-8660 • info@livinglessons.com

ISBN: 978-1-935949-05-3

Printed in China

The Living Lessons Yahadus Curriculum

carries the name and pays tribute to the memory of

Mrs. Sarah (Charlotte) Rohr (née Kastner) ע"ה
מרת שרה בת ר' יקותיאל יהודה ע"ה

Born in Mukachevo, Czechoslovakia to an illustrious Chassidic family,
she survived the fires of the Shoah to become the elegant and gracious
matriarch, first in Colombia and later in the United States, of generations
of a family nurtured by her love and unstinting devotion. She found grace
in the eyes of all those whose lives she touched and merited to see all her
children build lives enriched by faithful commitment to the spreading of
Torah and *ahavat Israel*.

Dedicated with love

by

The Rohr Family

New York City

CONTENTS

CONTENTS

INTRODUCTION

Welcome to the first volume of the **Living Lessons Yahadus Curriculum!**

Torah is different from any other subject. Torah is not just a subject which we study and memorize so we can pass a test; Hashem's Torah and mitzvos are our life! Living with Torah and mitzvos is what it means to live as a Jew! This curriculum will help you discover how every part of the Torah applies to you, even during these modern times.

Since following Hashem's Torah and mitzvos is the most important thing you can do, great effort was taken to make the material interesting and easy for you to learn and enjoy.

This curriculum will *iy"h* give those who study it a broad knowledge of every mitzvah in the Torah! There will be a total of five books, one to be studied during each of five years, starting in fourth grade and completing the curriculum in eighth grade.

It will be a fascinating five year journey which will leave you with a familiarity in every aspect of the Torah and its mitzvos.

How it works

There were many different way of how the 613 mitzvos of the Torah were organized. The Rambam organized all the mitzvos into 83 subjects, and grouped these subjects into fourteen different *sefarim*.

This curriculum follows the Rambam's order, and has broken down the 83 subjects into many smaller "units." A unit sometimes contains just one mitzvah and sometimes it is a group of two or more mitzvos.

For example, there is a *mitzvas asei* to create a *kiddush Hashem* and a *mitzvas lo sa'aseh* not to create a *chillul Hashem*. These two *mitzvos* are in one unit – a unit on the topic of *kiddush Hashem*.

Each mitzvah is so rich and has many more details than can be expected to be learned in a curriculum that is touching on every part of the Torah. **The goal of this curriculum is for you to learn the main details of each mitzvah and how to live with the mitzvah in your life.**

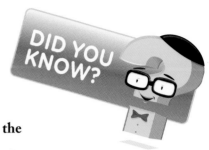

Each unit will also have lots of other interesting information relating to the mitzvah, for example, some words of wisdom from *Chazal*, stories and biographies of *Gedolei Yisrael*, historical facts and much more.

This first book contains 45 units which includes 86 mitzvos from the Torah, and two *mitzvos miderabanan.* They are all the mitzvos from the Rambam's first two *sefarim* called סֵפֶר מַדָּע and סֵפֶר אַהֲבָה which mean the "Book of Knowledge" and the "Book of Love."

Sefer Mada contains the *mitzvos* which are the very foundation of the Torah such as believing in Hashem, being a good person, learning Torah, distancing from *avodah zarah*, and doing *teshuvah*.

Sefer Ahavah contains the mitzvos which help us remember about and love Hashem, including reading *shema*, *davening*, wearing *tefillin* and *tzitzis*, and *bris milah*.

Just imagine, after learning this first book, you will already know so much about 86 mitzvos!

The books are yours to treasure for life.

LEARN IT!
KEEP IT!
LIVE IT!

UNIT 1

IN THIS UNIT YOU WILL:

EXPLORE

- Why do we have to believe that everything comes from Hashem?
- Why do all mitzvos depend on the mitzvos in this unit?

EXAMINE

- What is special about the mitzvos in this unit?
- What can a person do to show that he believes in Hashem?

EXTRACT

- Who is watching your every move?
- Which words would you use to show that you believe in Hashem?

בִּטָחוֹן
אֱמוּנַת ה'

KEY CONCEPTS

Book: Madda, Section: Foundations of the Torah

סֵפֶר מַדָּע הִלְכוֹת יְסוֹדֵי הַתּוֹרָה

אֱמוּנַת ה'

BELIEVING IN HASHEM

שָׁלֹשׁ מִצְוֹת

Look for a moment at the castle. Look closely at all its details: the towers, the doors, the windows, and the brickwork. Could this castle have built itself? Impossible! You never met the builder, but you know that someone talented built it, down to the very last detail.

אָנֹכִי

The letter א was upset. "It's so unfair!" it said. "Why should the Torah start with the letter ב? I am the first letter! The Torah should start with me!"

Hashem answered, "Do not worry; when I give the *Aseres Hadibros* to My people, I will begin with the letter *alef!*"[1]

HISTORY

First Things First

Since these mitzvos are so important, they were said by Hashem Himself to all the Jewish people at *Matan Torah!*

When Hashem spoke these words, the whole world stood still in anticipation and respect. Birds didn't chirp, and leaves didn't rustle.

Although there were close to three million people there, each person felt that Hashem was speaking to him or her alone.[2]

The Mitzvos

The unit of *Emunas Hashem* has three mitzvos.

1. Know there is a Hashem
2. Do not believe that there are other gods
3. Believe that there is only one Hashem

MITZVAH 1

לֵידַע שֶׁיֵּשׁ שֵׁם אֱלוֹקָה
Knowing that there is a G-d

אָנֹכִי ה' אֱלֹקֶיךָ אֲשֶׁר הוֹצֵאתִיךָ מֵאֶרֶץ מִצְרַיִם מִבֵּית עֲבָדִים
(שמות כ, ב)

I am Hashem your G-d, Who brought you out of the land of Egypt, from the house of slavery.

Believe and know that there is a G-d.

 ALL PEOPLE   ALL PLACES   ALL TIMES

MITZVAH 2

שֶׁלֹּא יַעֲלֶה בְּמַחֲשָׁבָה שֶׁיֵּשׁ שֵׁם אֱלוֹקָה זוּלָתִי ה'
Not thinking that there is a god other than Hashem

לֹא יִהְיֶה לְךָ אֱלֹקִים אֲחֵרִים עַל פָּנָי
(שמות כ, ג)

You shall have no other gods before Me.

Do not believe that there is any god other than Hashem.

 ALL PEOPLE   ALL PLACES   ALL TIMES   NO PUNISHMENT

MITZVAH 3

לְיַחֲדוֹ
Knowing the oneness of Hashem

שְׁמַע יִשְׂרָאֵל ה' אֱלֹקֵינוּ ה' אֶחָד
(דברים ו, ד)

Hear, O Israel: **Hashem is our G-d, Hashem is one**

Believe and know that Hashem is the only G-d.

ALL PEOPLE   ALL PLACES   ALL TIMES

DID YOU KNOW?

Believe

The Rambam established the "Thirteen Rules of Faith." Every Jew must believe in these thirteen rules.

The first four rules come from these three mitzvos of *Emunas Hashem*.

Mitzvah Messages

EXPLORE

It Can't Happen By Itself

You've never seen Hashem, but does that really mean He's not here? You've probably never met the builder of your house either, but you know that he's around somewhere, and you are grateful to him for building your home.

We think of Hashem, the master Builder of the entire world, in the same way. We can't see Him, but He is here and He created you and everything that is in this world. [3]

With My Own Eyes

Even though your physical eyes have never seen Hashem, there is one part of every person which **has** seen Hashem. We each have a *neshamah*, which is part of Hashem, so there is a part of Hashem in each of us.

Not only did all of *B'nei Yisrael* who stood at *Har Sinai* actually see Hashem with their eyes, but every *neshamah* that has existed, and will ever exist, was there and also saw Hashem. If you saw Hashem with your own eyes, how could you not believe in Him?

CHECKPOINT Why do we believe that Hashem exists?

PEARLS *of wisdom*

An Accidental Painting?

A Rabbi and an *apikores*, (someone who does not believe in Hashem) were having an argument. The *apikores* told the Rabbi to prove that Hashem exists and that He created everything. The Rabbi pointed to a painting on the wall and asked, "Who painted that picture?"

The *apikores* responded, "Why, a painter of course. Who else could have done it?"

The Rabbi answered, "What if I were to tell you that some bottles of paint accidentally spilled and created this beautiful picture?"

"That would be impossible," said the *apikores*.

"Aha," said the Rabbi... [4]

Always Switched On

Most mitzvos are only done at certain times, by certain people, or in certain places. There are six mitzvos which are called מִצְוֹת תְּמִדִיוֹת - "constant mitzvos." These mitzvos must be done always!

1. אֱמוּנַת ה׳ — Believing in Hashem.

2. לֹא יִהְיֶה לְךָ — Not believing in any other god.

3. אַחְדוּת ה׳ — Believing that Hashem is the only G-d.

4. אַהֲבַת ה׳ — Loving Hashem.

5. יִרְאַת ה׳ — Fearing Hashem.

6. לֹא תָתוּרוּ —Not following anything that will bring you further away from Hashem.[3]

DISCOVERY

Not So Simple

The world has so many details. Even things which seem so small and simple, really have so many details helping it exist and survive.

For example, a flower. Every single part of the flower is needed for the flower to live. The roots suck up water and nutrients from the ground, and the leaves let it breathe. The color and smell attracts insects who are able to spread the pollen and make new flowers.

Could a system as complicated as this happen by itself?

Details

Basis For All Mitzvos

Every mitzvah in the Torah comes from the mitzvah of believing in Hashem. How is this so?

If you believe that Hashem is the G-d over the world, then you must follow His rules and keep His commandments. Part of the mitzvah of *emunah* is believing that Hashem is in charge of the world, and we have to keep all of His laws, the mitzvos.[5]

What Makes These Mitzvos Different?

The three mitzvos in this unit are special in two ways.

1. מִצְוָה שֶׁבְּמַחֲשָׁבָה - These mitzvos are only done in your mind, not with an action.

2. מִצְוָה תְמִדִיוֹת - These mitzvos must be done at all times.

An *Aveirah* Without a Punishment?

The *aveirah* of believing in other gods is only done in the mind. An *aveirah* like this is called a לָאו שֶׁאֵין בּוֹ מַעֲשֶׂה - an *aveirah* that has no action. This kind of *aveirah* is not punishable by *Beis Din*.[6]

However, one who says that there is no Hashem or that there is something else besides Hashem is considered a *min* (a non-believer) and they lose their portion in *Olam Habba*.[7]

Non-Jews

Non-Jews are also required to fulfill the mitzvah of not believing in any other god. It is part of the שֶׁבַע מִצְוֹת בְּנֵי נֹחַ - the seven mitzvos that all people are required to keep.[8]

CHECKPOINT   What is special about the mitzvos of *emunas Hashem*?

SELECTED HALACHOS

When you say *shema*, you must have in mind that Hashem is the only G-d. How can you think about this? Every letter in the word *echad* should be said slowly, with these thoughts:

א: The *gematria* of *aleph* is one, and Hashem in the one ruler over the entire world.

ח: The *gematria* of *ches* is eight, and Hashem is the one G-d over the seven heavens and one earth.

ד: The *gematria* of *daled* is four, and Hashem is the one G-d over everything in the four directions.⁹

Since these thoughts are so important, be careful to say the word "*echad*" slowly. The *aleph* should be said normally, the *ches* a little more slowly, and the *daled* very slowly.¹⁰

OUR SAGES SAY...

כָּל הַמַּאֲרִיךְ בְּאֶחָד מַאֲרִיכִין לוֹ יָמָיו וּשְׁנוֹתָיו

Someone who says the word "echad" in shema slowly and remembers that Hashem is the **only** G-d, will have a long life.¹²

A STORY

Looking for G-d

As a small child, *Avraham Avinu* was troubled with the question of who created this wonderful world. He looked at the sun, mighty and powerful in the sky.

"Surely," he thought, "since the sun is so big and powerful, bringing light and warmth to the world, it must be the creator." But at night, the sun set and the moon came out. To Avraham, the moon seemed to be more powerful than the sun. He decided that the moon was the creator and not the sun. Then came morning, and the moon was gone.

Avraham continued his search for a creator, trying many things and giving up on all of them when he realized how limited their power was. Finally, he realized that there was an unseen Creator, Who is **always** present and Who creates and directs **everything** in the world we live in. In fact, the sun, moon, and the entire world is not something that exists separately which He must control; they are all Hashem's powers, and the entire world is part of Hashem.¹¹

DID YOU KNOW?

Hashem is Here, Hashem is There

The top of the letter זז (as written in a *Sefer Torah*) points upwards. This teaches us that the seven heavens and the earth point **up** to Hashem and should help us see how great Hashem is.¹³

It's Just Me in Here

Hashem told *B'nei Yisrael*, "I created everything in this world as a pair. I created heaven and earth, the sun and the moon, a husband and a wife, this world and the World to Come.

But as for Me, I am the only One and there is no other."[14]

PEARLS
of wisdom

Always Re-creating

The *Ba'al Shem Tov* explained that the *passuk*, לְעוֹלָם ה' דְּבָרְךָ נִצָּב בַּשָּׁמָיִם - "Your words are forever standing in the heavens," means that the words which Hashem used to create the world are being used again and again so that the world can stay in existence.[15]

EXTEND YOUR KNOWLEDGE

Think Good and it Will Be Good

According to the Rambam, it is a mitzvah not to be scared of the enemy when you are going out to war. You must have complete faith that Hashem will save you from the hands of the enemy.[16]

Rabbeinu Yonah explains this even more, and teaches us that we shouldn't ever be afraid when we are in trouble, because Hashem can always save us.[17]

There is one difficulty with this. We know that Hashem punishes us and rewards us based on our actions. What if we do *aveiros* and don't deserve to be saved? Should we be scared then?

Hashem does not only protect us because of our actions. Just by having complete trust in Hashem, we deserve to get the "reward" of being saved!

Live The Mitzvah
EXTRACT

Hashem is Always Here and Watching

When we know that someone is watching us, we are very careful to only do the right thing. We know that Hashem exists and that He sees and knows everything, so of course we are going to be on our best behavior at all times!

Also, when someone is watching us we feel more safe. Since we know that Hashem is always watching us, we also feel safe and know that He will protect us wherever we are.

 CHECKPOINT How can *emunas Hashem* make us feel safe?

What Else Comes From This?
EXTRACT

Who is in Charge?

We know that Hashem controls everything that happens, since He is the only G-d.

Mentioning Hashem's Control

Since we know that something can only happen with Hashem's help, when we are planning something, we say בְּעֶזְרַת ה' - with Hashem's help, or אִם יִרְצֶה ה' - if Hashem wants. We also make sure to thank Hashem after something happens by saying בָּרוּךְ ה' - Hashem is blessed.[18]

בִּטָּחוֹן - **Trust in Hashem**

We know that everything comes from Hashem, and we know that Hashem is only good. Therefore, we know that everything that Hashem does is for the best. Sometimes, we don't see how something that happens can be good, but when we remember that Hashem will only help us, we can be calm even if a situation seems terrible.

CHECKPOINT   How can you use your words to show that you know that Hashem controls the world?

A STORY

Never Suffer

A man once came to R' Dovber, the *Maggid of Mezritch*, with a question. "The *Gemara* says that 'A person is supposed to bless Hashem for bad things just as he blesses Him for good things.' How is this humanly possible? How can a person be as grateful for his troubles as he is for his joys?"

R' DovBer replied: "To find an answer to your question, you must go see my student, R' Zusha of Anipoli. Only he can help you in this matter."

He travelled to R' Zusha, who received him warmly, and invited him to make himself at home. The visitor decided to watch R' Zusha for a while to see if he can figure out the answer to his question without explaining why he had come. R' Zusha was extremely poor, there was never enough to eat in his home, and some of his family members were sick. He couldn't think of anyone who suffered more hardship in his life than R' Zusha did. Yet R' Zusha was always cheerful, and constantly thanking Hashem for all His kindness.

But what was his secret? How does he do it? The visitor finally decided to ask his question. He said to his host: "Our Rebbe advised me to come here so that you can help me with an answer."

'What is your question?' asked R' Zusha.

The visitor repeated what he had asked of the *Maggid*; and said that the *Rebbe* had sent him to learn the answer from R' Zusha.

R' Zusha looked at him in surprise, "Why did our *Rebbe* send you to **me**? How would I know? He should have sent you to someone who suffers. I have no suffering in my life..."

The guest understood why the *Maggid* had sent him. R' Zusha accepted everything in his life with such faith in Hashem, that he didn't even feel any suffering! This was the lesson he was to learn.

UNIT 1

I'm Getting You Out of This

When someone is *niftar* and they go up to *Shamayim*, Hashem will ask him, "Did you wait eagerly for *Mashiach* to come?" The person might say, "But I didn't know that I had to! Where does it say in the Torah that I have to wait for *Mashiach* to come?"

The Sma"k says, that when Hashem told us "*Anochi Hashem*," He said, "I am Hashem who took you out of Mitzrayim."

Included in this mitzvah is the mitzvah of knowing that just as Hashem saved us from the *galus* in Mitzrayim, Hashem will save us from any other *galus*, such as the one we are in now.

We have a mitzvah to believe that Hashem will send *Mashiach*, and to wait for him excitedly![19]

ENDNOTES:

1. בראשית רבה א, י
2. שמות רבה פרשה כח-כט
3. החינוך בהקדמתו "הערת המחבר"
4. חובת הלבבות שער היחוד פ"ו. ראה אוצר המדרשים אייזנשטיין ע' 583
5. חדא"ג מהרש"א מכות כג, ב ד"ה תרי"ג
6. רמב"ם הל' סנהדרין פי"ח ה"ב
7. רמב"ם הל' תשובה פ"ג ה"ו-ז'

8. רמב"ם הל' מלכים ריש פ"ט
9. ב"י או"ח סי' ס"א ד"ה וצריך להאריך
10. מג"א סי' ס"א ס"ק ה' בשם מגדל עוז על הרמב"ם
11. רמב"ם ריש הל' ע"ז
12. ברכות יג, ב
13. שו"ע או"ח סי' ס"א ס"ו
14. דברים רבה ב, לא

15. אגרא דכלה בראשית א, כב ד"ה עוד יתפרש
16. סה"מ ל"ת נ"ח
17. שערי תשובה שער ג' אות ל"ב
18. של"ה שער האותיות אות אמונה
19. סמ"ק מצוה א'

UNIT 2

IN THIS UNIT YOU WILL:

EXPLORE

- Why is it important to do Hashem's mitzvos with love?

- Why is it important for other people to see and feel our love for Hashem?

EXAMINE

- What makes a person love Hashem?

- What are the three ways in which we have to love Hashem?

EXTRACT

- How can you help other people love Hashem?

- How can you love Hashem in the best possible way?

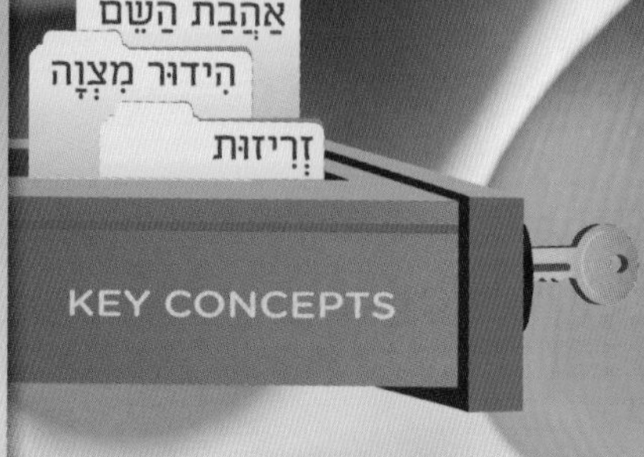

אַהֲבַת הַשֵּׁם

הִידוּר מִצְוָה

זְרִיזוּת

KEY CONCEPTS

Book: Madda, Section: Foundations of the Torah

סֵפֶר מַדָּע הִלְכוֹת יְסוֹדֵי הַתּוֹרָה

אַהֲבַת ה'
LOVING HASHEM

מִצְוָה אַחַת

Picture your favorite person in the world, the one you know so well, and love so much. If that person would ask you for a favor, how would you feel?

Out of Range

Most birds carry their babies with their feet so that no other birds can fly down and grab the baby. Eagles, however, fly higher than any other bird and do not need to worry that their babies will be grabbed. Eagles carry their babies on their backs so that an arrow shot from below won't hurt the baby.

When Hashem took us out of Mitzrayim, He carried us like an eagle carries her babies, protecting us and loving us as a mother loves her child. When we think about how much He loves us, it is easy to love Him back.[1]

DID YOU KNOW?

Can't Forget

The source of this mitzvah is in the *parshah* of *shema*. It is such an important mitzvah that we are reminded of it at least three times a day!

We say the *shema* in the morning and twice at night, and the *pessukim* of *shema* are in a *mezuzah*, and in both the *tefillin shel rosh* and the *tefillin shel yad*.

The Mitzvah

EXAMINE

The unit of *Ahavas Hashem* has one mitzvah.

You must love Hashem with your all heart, with all your soul, and with all of your abilities.[2]

MITZVAH
4

מִצְוַת אַהֲבַת ה'
Loving Hashem

וְאָהַבְתָּ אֵת ה' אֱלֹקֶיךָ בְּכָל לְבָבְךָ וּבְכָל נַפְשְׁךָ וּבְכָל מְאֹדֶךָ
(דברים ו, ה)

You shall love Hashem your G-d with all your heart and all your soul and all your abilities.

Love Hashem.

ALL PEOPLE   ALL PLACES   ALL TIMES

Mitzvah Messages

EXPLORE

Labor of Love

Children love their parents more than anyone else in the world. This is because parents do so much for them. They buy food, clothing and toys, and give them a lot of love. It is therefore only natural that children love their parents in return and want to please them. Children happily do what their parents ask of them, and give it their best shot. No job is too difficult or too boring to do for a parent.

We feel the same way about Hashem, who is our Father. Out of His love for us, He gives us everything, starting from our very life. In return, we happily do Hashem's mitzvos with love and care. Through your love for Hashem, a mitzvah becomes meaningful and exciting, and is no longer just something that has to be gotten over and done with.

CHECKPOINT How hard would you work to help somebody you love? What about somebody who hurts you?

Details

EXAMINE

Felt in the Heart

Have you ever felt so excited to do something or see someone that your heart felt like it was going to burst? The mitzvah to love Hashem is a mitzvah that must actually be felt in the physical heart.[3]

Constantly

The mitzvah to love Hashem is one of the six מִצְווֹת תְּמִדִיּוֹת - "constant mitzvos" that everyone must do at all times.

Even in Hard Times

The *passuk* says "וְאָהַבְתָּ אֵת ה' אֱלֹקֶיךָ.... בְּכָל מְאֹדֶךָ" – "*You shall love Hashem... with all your abilities.*" The word מְאֹדֶךָ can also mean מִידָה - measures (what you are given). Therefore, the *passuk* can be read as: "*You shall love Hashem.... with all your measures.*"

DID YOU KNOW?

Love that Kills

A famous example of strong love for Hashem is the story of Nadav and Avihu, the sons of Aharon who were killed by Hashem.

There is one explanation that the sons died because they did not listen to Hashem's instructions about bringing *korbanos*.

A deeper explanation is that their love for Hashem was so strong that their *neshamos* left their bodies and flew right up to Hashem.

Even though this is a very high level of love, the Torah calls it a "strange fire," because Hashem wants us to stay in this world to accomplish our mission.[4]

OUR SAGES SAY...

I'm a Better Person

A *"same'ach beyisurin"* is someone who is happy even when he is in pain or is going through a difficult time. He knows that everything Hashem does is good, so of course he will be happy!

People who love Hashem so much that they are even happy when they are in pain will get to feel the *Shechinah* like the blazing sun when *Mashiach* comes![5]

PEARLS
of wisdom

You're Worth It

"Ya'akov worked seven years to be able to marry Rochel, but they seemed to him like a few days because he loved her so much."

The *meforshim* ask: Shouldn't it have been the other way around? Since Ya'akov loved Rochel so much, seven years should have seemed like a very, very long time. How did it feel like a few days?

The *passuk* is not telling us that Yaakov didn't mind waiting. Rather, he knew how special Rochel was, and he was willing to work even for seven years for something that he loved.

When you love someone very deeply, no work is too hard to do for that person.[6]

DID YOU KNOW?

Hashem's Children

Hashem tells us many times that we are like His children, and He loves us like a parent loves his child.

Here are just a few examples :

בָּנִים אַתֶּם לַה' אֱלוֹקֵיכֶם (דברים יד, א)

בְּנִי בְכֹרִי יִשְׂרָאֵל (שמות ד, כב)

אָהַבְתִּי אֶתְכֶם אָמַר ה' (מלאכי א, ב)

Therefore, loving Hashem is connected with loving our fellow Jew. Hashem is our Father. If you love the Father, you love His children too!

This means that you have a mitzvah to love Hashem, no matter what He gives you. If Hashem gives you pain or happiness, you must love Him anyway.[7]

It should be easy to love Hashem, but sometimes, it's really hard. Something which seems terrible might happen to someone, and that person might wonder, "Why is Hashem doing this to me?" When that happens, it can be very difficult to feel love towards Hashem, and it takes a special extra effort to love Him.

Here are two thoughts which can help you love Hashem all of the time.

1. All that Hashem does is for the good. It might not be possible to see this right away, and sometimes you may never see it, but Hashem knows what He is doing and will only do what is good for us.

2. People may be in pain to erase their *aveiros* so that they can start over again with a clean slate. Hashem only made them have pain to help them get rid of their *aveiros* and become closer to Him.[8]

CHECKPOINT How could something that seems bad really be good for you?

A STORY

Accept with Love

R' Meir of Premishlan's daughter became sick on *Sukkos*, and by *Simchas Torah*, she was close to death.

As always, R' Meir was dancing joyously with the Torah, while he cried to Hashem: "Master of the universe! You commanded us to blow the *shofar* on *Rosh Hashanah*, and Meir'l blew. You commanded us to fast on *Yom Kippur* and Meir'l fasted. You commanded us to live in the *sukkah* and Meir'l did so. You commanded us to be happy on *Simchas Torah* and Meir'l is happy. You've caused my daughter to be sick and we are commanded to accept trouble with joy, Meir'l is therefore accepting this with joy.

"But, Master of the world, isn't there a *halachah* that says, 'One may not mix one joy with another.' How can I be happy with the Torah and with accepting my daughter's illness at the same time?!'"

Immediately after asking Hashem that question, news came from his home that his daughter's fever had gone down, and she recovered.[9]

EXTEND YOUR KNOWLEDGE

Two Forms of Love

There are two kinds of love that people feel.

1. When you **enjoy** something very much, you get a lot of **pleasure** from it, like food, games, and having friends. Since people love themselves, they love whatever makes them feel good. If something doesn't feel good anymore, you most probably won't love it anymore.

2. A **natural** love that you have for your parents, siblings, or children. This kind of love is a much higher level of love than the first. It never stops and will never change.

Children feel both kinds of love for their parents, because parents give their children what they want and need, and also just because children naturally love their parents.

In the same way, we love Hashem with both these types of love, because Hashem gives us everything that we need, and because Hashem is our Father and we are His children.[10]

OUR SAGES SAY...

Loving Example

וְאָהַבְתָּ - שֶׁיִּהְיֶה שֵׁם שָׁמַיִם אָהוּב עַל יָדְךָ

The *passuk* says, "And you shall love Hashem." This can be explained to mean "People should love Hashem because of you."

When people see a Jew who behaves nicely, and is honest and caring, they will think, "How special the Torah must be, if it trained such a special People." They too will begin to love Hashem and His Torah.[11]

Live the Mitzvah

EXTRACT

Bringing Others to Love Hashem

When we love someone or something, we make sure everyone else knows all about it. We want them to share in what makes us happy. This was what happened to *Avraham Avinu*. When he found Hashem, he loved Hashem so much that he spread the message far and wide, inviting other people to learn about Hashem and love Him also.

We can also help other people serve Hashem, so that they can see how special it is to know, believe, and love Hashem. When people see how we carry out Hashem's will with a loving and joyful attitude, they will be inspired to learn more about Hashem and His Torah, and will come to love Hashem as well.

 How can your love for Hashem change the way another person thinks?

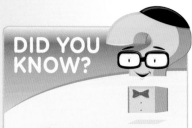

Show Me the Way

וְאָהַבְתָּ = הָאָבוֹת

The word וְאָהַבְתָּ from *shema* has the same letters as הָאָבוֹת. We learn about love for Hashem from the way in which the *Avos* loved Hashem:

בְּכָל לְבָבְךָ – This refers to *Avraham Avinu*, who served Hashem with much love. The *passuk* tells us that וּמָצָאתָ: "אֶת לְבָבוֹ נֶאֱמָן לְפָנֶיךָ" *"And You (Hashem) found his heart to be true to You."*

בְּכָל נַפְשְׁךָ – This refers to *Yitzchak Avinu*, who was ready to sacrifice his life (his soul) to Hashem at the *akeidah*.

בְּכָל מְאֹדֶךָ – This refers to *Ya'akov Avinu*, who gave one-tenth of his money to Hashem. The *Chachamim* explain that מְאֹדֶךָ can also mean מָמוֹנְךָ-your money. [12]

OUR SAGES SAY...

A Little Love Goes a Long Way

R' Shimon ben Elazar says: "Someone who serves Hashem out of love is greater than someone who serves Him out of fear."

"A person who serves Hashem out of fear is rewarded for one thousand generations, but someone who serves Hashem out of love is rewarded for **two** thousand generations!"[13]

Putting in That Extra Effort

When we love Hashem, nothing is too big, small or difficult to do for His sake. And the sooner the job can be done, the better!

Avraham Avinu's behavior when he was asked to sacrifice his only son was an example of *Ahavas Hashem*. We can learn from Avraham a very important way to show our *Ahavas Hashem*.

זְרִיזוּת – Eagerness

As a wealthy and respected person, Avraham could have asked his servants to prepare his donkey for him on the morning that he went to the *akeidah*. Instead, he was so excited to do what Hashem wanted that he woke up very early and saddled his donkey himself. Not a moment was wasted.

Avraham loved Hashem and was excited to do what Hashem asked. He was an example of זְרִיזִין מַקְדִּימִין לְמִצְווֹת – eager people do a mitzvah as soon as possible.[14]

הִידוּר מִצְוָה – Beautifying a Mitzvah

Another special way to show Hashem how much we love Him is by making sure that each mitzvah we do is done perfectly and beautifully. We don't try to take the easy way out and just do the basic mitzvah! We want to show Hashem that we love Him so much, we will make His mitzvos beautiful. There are many examples of this in our lives.

On *Sukkos*, we buy the most **beautiful** *esrog*, and on *Shabbos*, we wear **beautiful** clothing and use the most precious silver and dishes at our table.

When we love Hashem, we look for the best way to do a mitzvah, and certainly don't take any shortcuts![15]

 CHECKPOINT What are two special ways we can do mitzvos with love?

A STORY

A Full *Shul*

Once the *Ba'al Shem Tov* and his *chassidim* were on a journey when they passed an empty *shul* and decided to *daven minchah* there.

Just as the *Ba'al Shem Tov* was about to step into the *shul*, he stopped and would not cross the doorstep of the *shul*. His *chassidim* were very confused and wondered at his strange behavior. One of them was finally brave enough to ask the *Ba'al Shem Tov* why he would not enter the *shul*.

The *Ba'al Shem Tov* replied, "There is no room to go in because it is so crowded." His *chassidim* were shocked because the *shul* was empty!

The *Ba'al Shem Tov* explained, "When somebody *davens* with *kavanah*, his *tefillos* go straight up to Hashem. If someone *davens* without *kavanah*, his *tefillos* just stay in the room and do not go up. I can tell that the people who once *davened* here had no *kavanah*. Their *tefillos* had no wings and so they never went up. Now, the *shul* is so tightly packed with those *tefillos* that there is no room for us."[16]

Like a Bird

תּוֹרָה וּמִצְוָה בְּלָא דְחִילוּ וּרְחִימוּ לָא
יְכִילַת לְסָלְקָא וּלְמֵיקַם קֳדָם ה'

"Torah and mitzvos without love and fear cannot go up and stand before Hashem."

Yiras Hashem and *Ahavas Hashem* are like wings. Wings enable the bird to lift its body off the ground and soar into the sky. Without its wings, the bird would never be able to fly, as its body is too heavy.

Without love and fear of Hashem, mitzvos are heavy and burdensome. Love and fear for Hashem make the mitzvos we do full of life, and help them "soar" up to Him.[17]

PEARLS *of wisdom*

Pay to Lose

There was once a Jew called Shmuel who lived in a town next to a major highway in Russia. Often, Jewish travellers would stop at his home and Shmuel would always change the linen and prepare the guest room himself.

A friend, noticing him hard at work preparing for his guests, asked, "Why don't you hire someone for a few coins to set up the guest bedroom?"

Shmuel looked at him in surprise, "What? Not only I should lose out on the mitzvah, but I should **pay** someone to take it away from me?!"

UNIT 2

ENDNOTES:

1. רש"י שמות יט, ד ד"ה על כנפי נשרים
2. רמב"ם הל' תשובה פ"י ה"ו
3. ספר הערכים כרך א' ע' ער
4. אוה"ח ויקרא טז, א ד"ה וכל זה
5. שבת פח, ב
6. ספורנו בראשית כט, כ
7. ברכות נד, א

8. עי' רד"ק תהלים לג, ד
9. סיפורי חסידים - מועדים
10. מחקרי אבות ע' 132
11. יומא פו, א
12. ילקוט שמעוני רמז תתל"ז. ועי' ספר רוקח הל' חסידות שורש אהבת השם
13. סוטה לא, א

14. יומא כח, ב
15. סנהדרין קה, ב
16. באר משה, פרשת נ
17. תיקוני זוהר תקונא עשיראה כה, ב

UNIT 3

IN THIS UNIT YOU WILL:

EXPLORE

- Why does fearing Hashem help us do mitzvos?

EXAMINE

- What happens to a person who fears Hashem?

EXTRACT

- If a person wants to feel that Hashem is there every minute, what should he do?

כְּסוּי רֹאשׁ
יִרְאַת ה'

KEY CONCEPTS

Book: Madda, Section: Foundations of the Torah

סֵפֶר מַדָּע הִלְכוֹת יְסוֹדֵי הַתּוֹרָה

יִרְאַת ה׳
FEARING HASHEM

מִצְוָה אַחַת

Have you ever really wanted to do something that you know you should not do? What stopped you from doing it? Did you stop because you knew how embarrassing it would be if someone found out? Were you afraid of the punishment?

DISCOVERY

Watching Everywhere

Have you ever seen the security office in a building? Video cameras can record every movement and every sound we make. This makes it possible for a person in one place to watch and even listen to many places at once.

This technology helps us understand that Hashem can see, listen and know everything that happens... everywhere!

The Mitzvah

The unit of *Yiras Hashem* has one mitzvah.

You must fear Hashem.

MITZVAH
5

מִצְוַת יְרְאַת ה'
Fearing Hashem

אֶת ה' אֱלֹקֶיךָ תִּירָא אֹתוֹ תַעֲבֹד וּבוֹ תִדְבָּק וּבִשְׁמוֹ תִּשָּׁבֵעַ
(דברים י, כ)

You shall fear Hashem, you shall serve Him, and you shall cling to Him, and you shall swear with His name.

Fear Hashem.

 ALL PEOPLE   ALL PLACES   ALL TIMES

Hashem is Always Watching

If your principal was watching your classroom through a video camera one day, would you behave differently than you normally do? Of course! When we remember that Hashem is **always** watching, it will help us always act properly. Since He is watching, we are not only afraid of the punishment for doing an *aveirah*, we are also embarrassed to do something that He told us not to do. *Yiras Hashem*, being afraid of Hashem, helps us to keep all the mitzvos at all times.

CHECKPOINT   How does fearing Hashem help us stay away from *aveiros*?

Constantly

This mitzvah is one of the six *mitzvos temidiyos* that everyone must perform at all times.

Respect for the Mitzvos

Not only does fearing Hashem help prevent you from doing *aveiros*, it also helps you do all the mitzvos. There is a *passuk* which says, "Serve Hashem with fear." We learn from this that everything we do for Hashem, even positive mitzvos, should be done with fear and respect.[1]

STORY

Always in Mind

The famous brothers R' Elimelech of Lyzhensk and R' Zusha of Anipoli were once traveling with some of their *talmidim*. When night fell, they stopped at an inn where R' Elimelech, tired from the day's journey, went to sleep.

When it was time to go, R' Zusha and some of the *talmidim* went to wake up R' Elimelech. Instead of shaking R' Elimelech or calling his name, R' Zusha simply covered the *mezuzah* on the door of R' Elimelech's room with his hand, and R' Elimelech awoke at once.

The *talmidim* were amazed, and asked R' Zusha to explain what they had seen. What connection was there between a *mezuzah* and sleep?

R' Zusha replied, "Every person must constantly keep Hashem in mind to fulfill the *passuk* that says שִׁוִּיתִי ה' לְנֶגְדִּי תָמִיד—'I have placed Hashem in front of me always.' When you sleep and cannot always be thinking about Hashem, you must rely on the Name of Hashem that is written on the outside of the *mezuzah*. Therefore, when I covered Hashem's Name with my hand, my brother could no longer sleep, and he had to wake up immediately so that he could think about Hashem and have Hashem before him."

The *talmidim* realized that R' Elimelech was no ordinary person and continued to learn from his extraordinary ways.[2]

Fight or Flight

When your body is scared, it will react right away. There are two ways that your body might choose to deal with whatever you are scared of. Either your body will decide to fight what you are afraid of, or you will want to run away. For both of these, your heart starts to beat faster and send more blood to your muscles and brain. You will breathe much faster to send more oxygen to your body.

This is how Hashem designed your body to give you the energy you need to save yourself if something scary happens.

DID YOU KNOW?

The Whole Point

Shlomo Hamelech was the wisest of all people to ever live. He knew the special importance of *Yiras Shamayim*. That's why he ended both the *sefarim* of *Koheles* and *Mishlei* with a *passuk* that tells us how important *Yiras Shamayim* is.

Koheles ends with this important message: even after we have learned everything in the Torah, fearing Hashem and keeping His mitzvos is the most important.[3]

Mishlei ends with this *passuk*: "Charm is false and beauty is pointless; a woman who fears Hashem is to be praised."[4]

Doing *Teshuvah*

When someone does an *aveirah*, he has a special mitzvah of *teshuvah*, where he can fix what he did wrong.

If a person does not do *teshuvah*, it shows that he is not afraid of doing something against Hashem's instructions. The person now has done **two** *aveiros*, the *aveirah* that was done, and not fearing Hashem![5]

Only Fear Hashem

The only thing you should really fear is Hashem, not other people, or anything that might happen to you.[6] When you realize that anything else in the world, even something that seems really powerful, is not even close to how mighty and strong Hashem is, you will fear Hashem so much more.

CHECKPOINT Which mitzvos are easier to do when you have *Yiras Hashem*?

SELECTED HALACHOS

- You must learn Torah with a feeling of *Yiras Hashem*, just as the Jews trembled with fear when they received the Torah at *Har Sinai*. This is learned from the *passuk*, "וַיַּרְא הָעָם וַיָּנֻעוּ – The people saw and they trembled."[7]

- When you *daven*, you should imagine yourself standing in the presence of Hashem Himself, as it says, "שִׁוִּיתִי ה' לְנֶגְדִּי תָמִיד – I have placed Hashem in front of me always."[8]

- On *Rosh Hashanah*, you should eat only as much as your body needs, not so much extra, so that *Yiras Hashem* will always be on your mind and you will not be distracted by the delicious foods.[9]

- Fearing Hashem also prevents you from saying Hashem's name for no reason. Saying Hashem's name for no reason shows a lack of awe and respect for Hashem.

EXTEND YOUR KNOWLEDGE

It's Not Just About the Punishment

The simplest kind of *Yiras Hashem* is יִרְאַת הָעוֹנֶשׁ, being afraid of Hashem's punishments. But there are other levels that are higher than יִרְאַת הָעוֹנֶשׁ. This can be understood with the following story:

A simple farmer is invited to the king's palace to tour his royal gardens. He shyly enters the throne room and is immediately swept away by the sight of the king. Tall and broad-shouldered with piercing eyes and a flowing beard, the king looks amazing in his royal garments; a jewel-encrusted crown sparkling on his head, and a sword at his side. Never had the farmer seen anything so awe-inspiring as the vision of majesty and power before him. Overcome, he falls on his face before the king.

Like the simple farmer, when you think about how great and mighty Hashem is, you will become overcome with awe. You may even be more embarrassed to have done something against Hashem than you are scared to be punished! This is called יִרְאַת בּוֹשֶׁת.

There is another kind of fear called יִרְאַת חֵטְא - being scared of the actual *aveirah*.

Let's go back to the farmer in the story:

The king leads the farmer to the royal gardens. He sweeps his arm across the many trees laden with fruit, and declares that the farmer may take as much fruit as he likes to eat. However, the king points to one tree, and warns the farmer never to touch the fruit on that tree. If he does, he will never be allowed into the palace again.

As the farmer strolls around the orchard, his eyes are drawn to the fruit tree that the king has forbidden. A strong desire to eat from it overcomes him. As he stretches his arm to pluck the fruit, he stops. "How can I do something that would cause me to be separated from the king?" he says to himself. "No, I shall not go against the king's wishes!"

In the same way, doing an *aveirah* separates you from Hashem, and this is very painful for your *neshamah*. The fear of being separated from Hashem can stop you from doing an *aveirah*.[10]

STORY

Someone's Watching!

Before his death, R' Yochanan ben Zakkai was surrounded by his beloved students. Realizing that he was going to pass away soon, they begged him, "*Rebbe*, give us a *brachah*!"

R' Yochanan ben Zakkai then blessed them, "May you fear Hashem as much as you fear man."

"That's it?!" the students wondered.

R' Yochanan ben Zakkai explained that when you are doing something wrong, you do not want anyone to see you. Remember that Hashem is always watching and you will not do *aveiros*! [11]

PEARLS of wisdom

Hashem's Treasure

The *passuk* in *Yeshayah*[12] calls *Yiras Hashem* a "treasure." Why is it referred to as a treasure?

A king does not have a treasure because he worked for it himself. A king's treasure is taken from other people through taxes and wars.

The same is true with *Yiras Hashem*. The *Gemara*[13] says "Everything is in Hashem's hands except for *Yiras Shamayim (Hashem)*." Hashem gives us everything we need or want, except for *Yiras Hashem*. That's up to us to accomplish.

Since our *Yiras Hashem* is created by **us**, it is like Hashem's "treasure" that we give to Him![14]

DID YOU KNOW?

The word usually used for a head covering, "*yarmulka,*" has two meanings:

1. It can be a short version of the Aramaic words, "*yarei malka,*" meaning "fear of the King" [Hashem].

2. It can also be a short version of the Hebrew words, "*ya'arei m'Eloka,*" meaning "Fearful of Hashem."

A STORY

One G-d and Two Worlds

In 1920, R' Yosef Yitzchak of Lubavitch was summoned by the part of the Russian government famous for hating Jews, called the "Yevsektzia."

When he arrived at the building where so many Jews had been sentenced to death, he was led to a large room where about fifteen people sat along both sides of a long table. At the head of the table sat another two officers, and the *Rebbe* was seated opposite them at the foot of the table. Three guards sat behind him, left, right, and center.

The head officer announced that R' Yosef Yitzchak was arrested for spreading Judaism and for setting up *yeshivos, mikvaos,* and *shuls* around Russia. When R' Yosef Yitzchak made it very clear that he was not going to stop what he was doing, or tell on any of his friends, one angry officer lifted his gun.

"This gun of mine has made many people change their ways!" he shouted. "Even people who thought they would never surrender, listen once they are frightened by my gun!"

"You are totally wrong," R' Yosef Yitzchak calmly replied. "Your gun will only scare someone who believes in one single world and many gods. For me, a Jew, I believe in two worlds and only one Hashem, so I am not scared of your gun at all."[15]

Live the Mitzvah   EXTRACT

וְהִנֵּה ה' נִצָּב עָלָיו

Hashem is always watching our every action. He reads all our innermost thoughts. He sees our every move. How differently we should act, knowing that Hashem never stops watching, not even for a moment!

 CHECKPOINT   What changes about our actions when we know that Hashem is always watching?

What Else Comes From This?   EXTRACT

Remembering That Hashem is Always Here

How can we remind ourselves to always fear Hashem?

The *Gemara*[16] tells us that R' Nachman's mother told him to always cover his head so that he would always feel *Yiras Hashem*.

Jewish men and boys cover their heads, since it reminds them that Hashem is always with them.

Here are some *halachos* about boys and men covering their heads:

- You should not wear a wig as a head covering because it does not look like you are wearing a *yarmulka*.[17]

- A *yarmulka* should cover most of your head.[18]

- You should also wear a *yarmulka* at night while sleeping.[19]

- Young children should also cover their heads to train them to always remember to have *Yiras Hashem*.[20]

- If you do not have a covering for your head, you should put your sleeve on your head or have your friend cover your head with his hand. If you can't do any of the above, then you may put your own hand on your head.[21]

 CHECKPOINT How does a *yarmulka* help someone have *Yiras Hashem*?

A STORY

Scared to Death

The Jewish printing press in Slavita, Russia was owned by two Shapiro brothers. They were *Talmidei Chachamim* and had great *Yiras Shamayim*.

In 1853, enemies of the Jews convinced the Czar that the Jews had been involved in illegal activities.

The Czar became very angry. As a punishment, he decreed that the two brothers must run through two rows of five hundred soldiers all holding sticks. When the men would run through the lines of soldiers, the Jew-hating soldiers would beat them as forcefully as they could.

While the second brother was running, being beaten on both sides by the savage soldiers, his *yarmulka* fell off. Instead of continuing to run, he stopped to bend and pick it up.

Even though the soldiers continued beating him, he would not take one step without wearing his *yarmulka*![22]

A page from a *siddur* printed in the Slavita printing press seventeen years before the false accusation.

PEARLS of wisdom

What G-d Wants

"And now, Yisrael, what does Hashem your G-d want of you, other than to fear Hashem your G-d..."

Moshe Rabbeinu told these words to *Bnei Yisrael* before he died.

If you look at *Moshe Rabbeinu's* words to *B'nei Yisrael*, it seems like fearing Hashem is something easy to do. Is it really so simple? The *Gemara* explains that for *Moshe Rabbeinu*, fearing Hashem **was** simple.

This answer is difficult to understand. Wasn't *Moshe Rabbeinu* talking to the Jewish people? He was saying that for the **B'nei Yisrael** it is easy, not for himself!

The answer is that all Jews have a part of their *neshamos* which are on the level of *Moshe Rabbeinu*. Usually it is covered and we cannot feel it. However, if we can awaken this level of our *neshamah*, it becomes very easy to fear Hashem.

The *Gemara* is hinting that for the level of *Moshe Rabbeinu* inside each of us, it is an easy thing to fear Hashem. It is because of this level of the *neshamah* that we are able to fear Hashem in our day to day lives.[23]

UNIT 3

ENDNOTES:

‫1. ס׳ חרדים מ״ע מדברי קבלה פ״א אות ו׳‬

‫2. סיפורי חסידים פ׳ ואתחנן‬

‫3. קהלת יב, יג‬

‫4. קהלת רבה ג, יד‬

‫5. רדב״ז ב״טעמי המצות״ מצוה ה׳‬

‫6. סה״מ עשה ד׳‬

‫7. ברכות כב, א‬

‫8. סנהדרין כב, א‬

‫9. שו״ע או״ח סי׳ תקצ״ז ס״א‬

‫10. ילקוט מעם לועז דברים ב׳ ע׳ תקמז‬

‫11. (ברכות כח, ב)‬

‫12. ישעי׳ לג, ו‬

‫13. ברכות לג, ב‬

‫14. רבינו בחיי דברים כח, נב‬

‫15. סה״ש תר״פ ע׳ 4‬

‫16. שבת קנו, ב‬

‫17. משנה ברורה סי׳ ב׳ ס״ק י״ב‬

‫18. אגרות משה או״ח ח״א סי׳ א׳. שו״ת האלף לך שלמה או״ח סי׳ ג׳‬

‫19. משנה ברורה סי׳ ב׳ ס״ק י״א‬

‫20. מג״א סי׳ ב׳ ס״ק ו׳‬

‫21. משנה ברורה סי׳ ב׳ ס״ק י״ב‬

‫22. ספר הבעש״ט ע׳ רצט‬

‫23. לקו״א פמ״ב. וראה ילקוט מעם לועז דברים ב׳ ע׳ תקמז‬

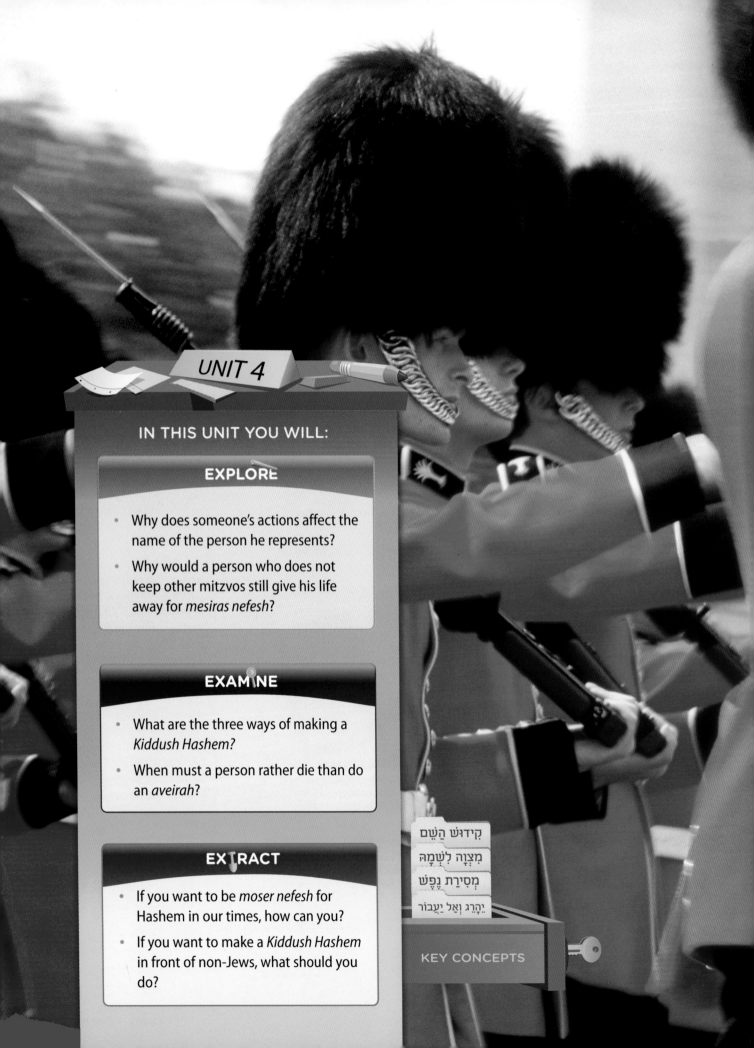

UNIT 4

IN THIS UNIT YOU WILL:

EXPLORE

- Why does someone's actions affect the name of the person he represents?
- Why would a person who does not keep other mitzvos still give his life away for *mesiras nefesh*?

EXAMINE

- What are the three ways of making a *Kiddush Hashem*?
- When must a person rather die than do an *aveirah*?

EXTRACT

- If you want to be *moser nefesh* for Hashem in our times, how can you?
- If you want to make a *Kiddush Hashem* in front of non-Jews, what should you do?

קִידוּשׁ הַשֵּׁם
מִצְוָה לִשְׁמָהּ
מְסִירַת נֶפֶשׁ
יֵהָרֵג וְאַל יַעֲבוֹר

KEY CONCEPTS

Book: Madda, Section: Foundations of the Torah

סֵפֶר מַדָּע הִלְכוֹת יְסוֹדֵי הַתּוֹרָה

קִידוּשׁ ה׳

SANCTIFYING HASHEM'S NAME

שְׁתֵּי מִצְוֹת

A soldier in an army represents his home country. People judge a country based on the actions of one or two people from that country.

The Mitzvos

The unit of *Kiddush Hashem* has two mitzvos.

1. Make the name of Hashem great and holy.

2. You may not do anything to bring shame to Hashem.

MITZVAH 6

לְקַדֵּשׁ שְׁמוֹ

Making the name of Hashem holy

וְלֹא תְחַלְּלוּ אֶת שֵׁם קָדְשִׁי וְנִקְדַּשְׁתִּי בְּתוֹךְ בְּנֵי יִשְׂרָאֵל אֲנִי ה' מְקַדִּשְׁכֶם (ויקרא כב, לב)

Do not disgrace My holy name. **I must be made holy among the Jewish people.** I am Hashem who makes you holy.

There are three kinds of actions which fulfill this mitzvah:

1. Give up your life when required to by the Torah.

2. Do a mitzvah just because Hashem commanded you to.

3. Act in a way that brings honor to Hashem.

 ALL PEOPLE   ALL PLACES   ALL TIMES

Nothing New

There were many times throughout history when thousands of Jews were killed just for being Jewish.

Some of the most famous of these are:

The Crusades: Starting from the year 1095, as Christian gangs traveled through Europe and other areas on their way to Eretz Yisrael, they killed thousands of Jews wherever they passed.

The Spanish Inquisition: Before the Jews were thrown out of Spain in 1492, many Jews were killed and sometimes even burned alive because they refused to convert to Christianity.

Chmelnicky: During the years 1648-1649, a cruel Ukrainian peasant lead many Cossacks through much of Eastern Europe. He and his men killed thousands of Jews, wiping out entire towns.

The Holocaust: When Nazi Germany tried to kill all the Jews, more than six million Jewish men, women and children were murdered between the years of 1938-1945.

The decree signed in 1492 by King Ferdinand and Queen Isabella expelling all the Jews from Spain.

MITZVAH 7

שֶׁלֹּא לְחַלֵּל שְׁמוֹ
Not disgracing the name of Hashem

וְלֹא תְחַלְּלוּ אֶת שֵׁם קָדְשִׁי וְנִקְדַּשְׁתִּי בְּתוֹךְ בְּנֵי יִשְׂרָאֵל אֲנִי ה' מְקַדִּשְׁכֶם (ויקרא כב, לב)

Do not disgrace My holy name. I must be made holy among the Jewish people. I am Hashem Who makes you holy.

There are three kinds of actions which are *oveir* this mitzvah:

1. Not giving up your life when required to by the Torah.

2. Doing *aveiros* just to go against Hashem's commandment.

3. Acting in a way that brings shame to Hashem.

ALL PEOPLE · ALL PLACES · ALL TIMES · NO PUNISHMENT

Mitzvah Messages

EXPLORE

מְסִירַת נֶפֶשׁ – Giving Away Your Life

Every Jew has a *neshamah* which is a part of Hashem. Our *neshamah* only wants to do what Hashem wants. Sometimes our *neshamos* can become a bit sleepy and we won't feel the strong need to stay connected to Hashem. However, when something happens that makes our *neshamos* feel that they are going to be separated from Hashem (like being forced to serve *avodah zarah*), the *neshamah* wakes up! It will never let us become disconnected from Hashem.[1]

Train tracks leading to a concentration camp in Poland during World War 2

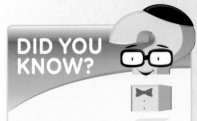

DID YOU KNOW?

Local Fast Day

In addition to the usual fast days, some communities fast on specific days to remember terrible events that happened there against the Jews.

For example in Cologne, Germany, the community chose the 23rd of *Nissan* as a day of fasting and mourning to remember the Jews of Cologne who were killed in 1147 during a Crusade.

DID YOU KNOW?

Two For The Price Of One

When one does a mitzvah purely for the sake of serving Hashem, he gets two mitzvos: the mitzvah that he did, and the added mitzvah of *Kiddush Hashem*.

Oooops!

Sometimes you can embarrass Hashem's name without realizing it. For example, when you do something thinking that no one else saw what was going on, or if you didn't know that you were doing something that is wrong. A person who sees you will still think badly about Jews and about Hashem because of what you did, whether you meant it or not!

You must always be very careful to act properly.[2]

לְשֵׁם שָׁמַיִם - For Hashem's Sake

If you let your friend ride your bicycle because you want your friend to let you play with her computer, then who are you really doing a favor for? For your friend, or for yourself?

If a Jew does a mitzvah only because he wants the reward, it is definitely better than not doing the mitzvah at all, but whom are they serving? Hashem or themselves?

Servants who really care what their master wants will fulfill the master's command simply because the master requested it.

We are loyal servants of Hashem and should try to do mitzvos only because Hashem wants us to do them, and not for the reward.[3]

Hashem's Representatives

People often look at the way someone acts and assume that all people in that same group act the same way.

If you see someone important from a different country acting nicely to other people, you will assume that all the people from his country must be nice like him. If he acted rudely, you would assume that the other people from that country are also rude.

A soldier represents his country. A businessman represents his company. **A Jew represents Hashem.** When a Jew behaves properly, people think that Hashem is good, since His people are good.

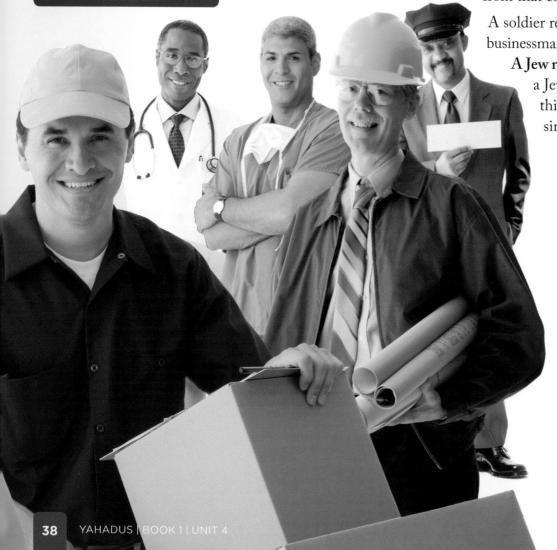

If a Jew behaves badly, people will say that Hashem and His Torah are not good because His people don't behave as they should.

It is important that we act and behave perfectly in order to show all the nations of the world how holy and special Hashem is.[4]

 CHECKPOINT What is the best reason to do a mitzvah?

Details

EXAMINE

מְסִירַת נֶפֶשׁ - Giving Up One's Life When Required To By The Torah

We are taught in the Torah that a human life is more important than almost anything else. The Torah tells us "וָחַי בָּהֶם" which means that we must "live" for the mitzvos and not die for them. Usually, saving a life is more important than any mitzvah. For example, if a very sick person needed to be *mechalel Shabbos* in order to go to the hospital or to get medicine, it is allowed. Also, if someone tells a Jew to "eat non-kosher food or I will kill you!" the Jew should eat the food to save his or her life.[5]

There are some exceptions to this rule. In some cases, a Jew must give up his life and not go against the Torah.

These situations are called "יֵהָרֵג וְאַל יַעֲבוֹר" - Be killed and do not be *oveir* the mitzvah.

1. The "Three *Aveiros*"

There are three *aveiros* for which a person must give up his life and not do the *aveirah*. They are:

עֲבוֹדָה זָרָה – Idol worship.

גִּילּוּי עֲרָיוֹת – Living as married with someone who is forbidden to you.

שְׁפִיכַת דָּמִים – Killing another person.

These *aveiros* are so severe that we must give our lives away rather than do them. For example, if someone tells a Jew, "Kill that person or I will kill you!" the Jew must let himself be killed rather than kill someone else.[6]

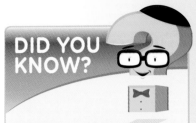

This is Different

Causing a *Chillul Hashem* is a very serious *aveirah*:

For other *aveiros*:

• Hashem does not punish the person right away, because he might do *teshuvah*. But for *Chillul Hashem*, Hashem punishes him right away.

• If a person did an equal amount of mitzvos and *aveiros* throughout their lifetime, Hashem will not punish them. However, if *Chilul Hashem* is among the *aveiros* that the person didn't do *teshuvah* for, then the person will be punished regardless - even if they did mostly mizvos.[8]

OUR SAGES SAY...

Painless

The Maharam from Rottenberg was put into jail for the last years of his life. While he was in jail, he continued to teach his students. One of the amazing things he revealed is that when people give up their lives *al Kiddush Hashem*, they do not feel any pain![9]

2. לְהַעֲבִירוֹ עַל הַדָּת - **To Remove Him from His Religion**

If someone is forcing you to do **any** *aveirah* in public (in front of at least 10 other Jews) just to go against Hashem, you are not allowed to do it. Since they are forcing you to do an *aveirah* only because they want to make fun of Hashem and show that Jews do not listen to Hashem, every *aveirah*, no matter what it is, becomes extremely important and you must give up your life for **any** *aveirah*.

If there are less than ten people present, you are allowed to do the *aveirah* to save your life.[10]

3. A Time When Jews are Being Killed for Following the Torah

There are times when our enemies try to force us to stop keeping mitzvos. This is called a time of "שְׁמַד." During such times we must sacrifice our lives for **any** mitzvah or *minhag*, even if no-one else is looking. For example, in the days of the *Gemara*, the Jewish people would tie their shoes differently than non-Jews. If those Jews would have been forced to tie their shoes like non-Jews, they would have had to sacrifice their lives not to change the way that they tie their shoes![11]

Brachah

When someone is about to be killed *al Kiddush Hashem* in public, he should say this *brachah*.

בָּרוּךְ אַתָּה ה' אֱלֹקֵינוּ מֶלֶךְ הָעוֹלָם אֲשֶׁר קִדְּשָׁנוּ בְּמִצְוֹתָיו וְצִוָּנוּ לְקַדֵּשׁ שְׁמוֹ בָּרַבִּים.[12]

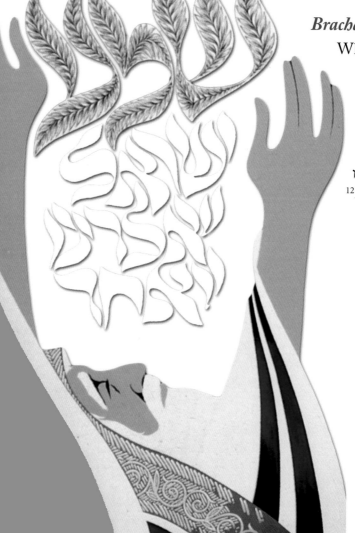

Representing Hashem:

We can bring praise to Hashem's Name every time we are in public and every time we interact with a non-Jew. We can do this by speaking nicely to people, greeting everyone with a smile, not offending others, honoring others, doing more than the law requires, doing business honestly, and acting calmly and well-behaved.

If you act in the opposite way, you are disgracing Hashem's Name and are doing the *aveirah* of *chillul Hashem*.[13]

 CHECKPOINT When do we have to give up our lives rather than do an *aveirah*?

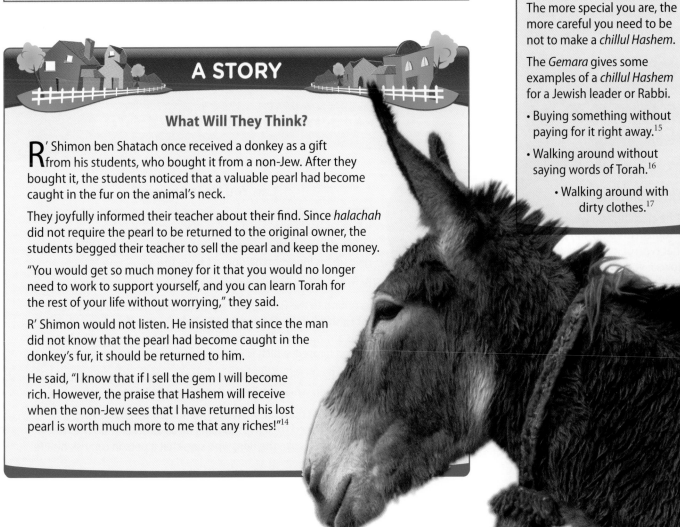

A STORY

What Will They Think?

R' Shimon ben Shatach once received a donkey as a gift from his students, who bought it from a non-Jew. After they bought it, the students noticed that a valuable pearl had become caught in the fur on the animal's neck.

They joyfully informed their teacher about their find. Since *halachah* did not require the pearl to be returned to the original owner, the students begged their teacher to sell the pearl and keep the money.

"You would get so much money for it that you would no longer need to work to support yourself, and you can learn Torah for the rest of your life without worrying," they said.

R' Shimon would not listen. He insisted that since the man did not know that the pearl had become caught in the donkey's fur, it should be returned to him.

He said, "I know that if I sell the gem I will become rich. However, the praise that Hashem will receive when the non-Jew sees that I have returned his lost pearl is worth much more to me that any riches!"[14]

First-Class Ticket

A person who gives their life away *al Kiddush Hashem* is called a *Kadosh* and their *neshamah* goes straight to the highest levels of *Gan Eden*. Even if a person went against the Torah their whole life, if they were killed *al Kiddush Hashem*, they go straight to *Olam Habba*![18]

- If one is being forced to do one of the three *aveiros* and is afraid they won't be able to withstand the test, they may take their own life first.[19]

- You should not lie and say "I'm not Jewish" in order to save your life. If you do this, you are showing that you do not believe in Hashem.[20]

- If someone knows that he will be forced to convert and will have to die, but he can escape and save his life, he should run away. Even though he is not going to do the mitzvah of dying for Hashem, he is getting the mitzvah of saving a life. If he chooses to die for Hashem to let everyone learn from his actions, he is allowed to stay and let himself be killed.[21]

Status Clothing

The clothing you wear represents who you are or what type of job you have. It shows if you are a boy or girl, wealthy or poor, policeman or firefighter.

In ancient times, only Roman Senators could wear purple clothing, and only high-ranking Hawaiian chiefs could wear feather cloaks or carved whale teeth. In ancient China, only the Emperor could wear yellow. This showed their special status.

We too have a special status as Hashem's representatives and must dress respectfully and accordingly.

Can You Do It Anyway?

The Torah does not want us to die for a mitzvah except for the few cases mentioned earlier. What if a person wants to do a mitzvah for which he does not have to give away his life? Can he give up his life when he doesn't **have** to?

There are different opinions about this.

According to the Rambam,[22] a person is not allowed to be killed for Hashem if the Torah doesn't say he has to. If a person does this anyway and dies when he does not have to, it is like he killed himself, which is a great *aveirah*.

The Ran[23] disagrees, and says that a person may sacrifice his life even when the Torah doesn't say he has to.

We find a number of stories mentioned by *Chazal* where people risked their lives to fulfill mitzvos other than the "three mitzvos." This is like the Ran, who says that a person can risk his life for any mitzvah.

However, the *Nimukei Yosef*[24] explains that although a regular person may not give up their life when he doesn't have to, a great person or leader is allowed to give up his life for any mitzvah. The reason for this is so that people will see and learn from him to love and fear Hashem.

Live the Mitzvah

Live on *Mesiras Nefesh*

Throughout history, Jews were often forced to choose between serving Hashem or giving up their lives. The response was always the same: Jews will never go against Hashem, even at the cost of their life. This is called מְסִירַת נֶפֶשׁ – "handing over your life."

Baruch Hashem, today this doesn't happen very often. Most Jews live in free countries where they can be Jewish in public.

But the idea of מְסִירַת נֶפֶשׁ is still very applicable in our times. The word נֶפֶשׁ can also mean "desire." *Mesiras nefesh* means to give up your desires. Every time you do something for Hashem that you don't want to, you perform *mesiras nefesh!*[25]

Another example of *mesiras nefesh* is to do what is right even when people make fun of it. This is what *Chazal* mean when they tell us to be as "bold as a leopard." A leopard is very brave and is not scared by larger animals. If we can be as bold as a leopard, we will always do the right thing and not worry about what people will say.

The temptations to do things that are against the Torah keep getting stronger. It can be extremely difficult at times, and can demand real *mesiras nefesh!*[26]

CHECKPOINT How can you have *mesiras nefesh* for Hashem without giving up your life?

Leopards are very brave hunters and not afraid to attack animals many times their size and strength.

PEARLS *of wisdom*

Last Minute Mitzvah

What happens if someone was ready to sacrifice his life for Hashem and at the last minute he was saved? Did he still do the mitzvah of *Kiddush Hashem?*

There is a difference of opinions as to whether he gets the mitzvah. Some say that this mitzvah is only fulfilled when the person **actually** dies *al Kiddush Hashem* because the person doesn't show how strong he is until he actually dies. With anything less, this mitzvah is not considered fulfilled.

Others say that the mitzvah of *Kiddush Hashem* is fulfilled also in a case when one is saved unexpectedly and was not actually killed. Everyone will see that Hashem saves those who believe in Him, and this itself will bring honor to Hashem's Name.[27]

UNIT 4

ENDNOTES:

1. לקו"א פי"ח-י"ט
2. אבות פ"ד מ"ד
3. רמב"ם הל' יסוה"ת פ"ה ה"י
4. רמב"ם הל' יסוה"ת פ"ה הי"א
5. סנהדרין עד, א. רמב"ם הל' יסוה"ת פ"ה ה"א כרוב הדינים שבנושא זו
6. סנהדרין עד, א. רמב"ם הל' יסוה"ת פ"ה ה"ב
7. לקו"א פי"ח
8. קידושין מ, א וברש"י שם ד"ה אין עושין לו כתנוני וד"ה שאם היתה
9. תשב"ץ סי' ת"ט
10. סנהדרין עד, א. רמב"ם הל' יסוה"ת

11. סנהדרין עד, א. רמב"ם הל' יסוה"ת פ"ה ה"ג
12. של"ה שער האותיות אות אמונה
13. רמב"ם הל' יסוה"ת פ"ה הי"א
14. ירושלמי בבא מציעא פ"ב ה"ה
15. יומא פו, א
16. יומא פו, א
17. שבת קיד, א
18. רמב"ם אגרת השמד פי"ט
19. הגהות סמ"ק סי' ג'. ש"ך יו"ד סי' קנ"ז ס"ק א'
20. שו"ע יו"ד סי' קנ"ז ס"ב

פ"ה ה"ב
פ"ה ה"ג

21. פתחי תשובה יו"ד סי' קנ"ז ס"ק ח'
22. רמב"ם הל' יסוה"ת פ"ה ה"ד
23. סמ"ק סי' ג'. וכן רבים, הובאו בב"י יו"ד סי' קנ"ז ד"ה ומ"ש רבינו
24. סנהדרין יח, א מדפי הרי"ף
25. ס' חרדים פ"ד (מצוות התלויות בראש הגויה) בסופו "מסרו נפשם כמו עולות ושלמים". ע"פ ס' ייטב פנים (טייטלבוים) להקפות ש"ע וש"ת אות י"ב
26. ע"פ טור או"ח סי' א'. וראה ב"י שם
27. ע"פ רמב"ם הל' יסוה"ת פ"ה ה"ד ורש"י ויקרא כב, לב

UNIT 5

IN THIS UNIT YOU WILL:

EXPLORE

- Why is it important to respect holy objects?

EXAMINE

- What kind of objects must be treated with respect?

EXTRACT

- If you are in a *shul* or other holy place, how should you behave?
- If a page is torn out of a *siddur* or another *sefer*, what should you do with the page?

שֵׁמוֹת

כְּבוֹד בֵּית הַכְּנֶסֶת

גְּנִיזָה

KEY CONCEPTS

Book: Madda, Section: Foundations of the Torah
סֵפֶר מַדָּע הִלְכוֹת יְסוֹדֵי הַתּוֹרָה

שֶׁלֹא לְאַבֵּד דְּבָרִים שֶׁנִּקְרָא שְׁמוֹ עֲלֵיהֶם

DO NOT DESTROY SOMETHING THAT REPRESENTS HASHEM

מִצְוָה אַחַת

What do a dollar bill, a flag and a police officer's badge have in common? In many countries, it is against the law to purposely damage or show disrespect to them.

They are symbols of the country and must be treated respectfully.

DISCOVERY

Messing With Me

Starting in the late 1800's, all of the States in America established laws of how to treat flags. These laws made it illegal to place any kind of marking on a flag of the United States, use the flag as a form of advertising, or to publicly damage the flag in any way.

Any material that a person would recognize immediately to be a flag of the US or to represent a US flag, is part of this law, as long as it is the right colors and has any number of stars and stripes!

The Mitzvah
EXAMINE

The unit of respecting something that represents Hashem has one mitzvah.

Do not destroy anything that represents Hashem, or is used to serve Hashem.

MITZVAH
8

שֶׁלֹּא לְאַבֵּד דְּבָרִים שֶׁנִּקְרָא שְׁמוֹ עֲלֵיהֶם
Not destroying something that represents Hashem.

לֹא תַעֲשׂוּן כֵּן לַה׳ אֱלֹקֵיכֶם
(דברים יב, ד)
You may not do this to Hashem your G-d.

Do not erase or destroy any object or place which represents Hashem or is used to serve Him.

 ALL PEOPLE   ALL PLACES   ALL TIMES   *MALKUS*

Flag of Hashem

When you salute the national flag, you aren't just saluting a piece of cloth on a pole. The national flag is actually a symbol of the country and everything the country stands for. By showing respect to the flag, you are honoring the country. Showing disrespect to the flag is disrespectful to the country.

In the same way, everything that represents Hashem must be treated with respect. This includes showing respect to the Torah, the mitzvos, and all holy objects such as a pair of *tefillin*. Showing disrespect to these items shows disrespect to what they represent: Hashem.

 CHECKPOINT Who are you really honoring when you show respect to something that is used for a mitzvah?

Details EXAMINE

Holy Words and Sacred Objects

There are two types of things that you are not allowed to destroy; holy words and objects dedicated to Hashem.

Holy Words

- These include Hashem's names and words of Torah. They may not be erased, and any books or papers with these words on them may not be thrown away.

- There are seven names of Hashem that may not be erased:

  1. י-ה-ו-ה   2. א-ד-נ-י   3. א-ל   4. א-ל-ו-ה

  5. א-ל-ה-י-ם   6. ש-ד-י   7. צ-ב-א-ו-ת

- Some opinions include the name א-ה-י-ה.[2]

- If you write any of these names on paper, parchment or any other surface (even a chalkboard or marker board) you are not allowed to erase it.[3]

- The letters written **before** the name of Hashem, such as the ל of לי-ה-ו-ה, or the ב of בא-ל-ה-י-ם, may be erased.[4]

- The letters written **after** the name of Hashem, such as the ך of א-ל-ה-י-ך or the כם of א-ל-ה-י-כם, may **not** be erased.[5]

Honor My Messengers

R' Shimon bar Yochai said: "Mitzvos of Hashem are like Hashem's messengers. The messenger of a person is like the person himself!"

However we treat the mitzvos - the messengers of Hashem - is how we are treating Hashem.[8]

- You may not erase even two of the letters of Hashem's name, like א-ל or י-ה, since they are also names of Hashem. Also, the letters א-ד should not be erased, since those letter make the sound of the way we say Hashem's name.[9]

An Object Specifically for Hashem

Anything which is used only for Hashem is considered to be Hashem's "property" and must be treated with respect. This includes any part of the *Beis Hamikdash* - Hashem's "home" in this world.

Even though today we do not have the *Beis Hamikdash*, the mitzvah still applies to *shuls* and *batei midrash*. Our *Chachamim* tell us that the *kedushah* of the *Beis Hamikdash* was spread out into all the *shuls* and places where Torah is studied around the world. Each of these places is called a *mikdash me'at*[10] (a mini *Beis Hamikdash*), and therefore must be treated with the same respect given to the *Beis Hamikdash* itself. For example, you may not damage a *shul* by removing a brick, or by even scratching off the paint. The furniture of a *shul*, such as benches, tables and stands may not be destroyed.

You may only destroy a part of a *shul* if you are fixing it.[11]

CHECKPOINT What types of objects have to be respected?

Two Holy

Before the *Mishnah* was written, all of the *Torah Sheba'al Peh* was passed down from teacher to student, not through *sefarim*. In those days, the only written words of Torah were the words of *Tanach* – the *Torah Shebichsav*.

Now that the *Torah Sheba'al Peh* has also been written down, these *sefarim* must also be treated respectfully, and we may not throw out any writings from the *Mishnah* and *Gemara*.

The Great Synagogue in Florence, Italy was completed in 1882. It was designed by famous Italian architects, and survived many attempts to destroy it. There are still Nazi knife marks visible on the *Aron Hakodesh*.

SELECTED HALACHOS

- When you write the word for Hashem in a different language (for example, "G-o-d" in English), you are allowed to erase it, since it is not a real name of Hashem.[12] However, you should not throw it out. Instead, it should be buried. For this reason, many people have the custom to write "G-d" without writing the complete word, so that they won't have this problem.

- Names of people that have Hashem's name in them, (such as יְשַׁעְיָהוּ) may be thrown out.

- According to most opinions, you are allowed to throw out CDs, computers or memory cards that have Torah words stored on them. This is because the actual words are not written there, just digital information which creates the sounds or images of words.[13]

HISTORY

The *Shaf V'yasiv Shul*

There was a *shul* in the town of Naharda'ah in Bavel called the שַׁף וְיָתִיב *shul*.

One of the reasons why it had this name is because this name means "the *shul* which travelled and settled." It was believed that the *shul* was made from stones that were taken from Eretz Yisrael.[16]

Some people mistakenly think that it was built with stones taken from the *Beis Hamikdash*. This could not be, because it is forbidden to take stones from the *Beis Hamikdash*![17]

EXTEND YOUR KNOWLEDGE

It's My Home

Keep the *Kosel* Whole

When people visit Eretz Yisrael, they often don't realize that places around the country are as holy as they were 2,000 years ago. The best known of these sites is the *Kosel Hama'aravi,* the remaining wall that was around the *Har Habayis* (the large courtyard around the *Beis Hamikdash*). Some people collect stones from the *Kosel* and take them home as souvenirs. They do not know that this is actually forbidden, since the *Kosel* is part of the *Beis Hamikdash* that once stood. Taking a stone, or even part of a stone, out of the *Kosel,* would be like destroying the *Beis Hamikdash* itself, and is forbidden.[14]

Shul Renovations

A *shul* is considered to be like a mini *Beis Hamikdash* and no part of it may be destroyed. Even making a small hole in any part of the building is forbidden. If you are fixing up or adding to the *shul*, can you make a permanent hole in the wall of the *shul* which will be used to connect it with the new addition?

The answer is that although it may look like the *shul* is being damaged, it is still allowed. This is because the intention is to **improve** the *shul*. Since you are just "fixing" the *shul,* it is not considered destroying it.[15]

A Great Reward

There are stories of people who received enormous rewards from Hashem because during their lifetime, they would always sweep the floor in front of the *aron kodesh* and keep the *shul* clean.[18]

Live the Mitzvah
EXTRACT

Keep Your *Shul* Beautiful

The next time you are in *shul*, have a look around. Is the *shul* a big mess, with crumpled tissues and pretzels on the floor? Is anything broken? Are there *siddurim* lying around instead of sitting neatly in their place? All these things are disrespectful to the "home" of Hashem.

What can you do to make sure the *shul* is treated with the proper respect?

You could make sure to always throw your trash in the bins provided, to wipe your feet on the mat before entering the *shul*, to put *siddurim* back on their shelf. You could point out the broken items to the people in charge and ask them to fix it.

It is these small things that make all the difference in keeping the *shul* looking its very best, as befitting a place dedicated to Hashem.

CHECKPOINT How can you show respect to Hashem's "home"?

What Else Comes From This?
EXTRACT

בס"ד

Many people have the custom to write B"H (or ב״ה), which stands for *baruch Hashem*, at the top of a piece of paper before starting to write. It shows that you are thanking Hashem before starting a project. If you wrote B"H and accidentally threw out the paper, it may be considered destroying or erasing Hashem's name.

To avoid this problem, you can instead write בס"ד which stands for *b'siyata d'shmaya*, which means, "with the help of Heaven." These words mean the same thing as B"H and do not have Hashem's name in them. Therefore, there is no problem with throwing it out.[19]

Sheimos

In addition to the mitzvah of not erasing or destroying Hashem's name, the *Chachamim* added that you may also not destroy words from Torah. Therefore, it is forbidden to throw away, burn or erase written words of Torah.[20]

Any books or papers with words of Torah that were written to learn from for a long time must be buried.[21] However, homework, *parshah* sheets,

notes and tests may be thrown out, as they are only meant for quick review, not intense study. Also, printing scraps, extra copies, misprints, etc. may be thrown out since they were not made for studying at all.[22]

Burying *Sheimos*

Burying anything which has the words of Torah is commonly known as "*sheimos*" (which literally means "names") because it comes from the *issur* to erase Hashem's name.

Often, large trucks called "*sheimos* trucks" pull up in communities with large Jewish populations. These special trucks collect old, worn, and no longer used *siddurim*, *sefarim*, papers and holy items. Once they are collected, the books, papers and items are taken outside of the city and buried near a Jewish cemetery. These items, though no longer needed, are still considered holy and therefore may not be thrown out with the garbage.

HISTORY

Genizah

Throughout history, when *sefarim*, *siddurim*, or papers were worn out or torn, they were stored away in a *genizah* (hiding place). Some Jews had the custom to bury them in the ground, or to keep them in the cellar or attic of the local *shul*. Some very famous and important *genizos* have been found which have very interesting stories connected to them.

Cairo *Genizah*

In the middle of the 1800's, a huge *genizah* was found in the *Ben-Ezra Shul* in Cairo, Egypt. There were almost 200,000 pages of handwritten papers, and some were written more than 1000 years ago!

Prague

The *Alteneu Shul* in Prague was built in 1208. The Maharal of Prague used this *shul*. In the attic, there is a large *genizah*. Some people say that the Golem of Prague is buried in that pile of *sheimos*.

A handwritten page from the Rambam's *Sefer Moreh Hanevuchin* found in the Cairo *Genizah*.

CHECKPOINT What is *sheimos* and what must be done with it?

UNIT 5

ENDNOTES:

1. שו״ת מנחת יצחק ח״ה סי׳ פ״ג
2. שו״ע יו״ד סי׳ רע״ו ס״ט. וכ״ה ברמב״ם הל׳ יסוה״ת פ״ו ה״ב לפי הנוסחא שבכ״מ
3. רמב״ם הל׳ יסוה״ת פ״ו ה״ה-ו׳
4. רמב״ם הל׳ יסוה״ת פ״ו ה״ג
5. רמב״ם הל׳ יסוה״ת פ״ו ה״ג
6. ט״ז יו״ד סי׳ רע״א ס״ק ח׳
7. יוסף אומץ (יוסף האן) ע׳ רעט, פסקי תשובות סי׳ קנ״ד הע׳ קכ״ו

8. מדרש תנחומא ויגש, ו
9. שו״ע יו״ד סי׳ רע״ו ס״י, ועי׳ בהגה
10. מגילה כט, א
11. שו״ע או״ח סי׳ קנ״ב ס״א
12. ש״ך יו״ד סי׳ קע״ט ס״ק י״א
13. אגרות משה יו״ד ח״א סי׳ קע״ג
14. אגרות משה יו״ד ח״ד סי׳ ס״ג אות י״ג
15. ט״ז או״ח סי׳ קנ״ב ס״ק ג׳
16. רש״י מגילה כט, א ד״ה דשף ויתיב

17. אגרות משה יו״ד ח״ד סי׳ ס״ג אות י״ג
18. שי״ק תשל״ד ע׳ 86
19. אגרות משה יו״ד ח״ב סי׳ קל״ח
20. רמב״ם הל׳ יסוה״ת פ״ו ה״ח
21. עי׳ שו״ע או״ח סי׳ קנ״ד ס״ה, ועי׳ במג״א ס״ק ט׳
22. אגרות משה או״ח ח״ד סי׳ ל״ט

Imagine that you are in China on an important mission. You can't understand or read a single word in Chinese, and their customs make no sense to you. You know what your mission is and you want to do it, but you don't know what to do. **Who would you ask for help? How do you know whom you can trust?**

UNIT 6

IN THIS UNIT YOU WILL:

EXPLORE

- Why does *nevuah* help us do *teshuvah*?
- Why does Hashem use *nevi'im*?

EXAMINE

- What are the signs of a true *navi*?
- Who can be a *navi*?
- How does a *navi* receive a *nevuah* from Hashem?

EXTRACT

- If someone asks you for advice, what should you do?
- When is the only time you are allowed to test Hashem?

הוֹרָאַת שָׁעָה
נְבוּאָה

KEY CONCEPTS

Laugh or Cry

R' Akiva and a group of other *Chachamim* went up to where the *Beis Hamikdash* used to stand. While they were there, a fox ran out from between the crumbled walls of the *kodesh kedoshim*.

The *Chachamim* who were with R' Akiva began to cry loudly, but R' Akiva began to laugh! "Why are you laughing?" the *Chachamim* asked. "Well, why are you crying?" asked R' Akiva.

"We are crying because the *kodesh kadashim* used to be so full of Hashem's *shechinah* that only the *kohen gadol* could go inside. Now there is an animal, a fox, running out!"

"But that is exactly why I am so happy," R' Akiva explained. "There were two *nevuos* said about the *Beis Hamikdash*. The *navi* Uriah said that the *Beis Hamikdash* would be destroyed and animals would run around on it, and Zecharia said that old men and women would be able to sit in the streets of Yerushalayim. Since Uriah's *nevuah* came true, so it must be that Zechariah's *nevuah* will also come true!"

When they heard this explanation, the *Chachamim* said, "עֲקִיבָא נִחַמְתָּנוּ, עֲקִיבָא נִחַמְתָּנוּ" "Akiva, you have comforted us!"[1]

The Mitzvos

The unit of believing *nevi'im* has two mitzvos.

1. Listen to and follow a *navi* of Hashem.
2. Do not test a *navi* of Hashem.

MITZVAH
9

לִשְׁמֹעַ מִן הַנָּבִיא הַמְדַבֵּר בִּשְׁמוֹ

Listening to a *navi* who speaks in the name of Hashem

נָבִיא מִקִּרְבְּךָ מֵאַחֶיךָ כָּמֹנִי יָקִים לְךָ ה' אֱלֹקֶיךָ אֵלָיו תִּשְׁמָעוּן
(דברים יח, טו)

Hashem will set up a navi who is like me (*Moshe Rabbeinu*) from someone among you, **and you must listen to him.**

Follow a *navi* who gives prophecies in the name of Hashem.

ALL PEOPLE   ALL PLACES   ALL TIMES

BIOGRAPHY

R' Akiva

R' Akiva ben Yosef, also called just R' Akiva, was one of the greatest Tannaim, who lived at the end of the second Beis Hamikdash. We assume that every single mishnah is according to what R' Akiva taught, unless the mishnah tells us that he did not agree. R' Akiva's father was a ger, and he was a shepherd who did not know any Torah until he was forty years old! After many years of learning, he became a great tzaddik and Talmid Chacham and had 24,000 talmidim!

R' Akiva was captured by the Romans and was killed because he was caught teaching Torah. He is one of the asarah harugei malchus who's cruel death in the hands of the Romans we read about on Yom Kippur.

R' Akiva lived for 120 years and is mentioned 226 times in Mishnayos, and 564 times in Gemara![2]

MITZVAH 10

שֶׁלֹּא לְנַסּוֹת נָבִיא אֱמֶת יוֹתֵר מִדַּאי
Not testing a *navi*

לֹא תְנַסּוּ אֶת ה' אֱלֹקֵיכֶם כַּאֲשֶׁר נִסִּיתֶם בַּמַּסָּה
(דברים ו, טז)

You shall not test Hashem your G-d
as you tested Him in Massah.

Do not test or doubt a *navi*.

ALL PEOPLE   ALL PLACES   ALL TIMES   MISAH BIYDEI SHAMAYIM

EXPLORE

Mitzvah Messages

Our Guides

If you needed to complete a mission in a new country where you don't know what to do or where to go, you would probably become frustrated. It's too hard to do something when you have no idea where to even begin!

Our lives in Hashem's world can sometimes feel like that. We know that we have to do the mitzvos and serve Hashem, but we sometimes forget how we are supposed to do that. We need help!

Hashem helps us by sending us *nevi'im*, people who can get messages from Hashem and tell us exactly what it is that He wants us to to, and how we should do it. If Hashem wants us to do *teshuvah*, a *navi* can help tell us exactly how to do *teshuvah* and become close to Hashem. Without *nevi'im*, it is hard to know exactly what Hashem wants, so we can become confused and sometimes do the wrong thing.

CHECKPOINT   How does a *navi* help us do the mitzvos and know what Hashem wants?

DID YOU KNOW?

The Ladder of *Nevuah*

Does everyone in the world think in the same way? Of course not! There are many levels of wisdom and understanding. So too, there are many different levels of *nevuah*. Moshe Rabbeinu received the highest level of *nevuah*.[3]

PEARLS *of wisdom*

Extra *Sefarim*

Most of the *nevuos* in the *sefarim* that make up "Nevi'im" are words of rebuke to people who did *aveiros*. *Nevi'im* warned of the terrible punishments that would follow if these people would not do *teshuvah*.

Chazal say that if B'nei Yisrael had not done any of the *aveiros* that made them need these *nevuos*, we would only have *Chumash* and *Sefer Yehoshua*, since the other *sefarim* are about rebuking B'nei Yisrael.[4]

Play It Again

Down in the dumps? Not the best place for someone who wants to be a *navi*! The *Chachamim* explain that a *navi* had to be happy in order to receive a *nevuah* from Hashem. Because of this, many *nevi'im* would have people playing musical instruments for them so that they would be happy and be able to get a *nevuah*.[5]

DISCOVERY

Tried and True

When doctors want to give people a new medicine to use, it has to be tested many times before it is safe for people to use. If it is only tested one time, maybe it just worked by accident and will be very unhealthy for other people.

The same thing applies to a *navi*. If he just shows one sign or miracle that he is a true *navi*, we cannot just believe him. He would have to show us many signs and miracles to prove that he is really a *navi* from Hashem. Once we believe him, we are not allowed to test him anymore.[6]

Who Can Become a *Navi*?

If you were thinking of becoming a *navi*, you may be a bit disappointed to learn that it takes quite a lot to become one. The *navi* must be a very wise person who knows all of the secrets of the Torah. He must be in constant control of his *yetzer hara*, and he has to distance himself from regular activities. For example, a *navi* would not spend his afternoon playing a game, because he has to always be prepared to receive a *nevuah* from Hashem. The *navi* is a special person who has worked on his *middos* so much that he is worthy of Hashem sending a message through him.[7]

How a *Navi* Receives *Nevuah*

A *navi* does not receive his message from Hashem with **words** like a regular conversation, rather in the form of a **vision**. The vision might come to him whenever he is in a deep sleep. While he is getting the *nevuah* from Hashem, his body becomes very weak and his arms and legs shake.[8]

The vision that the *navi* gets is in the form of a parable, a *mashal*. This is like a secret language between Hashem and the *nevi'im*. Hashem will not tell the *navi* exactly what the message is, but it will be explained with pictures of other things. For example, *Ya'akov Avinu* dreamt of a ladder with *malachim* going up and down. This did not just mean that *malachim* were coming and going, but it was also interpreted as a message about all of the non-Jewish nations who would be in control of *B'nei Yisrael*.

When a *navi* tells people his *nevuah*, he can either tell them exactly what images he saw (the *mashal*), or he can explain to them the *nimshal*, the **meaning** of the *mashal*. Sometimes, the *navi* will tell people both the *mashal* and the *nimshal*.[9]

How do We Know that the Person is a True *Navi*?

When a person says that he received a *nevuah* from Hashem, we will only believe him if:

1. He knows the secrets of the Torah, can control his *yetzer hara*, is not involved with regular activities, and has perfect *middos*.

2. He performs a miracle.

3. He predicts the future more than once, and **all** of his positive predictions come true.

4. A person who we already know as a true *navi* says that this man is a true *navi*.[10]

Not Testing a *Navi*

Once a *navi* has shown that he is a true *navi*, we are not allowed to doubt what he says. Also, we are not allowed to test him more than we have to in order to see if he is a true *navi*. Instead, we must believe in him, since we know that Hashem is with him.[11]

 CHECKPOINT What does a *navi* have to do so that people will believe that he is a true *navi*?

SELECTED HALACHOS

הוֹרָאַת שָׁעָה

A true *navi* will never change a mitzvah in the Torah forever. Sometimes, a *navi* will tell *B'nei Yisrael* that they have to do a specific *aveirah* just once, for a very important reason. This is called a "*hora'as sha'ah*," a rule that is only for a short time. This would only be okay if it was very clear that the mitzvah was being changed just for one occasion. If a *navi* says that a mitzvah will be gone forever, he is a false *navi*, even if he already met all of the signs and *nissim*.[12]

For example:

If a true *navi* tells us that we must go to war that is not necessarily to save lives on a specific Shabbos, we must listen to him, since it is only happening once.

If a *navi* says that from now on, we are supposed to put five *parshios* in our *tefillin* instead of four, he is a false *navi* since he is changing a mitzvah forever.[13]

The only time a *hora'as sha'ah* does not apply is for *avodah zarah*. We can never worship idols, even for one second! Any *navi* who says we can serve *avodah zarah* even just once is a false *navi*![14]

HISTORY

Just This Once

When *Eliyahu Hanavi* brought a *korban* on *Har Carmel*, he was acting on a "*hora'as sha'ah*."

Normally, one may not bring a *korban* outside of the *Beis Hamikdash*. However, when *Eliyahu Hanavi* brought the *korban*, he explained that Hashem told him to bring the *korban* on *Har Carmel* just for that one time. This was so that everyone would be able to see the great miracles that were happening there.[16]

Nevuah Fast Facts:

1. There were 48 *nevi'im* and 7 *nevios* (Sorah, Miriam, Devorah, Chanah, Avigail, Chuldah, Esther) recorded in the times of *Tanach*![17]

2. There were times when *nevi'im* brought people back to life.

3. There were seven non-Jewish *nevi'im*: Bilam and his father Be'or, Iyov, Eliphaz, Bildad, Zophar, and Elihu the son of Barachel.[18]

OUR SAGES SAY...

Prophet Of Evil

Why did Hashem make non-Jewish *nevi'im*? He did so, so that when Mashiach comes, the idol-worshippers would not be able to tell Hashem that they did not follow the proper path because they didn't have proper guidance.

But what happened? The non-Jewish *navi*, Bilam, tried to use his power to destroy our nation, which is something that our compassionate *nevi'im* would never have done to any nation. Therefore Hashem took away the gift of *nevuah* from the idol-worshippers.[19]

EXTEND YOUR KNOWLEDGE

The *Nevuah* Forecast

The weatherman on your local radio station may sometimes be right, but is often wrong. He thought it would rain? It didn't! But it doesn't really matter, he won't lose his job just because the weather did not turn out as expected. A *navi*, however, is a false *navi* if even **one** prediction does not turn out to be true, and he could be killed.

But does **everything** he says really have to come true?

No. A positive *nevuah* will always come true,[20] but a negative *nevuah* might be cancelled by Hashem.

This is because Hashem always wants to do good for us, so He will never cancel a positive decree which will be good for someone. But, if someone has a negative *nevuah* (for example, that the person will be punished), Hashem is just waiting for them to do *teshuvah*! Once they do *teshuva*, Hashem will "tear up" the bad decree and the *nevuah* will never happen!

This happened in *Sefer Yonah*. Yonah delivered a message from Hashem to the city of Ninveh, telling them that they would be destroyed if they did not do *teshuvah*. The people did *teshuvah*, and the city was not destroyed.[21]

Live the Mitzvah   EXTRACT

You Can Be a Guide

The *nevi'im* were appointed by Hashem to act as guides for us. Sadly, we don't have this special gift anymore. However, we can still find guidance for ourselves, even in our times. Our *Chachamim* tell us עֲשֵׂה לְךָ רַב - find a *Rav* for yourself who can help you make the right choices.[22]

Also, we should guide other people, and help them in whatever way we can to serve Hashem to the best of their abilities. For example, we can teach others about keeping kosher, or we can remind our friends to stop speaking *lashon hara* by setting an example for them.

 CHECKPOINT How can you act like a *navi* nowadays, when there is no real *nevuah*?

What Else Comes From This?

EXTRACT

Not Testing Hashem

In general, you may not test Hashem by saying that you will do a mitzvah only if Hashem will do something in return, like heal you or make you rich.

The only time that you may test Hashem is when you are giving *tzedakah*. You may give it expecting to become richer as a result, as the *passuk* says[23] "וּבְחָנוּנִי נָא בָּזֹאת" — "*Please test Me with this.*"[24]

According to some opinions, we may only test Hashem when we are giving *ma'aser*, as the *Chazal* explain the *passuk* "עַשֵּׂר תְּעַשֵּׂר" - "*you shall give ma'aser*" to mean "עַשֵּׂר בִּשְׁבִיל שֶׁתִּתְעַשֵּׁר" - "*give ma'aser in order to become rich.*" According to this opinion, it would not apply to any other form of *tzedakah*, and someone can only expect to become rich from giving *ma'aser*.[25]

CHECKPOINT | When is the only time that you are allowed to test Hashem?

A STORY

Mouth To Mouth Resuscitation

Elisha the *navi* regularly stayed at the home of a certain Shunnamite woman. She set up a room for him with a bed so that he would have a place to rest. Out of gratitude, he promised her that she would have a son. A year later, her son was born.

One day, several years later, her son suddenly became ill and died. His mother laid him on the bed in Elisha's room, and ran to get Elisha. She begged him to help, and he went with her to her home, where he found the lifeless boy on his bed. He prayed to Hashem, and then laid down on the boy, putting his mouth against the boy's mouth, his eyes against his eyes, and his hands against his hands. The boy soon came back to life![26]

HISTORY

Fantastic, Amazing Miracle

All Jews experienced *nevuah* at *Kriyas Yam Suf*.

At that incredible moment in history, even a simple maidservant experienced greater *nevuah* than the *nevi'im* Yeshayah and Yechezkel who saw the highest spiritual levels in their *nevuah*.[27]

DID YOU KNOW?

Heaven Sent

One of the *Ba'alei Hatosfos* named Rabbi Ya'akov would ask a *malach* the questions that he came up with as he learned Torah. He would write the question on a piece of paper and place it under his pillow before going to sleep.

He collected the answers he received and wrote them into a sefer called שְׁאֵלוֹת וּתְשׁוּבוֹת מִן הַשָּׁמַיִם – Questions and Answers from Heaven.

UNIT 6

ENDNOTES:

1. מכות כד, ב
2. אטלס עץ החיים ח"ד ע' 275
3. רמב"ם הל' יסוה"ת פ"ז ה'ו
4. נדרים כב, ב
5. רמב"ם הל' יסוה"ת פ"ז ה"ד
6. ספר העקרים מאמר א' פי"ח
7. רמב"ם הל' יסוה"ת פ"ז ה"א
8. רמב"ם הל' יסוה"ת פ"ז ה"ב
9. רמב"ם הל' יסוה"ת פ"ז ה"ג

10. רמב"ם הל' יסוה"ת פ"ז ה"ז. פ"י ה"א-ב', ו'
11. רמב"ם הל' יסוה"ת פ"י ה"ה
12. רמב"ם הל' יסוה"ת פ"ט ה"א, וג'
13. הקדמת הרמב"ם למשנה
14. רמב"ם הל' יסוה"ת פ"ט ה"ה
15. מגילה יד, א
16. רמב"ם הל' יסוה"ת פ"ט ה"ג
17. מגילה יד, א
18. בבא בתרא טו, ב

19. במדבר רבה כ, א
20. ירמיהו כח, ט
21. רמב"ם הל' יסוה"ת פ"י ה"ד
22. אבות פ"א מ"ו
23. מלאכי ג, י
24. טור יו"ד סי' רמ"ז
25. רמ"א יו"ד סי' רמ"ז ס"ד
26. מלכים ב' פרק ד
27. ילקוט שמעוני תורה רמז רמ"ב, ובכ"מ

BELIEVING PROPHETS **59**

Is there someone you admire so much that you wish you were more like him or her? What is it about that person that makes you feel this way? What would you do to become more like that person?

UNIT 7

IN THIS UNIT YOU WILL:

EXPLORE

- Why is Hashem the perfect role model?
- Why is it so important to be a role model to other people?

EXAMINE

- What should be your thoughts when you do an act of *chessed*?
- What are some of the *middos* of Hashem?

EXTRACT

- If you want to take the middle path to become closer to Hashem, how should you behave?
- If you want to change a certain *middah*, what do you have to do?

הֲלִיכָה בִּדְרָכָיו
דֶּרֶךְ הַיְשָׁרָה

KEY CONCEPTS

UNIT
7

Book: Madda, Section: Character
סֵפֶר מַדָּע הִלְכוֹת דֵּעוֹת

הֲלִיכָה בִּדְרָכָיו
GOING IN HASHEM'S WAYS
מִצְוָה אַחַת

OUR SAGES SAY...

Do As I Do

R' Chama, the son of R' Chanina, explains that to copy Hashem, we should do the same acts of kindness that Hashem did for our *Avos*.

Just as Hashem gave Adam and Chavah clothes in *Gan Eden*, we should also give clothes and other things to people who need it.

Just as Hashem comforted Yitzchak after his father Avraham passed away, we can comfort someone whose relative died.

And just as Hashem visited Avraham after his *bris milah* we can visit the sick.[1]

The Mitzvah

The unit of *Halichah Bi'drochov* has one mitzvah.

You have to copy the actions and *middos* of Hashem.

MITZVAH 11

לְהַדָּמוֹת בְּדַרְכֵי הַשֵׁם יִתְבָּרֵךְ הַטוֹבִים וְהַיְשָׁרִים
Copying the good and fair ways of Hashem

יְקִימְךָ ה' לוֹ לְעַם קָדוֹשׁ כַּאֲשֶׁר נִשְׁבַּע לָךְ כִּי תִשְׁמֹר
אֶת מִצְוֹת ה' אֱלֹקֶיךָ וְהָלַכְתָּ בִּדְרָכָיו
(דברים כח, ט)

Hashem will set you up for Himself as a holy people, as He swore to you if you observe the commandments of Hashem your G-d, **and you shall go in His ways.**

Do actions specifically to act like Hashem.

ALL PEOPLE · ALL PLACES · ALL TIMES

STORY

Following the Tradition

R' Shamshon Raphael Hirsch lived in Germany, where the cold, snowy winters made it difficult for animals to find food.

Wanting to be kind to animals as Hashem is, Rabbi Hirsch's wife would put out food on her windowsill every morning for the birds who gathered there. After she passed away, Rabbi Hirsch continued doing this until his last days.

When he was on his deathbed, he even told his sons not to forget to take care of the birds.

So much was his desire to be kind just like Hashem is.[2]

BIOGRAPHY

Rabbi Shamshon Raphael Hirsch

(1808 – 1888) תקס"ח - תרמ"ח

R' Shamshon Refael Hirsch was a great Rav in many cities in Germany. He worked very hard to save the Jews of his generation from losing their connection to the Torah, and wrote many sefarim explaining the beauty of Torah and mitzvos including a pirush on Chumash and the siddur that is used by many to this day.

The Ultimate Role Model

Because everyone thinks that different things are important, everyone has different role models. A boy who loves planes may think his uncle who is a pilot is the greatest person in the world. His sister, who doesn't care about planes, might not agree. However, she may look up to her teacher and try to copy her because she is so impressed with the way her teacher seems to know everything.

Since everyone is so different, is there a single role model that everyone can follow and everyone agrees is always doing the right thing?

Yes. Hashem, Who is completely perfect, is the best role model for everyone to follow. We cannot go wrong by following in the ways of Hashem, because all of His ways are always perfect.

 CHECKPOINT   Why is Hashem the best role model for every single person in the world?

Details   EXAMINE

The Ways of Hashem

The Torah describes Hashem's *middos* to show us how perfect He is. We are commanded to copy these *middos*.

DID YOU KNOW?

All Day Long

Because Hashem commanded us to copy His ways, we have an easy way of serving Hashem anytime, anywhere.

Anything we do, even eating or sleeping, becomes a way of serving Hashem, if we do it for a purpose.

For example, if we eat with the thought that we are keeping our bodies healthy so that we can learn Torah and do mitzvos, then we are serving Hashem, just by eating a meal![3]

Be Like Him

R' Simlai said: Hashem blesses *chassanim*, makes *kallos* beautiful, visits the sick, buries the dead, and comforts the mourners. Since we should try to be like Hashem, we should also do these mitzvos.[4]

PEARLS of wisdom

Setting an Example

One of R' Akiva's students was sick, and no one visited him. So, R' Akiva himself went to visit him. The students prepared the house for the arrival of the special guest. They swept the ground and cleaned all of the dirt. Since the house was cleaned, the sick person became better!

R' Akiva said that since you can make someone feel better just by visiting them, if you don't visit him, it is like you make them sick![5]

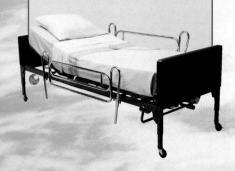

Some of these *middos* are:

רַחוּם - Merciful

Hashem is forgiving even when a person does not listen to Him again and again. Most people may only forgive someone who hurt them once, or even twice, but Hashem will show mercy to anyone who does *teshuvah*, no matter how many times they have done *aveiros*.

חַנוּן - Generous

Hashem gives people what they need even if they don't deserve it. No matter what type of person you are, Hashem wil take care of you.

אֶרֶךְ אַפַּיִם - Slow to anger

Some people lose their tempers easily, and will get angry as soon as anything goes wrong. Hashem does not do this. If we do something wrong, He gives us time to do *teshuvah*. We see this with what happened with Yonah and the city of Ninveh. They were supposed to be destroyed, but were saved because they did *teshuvah*.

רַב חֶסֶד - Extra kindness

One of the times when Hashem shows us extra kindness is when He tips the scale of our actions to the good side when we have an equal amount of mitzvos and *aveiros*.[6]

These examples teach us to be kind and patient with all people, no matter how difficult it might be. Even if someone is mean to you, or embarrasses you, you still have to be nice to them and do extra to help them out.

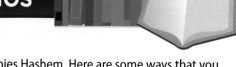

CHECKPOINT How can you copy the special *middos* of Hashem?

SELECTED HALACHOS

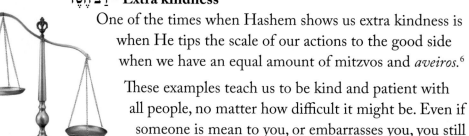

You must behave in a way that copies Hashem. Here are some ways that you can copy Hashem's ways in public:

- You should not eat on the street, or in a public place, except for a festive meal such as a wedding.[7]
- You should speak gently and not scream.[8]
- You should walk calmly in the street and not run or make noise.[9]
- You should not wear clothing that is torn or dirty.[10]

EXTEND YOUR KNOWLEDGE

Bonus for *Kavanah*

The mitzvah to copy Hashem seems to be very similar to the mitzvah of *Ahavas Yisrael*, because both *mitzvos* are about showing kindness to others. Since they are so similar, why do we need **both**?

The mitzvah of *Halichah Bidrachav* is different than that of *Ahavas Yisrael*, because we have to focus on our *kavanah*, instead of the actual action. For the mitzvah of *Ahavas Yisrael*, you don't need to have any special thoughts or *kavanah*. The most important thing is to do something nice to someone else no matter what the intention is.

The main mitzvah of *Halichah Bidrachav* is the **thoughts** and **kavanah** to try and "copy the ways of Hashem." When you have the *kavanah* to copy Hashem, you will naturally do kind actions.[11]

Live the Mitzvah

EXTRACT

You Are a Role Model Too

Even though you may have your own role models, you are also a role model to others, whether or not you realize it. Your younger siblings, if you have any, look up to you, and children in the younger grades think of you as a grown up. You have a responsibility to all these people to show your good *middos* and to behave nicely, so that they can look at you and decide to behave in a similar way.

By copying the ways of Hashem in your *middos* and actions, you can teach others to also follow in His ways.

CHECKPOINT — How can you be a role model for other people?

A Few Seconds of Happiness

R' Levi Yitzchak of Berditchev used to visit the sick people of Berditchev. He loved and cared for each patient so much, that even a patient who was extremely sick would feel better when R' Levi Yitzchok came to visit.

One time, R' Levi Yitzchok visited a patient whom he could not comfort. R' Levi Yitzchok asked the patient why he was so miserable. The man answered that he did not do so many mitzvos in his life and he did not think he would go to *Olam Haba* after he died.

Right away, R' Levi Yitzchok told the sick man "I will give you **my** share in *Olam Haba*." After the shock passed, a great happiness and relief came over the sick man and he died soon after, with a smile on his lips.

When R' Levi Yitzchok's *gabbai* asked him why he was willing to give away so much, R' Levi Yitzchok answered that it was worth giving away everything he has in this world and *Olam Haba*, just to give a few seconds of happiness to a fellow Jew!

The Middle Path

What Is It?

Everyone has different *middos*. Some people are calm and some get angry very easily, some are kind and some are selfish. Each *middah* can be done too much, or too little. Someone can have the *middah* of calm and be more calm than they should, or someone can have the *middah* of calm, but not be calm enough. Someone can be too nice, or not nice enough. Both extremes of *middos* are not the best.

The best way for a person to behave is to find the middle path of the *middah*. This is called the דֶרֶךְ הַיְשָׁרָה – the straight path. Following the middle path in each *middah* is following in the ways of Hashem.

Some Examples

- You should not want everything so much that you are never happy, but you should also not make your life unhappy by never having anything. The middle path is to want only the things that you need, but not to want anything extra.

- You should not be selfish and keep everything you have to yourself, but you should also not be too generous and give away more than you are able to. The middle path is to give to others based on what you are able to give, and based on what others need.

- You should not party and joke around all the time, but you should also not be sad and quiet all the time. The middle path is to always be happy and calm, with a smile at all times, but to be serious when you need to be.[12]

How to Get There

You can change a *middah* by acting properly over and over again until it becomes the way you act without thinking.[13]

This works when the *middah* that you are changing is not such a strong *middah*. However, when you have a very strong bad *middah*, you must go to the other extreme to fix it. For example, if you get angry easily, then you should go to the other extreme and never become angry, even when someone says something really mean to you or when someone hits you. Once that bad *middah* is gone, you can then find the middle path.[14]

When the Middle is Not Good

Although usually, you should follow the middle path, there are two *middos* which you should **not** follow the middle path.

These negative *middos* are arrogance and anger. Instead of taking the middle road, you should be very close to the bottom of the scale (but not all the way at the bottom).[15]

This means:

• You should not be arrogant and think that you are better than anyone else, but you should also not think that you are **totally** worthless. The middle path (to think that you are an average person) is also not good, because you will not be humble enough. The **best** way is to know that you are **far** from the best, but you should still not allow other people to "walk all over you" and make you feel bad.

• You should not get angry quickly, but you should also not be like a person who has no feelings and never feels anger. The middle path (to only get angry about something important) is also not good, because it will be too often. The **best** way is to only act angry in **extreme** cases, like when you see someone doing an *aveirah*, and you know that if you act angry, the person will not do that *aveirah* again.

 CHECKPOINT   How much of each *middah* should a person have?

UNIT 7

ENDNOTES:

12. רמב"ם הל' דעות פ"א ה"ד
13. רמב"ם הל' דעות פ"א ה"ז
14. רמב"ם הל' דעות פ"ב ה"ב
15. רמב"ם הל' דעות פ"א ה"ה, פ"ב ה"ג, ובלחם משנה שם
16. סיפורי חסידים מועדים סוכות

6. תוס' ר"ה יז, ב בהגה"ה
7. רמב"ם הל' דעות פ"ה ה"ב
8. רמב"ם הל' דעות פ"ה ה"ז
9. רמב"ם הל' דעות פ"ה ה"ח
10. רמב"ם הל' דעות פ"ה ה"ט
11. לקו"ש חל"ד ע' 153 ואילך

1. סוטה יד, א
2. Rabbi Samson Raphael Hirsch by Rabbi Eliyahu Meir Klugman - ArtScroll
3. רמב"ם הל' דעות פ"ג ה"ב
4. בראשית רבה ח, יג
5. נדרים מ, א

Extreme Control

R' Michel of Zlotchov was extremely poor, but had a beautiful pair of *tefillin* which he inherited from his father. He treasured the *tefillin* more than anything else in the world. His wife tried many times to convince him to sell the *tefillin* so they would at least have a little money, but R' Michel would not listen.

It was coming close to Sukkos and no one in the city had an *esrog*. Just when the town people thought they would not be able to perform the mitzvah of the *arba minim*, a stranger arrived in Zlotchov with a beautiful *esrog* for sale. However, his price was so high that no one could even think of buying it.

R' Michel thought for a moment, and then sold his *tefillin* for a large amount of money and used the money to buy the *esrog*. His wife was suspicious and asked R' Michel where he got the money to buy such a beautiful *esrog*.

When his wife found out that he had sold his *tefillin*, something she had begged him to do for years, she was so angry that she grabbed the *esrog* and bit off the *pittom*, making the *esrog* *passul*.

Although R' Michel now had neither his precious *tefillin* nor an *esrog*, he didn't say a word.

Later, R' Michel's father appeared to him in a dream and told him that for not becoming angry at his wife, he got a larger reward in *shamayim* than for buying the *esrog* with the money he had from selling his special *tefillin*.[16]

UNIT 8

EXPLORE

- Why is just watching how *Talmidei Chachamim* live and serving them more powerful than learning Torah from them?

- How are *Talmidei Chachamim* able to help you connect to Hashem?

EXAMINE

- What happens to you when you connect with *Talmidei Chachamim*?

- What are the different ways in which you can learn from and connect with *Talmidei Chachamim*?

EXTRACT

- How should you choose your friends?

- How can you learn from *Talmidei Chachamim* after they have passed away?

אֱמוּנַת חֲכָמִים

שָׁמוּשׁ תַּלְמִידֵי חֲכָמִים

KEY CONCEPTS

Book: Madda, Section: Character
סֵפֶר מַדָּע הִלְכוֹת דֵּעוֹת

הַדְּבֵיקָה עִם חַכְמֵי הַתּוֹרָה

CONNECTING TO TALMIDEI CHACHAMIM

מִצְוָה אַחַת

It is a beautiful morning. The sun is deliciously warm, and there are sweet smelling flowers nearby. Just by being outside, you feel that you are getting the strength you need to start your day. Would you feel the same way standing next to an overflowing trash bin in the dark?

Connect to Them

Hashem commanded us to connect to Him. But how can we possibly connect to Hashem when we have bodies and live in this world, and Hashem does not have a body?!

Chazal tell us that when we connect to *Talmidei Chachamim*, it is as if we have connected to Hashem Himself![1]

DISCOVERY

Scents that Empower

Our sense of smell is very powerful. We can even remember things only because of their smell. Smells can remind us of places we once were at and they can remind us of the same feelings we had a long time ago.

For example, imagine you were in a *matzah* bakery and were excited about seeing your big brother who was returning from *yeshivah* that evening. Years later, if you walked passed a *matzah* bakery and smelled the same smell, you might feel the same excitement you had back then when you were excited to see your brother.

Just like being around certain smells can change your mood, being around *Talmidei Chachamim* can affect you and change you to become a better person.

The Mitzvah

The unit of Connecting to *Talmidei Chachamim* has one mitzvah:

Connect to and learn from *Talmidei Chachamim*.

MITZVAH
12

הַחֲבֵרָה וְהַדְּבֵיקָה עִם חַכְמֵי הַתּוֹרָה
Connecting to *Talmidei Chachamim*

אֶת ה׳ אֱלֹקֶיךָ תִּירָא אֹתוֹ תַעֲבֹד וּבוֹ **תִדְבָּק** וּבִשְׁמוֹ תִּשָּׁבֵעַ
(דברים י, כ)

Fear Hashem your G-d, serve Him, **and cling to Him**, and swear in His Name.

Connect to *Talmidei Chachamim*.

ALL PEOPLE   ALL PLACES   ALL TIMES

Mitzvah Messages

Special Because of a Connection

As human beings, we learn a lot from where we are and who we are around. For example, being around a happy and cheerful person makes you feel refreshed and happy, while meeting an angry person might make you feel upset and angry. Therefore, it is important to be around those people who make you feel happy and have a good effect on you.

Talmidei Chachamim have a very good effect on others. Their excellent *middos* make it easier for us to see how we should behave, and their mitzvos help us to do more mitzvos ourselves. We should do our best to spend time with *Talmidei Chachamim*, so that we become better people![2]

CHECKPOINT How do you become a better person when you spend time with *Talmidei Chachamim*?

It Rubs Off On You

Some of the ways we can connect ourselves to *Talmidei Chachamim* are:

- Serving them. Not only is it a great honor to serve these holy people, but we have the chance to watch them and learn from their ways.

- Eating and drinking with them. Watching how *Talmidei Chachamim* eat and drink teaches us how to behave properly with food.

- Doing business with them.[3] This will inspire us to improve how we act and deal honestly in these areas.

- Learning Torah from them is also a good way to become wiser and smarter, much more so than learning on our own.[4]

CHECKPOINT What are some ways that you can connect and learn from *Talmidei Chachamim?*

SELECTED HALACHOS

- A man should try to marry the daughter of a *Talmid Chacham*.[5]
- A father should encourage his daughter to marry a *Talmid Chacham*.[5]
- You should allow a *Talmid Chacham* to make use of your personal possessions. This will help you have success in anything that you do.[6]
- You should not live in an area where people don't behave according to the ways of Torah, because it will be a bad influence on you.[7]

EXTEND YOUR KNOWLEDGE

Power Source

All the parts of the body are kept alive by the brain. If a body part is separated from the brain, it can no longer work. *B'nei Yisrael* are very similar. The *Talmidei Chachamim* are like the brain of the body, and all the Jewish people are like the body parts. The *neshamos* of the Jews are kept "alive" by the fire and mitzvos of the *Talmidei Chachamim*.[8]

DISCOVERY

Radiating Warmth

The average distance between the sun and the earth is 92,955,820.5 miles. This distance is so enormous that it takes 8 minutes and 20 seconds for the light rays to travel from the sun to the earth.

Therefore, when we look at the sun, we are actually seeing it as how it appeared 8 minutes and 20 seconds ago!

Yet, the sun is so powerful, that its heat comes all the way to us here on Earth and keeps us nice and warm.

This is similar to the positive effect that *Talmidei Chachamin* have on their surroundings.

OUR SAGES SAY...

A Lesson in Every Word

שִׂיחַת חוּלִּין שֶׁל תַּלְמִידֵי חֲכָמִים צְרִיכָה לִימוּד

Even the everyday conversations of Talmidei Chachamim must be studied.

In addition to **what** they are saying, there is much that can be learned from the **way** *Talmidei Chachamim* speak.[9]

Learning By Example

גְּדוֹלָה שִׁמּוּשָׁהּ שֶׁל תּוֹרָה יוֹתֵר מִלִּמּוּדָהּ

Serving those who study Torah is greater than studying Torah from them.[10]

Sometimes, watching how *Talmidei Chachamim* act throughout the day can teach you more about good *middos* than you would ever learn from listening to *shiurim* by those same *Talmidei Chachamim*.

We learn this from Elisha, who would pour water over the hands of Eliyahu.[11] Elisha's greatness came from serving Eliyahu, more than from learning with him.

DID YOU KNOW?

Substitute

Talmidei Chachamim are also compared to the *Beis Hamikdash*. The *Beis Hamikdash* was where the *Shechinah* rested. From there, its light spread to the entire Jewish nation. So too, the *Talmidei Chachamim* spread the light of the *Shechinah*, and we learn so much from them.

Therefore, *Chazal* tell us that שְׁקוּלָה מִיתָתָן שֶׁל צַדִּיקִים כִּשְׂרֵיפַת בֵּית אֱלֹקֵינוּ — The death of *tzaddikim* is equal to the burning of the *Beis Hamikdash*.[12]

Live the Mitzvah

EXTRACT

Good People Make Good Friends

Pick Your Friends

We all want friends. But sometimes, we need to stop and think: *Who* are the people I want to be friends with? Will it be good for me if I become friends with this person? Will I learn from their mitzvos, or will I end up rolling around in the mud of their *aveiros*? Will I be warmed by their *middos* and kindness, or will I be hurt by their arrogance and selfishness?

Choosing your friends is like choosing between being in the warm sun or in the cold night. Imagine yourself in the sun. Its light and warmth are working their magic on you, and you feel great. This is what good people are like. Their goodness shines out of them, giving strength to others. Like *Talmidei Chachamim*, our good friends bring out the best in us, and in the light of their wisdom and goodness, we are able to grow.

CHECKPOINT How should you choose your friends?

What Else Comes From This?

EXTRACT

Shechinah Is With Them

Because *Talmidei Chachamim* are connected to Hashem through their Torah learning, the *Shechinah* rests upon them. Even after they pass away, the *Shechinah* stays with their bodies. For this reason, people *daven* at the graves of *Talmidei Chachamim*, so that they can stand in the presence of the *Shechinah*.[13]

Me'aras Hamachpelah is where our *Avos* and *Imahos* are buried.

Tell Me A Story

The memories of *Talmidei Chachamim* remain with us even after they are no longer alive, since many of the great stories about them are written down for us to learn. Such stories can be found in *Gemara*, *Midrashim*, and *sefarim*, such as *sipurei tzadikim*, as well as the the many biographies of modern-day *tzadikim* and *Chachamim* available today. From these stories, people can learn how to improve their *middos* and serve Hashem in the best way possible.[14]

אֱמוּנַת חֲכָמִים - Trusting *Chachamim*

Talmidei Chachamim have a special connection to Hashem and are able to see things that ordinary people cannot. Some also have a special ability to give advice and *berachos* to those who need help. Because of their special connection to Hashem and His Torah, we trust their words and their advice.[15]

CHECKPOINT — Why do we trust the advice of *Talmidei Chachamim* more than anyone else?

A STORY

Wrong Problem, Right Solution

Two women went to see R' Yisrael of Ruzhin. One woman's husband was very sick, and the other's husband owed a lot of money to his landlord. The notes with their requests got mixed up and it looked like each wife got an answer which was good for the other one! The sick man's wife was told "May Hashem help you," and the wife of the man who owed a lot of money was told to use cupping glasses and leeches, a type of medicine.

The wife of the man who owed money believed in the *tzaddik's* advice, and she made her confused husband try the leeches and the cupping glasses.

The landlord's wife soon saw him bleeding in his bed and felt so bad for him that she begged her husband to cancel the debt.

This woman's belief in the *tzaddik* had saved them.[16]

UNIT 8

ENDNOTES:

1. חינוך מצוה תל"ד
2. רמב"ם הל' דעות פ"ו ה"א
3. רמב"ם הל' דעות פ"ו ה"ב
4. עירובין יג, ב
5. רמב"ם הל' דעות פ"ו ה"ב. שו"ע אה"ע סי' ב' ס"ו
6. סנהדרין צב, א

7. רמב"ם הל' דעות פ"ו ה"א
8. שו"ת חת"ס או"ח סי' קס"ו
9. סוכה כא, ב
10. ברכות ז, ב
11. מלכים ב' ג', יא
12. דרשות הר"ן הדרוש השמיני
13. דרשות הר"ן הדרוש השמיני

14. חינוך מצוה תל"ד
15. עי' מכתב מאליהו ח"א ע' 75 באריכות, ובכ"מ
16. סיפורי חסידים פ' בשלח
17. במדבר יא, כח
18. רלב"ג יהושע א, א
19. ברכות סד, א

Look at the many faces in this picture.

Now hold the book far away from your
face and look at all the faces together.
Do you see how all those small pictures
look like one single face?

UNIT 9

IN THIS UNIT YOU WILL:

EXPLORE

- Why is Hashem happy when you love all Jews?
- Why is it a problem if one Jew doesn't love another?

EXAMINE

- What can you do to show your love to another Jew?
- What are the five mitzvos that are part of the mitzvah of *ahavas yisrael*?

EXTRACT

- If you want to make sure that *klal Yisrael* is healthy, what do you have to do?
- If you want Hashem to answer your *tefillos*, what can you do?

אַהֲבַת יִשְׂרָאֵל
נִיחוּם אֲבֵלִים
הַכְנָסַת כַּלָּה
הוֹצָאַת הַמֵּת
בִּיקּוּר חוֹלִים
הַכְנָסַת אוֹרְחִים

KEY CONCEPTS

Book: Madda, Section: Character

סֵפֶר מַדָּע הִלְכוֹת דֵּעוֹת

אַהֲבַת יִשְׂרָאֵל
LOVE ALL JEWS

מִצְוָה אַחַת

Don't Rain on My People

In Eretz Yisrael, we begin *davening* for rain on the seventh day of *Cheshvan*. The *Chachamim* chose this day, and not an earlier day, because it would take some travellers as long as fifteen days to return home from Yerushalayim after the *Yamim Tovim*. If it would rain during this time, it would be very difficult for these Jews to travel.

So, although the farmers needed rain more than anything else, the rain is delayed until each Jew is home safely and comfortably. This shows the strong *ahavas yisrael* that we have for each other.[1]

The unit of *Ahavas Yisrael* has one mitzvah.

You must love every Jew as much as you love yourself.

MITZVAH
13

מִצְוַת אַהֲבַת יִשְׂרָאֵל
Loving every Jew

לֹא תִקֹּם וְלֹא תִטֹּר אֶת בְּנֵי עַמֶּךָ וְאָהַבְתָּ לְרֵעֲךָ כָּמוֹךָ אֲנִי ה'
(ויקרא יט, יח)

Do not take revenge or bear a grudge against the people of your nation. **You must love your friend as yourself.** I am Hashem.

Love every Jew the same way you love yourself.

ALL PEOPLE   ALL PLACES   ALL TIMES

One Big Body

The entire Jewish nation is like one huge body. Each body part is important, and together they make the body complete. Whatever happens to one part of the body is felt by all other parts of the body. If even one toe is infected, then the whole body is in danger as the infection can spread quickly! *B'nei Yisrael* are very similar. When one Jew is hurt, other Jews feel pain. When one Jew is happy, other Jews are happy too.[2]

United We Stand, Divided We Fall

Hashem is very happy when He sees His children loving and caring for each other. When we are united, Hashem sends us *brachos* and our enemies cannot destroy us. Therefore, when we care for each other, and *daven* or do mitzvos for other Jews around the world, we will have peace.[3]

 CHECKPOINT What happens when *B'nei Yisrael* act like one connected body?

Details   EXAMINE

Mitzvos That Are Part Of *Ahavas Yisrael*

The mitzvah of *ahavas yisrael* includes five specific mitzvos which you can do to show love for other Jews.[4]

הַכְנָסַת אוֹרְחִים – Welcoming Guests

You should make a special effort to invite guests from out of town, and treat them royally while they are in your house, especially with food and drink. When your guests leave, you should escort them out of the house.[5]

הַכְנָסַת כַּלָּה – Making a *Chassan* and *Kallah* Happy

If a *chassan* and *kallah* don't have enough money to pay for their wedding, it is a mitzvah to help them so that they can have a beautiful wedding.[6]

DISCOVERY

Strength in Numbers

Imagine that you have a small twig in your hand. You could break it very easily, couldn't you? But what if you had a big bunch of twigs all tied together. Is it still so easy to snap? The same twig which was so easy to snap by itself, is so hard to snap when it is with others.

Cables work the same way. A cable is made of many thin metal threads tied together. Cables can be so strong, that they can be used to hold up huge, heavy bridges.

The same thing applies to Jews. When one Jew is alone, he can easily be destroyed. However, when there are many Jews together, they can't be destroyed easily.

The **Golden Gate Bridge** in San Francisco, CA, is one of the longest bridges in the world to be supported by cables. Each cable is made of 27,572 wires and is 36 ⅜" (92.4 cm) thick.

Comfort, Comfort My People

When we visit an *avel* (someone who's close relative died), we ask that Hashem comfort the mourner together with all the Jews who are still mourning the destruction of the *Beis Hamikdash* and Yerushalayim.[7]

When the *Beis Hamikdash* was destroyed, only the physical building was destroyed, but the *kedushah* stayed.

We remind the *avel* that when a person passes away, only their physical body is gone, but the most important part – their *neshamah,* the Torah they have learned, and the mitzvos they have done – remain forever!

This mitzvah also includes dancing in front of a *chassan* and *kallah* to bring them joy on their special day.[8] Another way to bring happiness to a wedding is by walking with the *chassan* to his *kallah* when he covers her face with a veil.[9]

בִּיקוּר חוֹלִים – Visiting the Sick

It is a mitzvah to visit sick people, since it makes them feel better and helps them get well sooner. Another way you can fulfill this mitzvah is by *davening* for a sick person to get better.[10]

הוֹצָאַת הַמֵּת – Preparing and Burying Someone Who Died

It is a special mitzvah to help prepare and bury a person, and to walk with the *aron* on the way to the burial. This brings comfort to the *neshamah* and is a kind act of *ahavas yisrael* to the person who passed away. It is special because the person who passed away cannot repay you for your act of kindness.[11]

נִחוּם אֲבֵלִים – Comforting Mourners

When someone passes away, it is a mitzvah to comfort the person's relatives as they sit *shivah*.[12] When visiting the *aveilim*, the following is said: הַמָּקוֹם יְנַחֵם אֶתְכֶם בְּתוֹךְ שְׁאָר אֲבֵלֵי צִיּוֹן וִירוּשָׁלַיִם – *May Hashem comfort you amongst all the mourners of Tzion and Yerushalayim.*[13]

 CHECKPOINT What are the five mitzvos that are part of the mitzvah of *ahavas yisrael*?

R' Dovid Lelover

(1746–1814) ה'תק"ו–ה'תקע"ד

R' Dovid Lelover was the first Rebbe of the Lelover dynasty. He lived in the town of Lelow, Poland. He was a talmid of the famous "Chozeh of Lublin" and was known for his tremendous love for every Jew.

A STORY

No Jew Will be Left Behind

The entire town was nervous. R' Dovid of Lelov's young son was extremely sick. The entire *Sefer Tehillim* was divided up between people and everyone was *davening* for him.

Finally, their *tefillos* were answered and R' Dovid's son began to get better. When the boy was completely healed, the entire town was invited to a *se'udas hoda'ah* to thank Hashem for healing the young boy. As the festivities began, all the guests were shocked when their *Rebbe*, R' Dovid, started crying!

"Why are you crying?" Everyone asked. "This is such a happy time!"

"My dear son was very sick and everyone in Lelov was worried," cried the *Rebbe*. "*Tefillos* were said for his recovery, and people even fasted. *Baruch Hashem*, your *tefillos* were answered.

"But what happens when someone else, a simple Jew, becomes sick? Does everyone say *Tehillim* for him? Is everyone concerned in the same way? I am crying for all those people who are alone when they need others to *daven* for them."[14]

SELECTED HALACHOS

Many important details of *hachnasas orchim* can be learned from the story of *Avraham Avinu* and the *malachim* who came to visit him.

- You should make guests feel comfortable to enter your home. Avraham's tent had four doors so that the guests could find the doors easily and would come in from all directions.

- You should make an effort to find guests and be quick to greet them. Avraham searched for guests outside his home and when he finally saw some, he ran to greet them.

- You should provide your guests with everything they need. Avraham served his guests everything they needed; food, drink, and even water with which to wash their feet.

- You should offer your guests a comfortable place to sit or rest. Avraham gave his guests a comfortable place to rest under the tree.

- You should do more than expected for your guests. Avraham gave his guests meat and many other delicious foods.

- You should let other members of the family help you with the mitzvah of *hachnasas orchim*. Avraham asked his wife, Sorah, and his son, Yishmael, to help prepare food for his guests.[15]

OUR SAGES SAY...

Substitute *Korban*

In the days of the *Beis Hamikdash*, people would bring *korbanos* on the *mizbeiach* to be a *kaparah* for their *aveiros*.

Hashem loves *hachnasas orchim* so much, that when we have guests at our table, Hashem forgives our *aveiros*, just like He would forgive the *aveiros* of someone who brought a *korban* in the *Beis Hamikdash*![18]

EXTEND YOUR KNOWLEDGE

Love is a Blessing

Normally, you are not allowed to say a *brachah* if there is no need to. For example, you may not say a *brachah* on an apple if you just said a *brachah* on another apple a minute ago!

However, if you are helping someone else do a mitzvah, you can say a *brachah* again, even if you have already said the same *brachah* earlier. For example, someone who has already made *kiddush* may say *kiddush* again for another person, if the second person had not heard it yet and cannot make his own *brachah*. That *brachah* is not considered a *brachah* that is not needed, because "כָּל יִשְׂרָאֵל עֲרֵבִים זֶה בָּזֶה - All Jews are responsible for one another."[16]

If there is one Jew who has not yet been able to do a mitzvah, then all Jews are lacking in that mitzvah. Therefore, one must perform the mitzvah for the sake of the other person, so that all Jews can fulfill that mitzvah.[17]

DID YOU KNOW?

A Special Glow

The *Shechinah* rests with a sick person. That's why you should not sit higher than a sick person's head. That is where the *Shechinah* is resting, and you must show respect to the *Shechinah*.[19]

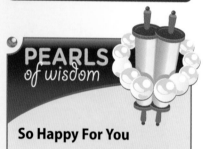
Destroyed By Hate

Megillas Eichah describes the destruction of the *Beis Hamikdash*. The first *passuk* reads:

"אֵיכָה יָשְׁבָה בָדָד הָעִיר רַבָּתִי עָם הָיְתָה"

The first letter of each of these words spell "אֵיבָה רָעָה" – "Hate is bad." Hate, specifically *sinas chinam*, was the reason why the *Beis Hamikdash* was destroyed.[20]

Just Like You Would Want

Here are just some of the many ways that you can fulfill the mitzvah of *ahavas yisrael*.

1. Act towards others with real love, instead of just pretending to love them.
2. Look for ways to make people happy.
3. Make people feel better when they are sad.
4. Greet people warmly.
5. Give others the benefit of the doubt.
6. Help someone who is working hard.
7. Lend or give money to someone who needs it, without making him feel bad about it.
8. Help others be successful.

One Big Happy Family

Parents are always very happy when they see their children getting along with each other. The mitzvah of *ahavas yisrael* does not only mean being nice to those in your classroom or *shul*, but also to your own family members! Yes, it can be difficult to show love for your little sibling if you are being annoyed by that sibling, but treating your sibling kindly means that you are showing love not only for your sibling, but for your parents as well. This is because you are making them happy when they see you treating your sibling, their other child, so nicely.

 CHECKPOINT How can you fulfill the mitzvah of *ahavas yisrael*?

So Happy For You

Sometimes, out of jealousy, you don't want a friend to be better than you. This mitzvah teaches you to be happy for your friends if they have something or do something better than you, and not to be jealous.[21]

What Else Comes From This?

EXTRACT

A Healthy Soul in a Healthy Body

The Jewish people are compared to a body. Every Jew has a special quality that no other Jew has, and when all Jews are united, the Jewish "body" is healthy and complete. If someone does not love another Jew, then it is like a body part has been cut off from the Jewish body.

In the days of the *Beis Hamikdash*, you could not bring a *korban* if the animal was missing any body parts. After the *Beis Hamikdash* was destroyed, we *daven* instead of bringing *korbanos*, and we must also not be missing anything for our *tefillos* to be answered.

This means that if you do not love every Jew, it is like you are not whole, and your *tefilos* may not be accepted in the same way.

For this reason, some people have certain *minhagim* that they do before *davening* to show their love for fellow Jews. Some people give *tzedakah* before *davening* and some announce their love for other Jews before *davening*. This is so that they will not be missing any "body parts," and then Hashem will accept their *tefillos*.[22]

  **CHECKPOINT** What are the similarities between bringing a *korban* and showing *ahavas yisrael*?

PEARLS of wisdom

The Pot Calling the Kettle Black

People usually ignore their own faults and concentrate on someone else's bad *middos* and mistakes. The mitzvah of *ahavas yisrael* teaches Jews to ignore other people's faults just as they would ignore their own.

When Hashem sees His children acting in such a matter, He will overlook their mistakes as well.[23]

OUR SAGES SAY...

Big Bundle of Love

When a non-Jew asked Hillel to teach him the whole Torah in a short amount of time - the time that he could stand on just one foot - Hillel replied: "Things that you hate being done to you, do not do to others! - This is the whole Torah; the rest is just an explanation!"

Since the mitzvah of *ahavas yisrael* has so many ways of doing the mitzvah, R' Akivah would call it a – כְּלָל גָּדוֹל בַּתּוֹרָה big rule of the Torah.[24]

UNIT 9

ENDNOTES:

1. תענית ה, ב

2. ירושלמי נדרים פ"ט ה"ד ובפני משה שם. וע"י רדב"ז הל' ממרים פ"ב ה"ד

3. ויקרא רבה ל, יב

4. רמב"ם הל' אבל פי"ד ה"א

5. סוטה מו, ב. רמב"ם הל' אבל ריש פי"ד

6. שו"ע יו"ד סי' רמ"ט סט"ו

7. פרישה יו"ד סי' שצ"ג אות ג'

8. כתובות יז, א

9. דרישה יו"ד סי' שס"א אות א'

10. שו"ע יו"ד סי' של"ה ס"א, וה'

11. רמב"ם הל' אבל פי"ד ה"א

12. רמב"ם הל' אבל פי"ד ה"א

13. פרישה יו"ד סי' שצ"ג אות ג'

14. Treasury of Chassidic Tales on the Torah pg. 351

15. אהבת חסד ח"ג פ"ב הובא באנציקלופדיה תלמודית ערך הכנסת אורחים הערה 55

16. שבועות לט, א

17. ר"ה כט, א. וברש"י שם ד"ה אע"פ

18. מנחות צז, א. ע"פ רש"י שם ד"ה שולחנו

19. שו"ע יו"ד סי' של"ה ס"ג

20. סמ"ק מצוה ח'

21. רמב"ן ויקרא יט, יח

22. כ"ה בנוסח אר"י ע"פ פע"ח שער עולם העשי' פ"א. וראה מג"א או"ח הקדמת סי' מ"ו

23. דרך מצוותיך מצות אהבת ישראל

24. ירושלמי נדרים פ"ט ה"ד ובפנ"מ שם

Have you ever been the new child in school? Did you wonder if you would have any friends, or if anyone would think that you were different? You probably felt very nervous about being in a new place. What would have made you feel more comfortable?

UNIT 10

IN THIS UNIT YOU WILL:

EXPLORE

- Why should you show *gerim* extra love?
- Why shouldn't you talk to a *ger* about what it was like before he became Jewish?

EXAMINE

- What can you do to make a *ger* feel welcomed?

EXTRACT

- If a new student joins your school, how should you make him feel?
- If you are playing a game, who should you make sure to include?

גֵּרִים

KEY CONCEPTS

UNIT
10

Book: Madda, Section: Character
סֵפֶר מַדָּע הִלְכוֹת דֵּעוֹת

אַהֲבַת הַגֵּר
LOVING A GER

מִצְוָה אַחַת

There were some very famous people who descended from or were *gerim*:

• *Mashiach* is a descendant of Rus, who was a *giyores*.[1]

• R' Akiva, one of the great *Tanaim* of the *Mishnah*, was the son of *gerim*.[2]

• Nevuzradan, the general for Nevuchadnetzar (the evil king who destroyed the first *Beis Hamikdash*), became a *ger*.

• The grandchildren of Haman learned Torah in Eretz Yisrael, and the grandchildren of Sisra (the evil king who fought Barak and Devorah) taught Jewish children in Yerushalayim.

• Shmaya and Avtalyon were great Torah leaders and they were the grandchildren of Sancheriv (the evil king who tried to wage war against Chizkiyahu).[3]

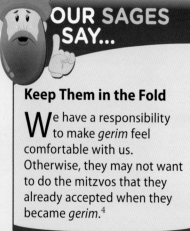

Keep Them in the Fold

We have a responsibility to make *gerim* feel comfortable with us. Otherwise, they may not want to do the mitzvos that they already accepted when they became *gerim*.[4]

The Mitzvah

EXAMINE

The unit of loving a *ger* has one mitzvah.

Love a *ger*.

MITZVAH
14

אַהֲבַת הַגֵּר

Showing love to a *ger*

וַאֲהַבְתֶּם אֶת הַגֵּר כִּי גֵרִים הֱיִיתֶם בְּאֶרֶץ מִצְרָיִם
(דברים י, יט)

You must show love toward the foreigner, since you were foreigners in the land of Egypt.

Love a *ger*.

ALL PEOPLE · ALL PLACES · ALL TIMES

Mitzvah Messages

EXPLORE

Caring For *Gerim*

It's Not So Easy Being A Child

Chazal tell us that גֵּר שֶׁנִּתְגַּיֵּיר כְּקָטָן שֶׁנּוֹלָד – "Someone who converts is like a newborn child."[5] A baby needs a lot of help to get used to the world he or she now lives in, and to learn how to walk and talk. A *ger* is very similar, and needs help to get used to this new way of life and to learn how to do everything.

Without Family, It's Harder

It is also very difficult for a family to move to a new city without any family or friends to help them. A *ger* has no Jewish relatives. Therefore, Hashem commands us to love *gerim* and be like family to them.[6]

CHECKPOINT How is a *ger* similar to a baby, or to a new student in school?

Showing Sensitivity

The mitzvah of *ahavas hager* means showing kindness and sensitivity to *gerim*, and being careful not to make them feel bad about their past life, or the people that they come from. Examples are:

- You must be careful not to remind *gerim* of their past and how they lived before they converted,[7] and you must not remind their children of their parents' past.[8]

- You may not make fun of *gerim*. For example, you are not allowed to say, "A mouth that ate *treif* will now learn Torah?!"[9] Instead, you must accept them as equal to anyone who was born Jewish.

- You may not speak badly of non-Jews in front of a *ger*, because it might make the *ger* feel bad.[10]

Two for One

Because the *ger* is a Jew, when you show love and sensitivity to a *ger*, you not only fulfill the mitzvah of *ahavas hager*, but you also fulfill the mitzvah of *ahavas yisrael*.[11]

CHECKPOINT — What must you be careful not to say or do to a *ger*?

EXTEND YOUR KNOWLEDGE

It's Tough On Their Kids Too

The mitzvah of loving a *ger* also applies to children of two *gerim*. Even though the children were born Jewish, since their parents have no Jewish relatives, their children do not either have any Jewish relatives other than their parents and siblings (for example grandparents or cousins), and they miss out on the love and support that they would have gotten from those relatives. Therefore, you also have to show extra love to these children as if they were *gerim* themselves.

However, if only one parent was a *ger*, then the extra mitzvah does not apply to the children, because the children will at least have some Jewish relatives from one side of the family.[12]

Like a Deer

Hashem's special love for *gerim* can be compared to a king who finds a beautiful deer grazing with his sheep and goats.

This king gives special instructions to his servants to make sure that the deer has plenty to eat and is safe. When the servants ask the king why he is giving the deer so much attention, the king said, "It is normal for sheep to eat and sleep in the field and be around people. However, deer usually sleep in the forest and is afraid of people. The deer is going against its nature just so that it can be in the king's field. The deer is special because it made that choice."

Gerim are like this deer. They are special because they have made the decision to leave everything behind to join the Jewish people, and it's special for us that we have these *gerim* with us.[13]

OUR SAGES SAY...

Keep Them in the Fold

Why was Avraham commanded to give himself a *bris* at 99 years old?

To teach us that someone who wants to convert shouldn't say "I'm too old to convert and have a *bris*." Rather, he should learn from Avraham who had his *bris* at 99 years old.[14]

DID YOU KNOW?

You're Special

The Rambam once wrote a long letter to a *ger* who had been insulted by someone.

He explained to the *ger* how special it is that he left everything to become a Jew and serve Hashem, and how beloved *gerim* are to Hashem.[15]

Life-Changing Journey

The *Ba'al Shem Tov* and a *talmid* of his travelled to Posen to spend *Shabbos*. Mysteriously, the *Ba'al Shem Tov* decided to spend the *Shabbos* at the home of a tailor in a very dangerous part of town where Jews were not allowed to enter.

When the Christians found out that there were Jews in their part of the city, they ran to the tailor's house to attack them. However, they were so awed by the presence of the *Ba'al Shem Tov* that they left the tailor and his guests alone.

When a certain professor at a nearby university heard about this amazing rabbi, he decided to go and see this person for himself. He slipped into the house quietly, and was instantly spellbound by the holy *Ba'al Shem Tov*. All *Shabbos*, the professor sat silently, amazed by the words of wisdom.

After *Shabbos*, he left the house a changed man. Eventually, he converted to Judaism and later became the *Rav* of a faraway city.[16]

Live the Mitzvah

EXT**RACT**

Welcome, Stranger

Since the word *ger* also means stranger, or someone from a different place, the mitzvah of *ahavas hager* tells us to show special kindness to anyone who is a stranger.[17]

Perhaps the new child from another country at your *shul* needs help finding the *siddurim*. Or maybe the new family next door needs someone to introduce them to the other neighbors. The new janitor at school may want all the students to treat him with respect and be considerate while he is trying to do his job. We should always greet any new arrivals warmly and make them feel at home as much as we can.

 CHECKPOINT To which people should you show extra kindness?

DID YOU KNOW?

Welcoming Them In

Part of the mitzvah[19] of loving a *ger* is helping a non-Jew actually convert after the *Beis Din* allows him or her to.[20]

A STORY

Onkelos the *Ger*

Onkelos was the nephew of the evil Roman emperor Titus. He ran away from Rome to Eretz Yisrael to convert, and he eventually became a *Talmid Chacham*.

When Titus found out that his nephew had converted, he was furious and sent a group of soldiers to bring him back. However, they were so impressed by Onkelos that they ended up becoming *gerim* themselves!

Titus sent two more units of soldiers, but they, too, converted.

After nothing worked, Titus finally gave up and left his nephew in peace.[18]

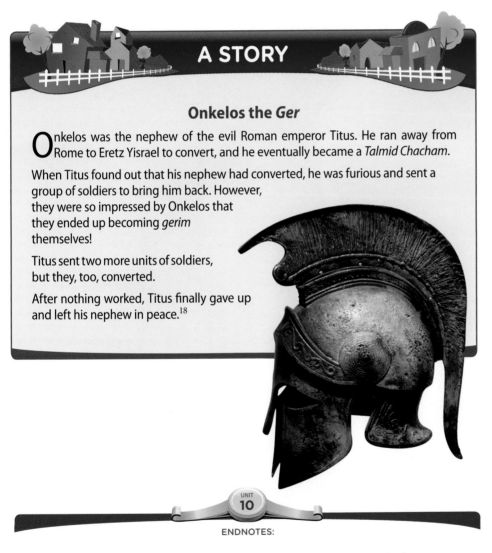

PEARLS *of wisdom*

From Birth

A person who converts is called a גֵּר שֶׁנִּתְגַּיֵּיר - a **convert** who converted, not a גּוֹי שֶׁנִּתְגַּיֵּיר - a non-Jew who converted.

This is because the *neshamah* of a *ger* was at *Har Sinai* together with the *neshamos* of all the Jewish nation. Therefore, the convert is considered to be a Jewish soul that was waiting to be revealed.[21]

UNIT
10

ENDNOTES:

17. חינוך מצוה תל"א. ורע' אנציקלופדיה תלמודית ערך אהבת הגר הע' 17

18. ע"ז יא, א. גיטין נו, ב

19. מהר"י פרלא לרס"ג עשין י"ט, הובא באנציקלופדיה תלמודית ערך אהבת הגר

20. ע"ע אנציקלופדיה תלמודית ערך אהבת הגר הע' 13

21. מדבר קדמות מערכת ג' אות ג'

8. שו"ע חו"מ סי' רכ"ח ס"ד

9. בבא מציעא נח, ב

10. סנהדרין צד, א. חינוך מצוה תל"א

11. רמב"ם הל' דעות פ"ו ה"ד

12. מנ"ח מצוה תל"א אות ב'

13. במדבר רבה ח, ב

14. תנחומא לך לך, כד

15. ילקוט מעם לועז שמות ע' תתסט

16. סיפורים נוראים ע' 24 ואילך

1. רות ה, יז. רמב"ם הל' מלכים פי"א ה"ד

2. הקדמת הרמב"ם לספר היד. וראה ברכות כז, ב עם פי' רב ניסים גאון על הש"ס שם

3. גיטין נו, ב

4. בבא מציעא נט, ב

5. יבמות מח, ב

6. רלב"ג דברים י, יט

7. חינוך מצוה תל"א

UNIT 11

IN THIS UNIT YOU WILL:

EXPLORE

- Why is it important to let someone know if they have done something wrong?

EXAMINE

- What should you do when you see another Jew doing something wrong?

EXTRACT

- Why is it your responsibility to rebuke someone else?
- If your friends are doing something that is not right, what should you do?

תּוֹכֵחָה

הַלְבָּנַת פָּנִים

עַרְבוּת

KEY CONCEPTS

Book: Madda, Section: Character

סֵפֶר מַדָּע הִלְכוֹת דֵּעוֹת

תּוֹכָחָה
REBUKING

שָׁלֹשׁ מִצְוֹת

Don't Keep it all bottled up inside.

The problem won't go away by itself,

and you might explode!

The unit of *tochachah* has three mitzvos. They are:

1. Do not keep hate for another Jew in your heart.

2. Rebuke a Jew if they have hurt you in any way and you are upset at them, or If they are not following the Torah and mitzvos.

3. Do not embarrass a Jew.

MITZVAH 15

שֶׁלֹּא לִשְׂנוֹא אַחִים

Not hating another Jew

לֹא תִשְׂנָא אֶת אָחִיךָ בִּלְבָבֶךָ
הוֹכֵחַ תּוֹכִיחַ אֶת עֲמִיתֶךָ וְלֹא תִשָּׂא עָלָיו חֵטְא
(ויקרא יט, יז)

Do not hate your brother in your heart. You must rebuke your friend, and don't carry an *aveirah* because of your actions toward someone else.

Do not keep hate for another Jew in your heart.

ALL PEOPLE   ALL PLACES   ALL TIMES   NO PUNISHMENT

BIOGRAPHY

The Maharil Diskin

תקע״ח - תרנ״ח (1818 - 1898)

R' Yehosua Yehudah Leib Diskin is known as Maharil Diskin or the Seraph of Brisk. He was a great gaon. Throughout his life he was a Rav in many cities including Mezritch, Kovno, Shklov, Brisk, and at the end of his life he moved to Yerushalayim.

He passed away on the 29th of Teves and is well known for protecting Torah Jewry from the negative influences of the time. He was very involved in supporting orphans and poor people.

All's Well That Ends Well

Avraham rebuked Avimelech because his servants stole Avraham's well. Avimelech did not know that this had happened, but when Avraham rebuked him, Avimelech made peace willingly.

We learn from Avraham and Avimelech that we should not avoid telling other people when they have done something wrong or hurtful.[1]

STORY

Sweet As Sugar

The *Maharil* Diskin, *Rav* of Brisk, needed to eat a lot of sugar. One night, during his *shiur*, the man who prepared his tea mistakenly put salt instead of sugar in his tea. This, of course, made the tea undrinkable. Incredibly, the *Maharil* drank the full cup of salty tea without a word.

When his wife found out what he had done, she was horrified, and rebuked him for endangering his health. He said calmly, "The *Chazal* say that it is preferable for one to throw himself into a fiery furnace than risk embarrassing someone else in public. Should I not risk my health so as not to embarrass another Jew?"[2]

MITZVAH 16

תּוֹכָחָה לְיִשְׂרָאֵל שֶׁאֵינוֹ נוֹהֵג כְּשׁוּרָה
Rebuking a Jew who is not behaving properly

לֹא תִשְׂנָא אֶת אָחִיךָ בִּלְבָבֶךָ הוֹכֵחַ תּוֹכִיחַ אֶת עֲמִיתֶךָ
וְלֹא תִשָּׂא עָלָיו חֵטְא
(ויקרא יט, יז)

Do not hate your brother in your heart. **You must rebuke
your friend,** and don't carry an *aveirah* because of your actions
toward someone else.

Rebuke another Jew in the following situations:

1. If they have hurt you in any way and you are upset at them.
2. If they are not following the Torah or mitzvos.

ALL PEOPLE   ALL PLACES   ALL TIMES

MITZVAH 17

שֶׁלֹּא לְהַלְבִּין פְּנֵי אָדָם מִיִּשְׂרָאֵל
Not embarrassing another Jew

לֹא תִשְׂנָא אֶת אָחִיךָ בִּלְבָבֶךָ הוֹכֵחַ תּוֹכִיחַ אֶת עֲמִיתֶךָ
וְלֹא תִשָּׂא עָלָיו חֵטְא
(ויקרא יט, יז)

Do not hate your brother in your heart. You must rebuke
your friend, and **don't carry an *aveirah* because of your
actions toward someone else.**

Do not embarrass another Jew.

ALL PEOPLE   ALL PLACES   ALL TIMES   NO PUNISHMENT

PEARLS
of wisdom

The Kindest Jab

Giving rebuke is like giving someone a shot. When a nurse gives a shot, the needle, your skin, and even the nurse have to be completely clean. If they aren't, germs can come into the body along with the medicine, and the medicine won't work at all. The person getting the shot might even get sicker because of the dirty needle.

Rebuke is like a shot because when you give rebuke, you have to be completely "clean" of any bad feelings, like jealousy or *gaavah*. You can only give rebuke if you are giving it with love and care, not a "dirty" feeling which will make the person feel "sick."

DID YOU KNOW?

Dead Embarrassing

There are only three *aveiros* in the Torah that we must always give our life away before doing. They are: killing another person, serving *avodah zarah* and living as married with someone who is forbidden.

Chazal say that embarrassing someone in public is just like killing them. Just as we must be prepared to be killed rather than to kill someone else, we must also be prepared to be killed rather than to embarrass someone else in public.[3]

OUR SAGES SAY...

Tragic Mistake

The *Beis Hamikdash* was destroyed because of two of these *aveiros*.

A person by the name of Bar Kamtza was once embarrassed and he went to the Romans and said *lashon hara* about the Jews, which led to the destruction of the *Beis Hamikdash*.[5]

The *Beis Hamikdash* was also destroyed because the people did not rebuke each other and let each other continue doing *aveiros*.[6]

Why Bottling Up Doesn't Help

Misunderstood

When people are angry or upset, it usually helps if they can talk to someone about their feelings.[7] Sometimes a person may be angry if he thinks that someone else was **trying** to hurt him. Talking with the other person may show that the other person wasn't trying to hurt anyone, and it was a mistake.

If the problem is not discussed at all, the problem will not be solved, and the anger and hurt will become stronger.[8]

Help Them Become Better

It is unfair to see someone do something wrong without letting them know so that they can do *teshuvah*. The person will need to ask for forgiveness, or learn from the mistake.[9] If you don't point out the mistake, how can it ever be fixed? This mitzvah reminds everyone that it is very important for people to communicate their feelings with each other, so that problems can be resolved and mistakes can be fixed.

 CHECKPOINT Why is it helpful for you to rebuke someone who did something hurtful?

Details   EXAMINE

How To Rebuke So People Will Listen

Look Who's Talking!

If you rebuke someone, make sure that you don't do the same *aveirah* about which you are rebuking the person. It will be very hard for someone to accept any rebuke from you if they know that you do the same thing.[10]

How To Rebuke

You should rebuke others in a soft and calm voice, and in private, so that the person won't be embarrassed. Make sure that the person knows that you are not pointing out the mistake to be mean, rather to help him do *teshuvah*.

Everybody gives rebuke differently, depending on the personality of the one who is being rebuked and the one who is giving the rebuke. If the person being rebuked is very sensitive and would feel bad very easily, you must make sure to use a soft tone that shows how much you care. If the person isn't very sensitive and can handle a stronger tone, then you can use a more serious voice.

When giving rebuke you have to make sure that you tell the person exactly what was done, and don't just tell them that they did "something" wrong. You must explain very clearly what was done wrong, so that the person will listen and take it to heart.[11]

Rebuking Teacher

You should even tell your teacher when he or she does something wrong,[12] but only in an extremely respectful way and only one time. For example, you should start with a question like, "Didn't you teach us...?"[13]

What If It Is Ignored?

If you are telling the person about something bad that was done to you, and they are angry and ignoring you, you should stop rebuking.[14]

If You Know They Won't Listen

If you know that a person will never listen when they are told about their mistake, there are many ways that you can respond.

1. If the person is doing an *aveirah* that is stated clearly in the Torah and it is being done in **private**, you should rebuke as many times as you can, even if you are being ignored.

2. If the person is doing an *aveirah* that is stated clearly in the Torah, and is doing the *aveirah* in **public**, you should rebuke only once.

3. If the person is doing an *aveirah* that is not stated clearly in the Torah, and not everyone knows about it, then you should not rebuke at all. Since they won't listen anyway, it is better for the person to to do the *aveirah* without knowing that it is wrong, rather than doing it purposely, knowing that it is forbidden.[15]

Don't Embarrass Me

It is forbidden to ever embarrass another person. It is a horrible thing to do and *Chazal* tell us that someone who embarrasses another person has no share in *Olam Haba*![16]

 CHECKPOINT How should you rebuke someone who is very sensitive? What about a teacher? How about someone who won't listen?

STORY

Better Not Said

R' Yisrael of Vizhnitz came to visit the home of a wealthy bank manager. R' Yisrael sat down, didn't say a word and after a while, he stood up and got ready to leave.

When his host asked him why he had decided to stop by, R' Yisrael replied:

"As part of the mitzvah to give rebuke, *Chazal* say that it is important **not** to give rebuke when you know that the person won't listen to you. Now, I have to tell you something to which I know you won't listen. So, I came to you so I can properly avoid telling you what I feel must be said, since you certainly won't listen!"

His curious host assured him that he would listen, but R' Yisrael said, "Oh, really?" The bank manager kept on pressing R' Yisrael to tell him what the rebuke was, until R' Yisrael finally gave in.

"Very well," he said. "A penniless widow is about to be thrown out of her home because she owes a lot of money to your bank. I hoped that you, as the bank manager, would ignore her debt, but I was sure you wouldn't listen, so I have a mitzvah to remain quiet."

The bank manager interrupted, "But, I can't do anything! I don't own the bank, and she owes an enormous amount of money!"

The *Rebbe* sighed, "See! You won't listen!" and left.

The bank manager was so inspired that he did not rest until he paid the widow's debt from his own money.[17]

Garlic Breath

Once, while R' Yehudah Hanassi was teaching his students, there was a strong odor of garlic in the room. Since it was disturbing the learning, R' Yehudah Hanassi requested, "Would the person who ate garlic please leave!" R' Chiya, one of the senior students, stood up and left. Upon seeing R' Chiya leave, everyone else also got up and left.

The next day, R' Chiya was approached by R' Shimon, the son of R' Yehudah Hanassi. "Was it you who annoyed my father yesterday?" he asked.

R' Chiya replied, "G-d forbid! I left so that everyone should follow me, and then the student who ate the garlic would not be embarrassed!"[18]

DISCOVERY

Red-Faced

One of the body's natural responses to embarrassment is blushing; the face turns red, and then turns white. Blushing is caused when the small blood vessels in the face widen to allow more blood to flow through them. These responses are something that we cannot control.

That's one of the reasons why *Chazal* say that if one embarrasses another Jew it is as if they "spilled blood."[19]

SELECTED HALACHOS

Rebuking

- If someone did something wrong to you, you may forgive the person without rebuking him for the wrong he did to you. You only have to rebuke someone when you are still upset about it.[20]

- You only have to rebuke someone you know, such as a friend or a relative, not a stranger who might be angry at you because of your rebuke.[21]

- You should immediately rebuke someone who does an *aveirah* in public, so that a *chillul Hashem* is not created.[22]

- If you rebuke someone and the person feels bad for what he did and asks you for forgiveness, you should forgive the person immediately.[23]

Embarrassing

- A person can become embarrassed even if no one else is around to hear or see what is happening. Therefore you may not embarrass someone even if no one else is around. For example, you should not remind another of something embarrassing that happened in the past.[24]

- You may not embarrass anyone, even a child.[25]

- You may not call someone an embarrasing name, even if it is a name that the person is used to and won't get upset.[26]

- Students should not ask their teacher a question about a topic that the teacher has not studied, because the teacher might feel embarrassed. However, if they are certain that their teacher will know the answer, they may ask.[27]

EXTEND YOUR KNOWLEDGE

Love and Rebuke

Some people may think that if you love someone, you should not rebuke them when they do something bad. This is wrong! Here are some things that our *Chachamim* tell us about the importance and love involved in rebuking.

"כָּל אַהֲבָה שֶׁאֵין עִמָּהּ תּוֹכָחָה, אֵינָה אַהֲבָה" - *"Any love which does not involve rebuking, is not real love."* If you really love someone, you will want them to become better, and try to help them by rebuking them.[28]

"אוֹת אֱמֶת לְאַהֲבַת הַבְּרִיּוֹת הִיא הַתּוֹכָחָה" - *"The true sign of really loving a person is rebuke."*[29]

"יֵשׁ לְךָ חֲבֵירִים, מִקְצָתָן מוֹכִיחִין אוֹתְךָ וּמִקְצָתָן מְשַׁבְּחִין אוֹתְךָ, אֱהוֹב אֶת הַמּוֹכִיחֲךָ וּשְׂנָא אֶת הַמְשַׁבֵּחֲךָ, מִפְּנֵי שֶׁמּוֹכִיחֲךָ מְבִיאֲךָ לְחַיֵּי הָעוֹלָם הַבָּא, וְהַמְשַׁבֵּחֲךָ מוֹצִיאֲךָ מִן הָעוֹלָם" - *"If some of your friends rebuke you and some of them praise you, love the ones who rebuke you, and hate the ones who praise you. For the rebuker is bringing you to Olam Haba, and the praiser is destroying you."*[30]

It is natural to hate being rebuked, and even to be upset at a person who rebukes you. Thinking about these wise words of our *Chachamim* can help overcome this, and let you appreciate the rebuke as bitter medicine making you healthy and strong.

Live the Mitzvah

EXTRACT

Don't Go With The Flow

If you are with some friends, and they want to do something that you know is not right, what would you do? Would you join in, because you don't want them to think that you are a goody-goody? Or would you just leave them and do your own thing? Neither way is going to help you or the others. Either you are going to do something wrong yourself, or you are letting your friends continue doing the wrong thing.

The best thing to do, for both you and your friends, is to tell them that what they are doing is wrong and explain why. They might not listen to you, but it is likely that they will later realize that you did the right thing and regret their actions.

CHECKPOINT What should you do if your friends want to do something that is wrong?

Low Blow

The pain of embarrassment is the worst kind of pain, and it remains with the person for a very long time.[32]

OUR SAGES SAY...

If It Won't Work, Don't Say It

If you can't rebuke in a way that the person will listen, you should not rebuke. It will only have negative effects, and it is not worthwhile.[33]

DID YOU KNOW?

Dead Wrong

One who says something embarrassing about a person who is not alive should fast, do *teshuvah,* and go to the grave of the dead person to ask forgiveness in front of ten people.[34]

Rebuking Made All The Difference

Hashem told Yonah to go to Ninveh and rebuke the people of the city, because they were wicked. Yonah did not want to go, so he tried to escape from Hashem by taking a ship to Tarshish.

While he was on the ship, a great storm arose, and the ship was in danger of sinking. The sailors realized that Yonah was responsible for the storm, so they said to him, "What have you done?! And what can we do to make the storm stop?" Yonah told them to throw him into the sea. They did so, and then the storm stopped.

Soon after that, Hashem sent a great fish to swallow Yonah, and Yonah stayed in the belly of the fish for three days and three nights. He *davened* to Hashem, and Hashem told the fish to bring Yonah back onto dry land.

Hashem again told Yonah to go to Ninveh. This time, Yonah went willingly. He entered the city and cried out, "In forty days Ninveh shall be destroyed!" The king and all the people heard this, and they did *teshuvah* for their wickedness, wearing sackcloth and ashes while fasting and praying. Hashem saw this, heard their prayers, and saved Ninveh.

Yonah was upset that Hashem had changed His mind about destroying Ninveh. So he sat outside the city, waiting to see if anything would happen in the city. Hashem sent a *kikayon* plant to shelter Yonah from the sun and Yonah was pleased.

But, in the morning, the *kikayon* was gone, destroyed by a worm. This upset Yonah very much, and Hashem asked him if he was really so sad about the *kikayon.* Yonah replied that he was, and Hashem said, "You took pity on this plant. Shouldn't I take pity on the people of the great city of Ninveh also?!"[35]

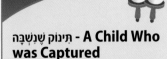

We're All In the Same Boat

The mitzvah of rebuking another Jew teaches you responsibility. When one Jew does an *aveirah*, no one can say, "It's not my problem. I won't worry about it."

Imagine a boat with a group of people in it. One person drills a hole under his seat, letting in enough water to sink the boat. What do the other people do? Do they let the person get away with it, because it's in "his" section of the boat? This is foolish! Water will fill the boat and **everyone** will sink.

Chazal[36] tell us that "כָּל יִשְׂרָאֵל עֲרֵבִים זֶה בָּזֶה - all Jews are responsible for each other." Since all Jews are affected by one Jew's *aveirah*, we all have the responsibility to try to prevent others from making mistakes.[37]

If you see someone doing an *aveirah*, and you do not stop them, it is as if you did the same *aveirah* that the person did![38]

Show Them the Way Home

There are many Jews who do not know about Torah and mitzvos. It is our responsibility to help guide them to love and serve Hashem. We must also remember that if we want to help people, our help must be given with a sincere love for the **other** person and in a real caring way.

We should not only care about saving ourselves from being responsible for other people's *aveiros*, but also care about the person who is doing an *aveirah* and want that person to do what is right and be a better Jew.

CHECKPOINT — What is your responsibility regarding another Jew who is not acting according to the Torah?

PEARLS *of wisdom*

תִּינוֹק שֶׁנִּשְׁבָּה - A Child Who was Captured

The mitzvah of rebuking someone about *aveiros* does not apply to most of the Jews of our time who do not follow the mitzvos. They are considered to be like a baby that was captured and raised by gentiles, who is not responsible for the fact that he does not keep mitzvos.

Even when these people become aware of the mitzvos, they cannot be blamed if they don't adopt the Jewish lifestyle since they were never raised with it.[39]

UNIT 11

ENDNOTES:

1. בראשית כא, כה

2. עמוד אש ע' קמט

3. שערי תשובה לר' יונה שער ג'

4. מנ"ח מצוה רל"ט אות ו'

5. גיטין נה, ב

6. שבת קיט, ב

7. רמב"ן ויקרא יט, יז

8. יד הקטנה ח"ב הל' דעות פ"ז ס"ד

9. רמב"ן ויקרא יט, יז

10. בבא מציעא קו, ב. ספר חסידים סי' ה'

11. רמב"ם הל' דעות פ"ו ה"ז

12. בבא מציעא לא, א

13. רמב"ם הל' ת"ת פ"ה ה"ט, ובכס"מ

14. משלי ט, ח

15. שו"ע הרב או"ח סי' תר"ח ס"ד-ה'

16. בבא מציעא נט, א

17. סיפורי חסידים פ' וארא

18. סנהדרין יא, א

19. בבא מציעא נח, ב

20. שו"ע הרב או"ח סי' קנ"ו ס"ו

21. שו"ע הרב או"ח סי' קנ"ו ס"ז

22. מג"א סי' תר"ח ס"ק ג'

23. שו"ע הרב או"ח סי' תר"ו ס"ד

24. שו"ע הרב חו"מ הל' אונאה וגניבת דעת ס"ל, ובפתיחה לחפץ חיים לאוין ס"ק י"ד

25. רמב"ם הל' דעות פ"ו ה"ח

26. שו"ע הרב חו"מ הל' אונאה וגניבת דעת סכ"ט

27. רמב"ם הל' ת"ת פ"ד ה"ו

28. בראשית רבה נד, ג

29. מגדל עוז עליית האהבה, פ"י

30. אבות דרבי נתן נוסחא א' פכ"ט

31. החפץ חיים חייו ופעלו ח"א ע' קעד

32. חינוך מצוה ר"מ

33. שו"ע הרב או"ח סי' תר"ו ס"ד-ו'

34. רמ"א חו"מ סי' ת"כ סל"ח

35. יונה פ"א-ד'

36. שבועות לט, א

37. כלי יקר ויקרא יט, יז ד"ה ולפי שנאמר

38. שבועות לט, ב

39. שו"ת יביע אומר ח"א יו"ד סי' י"א סי"ב

You have a rubber ball. You bounce it around the room, twirl it on your finger and then throw it at the wall so that it bounces back. Would you do the same if the object was a crystal vase? Certainly not! Why not?

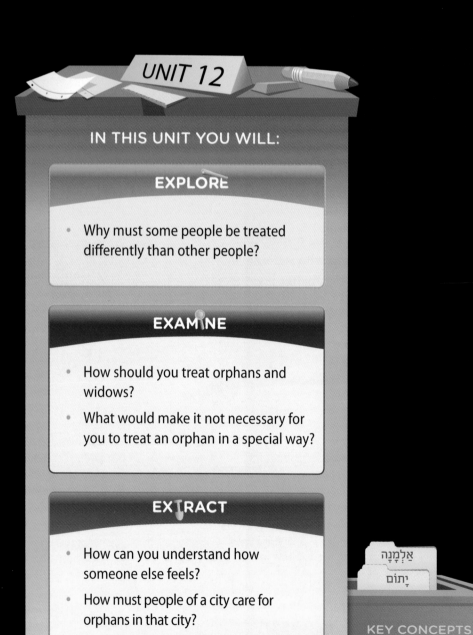

UNIT 12

IN THIS UNIT YOU WILL:

EXPLORE

- Why must some people be treated differently than other people?

EXAMINE

- How should you treat orphans and widows?
- What would make it not necessary for you to treat an orphan in a special way?

EXTRACT

- How can you understand how someone else feels?
- How must people of a city care for orphans in that city?

אַלְמָנָה

יָתוֹם

KEY CONCEPTS

שֶׁלֹּא לְעַנּוֹת יָתוֹם וְאַלְמָנָה

NOT CAUSING ORPHANS AND WIDOWS TO SUFFER

מִצְוָה אַחַת

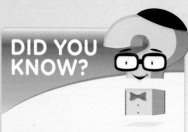

Measure For Measure

Even though *Beis Din* cannot punish a person for doing this *aveirah* because it can be done without any action, Hashem warns us that there is a very severe punishment to anyone who does it.[1]

If a man does this *aveirah*, his enemies will come and kill him, and his body will not be found. Since nobody knows for sure that he died, his wife might still be married, and can never get remarried to anyone else.[2]

If a woman does this *aveirah*, she will die and her children will be orphans.[3]

The Mitzvah   EXAMINE

This unit has one mitzvah.

You may not cause any suffering to widows or orphans.

MITZVAH
18

שֶׁלֹא לְעַנּוֹת יָתוֹם וְאַלְמָנָה
Not causing any suffering to a widow or an orphan

כָּל אַלְמָנָה וְיָתוֹם לֹא תְעַנּוּן
(שמות כב, כא)

Do not cause any suffering to any widow or orphan.

Do not cause suffering to a widow or orphan through speech, action or in any way.

| ALL PEOPLE | ALL PLACES | ALL TIMES | NO PUNISHMENT |

Mitzvah Messages   EXPLORE

Delicate Feelings

You can say the same thing to two different people, and each person will feel differently. The first person might laugh with you and forget about what you said, while another might feel very insulted and will be sad for a few days.

A widow or an orphan can become very lonely and very sensitive, and will be more easily hurt than other people. Since that person is all alone, there is no one to stand up for him or her when they need help. Therefore, the Torah commands us to be especially sensitive towards widows and orphans.[4]

 CHECKPOINT   Why can't we treat everyone the same way?

Who Needs Help?

An orphan is a child who has lost at least one parent, and a widow is a woman whose husband died. These people must be treated with extra care.

Caring for the Unfortunate

Showing Kindness

You must be very careful to treat a widow or an orphan with sensitivity and kindness. You should speak to them very gently, and never tease them. You should not make them do hard work, and you must never hit them.[5] You should take care of everything they need, even more than what you might do for yourself. Make sure that they have food, clothing, and a home to live in.

Poor Little Rich Kid

Even the widow or the orphan of a king must be treated with kindness, no matter how much wealth and power they still have, because even all of the money in the world cannot help the sadness of losing a parent or a husband.[6]

Poor No More

The mitzvah of being especially sensitive to orphans only applies when they need other people to take care of them, or if the orphans are not married. Once the orphans can take care of themselves, or are married and will be taken care of, this mitzvah does not apply.[7]

CHECKPOINT Who must be treated with extra care?

Father Of Orphans

Hashem is the Father of all orphans.

Just like a parent feels pain when the child gets hurt, Hashem is pained when an orphan is hurt.[8]

DID YOU KNOW?

Orphan Or Not?

A convert is like a newborn, and has no connection to his or her past life. Therefore a father and son who convert are not *halachically* related to each other.

Because of this, there is reason to consider a *ger* to be an orphan. However, he isn't really an orphan, because he can still turn to his non-Jewish father for support.[9]

EXTEND YOUR KNOWLEDGE

Why No *Malkus*?

The Rambam says that a person who makes a widow or an orphan suffer is not given *malkus*, because it can also be done without any action.

But what should happen if a person hits an orphan? Since hitting is an action and the person did the *aveirah* with an action, why should the person not receive *malkus*?

Two explanations why there is no *malkus* for making a widow or an orphan suffer are:

- Since most of the time the *aveirah* is done without any specific action, this *aveirah* is called a *lav she'ein bo ma'aseh*, an *aveirah* without an action. Since it is a *lav she'ein bo ma'aseh,* even if the *aveirah* was in this case done **with** an action, there is no *malkus*.[10]

- The Torah clearly says that the punishment for mistreating a widow or an orphan is *middah keneged middah*; that Hashem will punish the person with very harsh punishments. This takes the place of the usual punishment of *malkus*.[11]

Live the Mitzvah

EXTRACT

Put Yourself In Their Shoes

How can you be more sensitive to other people who are in very difficult situations? One way is to try to imagine as if you, G-d forbid, were experiencing the same thing. How would you feel? Terrible? Miserable? Wouldn't you want others to help you and look after you, while you work on feeling better? Now you know how they are feeling. Understanding how someone else feels is called **empathy**.

Don't Make Me Feel Like a *Nebach*

Even though you should try to treat orphans and widows with more care and kindness than you would treat others, you must never show them that you pity them. You should try to treat them as normally as possible, so that they don't feel bad that their husband or parent passed away.

 CHECKPOINT How can you understand how someone else feels?

What Else Comes From This?

EXTRACT

Community Responsibility

Since young orphans cannot take care of themselves, the leaders of the community must help them.

For example:

- If orphans have an argument with someone, the *Beis Din* must help them argue their case.

- The *Beis Din* appoints an אַפּוֹטְרוֹפּוֹס - a guardian to care for the orphans and for their property.

- Since orphans are all on their own and don't know how to take care of their money, a person is not allowed to collect a debt from an orphan, unless the person who is collecting the money first promises that the money is owed to him. This is a law that only applies to orphans.[12]

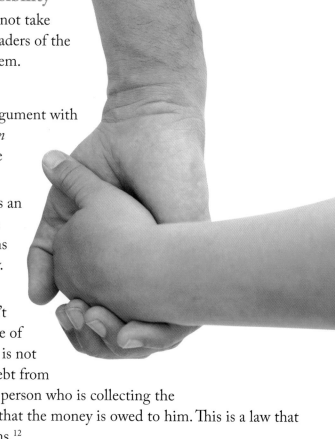

UNIT 12

ENDNOTES:

1. חינוך מצוה ס"ה
2. רש"י שמות כב, כג
3. חינוך מצוה ס"ה
4. חינוך מצוה ס"ה
5. חינוך מצוה ס"ה

6. רמב"ם הל' דעות פ"ו ה"י
7. רמב"ם הל' דעות פ"ו ה"י. שו"ת פנים מאירות ח"א סי' ל"ז
8. כלי יקר שמות כב, כב
9. מנ"ח מצוה ס"ה אות ט'

10. הגהת משנה למלך (ע"פ שי' החינוך בכ"מ) הובא במנ"ח מצוה ס"ה
11. קרית ספר (למבי"ט) הל' דעות פ"ו
12. חינוך מצוה ס"ה
13. ברכות יח, ב

Have you ever blown bubbles into the wind? Imagine trying to catch all of those bubbles and get them back into the bubble bottle. You would never, ever, be able to do it! Once those bubbles have flown away, they can never be placed back into the bottle!

UNIT 13

IN THIS UNIT YOU WILL:

EXPLORE

- Why is *lashon hara* so hurtful?
- How is *lashon hara* similar to bubbles and feathers?

EXAMINE

- What are the three ways that you are not allowed to talk about others?
- What is considered the "dust" of *lashon hara*?

EXTRACT

- If someone tells you a secret, what should you do with that information?
- How can you use the special power of words for a good purpose?

אֲבַק
לָשׁוֹן הָרַע

לָשׁוֹן הָרַע

רְכִילוּת

מוֹצִיא שֵׁם רַע

KEY CONCEPTS

UNIT
13

Book: Madda, Section: Character
סֵפֶר מַדָּע הִלְכוֹת דֵּעוֹת

לָשׁוֹן הָרַע
EVIL TALK

מִצְוָה אַחַת

STORY

Tongue at a Fork

"**G**o and bring me the best piece of meat from the market," said R' Gamliel to his servant Tavi. So, Tavi went to the market and brought him a piece of tongue. Another time, R' Gamliel asked Tavi to bring him the worst piece of meat. Once again, Tavi brought him a piece of tongue.

"Why did you bring me a piece of tongue for the best and the worst piece of meat?" asked the R' Gamliel.

The smart servant answered, "The tongue is the best, and also the worst. If it is a good one, there is nothing better; if it is a hurtful one, then there is nothing worse."

Shlomo, the wise king, said: "Life and death are dependent on the tongue."[1]

This unit has one mitzvah. Do not tell *lashon hara*.

MITZVAH 19

שֶׁלֹּא לְרַגֵּל

Not spreading *lashon hara*.

לֹא תֵלֵךְ רָכִיל בְּעַמֶּיךָ לֹא תַעֲמֹד עַל דַּם רֵעֶךָ אֲנִי ה׳
(ויקרא יט, טז)

Do not go around as a gossiper among your people.
Do not stand still when your neighbor's life is in danger,
I am Hashem.

Do not say or write anything bad about someone.

ALL PEOPLE   ALL PLACES   ALL TIMES   NO PUNISHMENT

OUR SAGES SAY...

Snake Bite

*L*ashon hara is like a snake-bite. When a snake bites, its posion spreads throughout the body and can hurt parts of the body that are far away from the actual place of the bite.

The same is true with *lashon hara*. What you say in one place can affect a person in a different country or even continent!

Mitzvah Messages   EXPLORE

Self Destructive

The *aveirah* of *lashon hara* rips apart the Jewish nation and stops us from having peace. When people say or write bad things about others, there can be many fights and arguments between them. Since Hashem wants us all to live in peace, He has commanded us not to tell *lashon hara* about others.[2]

Out of Control

Words of *lashon hara* have a very powerful effect. Once the words leave your mouth, they can go anywhere and cause a lot of harm to many people. Hashem warns us very strongly to be careful with what we say about others, since words that were spoken can never be taken back.

 CHECKPOINT   Why shouldn't you say bad things about other people?

Kinds of Negative Speech

There are three ways to be *oveir* the *aveirah* of *lashon hara*. They are:

1. רְכִילוּת – This is when you repeat to your friend what someone else said about your friend, or did to your friend, even if it is true and not even bad. For example: Reuven says to Shimon, "Levi said you are very strong!"[3]

2. לָשׁוֹן הָרַע - There are two kinds of *lashon hara*.

   • When you say anything bad about another person, even if the person will never find out about it.

   • When you say something about someone **on purpose** to be mean to them or hurt them. It doesn't matter if you are saying something good or bad. If your purpose was to be mean or to hurt, even a good piece of information is *lashon hara*.[4] For example, Aliza says to Rochi, "Shoshanah got a 99% on her *Chumash* test! Can you believe that someone like her was able to get such a good grade?" This is a good piece of information about Shoshanah, but it was meant to hurt her.

3. מוֹצִיא שֵׁם רַע - This is when you say something **not true** about someone.[5]

Staying Far, Far Away from *Lashon Hara*

There are some things that are not exactly *lashon hara*, but are very close to *lashon hara*. These are called אֲבַק לָשׁוֹן הָרַע – the "dust" of *lashon hara*, and these are also forbidden. Examples include:

• When you hint to someone that you know something bad about another person, but you won't say what it is. For example, "I know something about Reuven, but I can't say what it is."

• Saying something nice about "Shoshanah" in front of someone who doesn't like her. When that person hears you speaking nicely about her, she may want to say something bad about her because she doesn't like her.

• Making a joke about someone, or saying something just for fun, even if you don't want anyone to be hurt.[6]

Can You Ever Speak *Lashon Hara*?

There are some times when speaking or listening to *lashon hara* is allowed. For example, an employer is allowed to ask other people for information about a person who wants to

OUR SAGES SAY...

When Three Isn't A Lucky Number

Lashon hara is called לָשׁוֹן תְּלִיתָאֵי קָטִיל תְּלִיתָאֵי – the language of the third person that kills three:

It hurts the one who speaks it, it hurts the one who hears it, and it hurts the person who is being spoken about.[7]

DISCOVERY

Wildfires

Once a wildfire begins, it can travel more than 14 miles per hour (23 kph), burning everything in its path. Almost all wildfires begin with careless acts of humans, like not cleaning up a campfire or dropping lit cigarettes.

An average of 1.2 **million** acres of U.S. woodland burn every year. The term "wildfire" means that the fire is uncontrollable.

Therefore, people often use this term to describe the effect of *lashon hara*: "it spreads like wildfire!"

work for the business. In a time like this, you are allowed to share the truth about someone else, even if it is negative information, since this will help the employer decide if the person is right for the job.[10]

⚠ CHECKPOINT — What may not be said about another person?

Living Together

Hashem says that He cannot live together with someone who speaks *lashon hara*.[8]

PEARLS *of wisdom*

Death From Afar

The words of *lashon hara* are like arrows. Just like an arrow can hurt or kill someone who is far away from the archer, a word of *lashon hara* can hurt someone even when that person is far away from the speaker.[9]

BIOGRAPHY

The *Chafetz Chaim*
(תקצ״ח – תרצ״ג) 1838 - 1933

R'Yisrael Meir Hakohen Kagan was known as the Chafetz Chaim, the name of his famous sefer on the laws of lashon hara. He founded the Radin Yeshivah in 1869, and helped with a lot of Jewish causes. He travelled a lot (even as an old man in his 90's!) to encourage the observance of mitzvos amongst Jews. He wrote more than 20 sefarim, including the Mishnah Berurah, which explains the Shulchan Aruch, and Shemiras Halashon, a sefer discussing the importance of proper speech. The Chofetz Chaim passed away at the old age of 95.

SELECTED HALACHOS

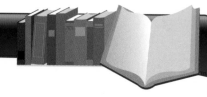

Rechilus

• You are not allowed to even **listen** to *rechilus*. Therefore, you can't ask your friend, "what have people been saying about me?" since this will cause you to listen to *rechilus*.[11]

• If you ask someone for a favor, and the person says no, you not allowed to ask, "Why did you do a favor for someone else but not for me?"[12]

Lashon Hara

• You should not stay around and listen while *lashon hara* is being spoken.[13]

• You may not write *lashon hara,* such as in a letter, email, or text message.[14]

• If people can figure out who you are talking about, it is considered *lashon hara*, even if the person's name is not mentioned.[15]

• You not allowed to say bad things about other people's belongings.[16]

• Parents are allowed to tell their children to stay away from someone with bad *middos* so that the child won't learn from that person's ways.[17]

A STORY

Even About Yourself

Travelling back home from a trip, the *Chafetz Chaim* met a man who told him that he was going to visit the great rabbi that everyone was talking about, the *Chafetz Chaim*.

The *Chafetz Chaim* told him, "Don't believe everything you hear about him! He's really not such a great rabbi! You're wasting your time."

The man was so angry to hear someone speaking about the rabbi this way that he slapped the *Chafetz Chaim*. Later, when the man found out that he had slapped the *Chafetz Chaim*, he nearly fainted.

From this incident, the *Chafetz Chaim* learned that you must not speak *lashon hara* about anyone, even about yourself![18]

EXTEND YOUR KNOWLEDGE

The Evidence Doesn't Hold Up In Court

Usually *Beis Din* needs to hear something from two witnesses for them to believe that the thing actually happened. If there is only one witness, then the *Beis Din* does not believe the testimony and does not do anything about it.

Since information heard from only one witness is not considered true in a *Beis Din*, if the person offers bad information in *Beis Din* he was *motzi shem ra*.[21]

Live the Mitzvah
EXTRACT

Far, Far Away

Once you speak, your words can never be taken back. They are like bubbles, which fly further and further away from you, spreading everywhere, and no one can stop them! Because the words of *lashon hara* travel far and wide, you can never imagine how much you can hurt someone with your words.[19]

This is especially true nowadays, with cellphones and e-mail, when something you say or write can be spread to thousands of people within seconds. And each of those people can spread it to thousands more. There is no way to take it back, so think very carefully before saying or writing **anything**!

Words of Peace

If speaking badly about someone can cause so much harm, think about how powerful speaking nicely about someone could be! When someone uses their words nicely and in a smart way, the words can bring people together.

For example, everybody loved Aharon the *Kohen Gadol*, because he made peace between people. Whenever there was a fight, he would speak to each person to tell them that the other person was sorry and wanted to be friends again.

His actions teach us that it is much more useful to talk to people about making peace, rather than taking sides in a fight and speaking in a bad way about another person. [20]

CHECKPOINT What is the special power of speech?

The Walls Have Ears

R' Yosi never said anything that would have caused him to look over his shoulder afterwards to make sure that no one had been listening.

We should never say things about other people that we wouldn't want them to find out about.

If you wouldn't say it to his face, don't say it at all![22]

STORY

Out of Your Mouth

The *Ba'al Shem Tov* sent some of his *talmidim* on a journey without telling them where they were going. They let their horse pull the wagon, taking them wherever it wanted to go. It stopped by an inn, and the *talmidim* went inside to have something to eat and get some rest.

Since they were so strict about *kashrus*, they asked the landlord many questions about the *kashrus* standards of the food served there. All through the meal, they loudly discussed each and every dish and how it had been prepared.

Eventually, a beggar called out to them, "Dear Jews, are you as careful with what comes **out** of your mouth as you are with what goes **into** your mouth?"

They became silent, as they understood that the *Ba'al Shem Tov* had sent them there to learn this message.

Burning With Rage

After certain coals are lit, they stay hot for a very long time, even if they look like they cooled down. In the same way, a person about whom *lashon hara* was spoken, may feel very hurt and upset for a long time, even if it looks like they don't care anymore.[23]

Poisonous Hatred

Doeg, the head of the *Sanhedrin* who was nevertheless evil, hated Dovid and made King Shaul jealous of him. Dovid eventually ran away to Nov, a city of *kohanim*. Achimelech the *kohen* gave Dovid food and a sword.

Doeg happened to see this, and immediately went to inform Shaul. Shaul called Achimelech and the other *kohanim* and asked them why they had helped Dovid. Achimelech said that he was not going against the king, but Shaul did not believe him. At Shaul's command, Doeg killed Achimelech, eighty five other *kohanim* and the entire city of Nov.[24]

All this happened because one person spoke when he should have kept quiet!

What Else Comes From This?   EXTRACT

Remember!

While travelling in the desert, Miriam told her brother Aharon that their brother Moshe had separated from his wife. Although she had not meant to harm Moshe, she was punished with *tzara'as*, the punishment for speaking *lashon hara*, because she spoke *lashon hara* that would have hurt Moshe if he would've heard it. Miriam was better off not having started that conversation at all.

The Torah[25] commands us to remember every day what happened to Miriam, and to learn from her that we always have to be careful when we speak about other people. When talking about other people, it is safer not to say **anything**. So, when in doubt, zip your lips![26]

My Lips Are Sealed

Sealing your lips is also the only way to keep a secret. Why should secrets be kept? Other than just respecting the person's privacy, secrets may hurt the person who told you the secret. In addition, sharing someone's secrets may also lead to *lashon hara* being said about that person.[27]

CHECKPOINT   Why is it important to keep someone else's secret?

A STORY

The Medicine of Long Life

A peddler travelling through the town of R' Yannai called out to the people in the marketplace, "Who wants a potion that makes you live longer?" R' Yannai's daughter overheard him and ran to tell her father about this exciting new medicine.

The peddler was invited in, and R' Yannai begged him to reveal the secret of the potion. The peddler asked him to bring a *Tehillim*, and he opened it to the *perek* where *Dovid Hamelech* says, "Who is the person that desires life… guard your tongue from evil talk…"

R' Yannai was so thrilled with the peddler's answer that he paid him six *selaim*.[28]

DID YOU KNOW?

Peddling Tales

The word רָכִיל is related to the word רוֹכֵל - a peddler. Just as peddlers buy items from one person and sell them to others, gossipers take what they hear from one person and tell it to others.[29]

PEARLS of wisdom

Either Way, It Hurts

The *Ba'al Shem Tov* said: When you hear bad information about another Jew, even if you do not know the person, you should feel very sad.

Two people might be doing *aveiros* now. The one who said the information is definitely doing an *aveirah*, even if the information is not true. And if it is true, then you should be sad that someone else did an *aveirah* in the first place.[30]

UNIT
13

ENDNOTES:

1. ויקרא רבה לג, א
2. חינוך מצוה רל"ו
3. רמב"ם הל' דעות פ"ז ה"ב, ע"פ כסף משנה וספר חפץ חיים
4. הגהות מיימוניות הל' דעות פ"ז אות ב', ובשו"ע הרב או"ח סי' קנ"ו ס"י
5. רמב"ם הל' דעות פ"ז ה"ב
6. רמב"ם הל' דעות פ"ז ה"ד
7. ערכין טו, ב
8. "היום יום" י"ב כסלו
9. ערכין טו, ב
10. ע"פ חפץ חיים ח"א הל' לשון הרע כלל ד' סי"א

11. חפץ חיים ח"ב הל' רכילות כלל ה' ס"ה
12. חפץ חיים ח"ב הל' רכילות כלל ה' ס"ג
13. חפץ חיים ח"א הל' לה"ר כלל ו' ס"ה
14. חפץ חיים ח"א הל' לה"ר כלל א' ס"ח
15. חפץ חיים ח"א הל' לה"ר כלל א' ס"ח
16. חפץ חיים ח"א הל' לה"ר כלל ה' ס"ז
17. חפץ חיים ח"א הל' לה"ר כלל ד' ס"י
18. פסחים קיג, ב
19. בראשית רבה צח, יט
20. תהילים קכ, ד ע"פ בראשית רבה צח, יט
21. בראשית רבה צח, יט

22. מעשיהם של צדיקים ח"ג ע' 242
23. דברים כג, ט
24. ספרי דברים פסקא רע"ה
25. ספר שערי התשובה לרבינו יונה פ"ג אות רכ"ה
26. שמואל א, פרק כא-כב
27. שבת קיח, ב. וברש"י שם ד"ה לא אמרתי
28. אבן עזרא ויקרא יט, טז
29. מדרש תנחומא פרשת מצורע סי' ה

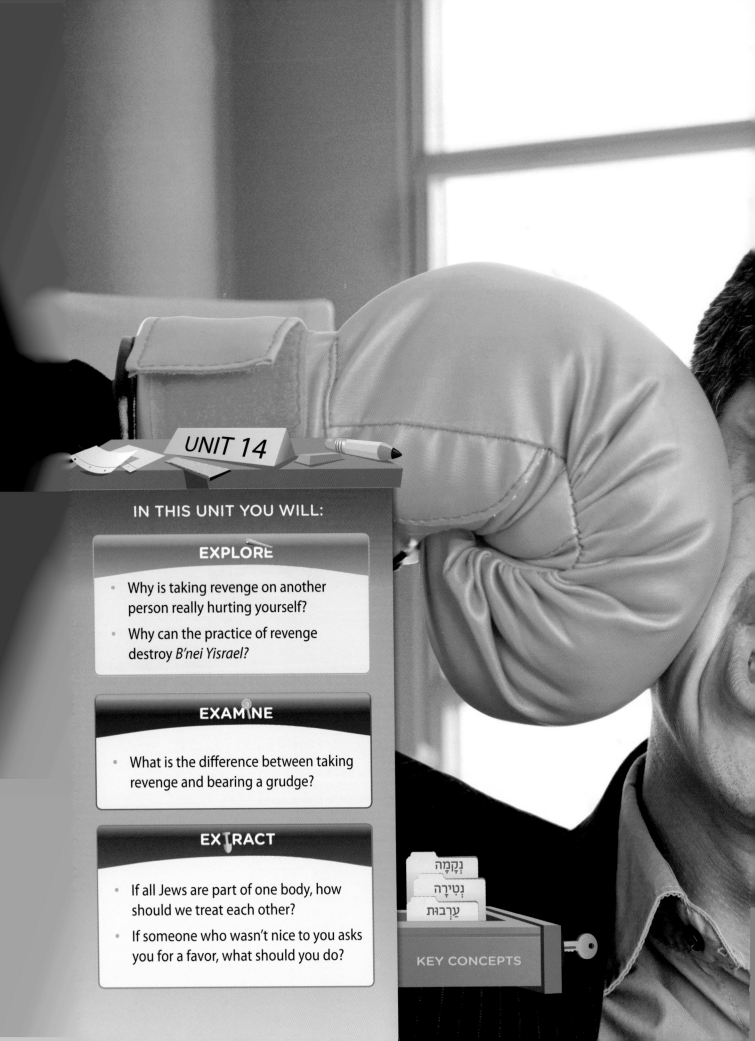

UNIT 14

IN THIS UNIT YOU WILL:

EXPLORE

- Why is taking revenge on another person really hurting yourself?
- Why can the practice of revenge destroy *B'nei Yisrael?*

EXAMINE

- What is the difference between taking revenge and bearing a grudge?

EXTRACT

- If all Jews are part of one body, how should we treat each other?
- If someone who wasn't nice to you asks you for a favor, what should you do?

נְקָמָה

נְטִירָה

עֲרֵבוּת

KEY CONCEPTS

Book: Madda, Section: Character

סֵפֶר מַדָּע הִלְכוֹת דֵּעוֹת

נְקָמָה וּנְטִירָה
REVENGE & GRUDGES

שְׁתֵּי מִצְוֹת

Ouch! You dropped your boiling cocoa all over your leg. Would you punch yourself in the face out of revenge?

Sweet Non-Revenge

A young man was sitting on a train next to R' Yisrael Salanter. Throughout the journey, the man bothered him, but R' Yisrael stayed patient with the man and never became angry.

When they arrived in Vilna, the young man found out that it was R' Yisrael whom he had been bothering. He was very embarrassed and went to beg R' Yisrael for forgiveness. R' Yisrael was more than forgiving and actually went out of his way to help the young man get certification as a *shochet*, and found him a job in another town.

When someone asked R' Yisrael why he had done so much for the man, R' Yisrael told him, "At first, I was happy to forgive him, but then I worried that I might still hold a tiny grudge against him. So, to cancel that grudge, I helped him so that I would grow to love him and not hold a grudge against him."[1]

BIOGRAPHY

R' Yisrael Salanter

(תק״ע - תרמ״ג) 1810 – 1883

R' Yisrael Lipkin, better known as R' Yisrael Salanter, started the Mussar movement, which helped Jews control their yetzer hara and improve their middos. He was a tremendous Talmid Chacham and famous Rosh Yeshivah. He passed away on כ״ה שבט.

The Mitzvos

The unit of *nekamah* and *netirah* has two mitzvos.
1. Do not take revenge against another Jew.
2. Do not hold a grudge against another Jew.

MITZVAH 20

שֶׁלֹא לִנְקוֹם
Not taking revenge

לֹא תִקֹּם וְלֹא תִטֹּר אֶת בְּנֵי עַמֶּךָ וְאָהַבְתָּ לְרֵעֲךָ כָּמוֹךָ אֲנִי ה׳
(ויקרא יט, יח)

Do not take revenge or bear a grudge against the people of your nation. You must love your neighbor as yourself. I am Hashem.

Do not take revenge against another Jew
who did wrong to you.

ALL PEOPLE · ALL PLACES · ALL TIMES · NO PUNISHMENT

MITZVAH 21

שֶׁלֹא לִנְטוֹר
Not holding a grudge

לֹא תִקֹּם וְלֹא תִטֹּר אֶת בְּנֵי עַמֶּךָ וְאָהַבְתָּ לְרֵעֲךָ כָּמוֹךָ אֲנִי ה׳
(ויקרא יט, יח)

Do not take revenge or **bear a grudge against the people of your nation**. You must love your neighbor as yourself. I am Hashem.

Do not hold a grudge against another Jew.

ALL PEOPLE · ALL PLACES · ALL TIMES · NO PUNISHMENT

Hurting Yourself

If your hand bangs against your foot, would your foot get angry and then take revenge against your hand by kicking it back? Not at all! That would be silly! Since *B'nei Yisrael* are like different parts of one body, when one person takes revenge against another, it is like one part of the body hurting another![2]

It Doesn't Stop

If we were allowed to take revenge, we would never be at peace. A person would take revenge for what his friend did to him the day before, then the friend will be mean back to him again to take revenge for the other person's revenge! Without a special mitzvah that tells us that we have to be nice to everyone even if they have been mean to us, the cycle of revenge would never end. It is much better to forgive and forget.[3]

Don't Get Upset About Small Things!

Too many times, people get angry over unimportant things. Should a three-year-old scream and yell and hit his friend if the friend knocked over his pile of blocks? For one minute, the little boy feels very angry and might **want** to hit his friend, but are the blocks so important that the boy should hurt someone? Will it be important in five days from now?

We should be quick to forgive and forget and to avoid getting into fights over anything, especially if it is not important.[4] The only truly important things in life are Torah and mitzvos which are our mission in life.

CHECKPOINT — Why is revenge so terrible for the Jewish nation?

Locked In

The word נְטִירָה also means guarding.

When you hold a grudge, it means that you are still holding the anger and "guarding" the memory of what happened in your heart, and will never forget it.

DISCOVERY

The Worst Enemy

A civil war is when people in the same country fight against each other. Sometimes, this kind of war can cause even more damage than a war fought against other countries.

In the American Civil War 620,000 people died, more than the total of all the wars that America fought against enemy countries.

In the same way, when we fight with each other, it can hurt us more than when enemies fight us. When we are united, it brings down special *brachos* from Hashem.

Nekamah

You cannot do something mean or hurtful to someone who hurt you. You cannot even just stop being nice to them to "get back" at them for being mean to you.

An example of an act of *nekamah* is when you refuse to lend your friend something just because they did not lend you something when you wanted to borrow it.[7]

Netirah

Do not stay angry and upset at a person who does something wrong to you, even if you do not actually take revenge.

An act of *netirah* is when you are nice to someone who was mean to you, but you say, "I am being nice to you even though you were mean to me." This shows that you are still holding a grudge in your heart, which is not allowed.[7]

 CHECKPOINT What is the difference between *nekamah* and *netirah*?

Pearls of Wisdom

Yosef Hatzaddik's Amazing Control

Yosef Hatzaddik forgave his brothers for the fact that they sold him as a slave.

Since he was second to the king of Egypt, he had the power to take revenge from his brothers and hurt them a lot. Instead, Yosef Hatzaddik chose to help and support his brothers.[5]

We should learn from him!

HISTORY

Good Revenge

When Zimri did an *aveirah* with Kozbi, Pinchas, the son of *Elazar Hakohen*, took revenge and killed both Zimri and Kozbi.

Since he was taking revenge for Hashem's honor, the brave act was a good thing, and the plague that Hashem had sent to punish the *Bnei Yisrael* was stopped.[6]

EXTEND YOUR KNOWLEDGE

Is it Ever Okay to Do *Nekamah* or *Netirah*?

Is a person ever allowed to take revenge or hold a grudge against someone?

The *Gemara*[8] says that a *Talmid Chacham* is allowed to take revenge if he is embarrassed in public.

R' Yerucham Fishel Perlow explains that this is because you are allowed to take revenge if **Hashem** has been insulted. Insulting a *Talmid Chacham* is like insulting the Torah and Hashem. Therefore, a *Talmid Chacham* **must** defend the honor of Hashem and the Torah by arguing with the person who embarrassed him.

Live the Mitzvah

EX**T**RACT

Cutting Off Your Nose To Be Mean To Your Face

Sometimes, when someone calls you a mean name, you say something mean right back to them, so that they will know how you felt. When you saw the pain and hurt on the other person's face, did it really make you feel good inside? Or did you feel bad that you did something mean, no matter how strongly you felt that the other person deserved it? You feel pain when someone else is in pain.

This is what Jewish *achdus* is all about. When you take revenge on other people, it is not only other people that are hurt, but **you yourself**, are hurt as well.

 CHECKPOINT Why do you feel pain when another Jew is in pain?

What Else Comes From This?

EX**T**RACT

Help Your Enemy

It is very easy to want to get even with someone who hurt you. However, there is a *halachah* that says that when you see two people who need help, and one is a friend and the other is an enemy, you should help the enemy first!

This is to help you get rid of any bad feeling towards that person, and become friends. It is the *yetzer hara* that is telling you to hate the "enemy." You should do extra to help the enemy, just to show your *yetzer hara* that you are not listening to him one bit.[9]

 CHECKPOINT How does helping your enemy help control your *yetzer hara*?

UNIT **14**

HISTORY

Shimshon's Revenge

In the time of the *Shoftim*, the enemies of *Bnei Yisrael* were extremely scared of *Shimshon Hagibor* because of his amazing strength. Shimshon's *Plishti* wife tricked him into telling her that the secret of his strength was in his hair. She had it cut off while he was sleeping, and then called the *Plishtim* to grab him. They made him blind and took him as their prisoner.

To celebrate their "catch," they made a huge feast to their idol, saying that their idol had defeated Shimshon. Shimshon had to dance for them, and when he was finished, he asked to rest against the two middle pillars that held up the building.

Shimshon *davened* to Hashem to give him back his strength so that he could take revenge on the *Plishtim*. Then, he pulled the pillars together, bringing down the building.

Thousands of *Plishtim* were killed, and Shimshon was able to make a big *Kiddush Hashem*.[10]

ENDNOTES:

7. יומא כג, א

8. יומא כג, א

9. בבא מציעא לב, ב. רמב"ם הל' רוצח ושמירת הנפש פי"ג הי"ג

10. שופטים פרק טז

3. חזקוני קדושים יט, יח. וראה רמב"ם הל' דעות פ"ז ה"ח

4. רמב"ם הל' דעות פ"ז ה"ז

5. אמרי יהוסף (על הסמ"ק) מצוה ח' ס"י

6. במדבר פרק כה

1. אור חדש זייטשיק קישוטי מדות ע' נג

2. ירושלמי נדרים פ"ט ה"ד, ובקרבן העדה שם

REVENGE & GRUDGES   **117**

UNIT 15

IN THIS UNIT YOU WILL:

EXPLORE

- How does Torah learning help us survive?
- Why is Torah different than any other subject a person learns?

EXAMINE

- What is the mitzvah of learning Torah?
- What is the best way to learn Torah?

EXTRACT

- If you don't have time to learn Torah all day and night, what can you do to fulfill this mitzvah?
- If a person doesn't have children of his own, what can he do to fulfill the mitzvah of teaching children Torah?

תַּלְמוּד תּוֹרָה

KEY CONCEPTS

Book: Madda, Section: Learning Torah

סֵפֶר מַדָּע הִלְכוֹת תַּלְמוּד תּוֹרָה

תַּלְמוּד תּוֹרָה
LEARNING TORAH

מִצְוָה אַחַת

It starts so high up, and comes all the way down, and the plants are lucky enough to benefit from its refreshing, life-giving power.

There is one mitzvah in the unit of *Talmud Torah*.
Learn and teach Torah.

OUR SAGES SAY...

Blueprint of Creation

The Torah is a special gift from Hashem that was around before the world was even created.

In fact, we know that אִסְתַּכֵּל בְּאוֹרַיְיתָא וּבָרָא עַלְמָא "Hashem looked into the Torah and created the world." A builder has a drawing of the building called a blueprint, which he follows to know how to build the building. Hashem used the Torah as His "blueprint" to create the world.[1]

The whole world was created just so that we can live according to the Torah, as *Chazal* say, בִּשְׁבִיל הַתּוֹרָה וּבִשְׁבִיל יִשְׂרָאֵל – the world was created for the Torah and for *B'nei Yisrael*![2]

OUR SAGES SAY...

The Writer and the Written

The word אָנֹכִי, the first word of the *Aseres Hadibros*, the first letters of the words אֲנָא נַפְשִׁי כְּתָבִית יְהָבִית, which means "I myself wrote and gave the Torah."[3]

These words can also mean that Hashem "wrote and gave Himself" in the Torah. Hashem put Himself into the Torah. When we learn Torah, we're connecting to Hashem Himself!

Mitzvah Messages   EXPLORE

Instructions for Life

Did you ever realize that the words תּוֹרָה and מוֹרָה or מוֹרֶה sound the same? That's because they come from the same root word, which means to teach and to guide. Hashem gave us the Torah, which teaches us exactly how we are to live and what we have to do.

Would you be able to use a complicated machine without any instructions? Would you be able to learn anything if you did not have a teacher to help you understand what your *sefarim* and textbooks are saying? In the same way, the Torah is our "teacher" for how to live our life.

Hashem created the world and all of the people in it. Just like you need an instruction booklet from the person who made the machine to know how to use it, we need the Torah to know how to live and to tell us how to act, what to do, and what not to do.

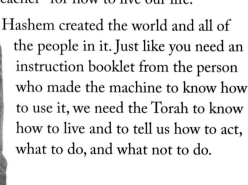

Precious Opportunity

The Torah is not a book which just tells you the story of our *Avos* and all of the mitzvos that we have to do. The Torah is a book of Hashem's wisdom[4] and is Hashem's special treasure.[5]

Obviously, Hashem's wisdom is much greater than ours, but we are able to understand part of Hashem's wisdom because He wrote it in the Torah for us to understand. Hashem took His wisdom and lowered it down to our level so that we would be able to learn from it.[6] Since the Torah is part of Hashem, when we learn Torah, we are connecting to Hashem in a very powerful way.

That's why it's a great mitzvah to learn all of the Torah, even about things which might never happen. We don't only learn Torah so that we should know what to do, but also because it is Hashem's wisdom, and by learning Torah, we are connecting to Hashem.[7]

CHECKPOINT   What is the Torah?

Details

EXAMINE

Who Must Learn Torah?

Every man has a mitzvah to learn Torah. There are no exceptions. The rich, the poor, the simple and the wise, all must learn Torah. No matter what is happening to a man or what is going on in his life, he must always find the time to learn Torah. Many *Chachamim* in our history had very busy lives as teachers, wood-choppers, water carriers and businessmen. Some were blind, crippled or very poor. But none of these things stopped them from learning Torah.[8]

To Whom are We Obligated to Teach Torah?

A father has a mitzvah to first teach Torah to his son. After that, a man has a mitzvah to teach his grandson. If a man cannot teach his children, he must pay someone else to teach them.[9]

There is more to this mitzvah! A man has a mitzvah to teach Torah to **everyone** whom he possibly can - not just to his own children or grandchildren.[10]

STORY

"כַּמָּה גְדוֹלִים מַעֲשֵׂי חִיָּיא"

How Great are the Actions of Chiya!

R' Chiya saw that people were forgetting the Torah because nobody was teaching it to them, so he found a way to teach Torah to the children of each city.

He would travel to a city, plant flax, collect it, and make it into ropes. He made the ropes into nets, and used those to trap deer. He then *shechted* the deer, giving the meat to poor orphans, and used the skins to make eleven scrolls of parchment. On five scrolls he wrote the five *Chumashim*, and on six scrolls, he wrote the *Shishah Sidrei Mishnah*.

He travelled like this from village to village. In every village, he gave each scroll to a different child and learned it with them. Each child then taught the other children, until they were all experts in all of *Chumash* and *Mishnah*, and then they went on to teach others. In this way, Torah was not forgotten.[11]

How Should You Learn Torah?

Three Parts

Every man has to learn Torah every day. A man's learning every day should be split into three parts: *Tanach*, *Mishnah* and *Gemara*.[16]

וְהָגִיתָ בּוֹ יוֹמָם וָלַיְלָה

A man has a mitzvah to learn Torah every day and every night of his life.[17] Really, he should learn at **all** times of the day and night. If this is impossible, he must at least set aside a specific amount of time to learn each day and night. The minimum amount he must learn is פֶּרֶק אֶחָד שַׁחֲרִית וּפֶרֶק אֶחָד עַרְבִית - one chapter in the morning and one chapter at night.[18]

Review

Reviewing what you learn is very important. You must know the Torah you have studied so well that if anyone would ask you a question about what you have been learning, you could immediately answer correctly without taking time to think about it.

If you learn and don't review, it's like someone who plants grain but does not harvest it. Even though you worked very hard, you aren't left with anything to show from your hard work.

The *Brachos*

There are three *brachos* said before learning Torah. One is a *brachah* for doing the mitzvah, just like we say for most mitzvos that we do. We continue with asking Hashem that we and our children should always learn and enjoy Torah. In the third *brachah*, we thank Hashem for choosing us to be the lucky nation to receive the Torah.[19]

 CHECKPOINT How and when must one learn Torah?

SELECTED HALACHOS

- As soon as a child can speak, his father should teach him the *passuk*, "תּוֹרָה צִוָּה לָנוּ מֹשֶׁה מוֹרָשָׁה קְהִלַּת יַעֲקֹב".[20]

- Someone who doesn't understand what he learns the first time should not be embarrassed to ask the teacher to explain it again.[21]

- Women have a mitzvah to learn the *halachos* that apply to them. For example, they must learn the laws of *Shabbos,* separating *challah,* not spreading *Lashon Hara,* etc, and things which will help them keep the mitzvos of *ahavas Hashem, yiras Hashem* etc.[22]

- The best place to learn Torah is in the same place where you *daven.*[23]

- You have to say a *brachah* before **saying** words of Torah, but if you are only **thinking** words of Torah, you do not need to say a *brachah.*[24]

- The best way to learn Torah is just for the sake of becoming closer to Hashem. If you cannot learn Torah only for this reason, you can learn Torah for any reason, as long as you want to eventually be able to learn for the right reason.[25]

- Torah is equal to all other mitzvos. If you can either do a mitzvah that can be done by someone else or learn Torah, you should learn Torah, and let another person do the mitzvah. If you are the only one who can do it, you should do the mitzvah yourself.[26]

EXTEND YOUR KNOWLEDGE

פַּרְדֵּס - The Orchard of Torah

The Hebrew word פַּרְדֵּס means an orchard. The four letters "ס" "ד" "ר" "פ" stand for the four levels of Torah learning. Although every word of Torah has a simple meaning, there are deeper ways of understanding it as well. The four levels are:

1. פְּשַׁט - the simple meaning of the words.
2. רֶמֶז - the hints or symbolic way of understanding the words of Torah.
3. דְּרוּשׁ - similar to *Midrash,* a much deeper way of explaining the Torah.
4. סוֹד - the deepest meaning of the Torah known as *Kabbalah.*[27]

Every Jewish *neshamah* must learn each one of these parts of Torah to fulfill the mitzvah properly![28]

STORY

R' Yehoshua ben Gamla

The *Gemara* says that if not for R' Yehoshua ben Gamla, we would have forgotten the Torah. What did he do?

Before the time of R' Yehoshua ben Gamla, children would only start learning with the local *Rebbi* at the age of 16 or 17.

R' Yehoshua realized that this wasn't such a good idea. He therefore decreed that a child must be brought to the teacher at the age of 6 or 7![29]

DID YOU KNOW?

Wine of Torah

Long ago, before there were *sefarim* and *yeshivos,* *talmidim* would sit before their teacher and listen to his words of Torah. They would then study what they learned by heart.

The students sat in rows facing their teacher, so that the seating arrangement made it look like a vineyard. For this reason, one of the *yeshivos* was actually called *"Kerem B'Yavneh"*- Vineyard in Yavneh.[30]

Absolute Limit

B'nei Yisrael were not sent into galus because they worshipped avodah zarah, killed people, or lied a lot. They were punished because they were disgusted with the Torah.

From this we see how important it is to Hashem that we hold the Torah precious, and learn it always.[31]

STORY

Fish Out Of Water

The Roman government once made a law that Jewish people may not study Torah. R' Akiva ignored this law and taught Torah anyway.

When someone asked him how he could do such a dangerous thing, he replied, "A fox was once walking near a stream and saw fish swimming quickly, as if they were running away from danger. 'What are you running away from?' asked the fox.

"The fish answered, 'From the nets of people who try to catch us.' The fox slyly said, "Why not come up onto dry land where you will be safe from the nets?"

"The fish laughed, 'Silly fox! Here, in the water, we have a **chance** to live, but on dry land, we will **surely** die!"

"Likewise," said R' Akiva, "the Torah is our life. With it, we may be in danger, but without it, we can surely not survive!"[32]

Live the Mitzvah

EX**T**RACT

"שֶׁלֹּא בֵּרְכוּ בַּתּוֹרָה תְּחִילָה"

The *Gemara*[33] tells us that the first *Beis Hamikdash* was destroyed because the Jews did not make *brachos* on the Torah before learning it.

The *Bach*[34] explains that this was not because people forgot to say the *brachos*. The problem was that the one who was learning Torah did not care about connecting to Hashem through learning His Torah. The person would just learn and not think about the fact that he was supposed to connect to Hashem through his learning.

The *brachos* that we say before learning Torah remind us of this, and help us focus on connecting to Hashem when we learn.

 CHECKPOINT Why is it important to say *brachos* before learning Torah?

What Else Comes From This?

EX**T**RACT

Partnership in Torah

Not everyone can learn Torah all day. How can a person get the benefit of doing the mitzvah of learning day and night if he cannot do it himself?

Yissachar and Zevulun show us how to do this! They were two of the *shevatim* with very different personalities and different jobs, yet they had a special arrangement through which they supported each other. Zevulun, a businessman, gave Yissachar enough money to live comfortably and learn Torah. Yissachar, in return, learned Torah on Zevulun's behalf.

Today, this kind of connection is continued by businessmen who support *Talmidei Chachamim*. These businessmen still have to learn once during the day and once during the night, and they also donate money to *yeshivos*; help *Talmidei Chachamim* and their families live comfortably, and pay people to learn Torah for them. These businessmen, who do not have time to study Torah all day, still get the mitzvah of learning Torah, and are considered as if they had learned the Torah themselves at the level of the great *Chachamim*.[35]

 CHECKPOINT How can someone who is a businessman still get the mitzvah of learning **all** day and night?

A STORY

Most Valuable Merchandise

A Talmid Chacham and some merchants were traveling on a ship. Each one bragged that his items were the best. The only person on the ship who did not brag was the Talmid Chacham – he sat and studied from his sefarim. The merchants asked him if he had anything good to sell, and the Talmid Chacham said, "My merchandise is more valuable than yours, but it is hidden and you will not see it until the time is right." The merchants laughed at him, because he had nothing but his sefarim.

Time passed, and the ship was attacked by pirates. They took everything, leaving the merchants with nothing. The ship reached land, and the merchants were left in the street with nothing to sell and no money to buy food. The Talmid Chacham however, went to the Beis Medrash, sat down and learned. Soon, he caught the attention of others, and they discovered his great Torah knowledge and wisdom. They begged him to be their Rabbi, and he agreed.

They led him royally to his new house, and he passed by the merchants who begged him for help. "You see," he told them, "my merchandise was better than yours. My Torah knowledge, my merchandise, cannot be taken away from me."

He asked the people to help the merchants and give them food, clothing and money to help them get home.[36]

ENDNOTES:

1. זוהר ח"ב קסא, ב
2. רש"י בראשית א, א ד"ה ד"ה בראשית ברא
3. שבת קה, א
4. עי' זוהר ח"ב ס, א. ושם ח"ג עג, א
5. שבת פח, ב, וראה מדרש משלי פרשה ח' ד"ה כלם נכוחים
6. תענית ז,
7. ראה סנהדרין עא, א לגבי עיר הנדחת
8. רמב"ם הל' ת"ת פ"א ה"ח-ט'
9. רמב"ם הל' ת"ת פ"א ה"ב-ג
10. רמב"ם הל' ת"ת פ"א ה"ב ע"פ כסף משנה
11. ב"ב פה, ב. כתובות קג, ב
12. אבות פ"ו מ"ד
13. ירושלמי ברכות פ"ה ה"א
14. עירובין נד, א. שו"ע יו"ד סי' רמ"ו סכ"ב
15. ספר "נועם המצות" ח"ד ע' 54
16. רמב"ם הל' ת"ת פ"א הי"א
17. רמב"ם הל' ת"ת פ"א ה"ח, שו"ע יו"ד סי' רמ"ו ס"א
18. שו"ע יו"ד סי' רמ"ו ס"א, ובהגה שם
19. שו"ע או"ח סי' מ"ז ס"א-ה'
20. שו"ע יו"ד סי' רמ"ו ס"ה
21. שו"ע יו"ד סי' רמ"ו סי"א
22. רמ"א יו"ד סי' רמ"ו ס"ו
23. שו"ע יו"ד סי' רמ"ו סכ"ב
24. שו"ע או"ח סי' מ"ז ס"ד
25. שו"ע יו"ד סי' רמ"ו ס"כ, ועי' הל' ת"ת בשו"ע הרב פ"ד ה"ג
26. שו"ע יו"ד סי' רמ"ו סי"ח
27. חדא"ג מהרש"א עירובין כא, א ד"ה עד שבא זכרי'
28. שער הגלגולים הקדמה י"א והקדמה ט"ז
29. בבא בתרא כא, א
30. ראה לדוגמא כתובות פ"ד מ"ו ותוי"ט
31. ירושלמי חגיגה פ"א ה"ז
32. ברכות סא, ב
33. בבא מציעא פה, ב
34. או"ח ריש סי' מ"ז
35. ויקרא רבה כה, ב
36. תנחומא תרומה, א
37. קידושין ל, ב
38. שבת פח, ב

Your mind is very hungry! What kind of information do you feed it? What happens to that knowledge once it is eaten up? Where does it go?

UNIT 16

IN THIS UNIT YOU WILL:

EXPLORE

- What happens to information that you learn?
- Why should we have more respect for our teachers than we have for our parents?

EXAMINE

- What should you do when you see a *Talmid Chacham*?
- What happens to a person who learns a lot of Torah?

EXTRACT

- If you learn Torah by heart, what do you become?
- If you see an older person, how should you treat him?

כְּבוֹד חֲכָמִים

KEY CONCEPTS

Book: Madda, Section: Learning Torah
סֵפֶר מַדָּע הִלְכוֹת תַּלְמוּד תּוֹרָה

כְּבוֹד חֲכָמִים
RESPECTING TALMIDEI CHACHAMIM

מִצְוָה אַחַת

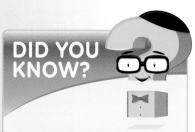
Honor Leads to Awe

Showing respect for *Talmidei Chachamim* can help you have *yiras shamayim*.[1]

STORY

Empty Wagon

R' Akiva Eiger and R' Ya'akov of Lissa had the greatest respect for each other. Once, they travelled to Warsaw together to meet with other Jewish leaders.

As their carriage drew near the city, a large crowd came out to greet them. Out of respect, they unhitched the horses and pulled the carriage themselves. Out of his great humility, it didn't occur to R' Akiva Eiger that everyone was honoring him — they must be honoring his esteemed friend! So, he secretly slipped out of the carriage to join the others in pulling the wagon.

Meanwhile, the humble R' Ya'akov of Lissa made the same conclusion, so he too snuck out from the other side, and cheerfully started pulling.

Only when they reached the city did everyone realize that they had been pulling an empty wagon![2]

The Mitzvah

EXAMINE

The unit of respecting *Talmidei Chachamim* has one mitzvah.

Respect a *Talmid Chacham*.

MITZVAH 23

מִצְוַת כְּבוֹד חֲכָמִים
Respecting *Talmidei Chachamim*

מִפְּנֵי שֵׂיבָה תָּקוּם וְהָדַרְתָּ פְּנֵי זָקֵן וְיָרֵאתָ מֵאֱלֹקֶיךָ אֲנִי ה'
(ויקרא יט, לב)

Stand up before the elderly and give respect to the old and you shall fear your G-d. I am Hashem.

Show respect to *Talmidei Chachamim*.

ALL PEOPLE   ALL PLACES   ALL TIMES

Mitzvah Messages

EXPLORE

BIOGRAPHY

R' Ya'akov M'Lissa
(1760 – 1832) תק"כ - תקצ"ב

R' Ya'akov ben Moshe Lorberbaum of Lissa is known as the "Nesivos Hamishpat" from the title of his most well-known sefer. He was the chief Rabbi of Lissa, Poland.

He was a great Rav and Posek who wrote many sefarim and fought fiercely against the Maskilim. He was one of the three Poskim on whom Rabbi Shlomo Ganzfried based his rulings in Kitzur Shulchan Aruch. He passed away on כ"ה אייר.

Plugged In

Learning Torah is a powerful tool that we can use to connect to Hashem. Since Hashem put Himself into the Torah, when you learn Torah and bring Torah into your mind, you are bringing Hashem into your mind. When you think words of Torah in your mind, you have part of Hashem with you at that moment. Since a *Talmid Chacham* has a lot of Torah in his mind, when you give respect to a *Talmid Chacham*, you are giving respect to Hashem.

This applies even when the *Talmid Chacham* is not actually learning Torah at the time, because he still has words of Torah stored in his mind.[3]

CHECKPOINT Why does respecting *Talmidei Chachamim* show respect for Hashem?

Stand Up

You must give respect to all *Talmidei Chachamim*, even if they are not your teacher.[4] If they are **your** teachers, you must be even more careful to give them respect.[5]

To show respect, you must stand up for all *Talmidei Chachamim*, when he passes you within a distance of four *amos*. Once the *Talmid Chacham* has passed, you may sit down.

Spiritual Parent

The mitzvah of giving respect to your Torah teacher is even greater than the mitzvah of respecting your parents! The reason for this is that while your parents brought you into this world, your Torah teacher helps you reach *Olam Haba*.[6]

There are many practical examples of this *halachah*. If you see two lost objects, one belonging to your Torah teacher and one belonging to your parent, you should return your Torah teacher's object first. The same is true with helping them with any bags or loads they are carrying, or to save them from prison; your Torah teacher comes first.[7]

At the Right Place at the Right Time

The *passuk* that teaches us about this mitzvah teaches us that you have to do two actions when you see *Talmidei Chachamim*. You have to "stand up" and you have to give "respect." *Chazal* learn that these two actions are connected, and that by standing up, you are showing respect.

Chazal also teach us that their laws are similar; since showing "respect" doesn't cost any money, so too, you only have to stand up for a *Talmid Chacham* when it will not cause you to lose money. This means that you don't have to stand up while you are at work, since it will take you away from your work and could cost you money.[8]

CHECKPOINT · How do we show respect for *Talmidei Chachamim*?

OUR SAGES SAY...

Nothing is Without Value

Achitofel taught *Dovid Hamelech* only two things; to learn together with other people rather than alone, and to walk together with other people, and with excitement when going to learn. For this, Dovid honored him and called him "my master."

From this we learn that we must respect someone who teaches us even the simplest idea.[9]

HISTORY

Unlikely Advisors

When King Achashverosh became angry at his wife Vashti for not following his orders, he did not know what to do. Who do you think he turned to first?

Not to his own ministers or advisors, but to the *Talmidei Chachamim* of the time! They did not want to give him advice, so he had to ask his own ministers.[10]

Advisor to Kings

The Roman Emperor, Antoninus, understood that *Talmidei Chachamim* are very wise, and he often asked advice from *R' Yehudah Hanassi*.

He once sent a messenger to R' Yehudah with this question: "The Royal Treasury is empty. What should I do?" R' Yehudah took the messenger into the garden, where he pulled out some plants and replaced them with others. He then sent the messenger back to the Emperor.

The messenger told the Emperor that R' Yehuda did not give any answer. Antoninus knew that R' Yehuda was very wise and would never send back a messenger with no answer. Antoninus asked the messenger if R' Yehudah did **anything** while he was there. The messenger described what he had seen with the plants.

The Emperor understood that R' Yehudah was sending him a message; he should fire some of his officers and replace them with others. Antoninus replaced several of his officers who were dishonest and soon the royal treasury was full again.[11]

SELECTED HALACHOS

Honoring all *Talmidei Chachamim*

- You do not have to stand up for a *Talmid Chacham* if you are sick.[12]

- You should stand up for a *Talmid Chacham* even while learning Torah.[13]

- *Talmidei Chachamim* should try not to bother people. Therefore, they should try to avoid causing people to stand up for them by walking in less public places.[14]

Honoring Your *Rebbe*

- You may not argue with your teachers, or even decide a *halachah* for someone else in front of them. You must be very careful to talk respectfully when you are learning with your teacher.[15]

- You may not call your teachers by their first names.[16]

- You may not sit in your teacher's designated place.[17]

- You must treat your teacher with the utmost respect; it is even forbidden to inquire after his welfare before he asks you first.[18]

EXTEND YOUR KNOWLEDGE

No Names

You may never refer to your teachers by their first names, whether it is front of them or even when they're not there. Not only that, but if your teacher has a unique name, then you can never use that name, even if you are talking about someone else who has that name, and even if the teacher is not around!

However, if you put a respectful title before the name (for example, "my teacher…," "my *Rebbi*…." etc.), then you can call the teacher by name.[19]

Not An Excuse

Do you have to stand up when a blind *Talmid Chacham* walks by? Since the *Talmid Chacham* can't see anything, is there any point in standing up?

The answer is yes! By standing up, he is showing respect to the *Talmid Chacham* and to the Torah, even if the *Talmid Chacham* can't see it.[20]

Live the Mitzvah

EXTRACT

Travelling with Torah

We give respect to a *Talmid Chacham* because of Hashem's Torah that they carry around in their mind. Whatever you learn and remember becomes a part of you, and stays in your brain even if you are not thinking about it at that moment.

This is one of the reasons why it is so special to learn parts of Torah by heart. When you learn Torah by heart, it is stored in your mind forever, and wherever you go, you have the holy words of Torah going with you!

CHECKPOINT   Why should you learn Torah by heart?

What Else Comes From This?

EXTRACT

Respect for Elders

Included in this mitzvah is the idea of respecting our elders, even if they are not *Talmidei Chachamim*. For example, if a seventy-year old person walks into the room, you must stand up for that person.[21]

Why must we give respect to older people? Some of the reasons are:

- They have become wiser from their life experiences.
- They have performed many more mitzvos than someone younger than them.[22]

CHECKPOINT   Why do older people deserve respect?

UNIT 16

ENDNOTES:

19. שו"ע יו"ד סי' רמ"ב סט"ו. ועי' ש"ך שזה רק שלא בפניו, אבל בפניו, נוהגין לקרותו רבי

20. עי' מנ"ח מצוה רנ"ז אות ה', ובפתחי תשובה יו"ד סי' ר"מ ס"ק ו'

21. רמב"ם הל' ת"ת פ"ו ה"ט, ובשו"ע יו"ד סי' רמ"ד ה"א

22. חינוך מצוה רנ"ז

23. שו"ע יו"ד סי' רמ"ב סל"ו

10. אסתר א, יג. מגילה יב, ב

11. בראשית רבה יא, ד. סז, ו

12. רמ"א יו"ד סי' שע"ו ס"א

13. שו"ע יו"ד סי' רמ"ד סי"א

14. שו"ע יו"ד סי' רמ"ד ס"ו

15. שו"ע יו"ד סי' רמ"ב ס"ב ואילך

16. שו"ע יו"ד סי' רמ"ב סט"ו

17. שו"ע יו"ד סי' רמ"ב סט"ז

18. שו"ע יו"ד סי' רמ"ב סט"ז

1. במדבר רבה טו, יז

2. דברות אליהו ח"א ע' קמח

3. לקו"ת פ' קדושים ל, ד ד"ה והדרת

4. שו"ע יו"ד סי' רמ"ד ס"א

5. שו"ע יו"ד סי' רמ"ד ס"א

6. רמב"ם הל' ת"ת פ"ה ה"א

7. שו"ע יו"ד סי' רמ"ב סל"ד

8. שו"ע יו"ד סי' רמ"ד ס"ה

9. אבות פ"ו מ"ג ע"פ מס' כלה רבתי פ"ה ה"ד

DID YOU KNOW?

Greatest Forever

*M*oshe Rabbeinu was the greatest *navi* who ever lived. He was a *navi*, a *Talmid Chacham*, and a *tzaddik*. Therefore, we give him great respect, even nowadays. If one were to tell a friend, "I wouldn't listen to you even if you were as great as *Moshe Rabbeinu*," this is considered to be disrespectful to *Moshe Rabbeinu*.[23]

PEARLS of wisdom

Monkeying Around

A non-Jewish person noticed that his Jewish neighbor's children showed great respect to their parents and to elders in general. Desperate to know the secret of success, he asked his neighbor, "How do you get your children to show respect to older people? My children don't show me any respect!"

The Jewish neighbor answered, "We teach our children that many years ago, Hashem revealed Himself to us on *Har Sinai* and gave us the Torah. Therefore, the children understand that each previous generation is one generation closer to that special moment.

"You, on the other hand, teach your children that people come from monkeys. According to you, parents are one generation closer to being a monkey! Why **should** they respect you?"

UNIT 17

IN THIS UNIT YOU WILL:

EXPLORE

- Why should you be careful to only look at good things?
- Why does looking and thinking about the wrong things make your life more difficult?

EXAMINE

- What are you not allowed to do with information about idols?
- What are you not allowed to stare at or even think about?

EXTRACT

- If you want to stay focused on your mission, what should you avoid?

לֹא תָתוּרוּ

אַל תִּפְנוּ

שְׁמִירַת הָעֵינַיִם

KEY CONCEPTS

Book: Madda, Section: Idol Worship

סֵפֶר מַדָּע הִלְכוֹת עֲבוֹדָה זָרָה

שֶׁלֹּא לִפְנוֹת אַחַר דְּבָרִים אֲסוּרִים

NOT SHOWING INTEREST IN FORBIDDEN THINGS

שְׁתֵּי מִצְוֹת

There are so many people and distractions in this place. **How can you keep track of the person you are trying to follow?**

OUR SAGES SAY...

A Dangerous Step

The *yetzer hara* is very smart. He knows that if he tells you to do something that you know for sure is wrong, you will never listen. Therefore he starts off very slowly and carefully. One day he will just tell you to do a tiny thing wrong. "It's such a small thing, it doesn't really matter," he will tell you.

The next day he will tell you to do something a little worse, and the next day even worse, and so on. In the end, he will convince you to do the most terrible *aveiros, chas v'shalom*.

Be smart and protect yourself from the small steps of the *yetzer hara*. Don't even let him get a word in![1]

In the unit of not showing interest in forbidden things there are two mitzvos.

1. Do not to show interest in *avodah zarah*.
2. Do not follow anything that goes against Torah.

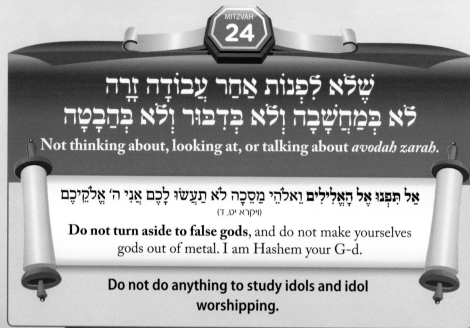

MITZVAH 24

שֶׁלֹּא לִפְנוֹת אַחַר עֲבוֹדָה זָרָה
לֹא בְּמַחֲשָׁבָה וְלֹא בְּדִבּוּר וְלֹא בְּהַבָּטָה

Not thinking about, looking at, or talking about *avodah zarah*.

אַל תִּפְנוּ אֶל הָאֱלִילִים וֵאלֹהֵי מַסֵּכָה לֹא תַעֲשׂוּ לָכֶם אֲנִי ה' אֱלֹקֵיכֶם
(ויקרא יט, ד)

Do not turn aside to false gods, and do not make yourselves gods out of metal. I am Hashem your G-d.

Do not do anything to study idols and idol worshipping.

 ALL PEOPLE   ALL PLACES   ALL TIMES   MALKUS

DID YOU KNOW?

Spies

The word "תָּתוּרוּ" literally means spies. The eyes and the heart spy for the *yetzer hara* so that it can cause you to do an *aveirah*. First the eyes see, then the heart wants it, and then the body finishes it off by doing the *aveirah*.[2]

MITZVAH 25

שֶׁלֹּא לָתוּר אַחַר מַחֲשֶׁבֶת הַלֵּב וּרְאִיַּת הָעֵינַיִם

Not following what your eyes and heart want.

וְהָיָה לָכֶם לְצִיצִת וּרְאִיתֶם אֹתוֹ וּזְכַרְתֶּם אֶת כָּל מִצְוֹת ה' וַעֲשִׂיתֶם אֹתָם
וְלֹא תָתוּרוּ אַחֲרֵי לְבַבְכֶם וְאַחֲרֵי עֵינֵיכֶם אֲשֶׁר אַתֶּם זֹנִים אַחֲרֵיהֶם
(במדבר טו, לט)

These shall be your *tzitzis*, and when you see them, you shall remember all of Hashem's commandments, and you shall keep them. **And you shall not explore after your heart and after your eyes, which cause you to go astray.**

Do not think about anything that goes against Torah.

 ALL PEOPLE   ALL PLACES   ALL TIMES   NO PUNISHMENT

Staying Focused

You might think that it's really not a big deal if once in a while you think about something that goes against Torah. You might think, "What harm can I do just by **thinking** a little bit?" After all, you're not actually **doing** anything, are you? You won't even realize that when these thoughts begin entering your mind, they have more power than you ever thought was possible. These thoughts will just get stronger and stronger, and it will be very easy to start doing the actions, and then to become totally lost from the path of Torah.

If you do not even let these thoughts come into your head in the first place, you will be able to stay focused on the Torah and do what Hashem wants from you, and you will not get distracted.[3]

Eyes on the Goal

Things that you see can distract you. It doesn't matter if, only seconds ago, you didn't know or care if these things existed. If you look for too long, you will chase after those things, leaving the path of Torah. These mitzvos teach us to focus our thoughts, and not to look at, or even think about, things that could bring us to do *aveiros* and leave the path of Torah.[4]

CHECKPOINT Why is it important to not even **think** about things which can distract us from Torah?

STORY

Double Standard

A merchant in the town of Stravisky used to sell his books near the town's shul, right next to a large oven. One day, the Rabbi, R' Chaim Leib Myszkovski took one look at the books and realized that they were about things which were against the Torah. Quickly, he opened the oven door and threw them into the fire.

The merchant was devastated. "Rabbi!" he cried. "That was my whole business! Now I have no money!" R' Chaim Leib answered calmly, "I'll find you a new job, have no fear."

R' Chaim Leib told the merchant that the priest of the city needed someone to help him ring the church bells. The merchant was shocked. "But Rabbi, I can't work for a church!"

R' Chaim Leib smiled and said, "So you don't want to be involved in other religions - but you are comfortable selling books that are against the Torah, and helping young children follow after *avodah zarah*. How is that any different?"[6]

Do Not Follow *Avodah Zarah*

How can you stay on the path of Torah if you are looking, thinking, and talking about *avodah zarah*? Hashem is protecting us from the *yetzer hara* by giving us the mitzvah of never showing interest in anything that has to do with *avodah zarah*. A simple example of this would be staring at an idol.

It is also forbidden to try and find out information about other gods. For example, you cannot read books about these gods, and how people worshipped them. You are also not allowed to ask people about *avodah zarah*, how they are served, and what it is like.[9]

Don't Go Too Far!

Avodah zarah is not the only idea we are warned not to think about. Any thought that would cause one to question, doubt, or not believe the truthfulness of the Torah is strictly forbidden.[10]

The Punishment

אַל תִּפְנוּ - Do not Show Interest in *Avodah Zarah*

If you do something to know more about an *avodah zarah* (like purposely moving a curtain to look at an idol), you are *chayav malkus*. If you only think about the *avodah zarah*, *Beis Din* would not give *malkus* because you did not do any **action**.[11]

לֹא תָתוּרוּ - Do not Think About Something that is Forbidden

There is no punishment from *Beis Din* for someone who does this *aveirah*, since the *aveirah* is only done through thought, not action. This is called a *lav she'ein bo ma'aseh*, an *aveirah* done without an action. Since the main *aveirah* is done through thought and cannot be punished, even if someone does this *aveirah* through an action, he will not get punished by *Beis Din*.[12]

 CHECKPOINT   What must we do to stay focused on serving Hashem?

OUR SAGES SAY...

Swallow Your Fear

A person should not spend any time with people who serve *avodah zarah*, even if it is at night and people who serve *avodah zarah* could save him from robbers.[7]

DID YOU KNOW?

Worshipping Nothing Gets You Nothing

Serving an *avodah zarah* is like going against the whole Torah. That's why *Moshe Rabbeinu* broke the *Luchos* when he saw the Jews worshipping the *Egel Hazahav*, because they were serving an *avodah zarah* and did not deserve to get the Torah and all of the mitzvos.[8]

SELECTED HALACHOS

- Your house should not have windows that face a church.[13]
- It is forbidden to stare at a statue that has been set aside for *avodah zarah*.[14]
- It is forbidden to worship idols, even in ways which they are not usually worshipped.[15]
- You may not do business by selling religious items, such as a cross, or something that represents an *avodah zarah*. [16]

DID YOU KNOW?

Constantly Resisting

The mitzvah of not following temptations is one of the six מִצְוֹת תְּמִידִיּוֹת - constant mitzvos which we must fulfill every second.[19]

EXTEND YOUR KNOWLEDGE

מוֹרֶה נְבוּכִים

The Rambam wrote a famous *sefer* called *"Moreh Nevuchim"* - *The Guide to the Confused*. This book explains many ideas about Hashem, using philosophy and science to explain and bring proof to Jewish ideas. It was written for people who did not understand Hashem or the Torah.

To be able to write this book, the Rambam must have read the other books that teach about non-Jewish ideas. How was he allowed to do this?

The *Gemara*[17] tells us about Acher. He was a great Rabbi, but he read many books about *avodah zarah* and was not careful to stay away from thinking about *avodah zarah*. Eventually, he left the path of mitzvos. Still, his student R' Meir continued learning from him. The *Gemara* explains that R' Meir was such a *tzaddik* and *Talmid Chacham* that he wasn't influenced from his teacher's ideas and only took the good things he taught. "He ate the fruit and threw away the peels."

Similarly, the Rambam was so great that he was able to read those books **only** for the purpose of helping people become closer to Hashem and to the Torah way of life, and did not become affected by them.

You can never try this on your own and think that you will not be influenced.[18]

HISTORY

Acher

In the times of the *Gemara*, there was a *Talmid Chacham* by the name of R' Elisha ben Avuya who became an *apikores* (someone who does not believe in Hashem) when he was older. The *Chachamim* would not call him by his real name, but by the name *"Acher,"* which means "the other one."

The *Gemara* tells us that when *Acher* would stand up when he was finished teaching, books about *avodah zarah* and other religions would fall from his lap. We see from what happened to him, that just reading books about *avodah zarah* can bring a person very far from Hashem.[20]

Lasered

Laser is used for many things, from reading bar codes to eye surgery.

Unlike an ordinary light bulb which gives light in all directions, a laser beam is a very strong, concentrated beam of light that moves toward a target.

Since it is so focused and intense, the laser beam is able to do many things an ordinary light can not do.

We can also be like a laser. By staying focused on our mission and concentrating on positive thoughts, we will follow them and succeed in always doing what's right!

DID YOU KNOW?

The "Wisdom" of Sira

The *Gemara* refers to a book called *"Ben Sira"* as a *"sefer chitzoni"* - an outside book.

This book was written by a man called *Ben Sira* in the times of the second *Beis Hamikdash* and is written in the same way as the books of *Tanach*. Although some of the book is quoted in the *Gemara*, the *Chachamim* decided that *Ben Sira* contains ideas that go against Hashem and is therefore completely unreliable![21]

Live the Mitzvah
EXTRACT

Information Age

The current period of time is called the "Information Age," because it is so easy to learn about anything that ever happened, just from the technology that exists. The internet and telephones can be used to read, talk, and learn about anything in the whole world. Often, if a person just uses technology to learn information and is not careful to stay away from information that is against the Torah way of life, they can go further away from the Torah instead of closer.

What Can You do About This?

You should only look at things that can bring you closer to Hashem, not the parts that will take you further away. You should only read things that will help you serve Hashem better. It is difficult to stay focused on Hashem and the mitzvos, but it will be easier if you remember that you will only be able to accomplish your goals in life if you can stay away from anything that will lead you away from Torah.

 CHECKPOINT How can you help yourself to stay focused on the right things?

What Else Comes From This?
EXTRACT

Avoiding the Trap

The mitzvah of אַל תִּפְנוּ includes not reading books about *avodah zarah*, or any books called *"sefarim chitzonim"* (books which include outside influences). These include books from priests or other religious people, and books on non-Jewish philosophy and what non-Jews believe.[22]

Not Just For Fun

The mitzvah of לֹא תָתוּרוּ teaches us that we should not follow whatever our heart desires. While many things are enjoyable, a Jew doesn't do them just because they are fun and enjoyable. We eat, sleep, exercise or wear beautiful clothes to give us more energy and make us happy so that we can serve Hashem better.[23]

 CHECKPOINT What kind of books should you stay far away from so that you do not do the *aveirah* of *Al Tifnu*?

A STORY

Exposed!

In Europe in the late 1700's, a movement called *Haskalah* was formed. The movement encouraged Jews to study secular subjects, to learn different languages, and to become just like the non-Jews in dress, language, manners and belief.

Shimon of Zamut worked for this group. He went to the city of Vilna to try and convince the Jewish people living there to become just like him. He acted as a *talmid chacham* and *yirei shamayim*, and so he was hired as the head of all *cheder* teachers in Vilna. He used this position to choose the best students and slowly talk to them about all of his non-Jewish ideas, He would then send them to schools run by *maskilim* in other cities, while telling the parents that their children were sent to study in better distant *yeshivos*.

The *Ba'al Hatanya*, realized what Shimon was doing, and sent a letter warning the leaders of Vilna to collect all the evidence needed to prove what he was really doing. The leaders sent a spy to search Shimon's house while he was away. Letters and other papers were found, proving everything that Shimon had done to lead students towards the *Haskalah* movement.

The leaders organized a public assembly. At the assembly, two witnesses stood up and declared that Shimon of Zamut was in fact an *apikores*, and that they had the evidence to prove it. The evidence was read before all the people, bringing grief to the parents who finally realized what had happened to the children Shimon had sent away. The *Beis Din* decreed that Shimon be put in jail for several weeks, after which he and his family would be sent away from the city.[24]

DISCOVERY

Blinders

Blinders are pieces of leather that are put on both sides of the horse's eyes so that the horse can only see directly ahead. This is to make sure that the horse does not become distracted by everything around it. Otherwise, the horse will get scared or distracted by crowds of people.

These two mitzvos are like our "blinders" helping us stay focused and not get pulled aside by our *yetzer hara*.

BIOGRAPHY

The Ba'al Hatanya
תק"ה - תקע"ג
(1745–1812)

R' Schneur Zalman of Liadi was the founder and first Rebbe of the Chabad-Lubavitch Chassidim. He was also known as the "Alter Rebbe," "the Rav," and the "Ba'al Hatanya." He was the author of a sefer called Tanya, and the Shulchan Aruch Harav. He taught that it is not enough to just believe in Hashem, but that we have to learn about Hashem and understand His ways as much as possible. He was born on ח"י אלול, *and passed away on* כ"ד טבת.

UNIT
17

ENDNOTES:

1. נדה יג, ב

2. רש"י במדבר טו, לט

3. חינוך מצוה שפ"ז ורי"ג

4. חינוך מצוה רי"ג

5. רש"י ויקרא יט, ד ד"ה אל

6. בירור הלכה ע' קו

7. תוספתא, הובא בסמ"ג לאוין י"ד. הגמ"י הל' ע"ז פ"ב אות א'

8. החינוך בהקדמתו "הערת המחבר"

9. רמב"ם הל' ע"ז פ"ב ה"ג

10. חינוך מצוה שפ"ז

11. חינוך מצוה רי"ג

12. חינוך מצוה שפ"ז

13. עי' בספר חסידים (מרגליות) סי' תל"א

14. שו"ע או"ח סי' ש"ז סט"ז ובמג"א ס"ק כ"ג

15. עי' רש"י סנהדרין סג, א ד"ה אבל המגפף. ועי' ס' יראים סי' שנ"א

16. שו"ת דברי יציב חלק יו"ד סי' מ"ה ד"ה וזאת התורה

17. חגיגה טו, ב

18. שו"ת ריב"ש סי' מ"ה

19. ראה שבת פז, א

20. חגיגה טו, ב

21. סנהדרין ק, ב

22. רמב"ם הל' ע"ז פ"ב ה"ב

23. חינוך מצוה שפ"ז

24. ספר התולדות אדמו"ר הזקן ח"ב ע' 546-565

How wrong is it to make fun of the one who cares for you and feeds you; the source of your existence!?

It is so wrong, that we don't even want to use the real word when talking about it, and instead we say the opposite; "blessing" Hashem!

UNIT 18

IN THIS UNIT YOU WILL:

EXPLORE

- Why is it wrong to "bless" Hashem?
- Why do we use the word "bless" in this mitzvah if we are really referring to the opposite of blessing?

EXAMINE

- What are the different punishments for "blessing" Hashem?
- What would happen at the trial of a person who "blessed" Hashem?

EXTRACT

- If you need to say a word that is not so nice, how should you say it?
- If you want to follow the ways of Hashem and use only nice words, what should you do?

בִּרְכַּת הַשֵּׁם

KEY CONCEPTS

Book: Madda, Section: Idol Worship
סֵפֶר מַדָּע הִלְכוֹת עֲבוֹדָה זָרָה

בִּרְכַת הַשֵּׁם
"BLESSING" HASHEM
מִצְוָה אַחַת

Smichah

Before the one who "blessed" Hashem received his punishment of *skilah*, the judges and witnesses would place their hands on top of his head. This action was called *smichah*.

This was the only time that *smichah* was done before the *Beis Din* carried out a death sentence![1]

HISTORY

Setting a Bad Example

The first time someone "blessed" Hashem was in the desert.

A man, whom the Torah describes as the son of a Jewish mother and an Egyptian father, got into an argument and was heard publicly "blessing" the name of Hashem. He was brought before Moshe, and was put in jail until his punishment would be made clear.

Hashem told Moshe to bring him outside of the camp, and have all the people stone him.[2]

The Mitzvah   EXAMINE

There is one mitzvah in the unit of *Birkas Hashem*.

Do not "bless" Hashem.

MITZVAH
26

לָאו דְּבִרְכַּת הַשֵּׁם
Not "blessing" Hashem

אֱלֹקִים לֹא תְקַלֵּל וְנָשִׂיא בְעַמְּךָ לֹא תָאֹר
(שמות כב, כז)

Do not "bless" Hashem. Do not curse a leader of your people.

Do not "bless" Hashem with one of His holy names.

| ALL PEOPLE | ALL PLACES | ALL TIMES | SKILAH |

Mitzvah Messages   EXPLORE

Hashem Our Parent

Would you curse your parents? How could you even think of doing such a thing?! They are the ones who feed you, clothe you, and take care of all your needs. They deserve your respect.

In the same way, everything that we have and everything that we are is only because of Hashem. We must speak about Him with great respect.

We don't even say the word "curse" when we speak about Him, even when we are discussing the *issur* to do so.

For this reason, the *Chachamim* called this mitzvah "Blessing Hashem," and this unit uses the word "bless" instead of the word "curse."

 CHECKPOINT Why should you never "bless" Hashem?

Details EXAMINE

The Court Case

The punishment for a person who "blessed" Hashem's name was a long process. After the court had come to a final decision, the crowd would be sent out of the courtroom. The judge would ask the older witness, "What did you hear?" and the witness would repeat the words of the person who "blessed" Hashem.

The judges who heard the "blessing" being repeated would tear their clothing. The other witnesses would then say "we heard the same thing," but would not actually say the terrible words that they heard.

When they were finished, the judges and the witnesses would place their hands on the head of the "blesser" and say, "Your blood is on your head for you caused this to yourself." They would then kill him with *skilah*.[3]

When *Skilah* Is Given

Not everyone who "blesses" Hashem's name receives the punishment of *skilah*. *Skilah* is only given if someone "blesses" the *Shem Hameforash (yud-kay-vav-kay)* using another name of Hashem that is not allowed to be erased (for example, by saying "may *Elokim* 'bless' *YKVK*").

Also, the person "blessing" Hashem must have been given a warning first, and there must be witnesses there when he does the *aveirah*.

Other Punishments

If the person who "blesses" Hashem had not been warned first, or if there were no witnesses, the person receives *kares* as a punishment. If the person "blesses" Hashem using a non-erasable name (but not the *Shem Hameforash*) against another non-erasable name, then his punishment would be *kares* if there is no warning, or *malkus* if there is a warning.[4]

 CHECKPOINT What is the process and punishment for someone who "blesses" Hashem?

DID YOU KNOW?

Euphemisms

The *Chachamim* were very careful not to use terms that were improper or insensitive. They would replace such words with expressions that have the opposite meaning.

For example, they used the expression "סַגִּי נָהוֹר" which in Aramaic means "great light," to refer to a blind person.

A cemetery is called a בֵּית הַחַיִּים - the House of the Living," and a *mesechta* in the *Gemara* on death and mourning was called מֶסֶכֶת שְׂמָחוֹת – Tractate of Happiness.

Also, if they wanted to discuss something negative in connection with *B'nei Yisrael*, they would refer to *B'nei Yisrael* as the "Haters of *Yisrael*." For example, "A solar eclipse is a bad sign for the non-Jews, and a lunar eclipse is a bad sign for the 'Haters of *Yisrael*' (i.e. *B'nei Yisrael*)."[5]

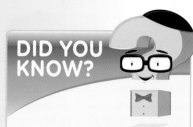
No Turning Back

In many cases of *halachah*, people can take back what they said within a few seconds of saying it. For example, if someone makes a promise to do something, he can take back his promise within a short amount of time.

"Blessing" Hashem is so terrible, that once you "bless" Hashem, you cannot take it back![6]

Shem Hameforash

The *Shem Hameforash* is the special name of Hashem that is rarely said out loud, except for a few exceptions, such as on *Yom Kippur*, by the *Kohen Gadol* in the *Beis Hamikdash*. When he would say it, the entire crowd of people who were in the *Azarah* would bow down on their faces, and proclaim בָּרוּךְ שֵׁם כְּבוֹד מַלְכוּתוֹ לְעוֹלָם וָעֶד.

Now that we don't have the *Beis Hamikdash*, this name of Hashem is never used.[7]

SELECTED HALACHOS

- If you hear Hashem's name being "blessed," you should tear your clothing as a sign of mourning for this tragedy.[8]

- You should tear your clothes even if someone "blesses" Hashem's name in any language (If it is one of the names that are meant to be holy, like "L-rd" or "G-d").[9]

- If you hear a non-Jew "blessing" Hashem, you do not have to tear your clothes.[10]

EXTEND YOUR KNOWLEDGE

Why Yossi?

When the witnesses tell the judges that they heard someone "bless" Hashem, they do not use the exact words of the "blessing" until the very end of the court case. During the court case, they will repeat the "blessing," but will use the word "יוֹסִי" instead of Hashem's name.

Why was the name "יוֹסִי" chosen? Rashi gives two reasons:

1. "יוֹסִי" has four letters, like Hashem's name.

2. The *gematriya* of "יוֹסִי" is 86, which is the same as "אֱ-לֹ-הִ-י-ם" - Hashem's name.[11]

Live the Mitzvah

EX**T**RACT

Living the Mitzvah

Have you ever caught yourself saying things like "Oh, my G-d?!"

Many people use expressions like that, but they don't realize that it comes very close to "blessing" Hashem's name, *chas v'shalom*!

You must be very careful not to use these expressions, because it is not respectful to Hashem. Also, if you

get used to saying Hashem's name without thinking, it might cause you to say worse things in the future.

When you get upset or frustrated, you have to be very careful to only use expressions that will not be disrespectful to Hashem.[12]

 CHECKPOINT Which kinds of expressions should be avoided when you are surprised or frustrated?

What Else Comes From This?   EXTRACT

Clean Speech

We can learn from the mitzvah of not "blessing" Hashem to always make sure that our speech is clean, polite and appropriate. This applies whether we are talking about someone else or not.

For example, some great *Chachamim* would never say the word "bad." Rather, they would say "not good," because "bad" was too harsh a word to use.[13]

 CHECKPOINT How can you have very refined and clean speech?

A STORY

Who Raised You?

Three *kohanim* were talking about how much of the *Lechem Hapanim* they had received.

One said, "I received as much as a bean." The second declared, "I received as much as an olive." The third claimed, "I received as much as a *halta'ah's* (one of the eight *tamei* insects) tail."

Since the third *kohen* spoke in an unrefined way, the *kohanim* suspected him of not being fit to serve as a *kohen*. They checked his history and saw that he was a *chalal*. Others say that they found out that he was involved with *avodah zarah*.[13]

UNIT 18

DID YOU KNOW?

No Exceptions

This mitzvah is one of the *Sheva Mitzvos B'nei Noach* – the seven mitzvos which non-Jews also have to keep.[14]

In fact, one of the few mitzvos that Hashem gave *Adam Harishon* was this mitzvah of "blessing" Hashem.[15]

OUR SAGES SAY...

Eight Extra Letters

The Torah is very careful about every single letter used. Sometimes we learn many *halachos* from a single extra word or even a single letter.

However, the Torah uses **eight** extra letters just to say something in a nicer way. When Hashem told Noach to take the animals into the *teivah*, Hashem described the non-kosher animals as "אֲשֶׁר אֵינֶנָּה טְהוֹרָה" - which is not *tahor*, even though it would take eight letters less to say "הַטְּמֵאָה" - the *tamei* one.

We see from this how important it is to use clean and refined language.[16]

ENDNOTES:

1. רמב״ם הל׳ ע״ז פ״ב ה״י
2. ויקרא כד, י-כג
3. רמב״ם הל׳ ע״ז פ״ב ה״ח-ה-י
4. עי׳ מנ״ח מצוה ע׳ אות ג׳
5. תוספתא סוכה פ״ב ה״ו
6. רמב״ם הל׳ ע״ז פ״ב ה״ט, ובמנ״ח מצוה ע׳ אות ח׳

7. יומא סו, א
8. רמב״ם הל׳ ע״ז פ״ב ה״ח, ובשו״ע יו״ד סי׳ ש״מ סל״ז
9. שו״ע יו״ד סי׳ ש״מ סל״ז. וראה שו״ע הרב או״ח סי׳ פ״ה ס״ג
10. שו״ע יו״ד סי׳ ש״מ סל״ז
11. סנהדרין נו, א. וברש״י ד״ה בכל יום

12. קשו״ע סי׳ ו׳ ס״ג
13. פסחים ג, ב. רש״י ותוס׳ שם ד״ה שמץ פסול
14. רמב״ם הל׳ מלכים פ״ט ה״ג
15. סנהדרין נו, ב
16. פסחים ג, א

"BLESSING" HASHEM   **145**

UNIT 19

IN THIS UNIT YOU WILL:

EXPLORE

- Why is serving idols so foolish?
- Why is doing any *aveirah* similar to serving *avodah zarah*?

EXAMINE

- What are the actions which one may not do to an *avodah zarah*?
- What was the idol of *Molech* and how was it served?

EXTRACT

- Why is a person has *ga'avah* similar to someone who serves *avodah zarah*?

עֲבוֹדָה זָרָה
מוֹלֶךְ
גַּאֲוָה

KEY CONCEPTS

Book: Madda, Section: Idol Worship

סֵפֶר מַדָּע הִלְכוֹת עֲבוֹדָה זָרָה

שֶׁלֹּא לַעֲבוֹד עֲבוֹדָה זָרָה

NOT SERVING AVODAH ZARAH

שָׁלֹשׁ מִצְוֹת

A father is standing under an apple tree with his child on his shoulders. The child reaches up and grabs an apple. Happily, the child says, "Look how tall I am! I reached up and picked this apple all by myself!"

Oh, really?

The unit of not serving *avodah zarah* has three mitzvos.

1. Do not worship an idol in the way that it is usually worshipped.

2. Do not bow down, offer sacrifices, burn a present, or pour anything for any idol.

3. Do not allow your child to be passed through a fire in order to worship the *Molech*.

STORY

How It All Began

Idol worship began with the people of the generation of Enosh, a grandson of *Adam Harishon*. They looked at the sun, the moon and the stars and saw that Hashem gave those creations honor by placing them high in the heavens. They decided that if Hashem is honoring those creations, they should also honor them.

As a result, the people built temples for them, and offered sacrifices, all because they thought that they were honoring Hashem by honoring the great creations. This was a serious mistake that led to even greater mistakes. Later generations came with false prophets who told everyone that the sun and others were really gods themselves, and made up different ways of worshipping them.

Eventually, everyone forgot that there was one true G-d, until Avraham came along.[1]

MITZVAH
27

שֶׁלֹּא לַעֲבוֹד אוֹתָהּ כְּדֶרֶךְ עֲבוֹדָתָהּ

Not serving an *avodah zarah* in the way that it is usually served

לֹא תִשְׁתַּחֲוֶה לָהֶם וְלֹא תָעָבְדֵם כִּי אָנֹכִי ה׳ אֱלֹקֶיךָ אֵ-ל קַנָּא פֹּקֵד עֲוֹן אָבֹת עַל בָּנִים עַל שִׁלֵּשִׁים וְעַל רִבֵּעִים לְשֹׂנְאָי

(שמות כ, ה)

Do not bow down to [such idols] **or worship them** for I am Hashem, your G-d. To those who hate Me, I visit the sin of fathers upon [their] children, to the third and fourth [generations].

Do not serve an *avodah zarah* in the way that it is usually served.

 ALL PEOPLE   ALL PLACES   ALL TIMES   *SKILAH*

שֶׁלֹּא לַעֲבוֹד עֲבוֹדָה זָרָה
Not serving idols

לֹא תִשְׁתַּחֲוֶה לָהֶם וְלֹא תָעָבְדֵם כִּי אָנֹכִי ה׳ אֱלֹקֶיךָ אֵ-ל קַנָּא פֹּקֵד עֲוֹן אָבֹת עַל בָּנִים עַל שִׁלֵּשִׁים וְעַל רִבֵּעִים לְשׂנְאָי
(שמות כ, ה)

Do not bow down to [such idols] or worship them for I am Hashem, your G-d. To those who hate Me, I visit the sin of fathers upon [their] children, to the third and fourth [generations].

Do not bow down, offer sacrifices, burn a present, or pour offerings to any idol.

| ALL PEOPLE | ALL PLACES | ALL TIMES | SKILAH |

שֶׁלֹּא נִתֵּן מִזַּרְעֵנוּ לַמּוֹלֶךְ
Not giving our children to the *Molech*

וּמִזַּרְעֲךָ לֹא תִתֵּן לְהַעֲבִיר לַמֹּלֶךְ וְלֹא תְחַלֵּל אֶת שֵׁם אֱלֹקֶיךָ אֲנִי ה׳
(ויקרא יח, כא)

Do not give any of your children to be passed [through fire] to *Molech*, so that you shall not desecrate Hashem's name; I am Hashem.

Do not give your child to be passed through fire to serve *Molech*.

| ALL PEOPLE | ALL PLACES | ALL TIMES | SKILAH |

Double Trouble

Anytime someone does any of these three *aveiros*, the person is also doing the *aveirah* of believing in *avodah zarah* - which is one of the *Aseres Hadibros*.

HISTORY

Mesiras Nefesh

Antiochus tried to convince each of Chana's seven sons to leave the ways of Torah. All of the children refused to go against the Torah and were killed.

The king tried to give the youngest child a chance to save his life by bowing down to pick up his ring in front of an idol, so that the people watching would think that he bowed to the idol. The boy refused to do even a meaningless action which did not involve any belief towards the idol.

The king was so angry that he ordered the boy to be killed.

This story teaches us to avoid anything even similar to *avodah zarah*, even if we don't mean what we are doing in any way.[2]

Bowl Once, Strike All

כָּל הַמּוֹדֶה בַּעֲבוֹדָה זָרָה כּוֹפֵר בְּכָל הַתּוֹרָה כּוּלָהּ

Worshipping *avodah zarah* means that you don't believe that Hashem created the world. It is a denial of Hashem's control over us and that we must follow only His commandments. Therefore, believing in *avodah zarah* is like denying the whole Torah.[3]

DID YOU KNOW?

Kemitzah

In the *Beis Hamikdash*, the *kohen* would scoop up some flour with his hand for the *korban minchah*. This was called קְמִיצָה.

Kemitzah has the same halachah as the *shechitah* of an animal. Therefore, doing this act for an *avodah zarah* is forbidden just like *shechitah* is forbidden to be done for idol worship.[4]

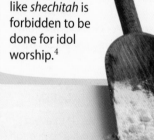

Mitzvah Messages

Insult and Be Insulted

Serving *avodah zarah* is more than just an insult to Hashem. By serving another god, it is like you are saying that Hashem did not create the world, and that Hashem did not even create you! By serving another god, in a sense you are saying that you don't exist, because Hashem doesn't exist!

 CHECKPOINT   Why is it foolish to worship another god?

Details

Serving Idols

Serving a Specific *Avodah Zarah*

Many years ago, different kinds of *avodah zarah* were worshipped in different ways. For some kinds of *avodah zarah*, people would burn animals, for other kinds, the people would sing songs, and some would even throw stones at their idols to serve them! The first mitzvah in this unit teaches that we must not serve an *avodah zarah* in the specific way that it was usually worshipped.

If someone would serve an idol in a way that it was **not** usually worshipped (like dancing in front of an idol that is usually worshipped by offering sacrifices), the person would not be punished with *skilah* or *kares*, but it is still forbidden.[5]

Serving Any *Avodah Zarah*

The second mitzvah in this unit teaches us that we are not allowed to serve **any** *avodah zarah* in the following four ways:

1. הִשְׁתַּחֲוָאָה – bowing down
2. זוֹבֵחַ – sacrificing an animal
3. מַקְטִיר – burning anything as a present to the idol
4. מְנַסֵּךְ – pouring liquid

Even if it is not the regular way of serving that *avodah zarah*, we are forbidden to do any of these four actions for any *avodah zarah*.[6]

Worshipping *Molech*

The third mitzvah in this unit forbids us from serving a specific kind of *avodah zarah* called *Molech*. This was a dangerous practice of passing a child through a fire to worship an idol. Anyone who does this terrible act does two *aveiros*: the *aveirah* of serving idols, **and** the *aveirah* of giving up a child to *Molech*.[7] The punishment for this *aveirah* is only given if the parent does each of these four things which are learned from the *passuk* telling us the mitzvah:

1. The father only sacrifices **some** of his children. If a person sacrifices **all** of them, the punishment is not given.
2. The child is given to the *Molech* priest first before passing him or her through the fire.
3. The child is only **passed** through the fire and not burned.
4. The child is passed through the fire with the legs going first, not the head.[8]

The Punishment

The punishment for doing any of these *aveiros* is *skilah*. This applies only if the person receives a warning and there are two witnesses who saw the person doing the *aveirah*. If one of these two conditions is missing, the punishment is *kares*. If someone does these *aveiros* by accident, the person has to bring a *korban chatas*.[9]

Accepting Another Power

If you do any action that shows that you think something other than Hashem created or controls the world, you are doing the first *aveirah* of believing in an *avodah zarah*. Even a silly action like picking up a brick and saying "this is my god" would be considered doing this *aveirah*.[10]

 CHECKPOINT Which acts are forbidden to do for an *avodah zarah*?

DID YOU KNOW?

Too Many Mouths To Feed

The *Molech* idol was a very strange looking idol, because it had seven mouths! The people who served it would do seven actions to worship it. They would burn spices, pour wine, sacrifice a bird, a sheep, a cow, an ox and a human.[11]

STORY

Fiery Argument

Nimrod invited Avraham to worship fire with him, but Avraham answered that it would be better to worship water, because it puts out fire. So Nimrod said, "Okay, let us worship water!" to which Avraham replied, "Better to worship the clouds which carry the water."

"Then let us worship the clouds!" exclaimed Nimrod. "Let us rather worship the winds which scatter the clouds." "Then worship the wind!" "No, better serve human beings who can stand before the wind."

Finally, Nimrod got fed up and threw Avraham into the fire, saying, "We'll worship the fire! Let your G-d come and save you from it!"

Hashem performed a great miracle and Avraham was not burned![12]

India

In India, the people would honor a certain *avodah zarah* by lighting candles in the courtyard of their homes.

Therefore, an Indian Jew who owned a home with a courtyard in those times was not allowed to light any candle in the courtyard, even if they have no intention of serving the idol.[13]

SELECTED HALACHOS

- הִשְׁתַּחֲוָאָה is when you spread out your hands and feet on the ground or lay your head on the ground.[15]

- The *aveirah* of זוֹבֵחַ is only if the animal that was sacrificed was perfect and was not missing any body parts, just as a *korban* must be complete.[16]

- **Throwing** (not just pouring) liquid is also considered מְנַסֵּךְ.[17]

- Anything burned as a present for an idol is considered מַקְטִיר.[18]

- If something was dropped in front of an idol, you may not bend down to pick it up because it looks like you are bowing down to the idol. Instead, you should sit down, and then pick it up.[19]

- It is forbidden to hug, kiss, or show any sort of respect or love to an idol, even if it isn't the normal way to worship that idol.[20]

STORY

Worth His While

The *Ba'al Shem Tov* once spent some time in the house of a non-Jew who had an idol in his home. He came out very happy, and said to his *talmidim*, "I am so happy because in one hour I was able to keep the whole Torah! I am not allowed to even think words of Torah in a filthy place. A house where people serve *avodah zarah* is a filthy place, and when I didn't even think words of Torah in such a dirty place, it was like I kept the entire Torah!"[14]

EXTEND YOUR KNOWLEDGE

Don't Thank Me, Thank My Boss

Hashem gave some of His creations special powers. For example, the sun was given the power to heal and to make things grow. Why can't you say thank you to the sun for doing these wonderful things, just like you would thank a doctor that helped heal you?

A person only deserves thanks if he had a **choice** whether or not to help you, and he chose to help you. Do we thank a spoon for putting food into our mouths? Of course not! The spoon itself does not **decide** to feed us. We use our hands to force the spoon to come up into our mouths! This is the same with the sun, rain, and other parts of nature. They are Hashem's tools that do what He wants. They have no choice whether or not to do their job. That is how they are made.

Therefore, there is no point in thanking them. We should thank Hashem for making them.

Who Runs Your Life?

Even if you don't actually serve an *avodah zarah*, any *aveirah* you do is like worshipping idols. This is because when you do an *aveirah*, you are not listening to Hashem. You are listening to your *yetzer hara* and other influences. You are making them your gods by allowing them to tell you what to do and how to live your life.[21]

It's All From Hashem

There is one *middah* that is even more like *avodah zarah* than any other *aveirah*. When you have *ga'avah* (you think of yourself as "amazing") and think that anything you do is because of your own talents, it is like you are worshipping *avodah zarah*. This is because you are not recognizing that Hashem is the One who gave you those gifts. It is like saying that you are talented all on your own.

What you must do instead, is recognize that all your good qualities and talents are a gift from Hashem and that you must use them to fulfill His will.

Unholy Rage

כָּל הַכּוֹעֵס כְּאִילּוּ עוֹבֵד עֲבוֹדָה זָרָה.
Anyone who gets angry is as if he serves avodah zarah.

If you really believe that everything that happens comes from Hashem, you wouldn't get angry at the person who did something wrong to you, since you would understand that this person is really only acting as a messenger from Hashem!

If you become angry at someone, you are forgetting that whatever happens to you comes from Hashem.[22]

DID YOU KNOW?

Disqualified

Any *kohen* who serves an idol in any way can never serve in the *Beis Hamikdash* again. This applies even if he did it by mistake, and even if he did complete *teshuvah*.[23]

CHECKPOINT How is the *middah* of *ga'avah* like serving *avodah zarah*?

UNIT 19

ENDNOTES:

17. סנהדרין ס, ב	8. רמב"ם הל' ע"ז פ"ו ה"ד ובכס"מ שם	1. רמב"ם הל' ע"ז פ"א
18. מנ"ח מצוה כ"ו אות ד'	9. סה"מ ל"ת ה'-ז'	2. ראה גיטין נז, ב ושם לא הוזכר
19. רמב"ם הל' ע"ז פ"ג ה"ז	10. רמב"ם הל' ע"ז פ"ג ה"ד	שם "חנה" במפורש, ומובא בס'
20. רמב"ם הל' ע"ז פ"ג ה"ו	11. שו"ת יכין ובועז ח"א סי' ק"ה	החשמונאים ח"ב פי"ז
21. לשון חסידים שער אמונה אות כ"ה	12. בראשית רבה לח, יג	3. רמב"ם הל' ע"ז פ"ב ה"ד
22. זוהר-רעיא מהימנא ח"ג רל	13. שו"ת חת"ס ח"ב סי' קל"ג	4. משנה למלך הל' ע"ז פ"ג ה"ג
23. רמב"ם הל' ביאת המקדש פ"ט הי"ג	14. סיפורי חסידים פ' וישלח	5. רמב"ם הל' ע"ז פ"ב ה"ב
	15. רמב"ם הל' ע"ז פ"ו ה"ח	6. רמב"ם הל' ע"ז פ"ג ה"ג
	16. ע"ז נא, א ע"פ הבנת המנ"ח מצוה כ"ו אות ב'	7. רמב"ם הל' ע"ז פ"ו ה"ג. וזה שחייב ב' לאוין מקורו במנ"ח מצוה ר"ח אות א'

UNIT 20

IN THIS UNIT YOU WILL:

EXPLORE

- Why should you not **own** certain objects?
- What is the best way to avoid doing something forbidden?

EXAMINE

- Which images are we not allowed to make?
- Which forms are we not allowed to make?

EXTRACT

- If you care too much about money, what are you like?
- If you're tempted to do something wrong, what should you do?

צוּרוֹת
אֲסוּרוֹת

KEY CONCEPTS

UNIT
20

Book: Madda, Section: Idol Worship
סֵפֶר מַדָּע הִלְכוֹת עֲבוֹדָה זָרָה

צוּרוֹת אֲסוּרוֹת
FORBIDDEN FORMS
שָׁלֹשׁ מִצְוֹת

You thought you would eat just one.

Now **all** the cookies for the *Shabbos* guests are gone.

Maybe you should have just left them alone.

Drop That Chisel!

It says in the Torah: "Cursed is the man who makes a stone or metal image."

From the very moment the image is made, even before it's worshipped, the man who created it is cursed.[1]

DID YOU KNOW?

We Didn't Mean To

According to many opinions, the Jews created the *Egel Hazahav* because they were scared that they didn't have a leader, so they wanted to make something to replace Moshe. They didn't really want to serve an *avodah zarah*. However, once they created the statue, they started worshipping it as an idol.[2]

The Mitzvos

EXAMINE

The unit of forbidden forms has three mitzvos.

1. Do not have anyone make an idol for you.

2. Do not create an idol.

3. Do not create any form or picture of people, the moon, stars, planets, sun, or angels.

MITZVAH
30

שֶׁלֹּא לַעֲשׂוֹת פֶּסֶל
Not having anyone make an idol for you

לֹא תַעֲשֶׂה לְךָ פֶסֶל וְכָל תְּמוּנָה אֲשֶׁר בַּשָּׁמַיִם מִמַּעַל וַאֲשֶׁר בָּאָרֶץ מִתָּחַת וַאֲשֶׁר בַּמַּיִם מִתַּחַת לָאָרֶץ
(שמות כ, ד)

Do not make any carved statue or picture of anything in the heaven above, or on the earth below, or in the water below the land.

Do not have anyone make an idol for you.

 ALL PEOPLE   ALL PLACES   ALL TIMES   MALKUS

MITZVAH 31

שֶׁלֹּא לַעֲשׂוֹת עֲבוֹדָה זָרָה לֹא לְעַצְמוֹ וְלֹא לְזֻלְתוֹ

Not making an idol for yourself or for someone else

אַל תִּפְנוּ אֶל הָאֱלִילִם וֵאלֹהֵי מַסֵּכָה לֹא תַעֲשׂוּ לָכֶם
אֲנִי ה' אֱלֹקֵיכֶם

(ויקרא יט, ד)

Do not turn aside to false gods, and **do not make yourselves gods out of cast metal.** I am Hashem your G-d.

Do not make an idol for anyone.

ALL PEOPLE · ALL PLACES · ALL TIMES · MALKUS

MITZVAH 32

שֶׁלֹּא לַעֲשׂוֹת צוּרוֹת אֲפִילוּ לְנוֹי

Not making any forms, even if only as a decoration

לֹא תַעֲשׂוּן אִתִּי אֱלֹהֵי כֶסֶף וֵאלֹהֵי זָהָב לֹא תַעֲשׂוּ לָכֶם

(שמות כ, כ)

Do not make a representation of anything that is with Me. Do not make silver gods or gold gods for yourselves.

Do not make forms or statues of people or planets, stars, and angels.

ALL PEOPLE · ALL PLACES · ALL TIMES · MALKUS

DID YOU KNOW?

Kiddush Hashem

Chur, the son of Miriam, tried to stop the Jews from making the *Egel Hazahav*, but was killed. As a reward for his bravery, Hashem chose his grandson, Betzalel, to build the *Mishkan*, which was a *kaparah* for the sin of the *Egel Hazahav*.[3]

OUR SAGES SAY...

Think You Know Yourself?

Chazal tell us "Do not believe in yourself until the day you die."

Do not to put yourself in a situation where you might do an *aveirah*, even if you are sure that nothing will happen. Hashem created you with a *yetzer hara* and as long as you are alive, your *yetzer hara* is trying to convince you to do *aveiros*.[4]

But, Officer…

Most states in America have "open container" laws. This means that no one is allowed to have an open container of any kind of alcohol inside a car, truck, or motorcycle. This is to stop people from drinking alcohol while they are driving, since it is very dangerous and can cause a terrible accident.

Mitzvah Messages

EXPLORE

An Ounce of Prevention

There are certain things that we do to prevent something worse from happening. For example, we dress warmly in the winter so that we should not get sick. We drive carefully so that we should not get into an accident. We might think that nothing will happen to us if we don't wear that coat or if we run a red light, but there is **always** the possibility that something might happen.

Making an idol, even if you promise not to worship it, is very similar. Even if you don't plan on worshipping it, there is a chance that you will if it is created. If you don't create it at all, there is **no way** that you will worship it!

CHECKPOINT   What is the best way to prevent yourself from doing something wrong?

Details

EXAMINE

Making Idols

The first mitzvah in this unit tells us that we are not allowed to have anyone make an idol for us. The second mitzvah tells us that we are not allowed to make an idol for anyone, even for non-Jews.

If you make an idol for yourself, then you committed two *aveiros*: One is the *aveirah* of making an idol, and one is the *aveirah* of having an idol made for yourself.[5]

Making Representations

The third mitzvah in this unit forbids us from creating pictures or sculptures of people, or of anything in the sky. Since it is very easy for people to end up worshipping other people, as well as the sun, moon, stars, planets and angels, Hashem gave us extra rules about creating these images so that we would never even come close to serving them as an *avodah zarah*.

DID YOU KNOW?

Honesty Is the Best Policy

It is an *aveirah* to cheat someone using weights that are not honest. Since this is such a serious *aveirah*, the Torah does not even allow us to **own** weights that are not honest, so that we will never come to use them.

Normally, when you look at something on earth, you see it in three dimensions, which means that it is does not look flat, and you can see it from all sides. When you look at something in the sky, it looks flat because you can only see how long and how wide it is, not how far back it goes.

The *halachos* about creating an image of something in the universe has a lot to do with the way we see these objects. Since you can see things on earth (people, animals, plants, objects) in three dimensions, there is only an *aveirah* to create a three-dimensional image of them, like a statue. Therefore, you are allowed to make a two-dimensional drawing of them.

Since you only see things in the sky as flat, you should not even make a flat picture of these things, and you surely can't make a statue or sculpture of them.[6]

How It's Learned from the *Passuk*

Two Types

There are two kinds of images that a person is not allowed to make: an image of a person, and an image of anything in the heavens. Both of these *aveiros* are learned from the same words in the Torah, which are explained in two different ways.

Representations of Other Beings

From the words "לֹא תַעֲשׂוּן אִתִּי" - "do not make with me…" the *Chachamim* teach us that Hashem is prohibiting the making of anything that is "**with Him**." This refers to the heavenly creations such as the angels, the sun, the moon, the stars, etc. which are "with" Hashem.[7]

Human Images

The words "לֹא תַעֲשׂוּן אִתִּי" literally mean "do not make with me…" However, the *Chachamim* teach us that we can also read the word to mean אֹתִי, which means, "do not make **Me**." This means that Hashem is commanding us not to make a statue of Him. But since we don't know what Hashem looks like, how is it possible to make a statue of Hashem? The Torah is therefore teaching us that it is forbidden to copy the image which Hashem used to reveal Himself to the *nevi'im*, which was the form of a man.[8]

 CHECKPOINT   Which things are we not allowed to make?

DID YOU KNOW?

Partners in Crime

It's usually not possible for two people to do an *aveirah* together and to both be *chayav* for the punishment. However, when two people make an idol together, they are both punished.

This is because the Torah says לֹא תַעֲשׂוּן - you shall not make, which is in the plural.[9]

Menashe's Evil Reign

King Menashe was the complete opposite of his father, the *tzaddik* King Chizkiyahu.

King Menashe brought back the idols that King Chizkiyahu had destroyed, and even brought idols into the *Beis Hamikdash* itself. Because of him, people forgot even the most basic teachings of the Torah.

King Menashe was eventually captured by the armies of *Ashur* and brought in chains to *Bavel*. There, he was tortured and embarassed. He called on all of his idols to save him, and when nothing happened, he cried to Hashem to save him.

He was set free by the king and he went back to Eretz Yisrael, where he ruled for another thirty-three years. This time, he ruled according to the Torah and listened to Hashem.[10]

- You are only not allowed to create a **complete** picture or sculpture of something. You are allowed to make a sun with a corner cut off, or a statue with an ear missing.[11]

- There is a different *halacha* for the moon. Since the moon appears in many sizes and shapes, any kind of image of the moon is forbidden,[12]

- You cannot own any of these pictures or statues, even if you did not make it.[13]

- You should not take a photograph specifically of the sun, moon, planets, or stars.[14]

- You cannot even **tell** a non-Jew to make one of these statues, even if you aren't going to keep it.[15]

- You are allowed to draw, carve, or sculpt any kind of animal, tree or plant, as long as the image that you are making will not be used as an idol.[16]

- You are allowed to make pictures of the sun, moon, stars, or planets, if it is for the purpose of learning, for example, to help understand the laws of *kiddush hachodesh*.[17]

EXTEND YOUR KNOWLEDGE

Constellations

Mazalos are constellations, or groups of stars that look like different things, including animals. Part of the mitzvah of not making idols is not to make pictures of these particular animals. One of the animals shown in the *mazalos* is a lion. Yet, we see lions everywhere, on the *Aron Kodesh,* on *Sifrei Torah* and so on - why is this allowed?

One answer is that you are not allowed to make all the *mazalos* together, but it is not a problem to make each *mazal* by itself.[18]

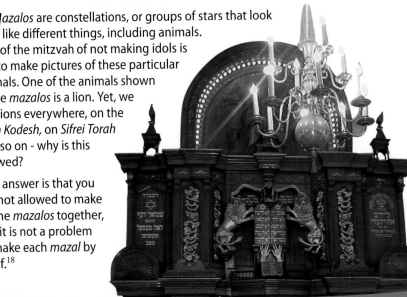

A Different Kind of Idol

People used to worship all kinds of idols – the sun, the moon, the *Molech* and many others. Today, people worship a very different type of idol. We know them as "fame," "beauty," "money," or "coolness." We think that we are smart enough not to get too carried away by these temptations, but if we get too involved with them, our *yetzer hara* will trick us into "worshipping" them and doing things that are wrong, just because "they" said so or because "they" are all doing it.

For this reason, the smartest thing to do is to stay away from them altogether. We ask Hashem every day: אַל תְּבִיאֵנוּ לִידֵי נִסָּיוֹן – don't bring us to a test - to a place where we will want to do an *aveirah*.

We can never trust ourselves enough not to want the idols of fame or beauty, so we ask Hashem again and again to keep us away from a place where we will want to do an *aveirah*.

CHECKPOINT   What are the types of *avodah zarah* in our lives today?

STORY

King Menashe's *Teshuvah*

A young man took the warning against the *aveirah* of making idols very seriously, so he decided to smash all the idols in his town. The night watchman caught him in the act, and he was eventually hanged by the government.

The *Chevra Kadisha* refused to help his widow from their fund for poor widows. They felt that the young man had caused his own death and could therefore be considered a suicide, which is a terrible *aveirah*. The case was brought for a ruling before R' Shmelke of Nikolsburg.

While R' Shmelke was looking for an answer, the *neshamah* of King Menashe, the king so well known for his terrible *avodah zarah*, appeared to him.

He told R' Shmelke that his *neshamah* had been in this young man and that the young man's act of *mesiras nefesh* had finally wiped away his *aveiros* of worshipping *avodah zarah*.

"Therefore," he said, "the young man should not be considered a suicide, but rather as someone who gave up his life, *al kiddush Hashem*."[19]

UNIT 20

ENDNOTES:

1. ע"ז נב, א
2. רמב"ן שמות לב, א. חזקוני ובכור שור שם. אבל עי' ראב"ע שם
3. שמות רבה מח, ג
4. אבות פ"ב מ"ד
5. רמב"ם הל' ע"ז פ"ג ה"ט
6. רמב"ם הל' ע"ז פ"ג ה"י, ובכס"מ שם בטעם האיסור
7. ר"ה כה, ב
8. ר"ה כה, ב. ריטב"א שם, וש"ך יו"ד סי' קמ"א ס"ק כ"א
9. מנ"ח מצוה ל"ט אות ט"ו
10. מלכים ב' פכ"א ובדברי הימים ב' פל"ג
11. מנ"ח מצוה כ"ז אות ד' ומצוה רי"ד אות ו'
12. מנ"ח מצוה ל"ט אות ט'
13. שו"ע יו"ד סי' קמ"א ס"ד
14. שו"ת מנחת יצחק ח"י סי' ע"ב
15. ש"ך יו"ד סי' קמ"א ס"ק כ"ג
16. שו"ע יו"ד סי' קמ"א ס"ו
17. שו"ע יו"ד סי' קמ"א ס"ד
18. ע"פ ש"ך יו"ד סי' קמ"א ס"ק ל'
19. שבחי צדיקים ע' נז

UNIT 21

IN THIS UNIT YOU WILL:

EXPLORE

- Why must you sometimes get rid of bad things?

EXAMINE

- What is an *Ir Hanidachas*?
- What are we supposed to do to an *Ir Hanidachas*?

EXTRACT

- How can you use the power of unity for good things?

עִיר הַנִדַחַת

KEY CONCEPTS

Book: Madda, Section: Idol Worship
סֵפֶר מַדָּע הִלְכוֹת עֲבוֹדָה זָרָה

עִיר הַנִּדַּחַת
IR HANIDACHAS

אַרְבַּע מִצְוֹת

You're sitting next to a man in a wheelchair, and you notice that he only has one leg. The man sees you looking, points downwards and says:

"Oh, you're wondering about my leg? **Thankfully**, my doctor cut it off."

Never Was and Never Will Be

According to one opinion in the *Gemara*, in all of history, there never was a city that became an *Ir Hanidachas*. Not only that, they say that there never will be one either!

If there will never be an *Ir Hanidachas*, why did Hashem give us these mitzvos and why should we learn about these mitzvos? The *Gemara* answers, "Learn about it and receive the reward for learning Torah."

If the Torah was only instructions on how to perform the mitzvos there would be no point in learning about things which will never happen. The Torah is Hashem's wisdom, and the learning itself is the goal![1]

The Mitzvos

The unit of *Ir Hanidachas* has four mitzvos.

1. Do not convince other people to serve *avodah zarah*.

2. Burn an *Ir Hanidachas* and everything in the city.

3. Do not rebuild an *Ir Hanidachas*.

4. Do not benefit from anything of an *Ir Hanidachas*.

MITZVAH **33**

שֶׁלֹּא לְהַדִּיחַ בְּנֵי יִשְׂרָאֵל אַחַר עֲבוֹדָה זָרָה

Not influencing Jews to follow *avodah zarah*

וּבְכֹל אֲשֶׁר אָמַרְתִּי אֲלֵיכֶם תִּשָּׁמֵרוּ וְשֵׁם אֱלֹקִים אֲחֵרִים לֹא תַזְכִּירוּ לֹא יִשָּׁמַע עַל פִּיךָ

(שמות כג, יג)

Be very careful to keep everything I have said to you. Do not say the name of another god, **and you must not let it be heard from your mouth.**

Do not persuade the people of a city to serve *avodah zarah*.

ALL PEOPLE · ALL PLACES · ALL TIMES · *SKILAH*

MITZVAH 34

מִצְוַת שְׂרֵיפַת עִיר הַנִּדַּחַת וְכָל אֲשֶׁר בָּה

Burning an *Ir Hanidachas* and everything inside of it

וְאֶת כָּל שְׁלָלָהּ תִּקְבֹּץ אֶל תּוֹךְ רְחֹבָהּ וְשָׂרַפְתָּ בָאֵשׁ אֶת הָעִיר וְאֶת כָּל שְׁלָלָהּ כָּלִיל לַה' אֱלֹהֶיךָ וְהָיְתָה תֵּל עוֹלָם לֹא תִבָּנֶה עוֹד

(דברים יג, יז)

Gather all [the city's] goods to its central square and burn the city along with all its goods, like a sacrifice to Hashem your G-d, and it shall remain an eternal ruin, never again to be rebuilt.

Burn and completely destroy an *Ir Hanidachas*.

 BEIS DIN HAGADOL   BEIS DIN IN LISHKAS HAGAZIS   ALL TIMES

MITZVAH 35

שֶׁלֹּא לִבְנוֹת עִיר הַנִּדַּחַת לְכְמוֹת שֶׁהָיְתָה

Not rebuilding a city where there was an *Ir Hanidachas*

וְאֶת כָּל שְׁלָלָהּ תִּקְבֹּץ אֶל תּוֹךְ רְחֹבָהּ וְשָׂרַפְתָּ בָאֵשׁ אֶת הָעִיר וְאֶת כָּל שְׁלָלָהּ כָּלִיל לַה' אֱלֹהֶיךָ וְהָיְתָה תֵּל עוֹלָם לֹא תִבָּנֶה עוֹד

(דברים יג, יז)

Gather all [the city's] goods to its central square and burn the city along with all its goods, like a sacrifice to Hashem your G-d, **and it shall remain an eternal ruin, never again to be rebuilt.**

Do not rebuild a city where there used to be an *Ir Hanidachas*.

 ALL PEOPLE   ERETZ YISRAEL   ALL TIMES   MALKUS

DID YOU KNOW?

Invalidated

If someone were to use a *shofar* or a *lulav* from an *Ir Hanidachas,* they have not fulfilled the mitzvah of *lulav* or *shofar*.

According to the Torah, since the *lulav* or *shofar* have to be burned, the Torah considers it as if it is **already** burned.

Ashes do not have the required size for a *kosher shofar* or a *kosher lulav*![2]

DISCOVERY

The Great Plague

The Great Plague (1665-1666) was a terrible disease in England that killed about 100,000 people. At one point, the plague reached a village called Eyam through a package of cloth from London that was infected. The villagers responded by putting themselves under quarantine in order to stop the plague from spreading. This means that they did not let anyone in or out of the city, so that nobody else would catch the disease.

Because they stayed separate, other cities did not get the diseases, but only 83 out of 350 people in the city stayed alive.

This is what is accomplished by destroying an *Ir Hanidachas*: Through destruction, the spread of *avodah zarah* is cut off.

MITZVAH
36

שֶׁלֹּא לֵיהָנוֹת בְּמָמוֹן עִיר הַנִדַּחַת

Do not gain anything from the money of an *Ir Hanidachas*

וְלֹא יִדְבַּק בְּיָדְךָ מְאוּמָה מִן הַחֵרֶם לְמַעַן יָשׁוּב ה' מֵחֲרוֹן אַפּוֹ וְנָתַן לְךָ רַחֲמִים וְרִחַמְךָ וְהִרְבֶּךָ כַּאֲשֶׁר נִשְׁבַּע לַאֲבֹתֶיךָ
(דברים יג, יח)

No part of the forbidden spoils shall remain in your hands. So that Hashem will turn back from His burning anger, and He will give you mercy and be merciful to you and multiply you, as He swore to your forefathers.

Do not benefit from the possesions of an *Ir Hanidachas*.

ALL PEOPLE   ALL PLACES   ALL TIMES   *MALKUS*

Mitzvah Messages

EXPLORE

Preventing Disease

Often, a doctor can heal a wounded or diseased part of the body with medicine or surgery. Other times, the damaged part has to be cut off totally, so that the infection does not spread to the rest of the body.

Avodah zarah is so terrible, that when a city becomes an *Ir Hanidachas*, it must be completely destroyed so that the disease of *avodah zarah* will not spread to other cities.[3]

CHECKPOINT   How are the mitzvos of *Ir Hanidachas* similar to a surgeon?

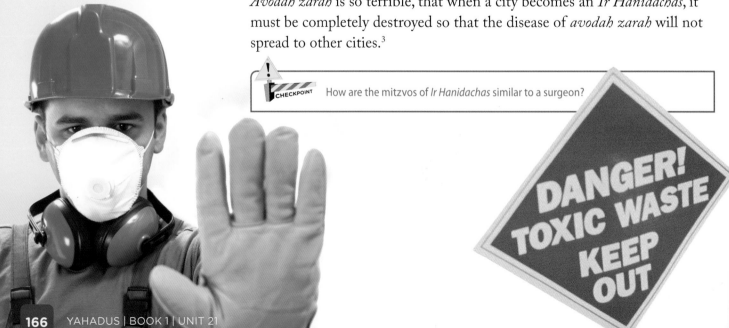

DANGER! TOXIC WASTE KEEP OUT

What is an *Ir Hanidachas*?

To become an *Ir Hanidachas*, a city must meet all of these conditions:

1. There must be at least two men trying to convince the people in the city to serve *avodah zarah*. These people are called *madichim*.

2. Both of the *madichim* must be men.

3. Both of the *madichim* must come from the same *shevet* as the people they influenced.

4. Both of the *madichim* come from the city that they influenced.

5. They must convince at least 100 people from their *shevet*.

6. They must convince less than the majority of their *shevet*.

7. They must convince at least most of the city.

8. They must include themselves when convincing the people, for example: "Let **us** go and serve *avodah zarah*" or, "Let **us** accept this *avodah zarah* on **ourselves**."

9. The people must be convinced and actually worship the *avodah zarah*.[4]

What Happens to an *Ir Hanidachas*?

The Investigation

When a city is suspected of being an *Ir Hanidachas*, there is a long process before the city and the people are punished:

1. The Great *Sanhedrin* sends messengers to the city to see if most of the city is worshipping *avodah zarah*.

2. If they see that most of the city really did serve *avodah zarah*, the Great *Sanhedrin* then sends two *Talmidei Chachamim* to try to persuade the people in the city to do *teshuvah*.
   If they do *teshuvah*, then the city is no longer an *Ir Hanidachas*.
   If they don't do *teshuvah*, then the Great *Sanhedrin* commands all of *B'nei Yisrael* to break into the city.

OUR SAGES SAY...

Saved by the Mezuzah

There is an opinion in the *Gemara* that says that an *Ir Hanidachas* that has even a single *mezuzah*, cannot be destroyed.

Why?

The Torah tells us that every single object in an *Ir Hanidachas* has to be burned, including everything in the houses.

However, a *mezuzah* is not allowed to be burned because it has Hashem's name in it. So, if a city has even a single *mezuzah* in it, the entire city will not be destroyed.[5]

DID YOU KNOW?

Safe City

עֲשָׂרָה דְבָרִים נֶאֶמְרוּ בִּירוּשָׁלַיִם... וְאֵינָהּ נַעֲשֵׂית עִיר הַנִּדַחַת.

One of the ten special facts about Yerushalayim is that it can never become an *Ir Hanidachas*.[6]

Staying Humane

"You shall not keep any of the spoils in your hand… and Hashem will give you mercy and be merciful to you."

What is the connection between destroying the spoils of an *Ir Hanidachas* and being merciful? Surely, mercy is not the quality we need when we have to destroy a city?

The *passuk* is telling us that Hashem blesses us to be able to keep our natural sense of mercy that we are born with, even after doing the sad and bitter task of destroying an entire city.[7]

DID YOU KNOW?

Just Obeying Orders

One reason why we destroy all the property of the city is so that it should be clear to everyone that the people of the city were killed only because Hashem commanded it, and not because people wanted to keep the property for themselves.[8]

3. Once they break in, small courts of judges are set up around the city and the people of the city are judged. Those who worshipped idols are put in a jail until they receive their punishment.

4. If the small courts see that only some of the people worshipped *avodah zarah*, not most of them, the people who served *avodah zarah* are stoned, but the rest of the city is not harmed.

The Punishment

If the investigation shows that **most** of the city worshipped idols, the city is declared an *Ir Hanidachas* and those who worshipped are taken to the Great *Sanhedrin* in Yerushalayim to finish the judgment:

1. The idol worshippers are put to death by **sword**, along with their wives, children, and all of their animals, but not anyone else in the city.

2. The *madichim* are **stoned** to death.

3. All of the spoils are collected and put into the main square of the city, even the things that belong to the people who did not serve *avodah zarah*. If there is no main square, then one is built.

4. The entire city is burned, along with all the spoils.[9]

 CHECKPOINT What is an *Ir Hanidachas* and what is the process of dealing with an *Ir Hanidachas*?

- Only the great *Beis Din* of seventy-one *Talmidei Chachamim* can carry out the laws of an *Ir Hanidachas*.[10]

- If the main square is outside the city, then a wall is built around it to make it part of the city.[11]

- Although you may not benefit from any possessions of the city's people, you are allowed to plant fields or gardens on the ruins of an *Ir Hanidachas*.[12]

- An animal of an *Ir Hanidachas* is not allowed to be eaten even if it was *shechted* properly.[13]

EXTEND YOUR KNOWLEDGE

The Punishment of Sedom

There is no city actually recorded as an *Ir Hanidachas* in history. However, the story of the punishment of Sedom looks very much like what would happen to an *Ir Hanidachas*.

For instance:

1. Hashem **burned** down the city.

2. Only **two** cities were burned down – Sedom and Amorah, but the surrounding cities were simply turned over because we do not burn three cities next to each other.

3. Lot was allowed to escape because he didn't worship idols. However, his property was burned to the ground.

4. The *passuk* says that Lot escaped to the city of Tzoar "because it was small." Since an *Ir Hanidachas* has to be at least 100 people from the same *shevet* (or nation, in this case), Lot was able to go to Tzoar, which had less than 100 people in it.[14]

Corrupted by Wealth

The people of Sedom were wicked, and rebelled against Hashem.

What caused the inhabitants of Sedom to become so corrupt?

They were very rich since the soil in the area was extremely good for growing food. The earth there also had natural treasures such as gold, silver, and precious stones. As their wealth grew, so did their greed, and they threw off Hashem's rulership.

They were selfish and did not want to share any of their wealth, so they did not allow strangers in their city. They were so selfish that all the trees growing on public property were pruned to remove their fruit so that the birds should not eat them.

These were some of the laws of Sedom:

1. Any stranger found in the city is allowed to be robbed.

2. It is the job of a judge to ensure that every traveller leaves the city penniless.

3. Anyone found giving food to a pauper or stranger will be put to death.

4. Anyone who invites strangers to a wedding will be punished by having all clothing removed from his body.[15]

Warning Rumbles

The destruction of Sedom did not happen suddenly without previous warning. Twenty-five years before it was destroyed, Hashem caused earthquakes throughout the area in order to awaken the people to do *teshuvah*, but they ignored these warnings from Hashem.[16]

HISTORY

Worst Place to Stay

A man from Sedom named Hedod invited a traveler who was carrying an expensive carpet to stay with him overnight, and offered to put away his carpet for storage.

When the guest asked for it back, Hedod claimed that he never received anything, and the man had dreamt that he gave him the carpet. Hedod even had the *chutzpah* to ask the guest for three gold pieces as payment for his interpretation of the dream!

The guest was very angry and brought Hedod before the judge. Of course, the judge ruled in favor of Hedod, and all the men of Sedom laughed as the poor man, now penniless, was chased out of town.[17]

STORY

Travels in Sedom

Eliezer, the servant of *Avraham Avinu*, once passed through Sedom. When he was walking in the street, he was attacked and beaten by one of the townspeople until he bled.

Eliezer went straight to the judge to demand justice. "What happened?" asked the judge. "This man hurt me!" complained Eliezer. "This is a clear-cut case," yelled the judge. "Pay the man immediately for performing the healing process of "bloodletting!"

Eliezer did not hesitate. He took a stick and beat the judge until the judge bled. Then he said to the judge, "Now you owe me money because I made you bleed. Instead of paying it to me, you can give it straight to the other man, since I owe him money!"

At night, the men from Sedom invited Eliezer to rest in one of their special guest beds. In the middle of the night, when the guests would be asleep, they would come with a knife. If the guest was too tall for the bed, they cut off his feet. If he was shorter than the bed, they stretched his body.

"Please stay in our guest house tonight," they begged Eliezer. Eliezer did not agree. "I'm sorry, but I am unable to accept your invitation," he answered. "Since the day my dear mother died, I promised never to lie down on a bed again!"

Eliezer had not eaten anything all day, since the people of Sedom refused even to sell him food for money. That day, there was a wedding in Sedom. Eliezer followed the crowd and sat down at the end of a table.

The law was that anyone who invited strangers to a wedding was punished by having all his clothes removed. People noticed the stranger and asked him, "Who invited you here?"

"The fellow over here," replied Eliezer, pointing at his neighbor. The neighbor hurriedly left, because he was afraid that he would get punished for inviting a stranger, and he would lose all his clothes. Eliezer moved to a different seat, and when asked again who invited him, he pointed to his new neighbor. He repeated this until everyone was gone. Eliezer sat down comfortably and ate his meal alone.[18]

הר סדום
جبل أسدوم
Mt Sodom

It's for Your Own Good

It's hard to have to give up something that you like or enjoy, and be told that "it's for your own good."

But it's the truth! If you hang on to something that is really bad for you just because it is enjoyable, you will get hurt. And what are the things you might have to give up? Junk food? Music? Staying up late? They are not the worst things in the world to be without! This is one of the lessons of the *Ir Hanidachas* – to get rid of anything that you do that is unhealthy for your body or your *neshamah*.

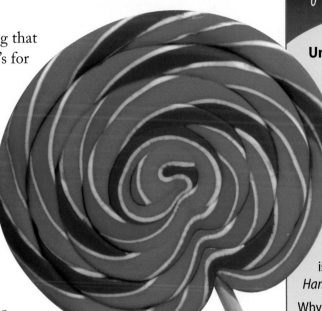

Unite for the Good

The *Ir Hanidachas* shows us how terrible it is when people unite to do bad things. Imagine how much good we can do if we unite to do good things!

Chazal tell us that anytime a group of ten Jews get together, the *Shechinah* rests there. We must be very careful any time we gather to act in a way that shows respect for the *Shechinah*. Also, when we learn and *daven* together, it has special power to bring Hashem's *brachah*.[19]

CHECKPOINT | How can you use the power of unity for a good purpose?

UNIT
21

ENDNOTES:

14. צפע"נ עה"ת בראשית פרק יט

15. סנהדרין קט ע"ב פדר"א כה כ"ב ר נ י'

16. בראשית רבה מט, ו

17. ספר הישר ע' 48

18. סנהדרין קט, ב

19. אבות פ"ג מ"ו

7. אוה"ח דברים יג, יח

8. בכור שור דברים יג, יח

9. רמב"ם הל' ע"ז פ"ד ה"ו

10. רמב"ם הל' ע"ז פ"ד ה"ג

11. רמב"ם הל' ע"ז פ"ד ה"ו

12. רמב"ם הל' ע"ז פ"ד ה"ח

13. רמב"ם הל' ע"ז פ"ד הי"ב

1. סנהדרין עא, א. וע" בתורת חיים שם ד"ה דרוש וקבל שכר

2. ר"ה כח, א. סוכה כט, ב

3. ילקוט מעם לועז דברים יג, יז

4. הכל ברמב"ם הל' ע"ז פ"ד ה"ב וה'

5. סנהדרין עא, א

6. בבא קמא פב, ב

PEARLS of wisdom

Unite to Right

A city is only an *Ir Hanidachas* if most of the Jews living there serve *avodah zarah*. Even though non-Jews are also forbidden to worship idols, a whole city of non-Jews who serve *avodah zarah* is not considered an *Ir Hanidachas*.

Why is this so?

Jewish *neshamos* always want to be together. Normally, Hashem wants this unity, because we can do so much good with it. However, in the case of an *Ir Hanidachas*, Jewish souls have united to do something wrong. This type of unity is deadly, and it must be torn apart.

Non-Jewish souls do not have this quality of unity; therefore, their city is not considered an *Ir Hanidachas*.

This mitzvah shows us how powerful Jewish unity is, and that we must only use it for good.

Do you find it difficult to say no to your friends? It is very hard to be different than everyone around you, and it makes you feel very uncomfortable. You should never try to convince another person to do the wrong thing.

UNIT 22

IN THIS UNIT YOU WILL:

EXPLORE

- Why is it so terrible to influence other people to do something wrong?

EXAMINE

- What is a *meisis* and what is a *madiach*?
- What is the special strict way the Torah treats a *meisis*?

EXTRACT

- With whom should you be friends?
- If your *yetzer hara* is like a *meisis*, how should you treat it?

מֵסִית

מוּסָת

KEY CONCEPTS

Book: Madda, Section: Idol Worship
סֵפֶר מַדָּע הִלְכוֹת עֲבוֹדָה זָרָה

מֵסִית
BAD INFLUENCE

שֵׁשׁ מִצְוֹת

In the unit of *Meisis,* (a person who convinces other people to worship *avodah zarah*) there are six mitzvos.

1. Do not convince someone else to worship *avodah zarah.*

2. The *musas* (the one who was convinced) may not love the *meisis.*

3. The *musas* and may not stop hating the *meisis.*

4. The *musas* may not rescue the *meisis* from death.

5. The *musas* may not defend the *meisis.*

6. The *musas* may not hold back any evidence against the *meisis.*

MITZVAH **37**

שֶׁלֹּא לְהָסִית אֶחָד מִיִּשְׂרָאֵל אַחַר עֲבוֹדָה זָרָה

Not to persuade any Jew to worship idols

וְכָל יִשְׂרָאֵל יִשְׁמְעוּ וְיִרָאוּן וְלֹא יוֹסִפוּ לַעֲשׂוֹת
כַּדָּבָר הָרַע הַזֶּה בְּקִרְבֶּךָ
(דברים יג, יב)

When all of Israel hears of this, they will be afraid, **and they will never again do such an evil thing among you.**

Do not persuade someone to serve idols.

 ALL PEOPLE   ALL PLACES   ALL TIMES   *SKILAH*

דִּין הַמֵּסִית
Laws about a *meisis*

לֹא תֹאבֶה לוֹ וְלֹא תִשְׁמַע אֵלָיו וְלֹא תָחוֹס עֵינְךָ עָלָיו
וְלֹא תַחְמֹל וְלֹא תְכַסֶּה עָלָיו.
(דברים יג, ט)

(38) **Do not agree with him and** (39) **do not listen to him.**
(40) **Do not let your eyes pity him,** (41) **do not show him any
mercy,** (42) **and do not try to cover up for him.**

38	שֶׁלֹּא לֶאֱהוֹב הַמֵּסִית The *musas* may not love the *meisis*.
39	שֶׁלֹּא לַעֲזוֹב הַשִּׂנְאָה מִן הַמֵּסִית The *musas* may not stop hating the *meisis*.
40	שֶׁלֹּא לְהַצִּיל הַמֵּסִית The *musas* may not rescue the *meisis* from death.
41	שֶׁלֹּא יְלַמֵּד הַמּוּסָת זְכוּת עַל הַמֵּסִית The *musas* may not defend the *meisis*.
42	שֶׁלֹּא יִשְׁתּוֹק הַמּוּסָת מִלְּלַמֵּד חוֹבָה עַל הַמֵּסִית The *musas* may not hold back any evidence against the *meisis*.

 THE MUSAS   ALL PLACES   ALL TIMES   NO PUNISHMENT

DID YOU KNOW?

Slippery Character

The first recorded *meisis* in the Torah was the snake who convinced Chavah to eat from the *Eitz Hada'as*.

We see how strict Hashem was with the snake, and how Hashem punished the snake and all snakes forever!

OUR SAGES SAY...

There's No Excuse

From where in the Torah do we see that we are not allowed to make excuses to save a *meisis*?

We learn this from the way Hashem dealt with the snake. Hashem could have used many excuses to save the snake, but He didn't, and was very strict with the snake's punishment![3]

DISCOVERY

Peer Pressure

Everyone is influenced by the people around them, even adults! This is called peer pressure, when you feel pressured by your friends. You feel peer pressure when your friends tell you to do things, and even if they don't tell you what to do, you still feel pressured to do what they do.

Sometimes, peer pressure is good for you. If you are friends with the right people, it can help you become better. If you are around people who are doing the wrong things, you will have to work very hard not to listen to them and not to get influenced by them.

PEARLS of wisdom

In a Good Place

"He who walks with the wise will become wise, while one who mixes with fools will suffer."[4]

You should try to live only near people who will influence you to do good things, not bad things. If you must choose between living with people who will influence you in a bad way, or living alone, you should choose to live alone.

Better to live alone in a cave or in a forest than be influenced to do the wrong things![5]

The *Aveirah* That Never Ends

You know that you should not do *aveiros*, and that every *aveirah* that you do takes you a little further away from Hashem. You also know that you are lucky since you are able to do *teshuvah*! You can undo your actions and be just as close to Hashem as you were before you did the *aveirah*.

If you would help other people do *aveiros*, you would not be able to do *teshuvah*, because you took other people far away from Hashem. How will you ever be able to fix that mistake?[6]

CHECKPOINT   Why is it so bad to influence other people to do *aveiros*?

Details   EXAMINE

Evil Like No one Else

Madiach vs. *Meisis*

A *meisis* and a *madiach* (who we learned about in the previous unit about an *Ir Hanidachas*) are both people who convince others to worship *avodah zarah*, but they are different. A *madiach* is someone who tries to influence a **large number** of people, while a *meisis* is someone who influences even one **single** person.

Another difference is that the *madiach* is only punished if the group of people he was convincing actually served idols after he convinced them to. The *meisis* however, is punished just for trying, even if he is not successful in influencing the other person.

The Trap

Normally, the Torah has a lot of mercy in a court case for a person who did an *aveirah*, and always tries to find the person innocent. There must be a warning, the court has to question the witnesses very carefully, and the one who did an *aveirah* is certainly never tricked into doing it just to punish him. The *meisis* is different. The Torah gives us details on how to set the *meisis* up so that people can witness his *aveirah*, and he does not even need to be warned:

If you are alone when the *meisis* tries to persuade you to do something, and you need witnesses to see him in action, you should tell the *meisis* that your

friends would be interested in his idea also. When the *meisis* repeats his ideas to your friends, you will have the witnesses that you need to bring the *meisis* to court to be judged. If you think that the *meisis* would get nervous with other people around, then you can even ask your friends to hide from the *meisis* when he repeats the plan, so that they can be witnesses.[7]

The Punishment

A *meisis* is punished with *skilah*. There is no punishment given by *Beis Din* for going against the five mitzvos that the *musas* has to do.

Why are these mitzvos not punishable by the *Beis Din*?

1. **Do Not Love a *Meisis*:** This is something that happens only in the *musas's* heart and is a *lav she'ein bo ma'aseh*, an *aveirah* that has no action.[8]

2. **Do Not Stop Hating a *Meisis*:** This *aveirah* can be done in the mind and heart of the *musas*, so it is also a *lav she'ein bo ma'aseh*.

3. **Do Not Rescue a *Meisis*:** The *musas* can not be punished for having pity on the *meisis*, because it could be that the *musas* was only "pretending" to have pity so that he could trap the *meisis* and bring him to court to be judged.[9]

4. **Do Not Defend a *Meisis*:** This *aveirah* can be done by speaking, so it is a *lav she'ein bo ma'aseh*.[10]

5. **Do Not Hold Back From Proving the Guilt of a *Meisis*:** This can only be done by **not** giving evidence to the *Beis Din*, so it is a *lav she'ein bo ma'aseh*."

CHECKPOINT   What does *Beis Din* do differently with a *meisis* than with every other person who does an *aveirah*?

DID YOU KNOW?

Spread the Wealth

If you know a wealthy person who gives *tzedakah*, you should not keep this information a secret from others so that you will be the only one who gets *tzedakah*.

Not only is that selfish, but it is also like being a *meisis* to the rich person. This is because when you take away the opportunity for the rich person to give more *tzedakah*, you are actually "influencing" this person not to do a mitzvah![13]

Positive Influence

From the strict punishment of a *meisis*, we see that the Torah knows how much a person can influence other people. Imagine how much power you have to influence people in a good way.

And if the Torah punishes the *meisis* so strictly for trying to influence others in a bad way, how much more so will the Torah reward you for influencing others in a good way![14]

HISTORY

Stay Over There

Avraham Avinu is also called "*Avraham Ha'ivri.*" This means, "Avraham from across [the river]." The *Midrash* explains that he was called this because he stood on one side, while the rest of the world stood on the other side.

The whole world was serving idols, yet Avraham wouldn't let himself be influenced by them. He was not afraid, and had the courage to stand against the entire world because he knew he was right![15]

SELECTED HALACHOS

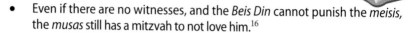

- Even if there are no witnesses, and the *Beis Din* cannot punish the *meisis*, the *musas* still has a mitzvah to not love him.[16]

- If a *musas* was convinced by a *meisis* to worship *avodah zarah*, his punishment is not as strict as the punishment given to the *meisis*, e.g. we do accept evidence for his innocence in court.[17]

- Even though the *musas* is not allowed to praise or defend the *meisis*, if he tells the *Beis Din* information to save the *meisis*, the *Beis Din* has to listen.[18]

- The *musas* should be the one to kill the *meisis*.[19]

- After the *Beis Din* kills the *meisis*, they send messengers throughout the land announcing that the *meisis* was killed in court.[20]

EXTEND YOUR KNOWLEDGE

Stuck With the Wrong Owner

In *Parshas Mishpatim*, the Torah gives us a mitzvah to help someone if their animal is having difficulty with a heavy load. However, if the owner is a *meisis*, the *musas* is forbidden to help him. This *halachah* is based on the third mitzvah of our unit.

It is unusually strict, for usually the Torah commands us to care for animals and not cause them pain. Here, by not helping the *meisis*, we harm not only the *meisis*, but the animal as well![21]

A STORY

Fire!

The *Gemara* tells us what R' Amram Chasida would do to stop his *yetzer hara* from convincing him to do *aveiros*. When he realized that his *yetzer hara* was trying to convince him to do an *aveirah*, he screamed out loud, "There's a fire in my house!" His students came running, and now there were people around, so R' Amram would be embarrassed to do the *aveirah*.

When the students saw no fire, they said, "Rebbi, how come you let yourself be embarrassed in front of everyone?" R' Amram calmly replied, "Better that I embarrass myself here than embarrass myself in *Olam Haba*."[22]

Live the Mitzvah

Choose Light

A *meisis* can mean a lot more than someone who influences you to serve *avodah zarah*. Anyone who influences you to do something wrong is a *meisis*. The Torah is very strict with how a *meisis* is to be treated. This is a wake-up call for you to think carefully about how you influence your friends and family.[23]

Your real friends are like the warm sun that does only good for you and helps you grow. These people would never ask you to do something wrong. If people do ask you to do something wrong, then that means that these so-called friends do not really care about you. They will let you sit in the darkness so long as they can get you to do what they want.

The choice is yours: where will you sit? In the warm sun, or out in the cold night? And, what would you do for your friends? Shine your rays on them, or bring them into darkness? Your power to influence is so great. You must use it wisely.

CHECKPOINT How can you use the power of friendship for good purposes?

What Else Comes From This?

Yetzer Hara

We all have our own *meisis* inside of us. It is the *yetzer hara*. It tries very hard to convince us to do the wrong thing, and it won't stop until we listen to it. The Torah commands us to show no mercy to a *meisis*. Therefore, the next time you hear that little voice telling you to go the wrong way, you should not be afraid to squash it firmly!

CHECKPOINT Who is your personal *meisis*?

UNIT 22

ENDNOTES:

15. בראשית רבה מב, ח
16. מנ"ח מצוה תנ"ז אות ב'
17. מנ"ח מצוה תס"ב אות י"ב
18. מנ"ח מצוה ת"ס אות ג'
19. רמב"ם הל' ע"ז פ"ה ה"ד
20. רמב"ם הל' ממרים פ"ג ה"ח ע"פ כס"מ שם
21. מנ"ח מצוה תנ"ח אות א'
22. קידושין פא, א
23. שו"ת אגרות משה או"ח ח"א סי' צ"ט

5. רמב"ם הל' דעות פ"ו ה"א
6. עי' רמב"ם הל' תשובה פ"ג ה"י. שם פ"ד ה"א
7. רמב"ם הל' ע"ז פ"ה ה"ג
8. מנ"ח מצוה תנ"ז אות ג'
9. מנ"ח מצוה תנ"ט אות ב'
10. מנ"ח מצוה ת"ס אות ב'
11. נגעים פי"ב מ"ו
12. רש"י במדבר ג, כט. ורש"י שם פסוק לח
13. שו"ת אגרות משה יו"ד ח"ג סי' צ"ה
14. ה"אלטער" מקעלם

1. מנחות צט, ב
2. ויקרא רבה כו, ז. סה"מ קונטריסים ח"א ע' 106.
3. סנהדרין כט, א
4. משלי יג, כ

Imagine yourself standing at a place on the road and you **have a choice to go to the right or to the left**. You don't know which direction to take. There are two men standing nearby, and you ask them for help. One tells you to go right, the other tells you to go left. How confusing! Who should you listen to? Whom can you trust? **Can you trust anyone now?**

UNIT 23

IN THIS UNIT YOU WILL:

EXPLORE

- Why is a false *navi* so dangerous for our *emunah*?

EXAMINE

- What happens to a false *navi*?
- What are the various types of false *nevi'im*?

EXTRACT

- If you're asked for advice and you don't know what advice to give, what should you do?
- If you get excited about something, what shouldn't you say?

נְבִיא שֶׁקֶר

KEY CONCEPTS

Book: Madda, Section: Idol Worship

סֵפֶר מַדָּע הִלְכוֹת עֲבוֹדָה זָרָה

נְבִיא שֶׁקֶר

FALSE NAVI

אַרְבַּע מִצְוֹת

OUR SAGES SAY...

No Power to the Wicked

R' Yosi Haglili said: When teaching us about a false *navi*, the Torah says, "If a *navi* will come and show you a *nes* or sign, do not listen to him." If he's fake, why does the Torah call the act of a false *navi*, a "*nes?*"

Hashem knew that people might be convinced by the *nissim* of a false *navi*. Hashem tells us that there will be miracles, and that they will look real, but we shouldn't listen to that *navi* and don't be convinced by the miracles he performs!"[1]

The Mitzvos

EXAMINE

The unit of a false *navi* has four mitzvos.

1. Do not tell anyone to do anything in the name of an *avodah zarah*.
2. Do not listen to someone who says a *nevuah* from an *avodah zarah*.
3. Do not say a false *nevuah*.
4. Do not be scared to point out and kill a false *navi*.

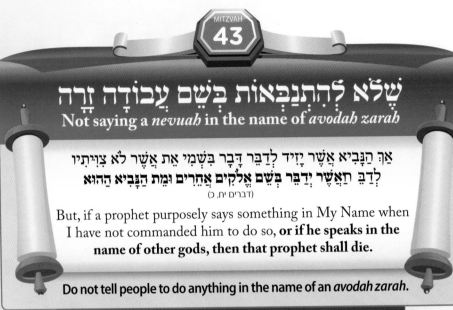

MITZVAH 43

שֶׁלֹּא לְהִתְנַבְּאוֹת בְּשֵׁם עֲבוֹדָה זָרָה
Not saying a *nevuah* in the name of *avodah zarah*

אַךְ הַנָּבִיא אֲשֶׁר יָזִיד לְדַבֵּר דָּבָר בִּשְׁמִי אֵת אֲשֶׁר לֹא צִוִּיתִיו
לְדַבֵּר וַאֲשֶׁר יְדַבֵּר בְּשֵׁם אֱלֹקִים אֲחֵרִים וּמֵת הַנָּבִיא הַהוּא
(דברים יח, כ)

But, if a prophet purposely says something in My Name when I have not commanded him to do so, **or if he speaks in the name of other gods, then that prophet shall die.**

Do not tell people to do anything in the name of an *avodah zarah*.

 ALL PEOPLE   ALL PLACES   ALL TIMES   CHENEK

MITZVAH 44

שֶׁלֹּא לִשְׁמוֹעַ מִמִּתְנַבֵּא בְּשֵׁם עֲבוֹדָה זָרָה
Not listening to someone who says *nevuos* in the name of an *avodah zarah*

לֹא תִשְׁמַע אֶל דִּבְרֵי הַנָּבִיא הַהוּא אוֹ אֶל חוֹלֵם הַחֲלוֹם הַהוּא
כִּי מְנַסֶּה ה' אֱלֹקֵיכֶם אֶתְכֶם לָדַעַת הֲיִשְׁכֶם אֹהֲבִים אֶת ה' אֱלֹקֵיכֶם
בְּכָל לְבַבְכֶם וּבְכָל נַפְשְׁכֶם
(דברים יג, ד)

Do not listen to the words of that prophet or dreamer, for Hashem your G-d is testing you to see if you are truly able to love Hashem your G-d with all your heart and all your soul.

Do not listen to a *navi* of an *avodah zarah*.

 ALL PEOPLE   ALL PLACES   ALL TIMES   NO PUNISHMENT

שֶׁלֹא לְהִתְנַבְּאוֹת בְּשֶׁקֶר
Not saying a false *nevuah*

אַךְ הַנָּבִיא אֲשֶׁר יָזִיד לְדַבֵּר דָּבָר בִּשְׁמִי אֵת אֲשֶׁר לֹא צִוִּיתִיו לְדַבֵּר
וַאֲשֶׁר יְדַבֵּר בְּשֵׁם אֱלֹקִים אֲחֵרִים וּמֵת הַנָּבִיא הַהוּא
(דברים יח, כ)

But, if a prophet purposely says something in My Name when I have not commanded him to do so, or if he speaks in the name of other gods, **then that prophet shall die.**

Do not say a *nevuah* in the name of Hashem if Hashem has not commanded the *nevuah*.

ALL PEOPLE · ALL PLACES · ALL TIMES · CHENEK

שֶׁלֹא נִמְנַע מֵהֲרִיגַת נָבִיא שֶׁקֶר וְלֹא נָגוּר מִמֶּנוּ
Not being scared to kill a false *navi*, and not fearing him

אֲשֶׁר יְדַבֵּר הַנָּבִיא בְּשֵׁם ה' וְלֹא יִהְיֶה הַדָּבָר וְלֹא יָבֹא הוּא הַדָּבָר
אֲשֶׁר לֹא דִבְּרוֹ ה' בְּזָדוֹן דִּבְּרוֹ הַנָּבִיא לֹא תָגוּר מִמֶּנוּ
(דברים יח, כב)

If the prophet predicts something in Hashem's name, and the prediction does not come true, then that message was not spoken by Hashem. That prophet has spoken wrong, **and you must not fear him.**

Do not be scared to point out and kill a false *navi*.

ALL PEOPLE · ALL PLACES · BEIS DIN · NO PUNISHMENT

DID YOU KNOW?

Tammuz

The Rambam tells the story of Tammuz, a false *navi*. This false *navi* was tortured to death by a certain king. After Tammuz died, his followers made up a story that on the night of his death some gods came to crown him, and then flew away the next morning.

This story was turned into a play. This play became so popular that the *navi* Yechezkel tells us that even while the *Beis Hamikdash* still stood, the play was shown regularly in Yerushalayim, and the women of Yerushalayim would watch the play and cry.[2]

OUR SAGES SAY...

Don't Fall For the Fireworks

R' Avahu said in the name of R' Yochanan: You must always listen to a *navi* of Hashem. But if he tells you to worship *avodah zarah*, you may never listen to him, even if he tries to prove himself by doing great miracles such as forcing the sun to stop moving in the sky.[3]

The Contest

King Achav of the *Aseres Hashevatim* was completely under the influence of his evil wife, Izevel. She spread the worship of *Ba'al* and *Asheirah* idols around the land of Eretz Yisrael and killed many true *nevi'im* until Eliyahu was the only one left. Eliyahu challenged the king to a public contest between the *nevi'im* of *Ba'al* and *Asheirah* and himself, to see who was the true G-d.

On the morning of the contest, Eliyahu told the eight hundred and fifty *nevi'im* of *Ba'al* and *Asheirah* to prepare a sacrifice to be laid on the *mizbeiach*, but not to light a fire, and he would do the same. The *nevi'im* prepared their sacrifice, and called on their gods from morning to noon to light the fire, but they were not answered. Then, Eliyahu prepared his *korban*, and *davened* to Hashem. Immediately, a fire flew down from Heaven and burned the animal.

B'nei Yisrael saw this and did *teshuvah*. At Eliyahu's command, the false *nevi'im* were killed.[4]

Giving *Nevuah* a Bad Name

The Torah tells us to trust our *nevi'im* and to follow what they say, as long as they are true to Torah. A fake *navi* causes us to lose our trust in all *nevi'im*. This is terrible, because we need *nevi'im* to guide us. Without a *navi* telling us what to do, we might get confused and do the wrong things. Even worse, if a false *navi* lies to us and we believe him, we will be led away from the path of Torah.

Therefore, we are commanded to kill false *neviim*, not to listen to them, and certainly not to be a false *navi* ourselves.

> **CHECKPOINT**   How can one false *navi* ruin your trust in all *nevi'im*?

Details   EXAMINE

Dealing With a False *Navi*

False *Navi* of Hashem

We have a mitzvah not to listen to a false *navi*. But how do we know who is a false *navi*? A true *navi* follows Hashem and His Torah that was given to Moshe on *Har Sinai*. A false *navi* is someone who either tries to change something in the Torah by explaining it in an incorrect way, by adding or taking away a mitzvah from the Torah, or by saying something in the name of an *avodah zarah*.[5]

Anyone who tells you to worship *avodah zarah*, or tries to change something in the Torah, is a false *navi* who must be killed before he convinces other people to leave the Torah.

Navi of *Avodah Zarah*

A person who worships an *avodah zarah* and tries to convince other people to do actions for that *avodah zarah*, or gives people messages "from" the *avodah zarah*, is even more dangerous! These messages can bring a person away from Torah even faster than a false *navi* of Hashem. This *navi* must be killed before he can convince anyone to leave the Torah.

Don't Even Think About It

Once you know that someone is a false *navi*, not only are you not allowed to listen to him, but you are not allowed to even **think** about listening to him. You cannot say to yourself, "If this *navi* proves that he can do a *nes*, then I will listen to him." You are also not allowed to ask the *navi* to do a *nes* for you. Even if the false *navi* does do a miracle, you are still not allowed to pay any attention to him.[6]

Don't Be Afraid

In the time of the *Beis Hamikdash*, there were many *nevi'im*. There were even schools for *nevi'im*. These *nevi'im* had great stature and demanded much respect. Therefore, the Torah specifically warns us not to fear a false *navi*'s status. Instead, you must do everything in your power to catch him and bring him to court.[7]

 CHECKPOINT What must we do with a false *navi*?

SELECTED HALACHOS

- Unlike a *meisis* who does not need to be warned in order to be punished, a *navi* of an *avodah zarah* must be warned in order for him to be punished.[8]

- It is forbidden to give a *nevuah* in the name of *avodah zarah,* even if it is to tell people to do a mitzvah.[9]

- The punishment of a **navi of avodah zarah** can be given by a smaller court of 23 judges, and does not need to be by the Great *Sanhedrin* of 71 judges.[10]

- The punishment for a **false navi** is different; only the Great *Sanhedrin* can give the punishment.[11]

- If a *nevuah* was told to someone else and you happened to find out about it, you may not say it over as if you had heard it yourself.[12]

DID YOU KNOW?

Once Bitten, Twice Shy

Before Yonah was sent to Ninveh, Hashem told him to go and tell the people of Yerushalayim that they would be destroyed if they did not do *teshuvah*. The people in Yerushalayim listened to Yonah's warning, did *teshuvah*, and Hashem saved the city.

After this, people started calling Yonah a false *navi* because he said that the city would be destroyed and it wasn't! This is why, later on, Yonah did not want to go to Ninveh when Hashem told him to do so. He was afraid that the same thing would happen there, and then even the *goyim* would think he was a false *navi*![13]

Avodah Zarah Trumps All

If someone who you know is a *navi* says a *nevuah* in the name of *avodah zarah*, even if he is not changing anything in the Torah, he must be killed.[14]

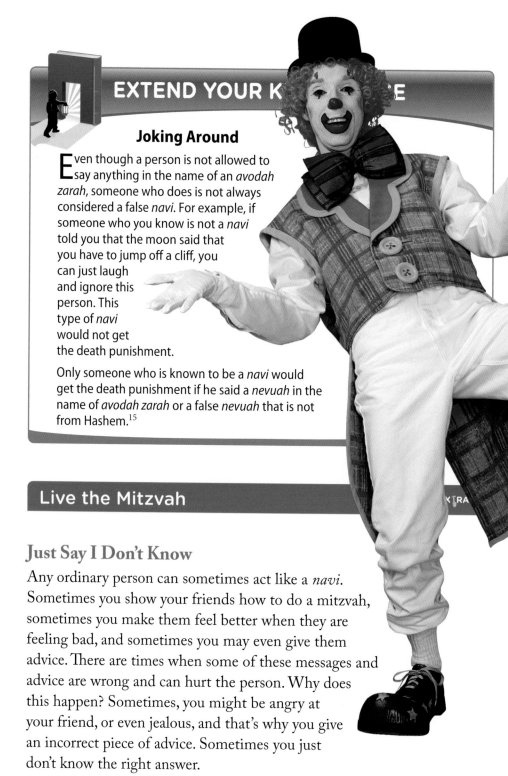

EXTEND YOUR KNOWLEDGE

Joking Around

Even though a person is not allowed to say anything in the name of an *avodah zarah*, someone who does is not always considered a false *navi*. For example, if someone who you know is not a *navi* told you that the moon said that you have to jump off a cliff, you can just laugh and ignore this person. This type of *navi* would not get the death punishment.

Only someone who is known to be a *navi* would get the death punishment if he said a *nevuah* in the name of *avodah zarah* or a false *nevuah* that is not from Hashem.[15]

Live the Mitzvah

Just Say I Don't Know

Any ordinary person can sometimes act like a *navi*. Sometimes you show your friends how to do a mitzvah, sometimes you make them feel better when they are feeling bad, and sometimes you may even give them advice. There are times when some of these messages and advice are wrong and can hurt the person. Why does this happen? Sometimes, you might be angry at your friend, or even jealous, and that's why you give an incorrect piece of advice. Sometimes you just don't know the right answer.

Stop and think! How would these people feel if they realize you purposely gave them the wrong answer? Can they ever trust you again? Because of you, they did the wrong thing, or something bad happened to them. Therefore, when you can't give your friends the right advice for any reason, you should tell them that you don't know the answer, or tell them to ask someone else who may be able to help them.

 CHECKPOINT How can you be like a true *navi* for your friends?

Just Ignore Them

Hashem warns us not to argue with false *nevi'im*. This means we can't get into debates with them. Today, missionaries try to convince others to convert to their religion. Often, they bring sources for their arguments, which can even be incorrect quotes from the Torah, or wrong explanations of the *mitzvos*. We should not argue with them and just ignore them.[17]

Leave Him Out of This

Sometimes, when people are excited, they slip up and say things like "In the name of G-d!" We have learned before that using these expressions is like "blessing" Hashem's name. It could also be like giving a *nevuah* in Hashem's name. Therefore, you should stay far away from using such expressions![18]

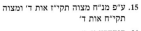

CHECKPOINT   What should you do if you meet a missionary?

OUR SAGES SAY...

No Exceptions for *Avodah Zarah*

If a *navi* tells you to get rid of a mitzvah completely, he should be killed. However, if he tells you to not do a mitzvah only one time, or to change the mitzvah just this once, he is not killed.

In the case of a *navi* telling you to serve an *avodah zarah*, the rules change: even if he tells you to worship *avodah zarah* for just one moment, he is killed.[16]

UNIT **23**

ENDNOTES:

1. סנהדרין צ, א ע"פ ערוך לנר שם
2. מורה נבוכים ח"ג פכ"ט
3. סנהדרין צ, א
4. מלכים א' פרק יח
5. רמב"ם הל' יסוה"ת פ"ח ה"ג ופ"ט ה"א
6. רמב"ם הל' ע"ז פ"ה ה"ז
7. רמב"ם הל' ע"ז פ"ה ה"ט, וע"פ רמב"ם הל' יסוה"ת ריש פ"ז

8. רמב"ם הל' ע"ז פ"ה ה"ו
9. רמב"ם הל' ע"ז פ"ה ה"ו
10. מנ"ח מצוה תקי"ח אות ג'
11. רמב"ם הל' ע"ז פ"ה ה"ט
12. רמב"ם הל' ע"ז פ"ה ה"ח
13. פרדר"א פ"ט
14. רמב"ם הל' ע"ז פ"ה ה"ו

15. ע"פ מנ"ח מצוה תקי"ז אות ד' ומצוה תקי"ח אות ד'
16. סנהדרין צ, א
17. ראה משלי כו, ד
18. יראים השלם סי' רמ"א

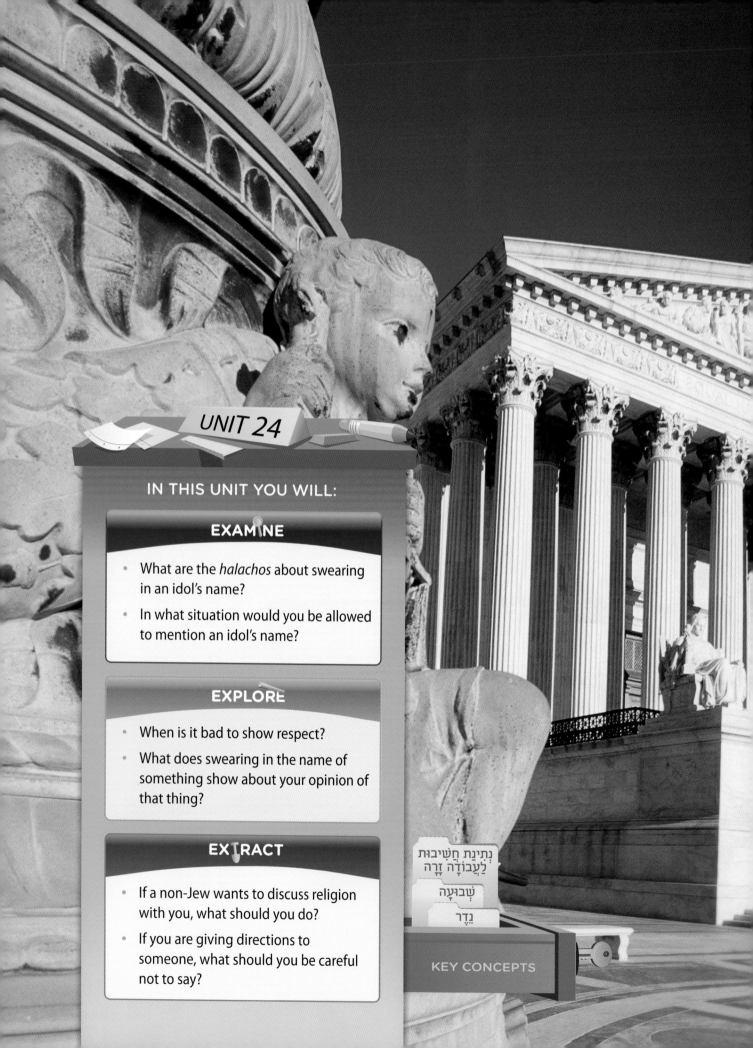

UNIT 24

IN THIS UNIT YOU WILL:

EXAMINE

- What are the *halachos* about swearing in an idol's name?
- In what situation would you be allowed to mention an idol's name?

EXPLORE

- When is it bad to show respect?
- What does swearing in the name of something show about your opinion of that thing?

EXTRACT

- If a non-Jew wants to discuss religion with you, what should you do?
- If you are giving directions to someone, what should you be careful not to say?

נְתִינַת חֲשִׁיבוּת
לַעֲבוֹדָה זָרָה

שְׁבוּעָה

נֶדֶר

KEY CONCEPTS

Book: Madda, Section: Idol Worship

סֵפֶר מַדָּע הִלְכוֹת עֲבוֹדָה זָרָה

שֶׁלֹּא לִישָּׁבַע בַּעֲבוֹדָה זָרָה

NOT SWEARING IN THE NAME OF AN AVODAH ZARAH

מִצְוָה אַחַת

The witness says to the judge, "Your Honor, with all due respect, I refuse to do that because I am a Jew!"

What is the witness refusing to do, and why?

OUR SAGES SAY...

Idolatry Ruins Everything

Before the Torah tells us the issur of *avodah zarah*, it says, "And **everything** I have told you, you should guard." This teaches us that someone who serves *avodah zarah* is as if he has gone against the entire Torah, and someone who is careful with staying away from *avodah zarah*, is as if he has kept the entire Torah.[1]

STORY

A Dog's Life

A certain philosopher asked *Rabban Gamliel*, "It is written in your Torah: 'I, the Eternal, your G-d, am a jealous G-d.' If *avodah zarah* really bothers Hashem, why does He not destroy it all?"

Rabban Gamliel answered, "If a person called a dog with the name of the king, who insulted the king? At whom would the king be angry? At the dog, or at the person who called it with the king's name? Of course, he would be angry at the person, not the dog who didn't do anything wrong!

"Hashem is not angry at the things being served as *avodah zarah*, as they didn't do anything wrong. He is angry at the *B'nei Yisrael*, who believe in them."[2]

The Mitzvah

The unit of swearing in the name of an *avodah zarah* has one mitzvah.

Do not make a promise or swear in the name of an *avodah zarah*.

MITZVAH 47

שֶׁלֹּא לִישָּׁבַע בַּעֲבוֹדָה זָרָה
Not swearing in the name of *avodah zarah*

וּבְכֹל אֲשֶׁר אָמַרְתִּי אֲלֵיכֶם תִּשָּׁמֵרוּ וְשֵׁם אֱלֹהִים אֲחֵרִים לֹא תַזְכִּירוּ לֹא יִשָּׁמַע עַל פִּיךָ
(שמות כג, יג)

Be very careful to keep everything I have said to you. **Do not say the name of another god**, and you must not let it be heard from your mouth.

Do not make any promises in the name of an *avodah zarah*.

ALL PEOPLE　　ALL PLACES　　ALL TIMES　　*MALKUS*

Mitzvah Messages

Misplaced Respect

Sometimes, people who want to prove to others that they are really telling the truth will swear in the name of something that they respect and believe in. For example, somebody in America might say, "I swear by the President that I am telling the truth!" Since many people believe in the President and respect him a lot, they will believe what the person is saying.

Therefore, you are not allowed to swear in the name of idols or gods, because it shows others that you respect these idols or gods and believe in them.[3]

Not Worth Their Respect

Even though you should show respect for others and their opinions, you are not allowed to make people think that you believe in and respect *avodah zarah* just because you want to be polite and respectful to non-Jews. Therefore, you are not allowed to swear in the name of an *avodah zarah* in any situation, including in court, or when you are doing a business deal with a non-Jew.

 CHECKPOINT Why can't you swear in the name of an *avodah zarah* if you really don't believe in it?

Details

EXAMINE

Vows and Oaths

There are two types of promises that a person is allowed to make:

1. A נֶדֶר - **vow**. This is when you promise never to do something in the future. For example, "I promise never to eat cake again."

2. A שְׁבוּעָה - **oath**. This is when you swear that something happened in the past, or that something will happen in the future or the opposite: you swear that something did not happen or will not happen. For example, "I swear that I ate cereal for breakfast yesterday." Or, "I swear that an apple will grow on this tree in three months.[4]

With both types (נֶדֶר and שְׁבוּעָה) you are not allowed to use the name of an *avodah zarah*. Even if you don't believe in the *avodah zarah* yourself, but you want non-Jews to believe that you are serious, you are still not allowed to use the name of any *avodah zarah* when making a promise.[5]

Business Sense

Not only are **you** not allowed to swear in the name of an *avodah zarah*, but you are also not allowed to make a non-Jew swear in the name of an *avodah zarah*.[6] Therefore, you cannot start a business with a non-Jew who believes in an *avodah zarah*, because the non-Jew might be forced to swear in the name of his *avodah zarah* if you have an argument about the business.[7]

However, most non-Jews nowadays do not serve *avodah zarah*, and you are allowed to do business with them.[8]

 CHECKPOINT What may we not promise in the name of *avodah zarah*?

Mock Them

רַבִּי אוֹמֵר, וְשֵׁם אֱלֹהִים אֲחֵרִים לֹא תַזְכִּירוּ, לְשָׁבַח, אֲבָל לִגְנַאי, תַּלְמוּד לוֹמַר שַׁקֵּץ תְּשַׁקְּצֶנּוּ

"The name of other gods you cannot mention" – This means that you are not allowed to mention them in a respectful way, but you are allowed to mention them if you are really making fun of the *avodah zarah*, as it says, "You should surely disgrace it."[9]

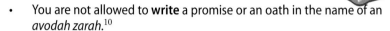

SELECTED HALACHOS

- You are not allowed to **write** a promise or an oath in the name of an *avodah zarah*.[10]

- You are allowed to use the name of an idol so that you can show how ridiculous and untrue it is.[11]

- You are allowed to say the names of idols or gods that are mentioned in the Torah, like *Pe'or*.[12]

- You should change the name of an idol when writing or saying it.[13]

- You are only not allowed to mention the name of an idol if you are talking about the idol. However, if someone or something happens to have the same name as an idol, you are allowed to say the name.[14]

EXTEND YOUR KNOWLEDGE

Just For Fun

You are allowed to say the name of an idol in order to make fun of it or show it disrespect. Therefore, if you swore in the name of an idol about something very silly or very obvious , it is not forbidden.

For example, you can say "I swear in the name of... that the earth is flat," or, "I swear in the name of... that the sun rose today."[15]

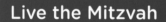

Live the Mitzvah

EXTRACT

Don't Be Mean!

It is certainly not nice to make fun of non-Jews about what they believe, but it is also not smart to pretend that their religion means something to you. It will **not** make them respect you more if you try to show them that you think their beliefs are just as good as your own, because it only shows them that your own religion is weak. While not putting down others, we have to be strong and proud in our faith.

You are allowed to make fun of other religions when people of that religion are not around. Do not say mean and insulting things in their presence, and especially do not show how ridiculous their religion is in their presence. That is mean and would cause a very great *chillul Hashem*.

CHECKPOINT How should you respond if someone asks you about another religion?

What Else Comes From This?

EXTRACT

Don't Mention It

You are not allowed to swear using a name of an idol, and you are also not allowed to use an idol to refer to something else, even if you are not making a promise.[16] For example, you can't say, "Meet me tomorrow by the idol on the corner of so-and-so street."[17]

This *halachah* also refers to churches. You are not allowed to say, "Make a right turn at the big church and go three blocks until you find my house."

It is also forbidden to mention *avodah zarah* for no reason.[18]

CHECKPOINT What do you have to be very careful about when you are giving directions?

UNIT 24

ENDNOTES:

9. מכילתא דרבי ישמעאל משפטים מסכתא דכספא פרשה כ׳ ד״ה ושם אלקים אחרים

10. מנ״ח מצוה פ״ו אות ד׳

11. סנהדרין סג, ב. שו״ע יו״ד סי׳ קמ״ז ה״ה

12. סנהדרין סג, ב. שו״ע יו״ד סי׳ קמ״ז ס״ד

13. שו״ת משנה הלכות ח״ט סי׳ קס״ט

14. הגהות מיימוניות פ״ה מהל׳ עכו״ם אות ג׳

15. מנ״ח מצוה פ״ו אות ג׳

16. רמב״ם הל׳ עכו״ם פ״ה ה״י

17. רמב״ם הל׳ עכו״ם פ״ה הי״א

18. שו״ע יו״ד סי׳ קמ״ז ס״א. וראה ט״ז ס״ק א׳

19. תורת הפרשה פ׳ בא

1. רש״י שמות כג, יג ד״ה לא תזכירו

2. ילקוט שמעוני תורה רמז רפ״ח

3. מנ״ח מצוה פ״ו אות ב׳ קרוב לסופו

4. רש״י סנהדרין ס, ב ד״ה הנודר בשמו, והמקיים בשמו

5. רמב״ם הל׳ עכו״ם פ״ה ה״י

6. רמב״ם הל׳ עכו״ם פ״ה ה״י

7. סנהדרין סג, ב

8. רמ״א או״ח סי׳ קנ״ו

Would you use a laundry bag to bring your books to school? Would you pack your toothbrush in a used pencilcase?

UNIT 25

IN THIS UNIT YOU WILL:

EXPLORE

- Why is it disrespectful to serve Hashem in the same way that the non-Jews serve their *avodah zarah*?

EXAMINE

- What are three ways in which you are not allowed to serve Hashem?

EXTRACT

- If your *shul* has a stone floor, how should you bow down on *Rosh Hashanah* and *Yom Kippur*?

מִצְוָה

אֶבֶן מַשְׂכִּית

הִשְׁתַּחֲוָאה

KEY CONCEPTS

Book: Madda, Section: Idol Worship
סֵפֶר מַדָּע הִלְכוֹת עֲבוֹדָה זָרָה

שֶׁלֹּא לַעֲבוֹד ה' בְּדֶרֶךְ הַגּוֹיִם

NOT SERVING HASHEM THE WAY AN AVODAH ZARAH IS SERVED

שָׁלֹשׁ מִצְוֹת

Replacements

After *Shlomo Hamelech* died, the kingdom of Eretz Yisrael was split into two parts. The half with the *Beis Hamikdash* in it was under King Rechavam, the son of Shlomo, and the other half was under King Yeravam.

King Yeravam was very worried that the people in his kingdom would go to the *Beis Hamikdash* in King Rechavam's land, and would end up liking King Rechavam better. To stop this, King Yeravam built new buildings and hired many priests to work in them. He told his people that they could worship Hashem in these new buildings and didn't have to travel to Yerushalayim.

The people listened, and they began to serve idols instead of Hashem in those new buildings. The desire to serve *avodah zarah* was so strong that even the death of King Yeravam's son did not stop him from serving the idols.[1]

The Mitzvos

This unit has three mitzvos.

1. Do not build a pillar of stone in order to serve Hashem.

2. Do not bow down to Hashem on a stone floor.

3. Do not plant a tree in the *azarah* of the *Beis Hamikdash*.

MITZVAH
48

שֶׁלֹּא לְהָקִים מַצֵּבָה

Not setting up a stone pillar to serve Hashem

וְלֹא תָקִים לְךָ מַצֵּבָה אֲשֶׁר שָׂנֵא ה' אֱלֹקֶיךָ

(דברים טז, כב)

Do not put up a monument, since this is something that Hashem your G-d hates.

Do not build a stone pillar to serve Hashem.

ALL PEOPLE   ALL PLACES   ALL TIMES   *MALKUS*

MITZVAH 49

שֶׁלֹּא נִשְׁתַּחֲוֶה עַל אֶבֶן מַשְׂכִּית אֲפִילוּ לַשֵׁם

Not bowing to Hashem on a stone floor

> לֹא תַעֲשׂוּ לָכֶם אֱלִילִם וּפֶסֶל וּמַצֵּבָה לֹא תָקִימוּ לָכֶם וְאֶבֶן מַשְׂכִּית
> לֹא תִתְּנוּ בְּאַרְצְכֶם לְהִשְׁתַּחֲוֹת עָלֶיהָ כִּי אֲנִי ה' אֱלֹקֵיכֶם
>
> (ויקרא כו, א)

Do not make yourselves false gods. Do not raise up a stone idol or a sacred pillar for yourselves. **Do not place a kneeling stone in your land to bow down on it**. I am Hashem your G-d.

Do not bow down to Hashem on a stone floor.

ALL PEOPLE | OUTSIDE THE *BEIS HAMIKDASH* | ALL TIMES | MALKUS

PEARLS of wisdom

The Same

Another reason why we don't bow down on stones is because we already bow down to Hashem in the *Beis Hamikdash* on a stone floor. Therefore, we may not do this anywhere else.

This is similar to not being allowed to make an exact copy of the *menorah*.[2]

MITZVAH 50

שֶׁלֹּא לָטַעַת אִילָן בַּמִּקְדָּשׁ

Not planting a tree in the *Beis Hamikdash*

> לֹא תִטַּע לְךָ אֲשֵׁרָה כָּל עֵץ אֵצֶל מִזְבַּח ה' אֱלֹקֶיךָ אֲשֶׁר תַּעֲשֶׂה לָךְ
>
> (דברים טז, כא)

Do not plant for yourself an *asheirah* or any other tree near the altar that you will make for Hashem your G-d.

Do not plant any kind of tree in the *azarah* of the *Beis Hamikdash*.

ALL PEOPLE | AZARAH | ALL TIMES | MALKUS

DID YOU KNOW?

Still Forbidden

Even nowadays, when there is no *mizbeiach*, we are still not allowed to plant a tree where the *azarah* used to be.[3]

DID YOU KNOW?

Careful Where You Put That Tree

If you plant an *asheirah* tree without even serving it, you have done an *aveirah* and can get a punishment.[4]

Air Force One

Air Force One is the name used for the plane set aside especially for the President (or any US Air Force plane in which the President of the United States is onboard).

The planes actually used for the President are two modified Boeing 747-200 jets which can be used as a White House in the sky. Each plane costs $325 million and costs about $68,000 an hour to use. The purpose of these planes is only to serve the President and his needs and is rarely used by anyone else, even the Vice President.

It is not befitting for the President to use a regular plane used by regular travelers.

What an Insult!

Can you imagine how insulting it would be to serve Hashem, the King of Kings, in the same way as worthless idols are served? Those pieces of stone, wood or metal have nothing to them, and serving Hashem in the same way that those idols are served is extremely insulting and disrespectful.

Hashem gave us the Torah and mitzvos which are special ways by which to serve Him. We must never copy the way non-Jews serve their idols.[6]

CHECKPOINT Why is it insulting to serve Hashem the same way non-Jews serve *avodah zarah*?

Serving *Avodah Zarah*

The following three actions were used often to serve different types of *avodah zarah*. You are never allowed to do any of these actions to serve Hashem.

1. Building a *Matzeivah*

A *matzeivah* is a stone pillar made of a single stone. It is usually set up so that people will know where to gather around and pray. Since this is what people who serve *avodah zarah* do, we are not allowed to build a *matzeivah* ourselves, even if we want people to gather around to serve Hashem.[7]

You are not allowed to build any kind of *matzeivah* that will be used for *davening* to Hashem, or serving Hashem.

2. Bowing on a Stone Floor

An "*even maskis*" is a natural stone that has been carved and smoothed to be used to pave a floor that people will bow down on.[8] Bricks, which are man-made of clay, mud, etc. are not included in this *issur* and can be used as a floor that will be used to bow down to Hashem.[9]

HISTORY

Never Again

Long ago, before the *Mishkan* was built, building a *matzeivah* was allowed. When Ya'akov travelled to see Lavan, he built a *matzeivah* on the road.

Later, when the non-Jews started building *matzeivos* for *avodah zarah*, Hashem said that we are no longer allowed to build and use *matzeivos*.[5]

There are two kinds of bowing:

הִשְׁתַּחֲוָאָה – Lying on the floor and spreading out your hands and feet, known as "*pishut yadayim v'raglayim*." [10] The Torah does not allow us to bow in this way on a stone floor. Anyone who does this would be punished with *malkus*.

כְּרִיעָה - Kneeling on both knees. The *Chachamim* do not allow us to bow this way on a stone floor.

You are allowed to bend your head and knees while standing on stone, like you do during *Shemonah Esrei*, since this is not considered bowing down. [11]

3. Planting a Tree in the *Beis Hamikdash*

You are not allowed to plant any trees in the *Beis Hamikdash*, even if it is only to make it look more beautiful. [12]

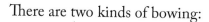

CHECKPOINT What are the three actions you cannot do to serve Hashem?

SELECTED HALACHOS

- You are allowed to use an *even maskis* for anything that is not kneeling or bowing down. [13]

- The *Chachamim* ruled that we are also not allowed to bow down completely with "*pishut yadayim v'raglayim*" on **any** kind of floor. [14]

- You are *oveir* the *aveirah* of planting a tree in the *azarah* as soon as you plant the tree, even before it starts growing. [15]

- The *Chachamim* didn't let anyone build anything wooden in the *Beis Hamikdash* because it was too similar to planting trees. [16]

EXTEND YOUR KNOWLEDGE

Don't Fall For Good Looks

Reish Lakish said: If someone appoints a bad judge to rule over a city, it is like he planted an *asheirah* tree.

R' Ashi says that it is like an *asheirah* tree was planted in the *Beis Hamikdash*, right next to the *mizbeiach*![19]

What is the connection between appointing an unworthy judge and planting an *asheirah* tree near the *mizbeiach*?

Trying to beautify the *Beis Hamikdash* by planting trees in it is insulting, because the beauty of the place comes from its holiness, not from the decorations.

This is like someone who appoints a new judge because of the judge's money, good looks, charm, or nice speeches. This new judge is being respected for the wrong reasons.

The only thing that is really important for a judge is his Torah knowledge and fear of Hashem.[20]

The Holocaust

Not too long ago, there was a terrible tragedy called the Holocaust. Millions of Jews all over Europe were killed in terrible ways. In certain areas, big stone pillars were put up to remember the people who were killed there. How is this allowed? Didn't we learn that any pillar, even if it is not designed for *avodah zarah*, is not allowed?

The answer is that since these *matzeivos* are not made for any religious reason, or any regular gathering, they are allowed to be made.

Tombstones

There are other stone *matzeivos* that we have to use, according to *halachah*, such as the *matzeivah* on a grave. The reason why these are allowed is because they are only a sign that the person is buried there, and are not meant to be a sign for people to gather around it and *daven*.

When people come and *daven* there, they are *davening* to Hashem, and asking the person buried there to also *daven* to Hashem.[21]

Not Bowing Down

You may have noticed that some people bring a little mat or sheet to shul for *Rosh Hashanah* and *Yom Kippur*. This is because some *shuls* have a stone floor, and there might be a problem when we bow down to Hashem on the floor. When you bow down in a shul with a stone floor during *mussaf* on *Rosh Hashanah* or *Yom Kippur*, you should either put a mat on the floor, or turn your head a little bit to the side so that your forehead does not touch the floor.[22]

 CHECKPOINT How should you bow down on *Rosh Hashanah* and *Yom Kippur* if your *shul* has a stone floor?

A STORY

Rebel with a Cause

Gideon was one of the few people who did not serve *avodah zarah,* even though there was a *mizbeiach* for the idol Ba'al with an *asheirah* tree next to it in his father Yoash's house. Because of this, Hashem chose him to lead *B'nei Yisrael.*

Hashem sent Gideon a *malach* to tell him to destroy the *mizbeiach* of Ba'al, together with the *asheirah* tree. He was then to build a *mizbeiach* to Hashem, and then bring a *korban,* using the wood of the *asheirah* tree for the fire.

Gideon did this, and in the morning, when everyone found out what Gideon did, the men of his town surrounded his father's house demanding to kill Gideon for what he had done.

Yoash wanted to rescue his brave son and answered, "Why do you stand up to defend the honor of Ba'al? If he is a god, let him fight for himself, since someone has destroyed his *mizbeiach.*"

They were silenced, and Gideon received the name יְרֻבַּעַל - "Let Ba'al fight him."[23]

Woodn't Stay Long

Every seven years, the *Hakhel* ceremony was celebrated in the *Beis Hamikdash*. On the first day of *Chol Hamoed Sukkos,* the Torah would be placed on a wooden *bimah* in the *Beis Hamikdash* and the king would read from it to the entire nation.

How could they build a wooden structure in the *Beis Hamikdash?* Some *Poskim* explain that it wasn't made out of wood, rather of stone. Other *Poskim* explain that it was made out of wood but it wasn't a problem because it was only temporary. Another explanation why it was allowed is because it wasn't connected or "planted" in the ground.[24]

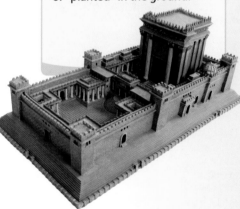

UNIT 25

ENDNOTES:

17. תמיד כח, ב

18. חינוך מצוה שמ"ט

19. סנהדרין ז, ב

20. אבן האזל

21. שו"ת מנחת יצחק ח"א סי' כ"ט

22. רמב"ם הל' ע"ז פ"ו ה"ז

23. שופטים פרק ו'

24. רמב"ם ורא"ד הל' ע"ז פ"ו ה"י. עבודת המלך על הרמב"ם שם

משכית

9. מג"א סי' קל"א ס"ק כ'

10. מגילה כב, ב

11. כסף משנה הל' ע"ז פ"ו ה"ו בסופו

12. סה"מ ל"ת י"ג

13. ירושלמי ע"ז פ"ד ה"א

14. משנ"ב סי' קל"א ס"ק מ'

15. מנ"ח מצוה תצ"ב אות ג'. נר מצוה סי' י' אות ה' ד"ה ודע

16. רמב"ם הל' ע"ז פ"ו ה"י, וע"י כס"מ

1. מלכים א' פרק י"ב-י"ד

2. רש"י מגילה כב, ב ד"ה לא אסרה תורה, וראה מנ"ח מצוה שמ"ט אות א'

3. מנ"ח מצוה תצ"ב אות א'

4. רש"י דברים טז, כא

5. ויצא כח, יח. ובפי' הרמב"ן עה"ת דברים טז, כב

6. חינוך מצוה תצ"ב בשם הרמב"ם

7. רמב"ם הל' ע"ז פ"ו ה"ו

8. אנציקלופדיה תלמודית ערך אבן

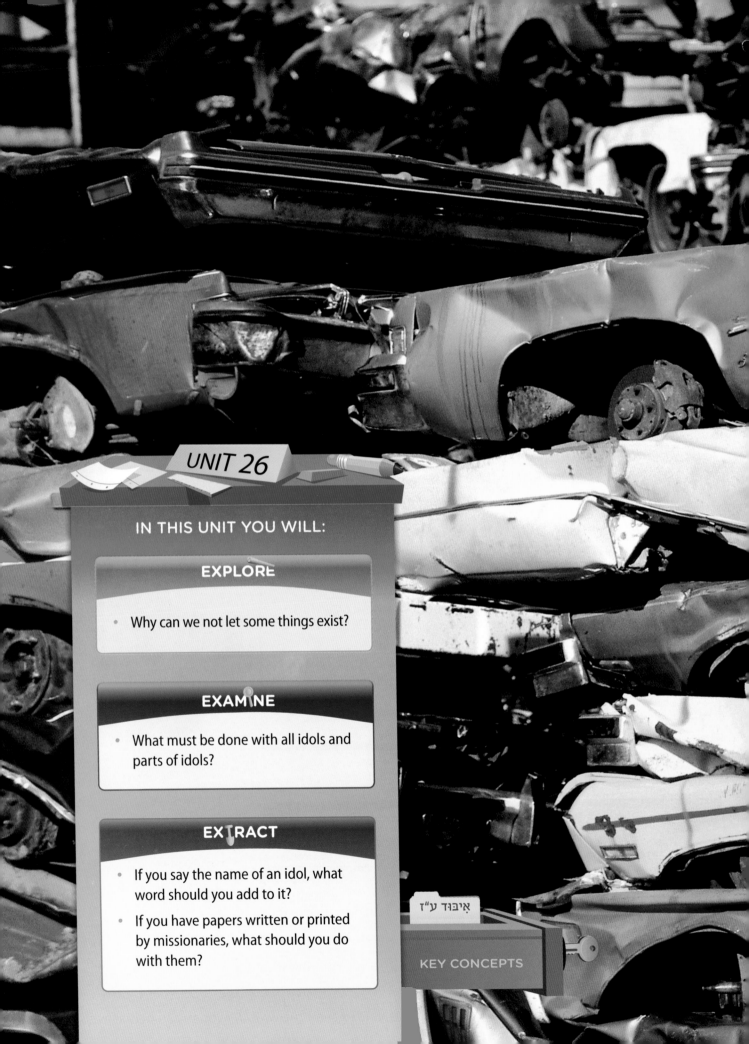

UNIT 26

IN THIS UNIT YOU WILL:

EXPLORE

- Why can we not let some things exist?

EXAMINE

- What must be done with all idols and parts of idols?

EXTRACT

- If you say the name of an idol, what word should you add to it?
- If you have papers written or printed by missionaries, what should you do with them?

אִיבּוּד ע"ז

KEY CONCEPTS

Book: Madda, Section: Idol Worship
סֵפֶר מַדָּע הִלְכוֹת עֲבוֹדָה זָרָה

אִיבּוּד עֲבוֹדָה זָרָה
DESTROYING AVODAH ZARAH
מִצְוָה אַחַת

Some dangerous things in this world can be fixed, and changed to become good. Some things can be ignored, and if you don't bother them, they won't bother you. And **some things must be crushed, or they will crush you.**

Worthless Lumps

Terach, *Avraham Avinu's* father, made idols and sold them. One time, Terach had to leave, so he put Avraham in charge of the store while he was away. Avraham took a hammer and smashed all of the idols except for the biggest one, and then put the hammer in the hand of the only idol that was not smashed.

When Terach came back and saw all of his idols in pieces, he was horrified. "Who did this?" he cried. Avraham answered calmly, "These idols just got into a fight over some food that was given to them. The biggest one took this hammer and smashed all the others to pieces."

"Are you making fun of me?" asked Terach. "The idols can't move like that! They have no minds of their own!" Avraham smiled. "If you yourself say that the idols don't have any powers, why are you serving them?"[1]

HISTORY

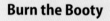

Burn the Booty

After Shimon and Levi killed all the men of Shechem, Yaakov told them to make sure that no objects or tools of *avodah zarah* were with the spoils that they took from the city.[2]

The Mitzvah

The unit of destroying *avodah zarah* has one mitzvah. You must completely destroy any *avodah zarah*, and anything used to serve an *avodah zarah*.

MITZVAH
51

לְאַבֵּד עֲבוֹדָה זָרָה וּמְשַׁמְשֶׁיהָ

Destroying *avodah zarah* and anything used to serve it

אַבֵּד תְּאַבְּדוּן אֶת כָּל הַמְּקֹמוֹת אֲשֶׁר עָבְדוּ שָׁם הַגּוֹיִם אֲשֶׁר אַתֶּם יֹרְשִׁים אֹתָם אֶת אֱלֹהֵיהֶם עַל הֶהָרִים הָרָמִים וְעַל הַגְּבָעוֹת וְתַחַת כָּל עֵץ רַעֲנָן

(דברים יב, ב)

You shall destroy completely all the places where the nations that you are driving away worshipped their gods: on the high mountains and on the hills, and under every leafy tree.

Destroy *avodah zarah* and anything used to serve *avodah zarah*.

ALL PEOPLE | ALL PLACES | ALL TIMES

Mitzvah Messages

Their Problem is Our Problem Too

When you look around the city you live in, at the people around you, and even at yourself, you will see many actions, behaviors, or objects that can hurt people or lead them to do *aveiros*. Sometimes, you can change the behavior or object so that it won't bother anyone. For example, you can help your friend stop a bad habit, or you can throw out a broken glass bottle so that no one gets hurt from it.

Sometimes, if something isn't so terrible, and you can't do anything to change it, you can just ignore the bad object or behavior. For example, if you know that someone much older than you always drops wrappers on the floor, and you know for sure that this person would not listen to what you say, you can ignore the disrespectful behavior.

Some things are so destructive and harmful that they **must** be destroyed before they can really hurt someone. If you knew that someone was putting poison into your family's water, would you just ignore them? *Avodah zarah* is just as terrible as poison that can kill you, and must be destroyed before it can harm you or anyone.

Even if you are not the one who is serving the *avodah zarah*, it can still hurt other people, so the Torah gives you a mitzvah to destroy it completely.[3]

 CHECKPOINT Why do you have to destroy *avodah zarah* even if you are not serving it?

Details   EXAM**I**NE

Destroying *Avodah Zarah*

When *B'nei Yisrael* are in control of Eretz Yisrael and can make the laws, we are commanded to find and destroy all *avodah zarah* from Eretz Yisrael. Outside of Eretz Yisrael, or even in Eretz Yisrael when there is no Jewish government, you do not have to **search** for idols to destroy them, but you have to destroy any idol that you come across.[4]

Hashem also gave us a mitzvah to destroy everything that has to do with serving *avodah zarah*. This includes anything used to worship the idols, the utensils used in their worship, and even the buildings in which they are worshipped.[5]

How to Destroy it
The destruction should be done quickly, so that there is nothing left from the idol that was worshipped, or from the objects used for the idol.[6] Idols of wood and *asheirah* trees must be burned, and the ashes should be scattered in any way that totally gets rid of them.[7]

Idols made from other materials like stone, gold, silver, or anything else, can be destroyed in any way.[8] Once they have been destroyed, you must grind them and then scatter the dust to the wind or into water, so that you cannot benefit from it at all.[9]

 CHECKPOINT How must idols be destroyed?

Unusable

A lulav from an *asheirah* tree or from an *Ir Hanidachas* is not allowed to be used for the mitzvah of *lulav*. Since the *lulav* or *shofar* have to be burned, the Torah considers it as if it is **already** burned.

Ashes do not have the required size for a *kosher lulav*![11]

STORY

Let Him Burn

King Nevuchadnetzar of Bavel had a Jewish advisor, Daniel, whom he respected very much. Sometimes, King Nevuchadnetzar would even bow down to Daniel as if he were a god.

One day, Nevuchadnetzar decided to test the three Jewish servants in his palace – Chananyah, Mishael and Azaryah. He made them choose between bowing down to an idol or being thrown into a fiery furnace. They did the right thing and refused to bow down to the *avodah zarah*. Outraged, Nevuchadnetzar threw them into the fire. Everyone was invited to watch them burn.

Daniel ran away because he was afraid that Nevuchadnetzar might also throw him into the furnace. Even if Hashem would save Chananyah, Mishael and Azaryah, Hashem might not save him, because Hashem might be happy to let an idol of a king burn.[12]

SELECTED HALACHOS

- You should use words to destroy the name of an *avodah zarah* by using an embarrassing name for it instead of the real name.[13] For example, if a building for idol worship was called *Beis Galya* - "the high place," you should call it "*Beis Karya*- "the low place."[14]

- If you destroy *avodah zarah* in Eretz Yisrael you should say a *brachah* just as you say a *brachah* before performing most mitzvos![15] This *brachah* is: "אֲשֶׁר קִדְּשָׁנוּ בְּמִצְוֹתָיו וְצִוָּנוּ לַעֲקֹר עֲבוֹדָה זָרָה מֵאַרְצֵינוּ..."

EXTEND YOUR KNOWLEDGE

Because They Agreed

There is a *halachah* that you are not able to make someone else's property forbidden to him. Usually, if you would worship something as an *avodah zarah*, then that object would have to be destroyed. However, if that object belongs to someone else, it would not have to be destroyed. Since you did not have permission from the owner to serve it, you cannot make it *assur*.

This *halachah* raises a question. When *B'nei Yisrael* went into Eretz Yisrael, Hashem told them that they had to destroy all of the trees that the *Canaanim* had worshipped. But why did the trees have to be destroyed? Since Eretz Yisrael belonged to the *B'nei Yisrael* from when Hashem promised it to Avraham, the trees never belonged to the *Canaanim*, they always belonged to *B'nei Yisrael*! Why did they need to be destroyed?

The *Gemara* explains that when *B'nei Yisrael* worshipped the *Egel Hazahav* in the *midbar*, they showed that they really agreed with worshipping *avodah zarah*. Because of this, when the *Canaanim* worshipped the trees in Eretz Yisrael that belonged to *B'nei Yisrael*, it was as if they were doing the *avodah zarah* with the permission of *B'nei Yisrael*.

This is why the *avodah zarah* needed to be destroyed.[16]

Live the Mitzvah

EXTRACT

Don't Just Stand There

If you saw your classmates making fun of someone in your class, would you stand by and let them do it? Would you shrug and think that it is not your business, as long as you're not the one making fun of this person? The person's feelings are being hurt terribly, and you cannot allow that to happen! In situations like this, you have to stand up and put an end to the meanness that you see happening around you.

 CHECKPOINT How can you get rid of a hurtful behavior in your everyday life?

What Else Comes From This? EXTRACT

It's a Disgrace!

Destroying *avodah zarah* is so important that you are allowed and even supposed to destroy words of Torah if they are used for an *avodah zarah*! Therefore, if missionaries use the words of Torah in their pamphlets, you must burn the papers. It's not enough to bury them, for this shames the holy words that are written there, therefore it should be burned.[17]

 CHECKPOINT What should you do with a missionary's pamphlets if you get them?

A STORY

The Real Diamond

A very poor, childless Jew named R' Yitzchak once found a rare diamond. The local bishop heard about it, and offered to buy it for a huge amount of money. When R' Yitzchak found out that the bishop wanted to use the diamonds to decorate a cross, he refused to sell it.

The bishop wouldn't give up and tricked R' Yitzchak into getting on a boat. The bishop and his men tried to force him to sell it, but R' Yitzchak threw it into the sea instead.

For this selfless act, R' Yitzchak was rewarded with the birth of a son the following year. This child grew up to be the famous Rashi (R' Shlomo Yitzchaki – the son of Yitzchak) who was a true diamond, lighting up the world with his brilliance![18]

UNIT
26

HISTORY

Nechushtan

While the Jews were still in the desert, they spoke against Hashem and Moshe. This made Hashem very angry and He sent poisonous snakes to warn them to do *teshuvah*. Most of *B'nei Yisrael* listened to the warning and immediately did *teshuvah*. For the ones who had not done *teshuvah* yet, Hashem told Moshe to make an image of a poisonous snake and put it on a pole. When those who had been poisoned by the snakes looked up at this snake, they would raise their eyes to *shamayim*, which would help them do *teshuvah* so that they could be cured.

Many years after entering Eretz Yisrael, the *B'nei Yisrael* began to worship the copper snake, calling it "*Nechushtan*" from the word *nachash* - snake. To stop this *avodah zarah*, *Chizkiyahu Hamelech* destroyed the snake.[19]

ENDNOTES:

14. ע"ז מו, א

15. חדא"ג מהרש"א ברכות נז, ב ד"ה הרואה

16. ע"ז נג, נ, ועי' שו"ת נודע ביהודה תניינא יו"ד סי' קמ"ח

17. שו"ת אגרות משה יו"ד ח"ב סי' קל"ז

18. שלשלת הקבלה ע' קיא

19. במדבר כא, ד-ט, מלכים ב' יח, ד

8. סה"מ עשה קפ"ה

9. קרית ספר (למבי"ט) הל' ע"ז פ"ח, וראה רמב"ם שם, שו"ע הרב או"ח סי' תמ"ה קו"א ב'

10. שמות לב, כ

11. סוכה לא, ב וברש"י ד"ה באשרה דמשה

12. סנהדרין צג, א

13. שו"ע יו"ד סי' קמ"ו סט"ו

1. בראשית רבה לח, יג

2. וישלח לה, ב-ד וברש"י. ועי' רמב"ן שם

3. חינוך מצוה תל"ו

4. רמב"ם הל' ע"ז פ"ז ה"א

5. רמב"ם הל' ע"ז פ"ז ה"ב. סה"מ עשה קפ"ה

6. חינוך מצוה תל"ו

7. שו"ע הרב או"ח סי' תמ"ה קו"א ב'

The mess in here is unbelievable! What are you going to do with all that junk? **If you can't use it, don't keep it!**

UNIT 27

IN THIS UNIT YOU WILL:

EXPLORE

- Why should you get rid of something that has no use?

EXAMINE

- What objects of *avodah zarah* are you not allowed to get any benefit from?
- What is the right way to cancel any *avodah zarah*?

EXTRACT

- If you want to protect your mind from being filled with harmful thoughts and ideas, what should you avoid?
- If you want to fill your mind with treasures, what should you do?

אָסוּר בַּהֲנָאָה

KEY CONCEPTS

Book: Madda, Section: Idol Worship
סֵפֶר מַדָּע הִלְכוֹת עֲבוֹדָה זָרָה

שֶׁלֹּא לֵיהָנוֹת מֵעֲבוֹדָה זָרָה
NOT BENEFITING FROM AVODAH ZARAH
שְׁתֵּי מִצְווֹת

In the unit of not benefitting from *avodah zarah* there are two mitzvos.

1. Do not benefit from an *avodah zarah*.

2. Do not benefit from the decorations of an *avodah zarah*.

DID YOU KNOW?

An Irresistible Urge

During the times of the second *Beis Hamikdash*, when *Ezra Hasofer* was the leader, the Jewish people gathered together and cried out to Hashem. They begged Hashem to take away the *yetzer hara* to serve *avodah zarah*! They knew that *avodah zarah* was the reason why the first *Beis Hamikdash* was destroyed, and they didn't want the same thing to happen again.

A note fell from Heaven with the word "true" on it. Hashem had agreed to their plan.

After all the leaders fasted and *davened* for three days, the image of a fiery lion came out from the *Kodesh Hakadashim*. *Zecharia Hanavi* told them "this is the *yetzer hara* of *avodah zarah*!" These *tzaddikim* were able to destroy the *yetzer hara* so that it would never bother people again.

Thankfully, we don't understand the urge for *avodah zarah* nowadays. But there are other silly things that we love, like money. In the times of the *Beis Hamikdash*, they wanted *avodah zarah* the same way we want money![1]

MITZVAH
52

שֶׁלֹּא לֵיהָנוֹת בַּעֲבוֹדַת כּוֹכָבִים וּמַשְׁמְשֶׁיהָ

Not benefitting from *avodah zarah* or something used to serve it

וְלֹא תָבִיא תוֹעֵבָה אֶל בֵּיתֶךָ וְהָיִיתָ חֵרֶם כָּמֹהוּ
שַׁקֵּץ תְּשַׁקְּצֶנּוּ וְתַעֵב תְּתַעֲבֶנּוּ כִּי חֵרֶם הוּא
(דברים ז, כו)

Do not bring any offensive idol into your house, for you may become just like it. Shun it completely and consider it absolutely offensive, for it is taboo.

Do not keep *avodah zarah* in order to have benefit from it in any way.

| ALL PEOPLE | ALL PLACES | ALL TIMES | DOUBLE *MALKUS* |

MITZVAH 53

שֶׁלֹּא לֵיהָנוֹת מִצִּיפּוּיֵי עֲבוֹדָה זָרָה

Not benefitting from the ornaments of *avodah zarah*

פְּסִילֵי אֱלֹהֵיהֶם תִּשְׂרְפוּן בָּאֵשׁ **לֹא תַחְמֹד כֶּסֶף וְזָהָב עֲלֵיהֶם וְלָקַחְתָּ** לָךְ פֶּן תִּוָּקֵשׁ בּוֹ כִּי תוֹעֲבַת ה' אֱלֹקֶיךָ הוּא

(דברים ז, כה)

You must burn their idolatrous statues in fire. **Do not desire the gold and silver on these statues** and take it for yourselves lest it bring you into a trap, for it is offensive to Hashem your G-d.

Do not benefit from the decorations of *avodah zarah*.

ALL PEOPLE · ALL PLACES · ALL TIMES · *MALKUS*

Mitzvah Messages

EXPLORE

Clear Them Out

Like many other mitzvos of *avodah zarah*, the reason for this mitzvah is so that we will not *chas veshalom* come to worship idols.[2]

When we have no use for something, it should be thrown out and not kept around. Hashem gave us a special mitzvah not to have any benefit from *avodah zarah*. Since we have no use for it, we will not keep it in our home, and if it's not in our home, we won't serve it![3]

CHECKPOINT Why do you have to get rid of any objects of *avodah zarah* even if you aren't using them?

Cheeky Little Critters

Hamsters have small flaps in their cheeks, called pouches, which allow them to store food. A normal hamster will pouch any food he finds and bury it in a safe place. The collecting and saving is so much in the nature of the hamster that a hamster in Hebrew is called אוֹגֵר, which stems from לֶאֱגוֹר - to collect.

Hamsters don't know when to stop collecting and saving food, so they just keep collecting food and hide much more than they actually need. Hamsters store so much food that farmers around the world used to dig up wild hamster burrows to use the food to feed the farm animals!

Humans are much smarter than this! If you have no need for something, give it away or throw it out!

Details

Not Benefitting From *Avodah Zarah*

Idols, and any items used to worship idols, are אָסוּר בְּהַנָאָה - you are not allowed to get any benefit from them. This includes anything that was used to prepare the *avodah zarah*, any jewelry or decorations that were put on the *avodah zarah*, or even a piece of a present that was given to the *avodah zarah*.[5]

When Does It Become *Assur B'hana'ah*?

Idols of non-Jews become *assur b'hana'ah* as soon as they are made, even if they are not actually served. An idol that is made by a Jewish person only becomes *assur b'hana'ah* once it is worshipped.

The **utensils** of *avodah zarah* (the special shovels, cups, or other objects used to serve the idol), become *assur b'hana'ah* only after they are used, no matter who made them, Jew or non-Jew.[6]

Presents given to an *avodah zarah* also become forbidden only after they are given to the idol. Before they are actually given to the idol, you are allowed to use them and definitely get benefit from them, even if they were supposed to be given to the *avodah zarah*.[7]

Any present that you find inside a building that is used for *avodah zarah* is forbidden, even if the present was not yet given. Just by being in the building, it is like the present was already given to the idol, and you can never get benefit from something that was already given to an *avodah zarah*.[8]

The Punishment

Someone who benefits from an *avodah zarah* gets punished with two sets of *malkus*, because there are actually **two** separate *aveiros*:

1. **Bringing** *avodah zarah* into your home. This is learned from the words of the *passuk* "לֹא תָבִיא תוֹעֵבָה אֶל בֵּיתֶךָ – Do not bring any idol into your house," which teaches you not to bring any kind of *avodah zarah* into your home, even if you don't benefit from it.

2. **Actually benefitting** from *avodah zarah*, which we learn from this mitzvah.

No *malkus* is given if you only did the first part of the *aveirah*, but not the second. However, if you do both *aveiros*, you would get two sets of *malkus*.[9]

Can You Ever Benefit From *Avodah Zarah*?

You **are allowed** to benefit from an *avodah zarah* if the person who made the *avodah zarah* doesn't believe in it anymore and cancels it. As proof that this person doesn't believe in the idol anymore, the *avodah zarah* must be smashed or broken.[10] If the person just says that he wants to smash the idol, that is enough to cancel it,[11] and you are allowed to benefit from the *avodah zarah* and its objects. However, only **non-Jews** can cancel an *avodah zarah*.

If the idol was made or owned by a **Jew**, it remains אָסוּר בַּהֲנָאָה forever and must be buried after it is destroyed.[12]

Can **every** part of the *avodah zarah* be cancelled?

It depends: **presents** given to an *avodah zarah* can **never** be cancelled and have to be destroyed. The *avodah zarah* itself **can** be cancelled. The **jewelry** or other objects that were used for the *avodah zarah* can also be cancelled and used.

If only the jewelry or objects were cancelled, but not the actual idol, then the idol itself is still forbidden, but you can use the jewelry.

The Jewelry of an *Avodah Zarah*

The first mitzvah that forbids benefiting from *avodah zarah* already includes that you are not allowed to get benefit from the jewelry of the *avodah zarah*.

Why does the Torah need a separate mitzvah to teach you that you are not allowed to benefit from the **jewelry** of *avodah zarah*?

The second mitzvah teaches us about a different kind of *avodah zarah* that is not a statue or object that someone made. Sometimes, people served the mountains, trees, plants, animals or other natural objects on earth as a god. They would put all kinds of decorations and jewelry on whatever they were serving to show how special it was to them. Since they have no power to make such things *assur*, you are allowed to benefit from the things themselves (e.g. to use rocks from the mountains), but you cannot benefit from the jewelry and decorations that were put onto the *avodah zarah*.

If a plant was planted specifically so that it would be served as an *avodah zarah*, you must destroy it and you can not benefit from it at all.

CHECKPOINT From what kind of object are you not allowed to benefit?

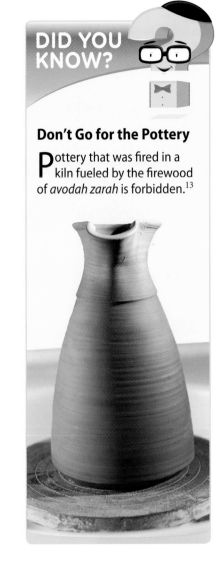

DISCOVERY

Compulsive Hoarding

There is a mental sickness where people collect and save thousands of objects without using or throwing them away. This is called hoarding. Some people hoard huge amounts of junk such as bottle caps, old records and even lint. Many hoarders think about how guilty they will feel if they need something that was thrown out, so they never throw anything away.

Having so much clutter can even kill a person! A man was once crushed under his own stuff, and a woman once died when firefighters were blocked by her piles and couldn't reach her in time to save her.

SELECTED HALACHOS

- You are allowed to benefit from a statue that is only made for people to enjoy and to look at, and not for *avodah zarah*.[14]

- If you sell an *avodah zarah*, its jewelry, or any of the presents that were given to it, you are not allowed to benefit from the money at all. If even a little bit of the money gets mixed up with other money, all of the money becomes forbidden, and you can not use any of it.[15]

- You are not allowed to purposely listen to the music used for *avodah zarah*, look at the beautiful decorations, or smell the beautiful smell of the spices and flowers that were given as presents.[16]

- You are not allowed to sit in the shade or have other benefit from trees that are planted in front of *avodah zarah*.[17]

- You are not allowed to benefit from the ashes of a burnt *avodah zarah*.[18]

EXTEND YOUR KNOWLEDGE

The *Egel Hazahav*

To destroy the *avodah zarah* of a Jew, it does not need to be completely destroyed, rather it can be buried.[19]

If so, why did Moshe crush and scatter the *Egel Hazahav*? Wasn't it an idol that was made by Jewish people that could have just been buried!

There are two explanations for this.

1. The *Egel Hazahav* was an embarrassment to the *B'nei Yisrael*, so Moshe wanted to destroy it completely so that it would not be remembered.

2. Moshe wanted to find out who had actually served the *Egel Hazahav* as an *avodah zarah*. Therefore, he made a mixture from the dust of the *Egel Hazahav*, and gave it to everyone to drink. Those who had done the *aveirah* died after drinking the mixture.[20]

Trash or Treasure

The space in your mind is precious and special. You wouldn't want to fill it with garbage that you have no use for, would you? Right now you might feel that it's really important to memorize all the songs from the new CD. Do you really think that they will be useful to you in twenty years? Of course not! It will just clutter your mind and make it harder for you to think straight and understand things properly.

What **will** really be useful to you is all the Torah knowledge that you gained so that you will have the tools you need to live a life filled with mitzvos.

Especially today, when there is so much information available, it os very important that you don't let useless junk into your mind!

 CHECKPOINT   How can you keep your mind clear and sharp?

DID YOU KNOW?

Giving it the Cold Shoulder

On a cold day, you may not warm yourself by the fire of a burning *avodah zarah*![21]

UNIT
27

ENDNOTES:

1. יומא סט, ב וברש"י שם
2. בכור שור דברים ז, כה
3. בכור שור דברים ז, כה
4. חינוך מצוה תכ"ט
5. רמב"ם הל' ע"ז פ"ז ה"ב
6. רמב"ם הל' ע"ז פ"ז ה"ד
7. רמב"ם הל' ע"ז פ"ז הט"ו
8. כס"מ הל' ע"ז פ"ז הט"ז

9. חינוך מצוה תכ"ט
10. רמב"ם הל' ע"ז פ"ח ה"ח-י'
11. רמ"א יו"ד סי' קמ"ו ס"ז, ובש"ך ס"ק ח'
12. רמב"ם הל' ע"ז פ"ח ה"ט
13. שו"ע יו"ד סי' קמ"ב ס"ה
14. רמב"ם הל' ע"ז פ"ז ה"ו
15. רמב"ם הל' ע"ז פ"ז ה"ט
16. שו"ע יו"ד סי' קמ"ב סט"ו ובש"ך

ס"ק ל"ב
17. שו"ע יו"ד סי' קמ"ב סי"ג, ט"ז ס"ק י"ח, ורש"ך ס"ק כ"ט
18. רמב"ם הל' ע"ז פ"ז ה"י
19. רמב"ם הל' ע"ז פ"ח ה"ט
20. תורת חיים (שור) ע"ז נב, א ד"ה מנין
21. ט"ז יו"ד סי' קמ"ב ס"ק ג'

You can't get that tune out of your head.

It makes you think about things you really
don't want to be thinking about.
You wish you hadn't bought that CD.
Now it's all that you can think about!

UNIT 28

IN THIS UNIT YOU WILL:

EXPLORE

- Why do you have to be careful with
  who your neighbors are?

EXAMINE

- What are the three mitzvos that teach
  you how you should act with people who
  serve *avodah zarah*?
- What are the ways you should keep yourself
  away from people who serve *avodah zarah*?

EXTRACT

- If someone who serves idols wants to buy
  land in Eretz Yisrael, what should you do?
- If you are invited to join a non-Jewish
  party that is all about non-Jewish
  ideas, what should you do?

שְׁמִירַת עֵינַיִם
לֹא תְחָנֵם

KEY CONCEPTS

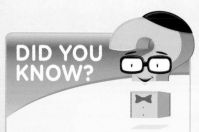

DID YOU KNOW?

Double Disadvantage

If a field in Eretz Yisrael is sold to a person who serves *avodah zarah*, there are two issues. Firstly, we are giving a non-Jew ownership of land in Eretz Yisrael. Secondly, there will be no *ma'aser* coming from that field, since a non-Jew doesn't give *ma'aser*.[1]

HISTORY

Fair Treatment

Before Yehoshua captured Eretz Yisrael from the Canaanim, he gave each of the seven nations who lived there three choices: Either they could stay in Eretz Yisrael and agree to keep the *Sheva Mitzvos B'nei Noach,* or they could leave Eretz Yisrael completely, or they could stay, fight, and be killed.

The *Girgashim* were the only nation to leave peacefully, and Hashem rewarded them by giving them a beautiful new land - Africa. The other six nations chose to fight, and, with Hashem's help, were completely destroyed.[2]

The Mitzvos

EXAMINE

The unit of staying away from people who serve *avodah zarah* has three mitzvos.

1. Do not make a peace treaty with a non-Jewish person or nation who serves *avodah zarah*.

2. Do not show kindness or be gracious to non-Jews who serve *avodah zarah*.

3. Do not allow a non-Jew who serves *avodah zarah* to live in Eretz Yisrael.

MITZVAH 54

שֶׁלֹּא לִכְרוֹת בְּרִית לְעוֹבְדֵי עֲבוֹדָה זָרָה

Not making a treaty with non-Jews who serve *avodah zarah*

וּנְתָנָם ה' אֱלֹקֶיךָ לְפָנֶיךָ וְהִכִּיתָם הַחֲרֵם תַּחֲרִים אֹתָם לֹא תִכְרֹת לָהֶם בְּרִית וְלֹא תְחָנֵּם (דברים ז, ב)

When Hashem your G-d gives them to you, and you defeat them, you must completely destroy them. **Do not make any treaty with them** nor show them any favor.

Do not make a peace treaty with a non-Jewish nation who serves *avodah zarah*.

ALL PEOPLE | ALL PLACES | WHEN JEWS RULE ERETZ YISRAEL | NO PUNISHMENT

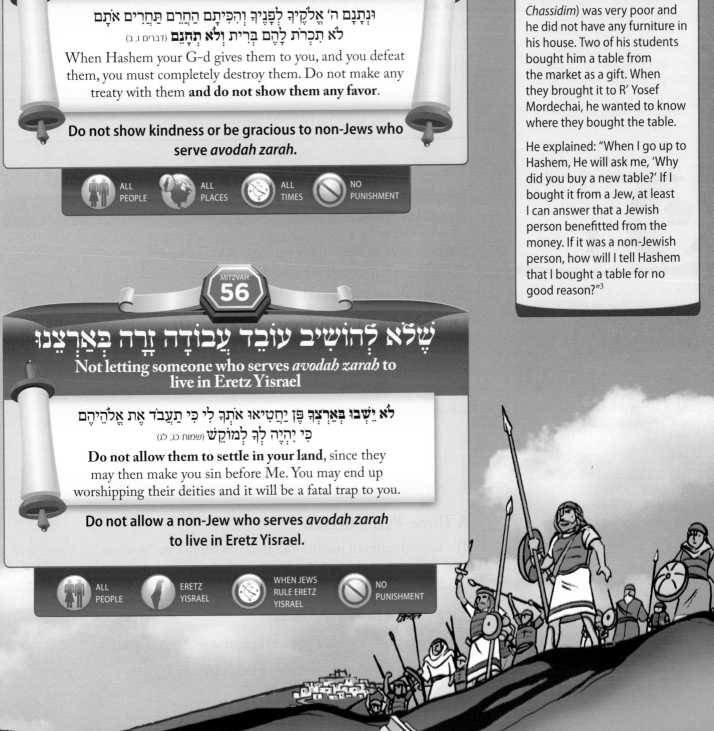

MITZVAH 55

שֶׁלֹּא לָחֹן עַל עוֹבְדֵי עֲבוֹדָה זָרָה
Not being gracious to people who serve *avodah zarah*

וּנְתָנָם ה' אֱלֹקֶיךָ לְפָנֶיךָ וְהִכִּיתָם הַחֲרֵם תַּחֲרִים אֹתָם
לֹא תִכְרֹת לָהֶם בְּרִית **וְלֹא תְחָנֵּם** (דברים ז, ב)

When Hashem your G-d gives them to you, and you defeat
them, you must completely destroy them. Do not make any
treaty with them **and do not show them any favor**.

**Do not show kindness or be gracious to non-Jews who
serve *avodah zarah*.**

| ALL PEOPLE | ALL PLACES | ALL TIMES | NO PUNISHMENT |

MITZVAH 56

שֶׁלֹּא לְהוֹשִׁיב עוֹבֵד עֲבוֹדָה זָרָה בְּאַרְצֵנוּ
Not letting someone who serves *avodah zarah* to
live in Eretz Yisrael

לֹא יֵשְׁבוּ בְּאַרְצְךָ פֶּן יַחֲטִיאוּ אֹתְךָ לִי כִּי תַעֲבֹד אֶת אֱלֹהֵיהֶם
כִּי יִהְיֶה לְךָ לְמוֹקֵשׁ (שמות כג, לג)

Do not allow them to settle in your land, since they
may then make you sin before Me. You may end up
worshipping their deities and it will be a fatal trap to you.

**Do not allow a non-Jew who serves *avodah zarah*
to live in Eretz Yisrael.**

| ALL PEOPLE | ERETZ YISRAEL | WHEN JEWS RULE ERETZ YISRAEL | NO PUNISHMENT |

STORY

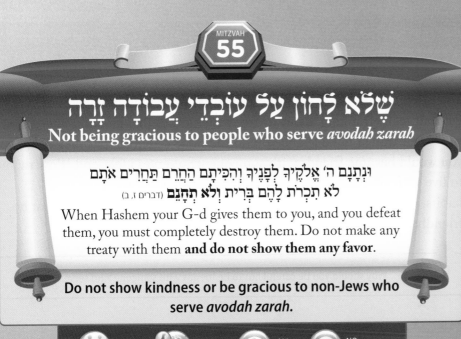

Buy Jewish

R' Yosef Mordechai Mordkofsky of Meichat (a *Rosh Yeshivah* of the *Slonimer Chassidim*) was very poor and he did not have any furniture in his house. Two of his students bought him a table from the market as a gift. When they brought it to R' Yosef Mordechai, he wanted to know where they bought the table.

He explained: "When I go up to Hashem, He will ask me, 'Why did you buy a new table?' If I bought it from a Jew, at least I can answer that a Jewish person benefitted from the money. If it was a non-Jewish person, how will I tell Hashem that I bought a table for no good reason?"[3]

Keep Your Distance

You often act like other people, especially your friends and neighbors, without really thinking about it. You wear clothes that look like theirs, you copy their way of talking, and you do the same activities that they do. If you would become friends with someone who serves idols, and allow them to live with you, then there is a good chance that you will pick up their habits, which might cause you to do an *aveirah*. Therefore, you cannot be friendly towards them, and definitely not let them live in your land.[5]

 CHECKPOINT Why should you be careful not to be friends with someone who serves idols?

Details   EXAMINE

Hashem gave us these three mitzvos to make sure that we always have a "fence" between us and the non-Jewish way of life. These three mitzvos and their details are explained below.

Don't Make a Peace Treaty with Non-Jews who Serve Idols

You cannot make a peace treaty with non-Jews who serve idols, since you are supposed to destroy them in war. The only way you **can** make a peace treaty with a nation that worships *avodah zarah* is if they accept the following three conditions:

1. They will keep the *Sheva Mitzvos B'nei Noach*.
2. They will pay tax to the Jewish government.
3. No one from their nation will be in a position of authority.[6]

A Three-Part Mitzvah

The second mitzvah teaches you that you cannot be "gracious" to a non-Jew who serves *avodah zarah*. There are really three ways that you can do this one mitzvah, because the word "תְחָנֵּם" can be translated in three different ways.[7]

לֹא תִתֵּן לָהֶם חֵן – Do not **like** them.

לֹא תִתֵּן לָהֶם חֲנָיּ' בְּקַרְקַע – Do not let them **rest** in Eretz Yisrael.

לֹא תִתֵּן לָהֶם מַתְּנַת חִנָּם – Do not give them a **free** gift.

1. Do not be Gracious to Idol Worshippers

You are not allowed to show mercy to someone who serves idols when you are fighting them in war, and you are not allowed to show mercy to them in everyday life. If someone who serves idols is in danger, you are not allowed to save him. Of course, you cannot actually kill him.[8] All this only applied to the *avodah zarah*-believeing nations in the time of the *Beis Hamikdash*, who did not believe in a G-d Who created the world and took the Jews out of Mitzrayim to give them the Torah.[9]

You are not allowed to compliment or show that you like the actions, possessions or appearance of someone who serves *avodah zarah*.[10]

2. Do not Let an Idol Worshipper Live in Eretz Yisrael.

You are not allowed to sell a house in Eretz Yisrael to a non-Jew who serves *avodah zarah*. You are allowed to rent houses to them to be used to store objects, but you cannot rent them a house to live in, because they might bring idols inside Jewish property.[11] *Miderabanan*, there is an extra rule that you cannot rent a field in Eretz Yisrael to a non-Jew who serves *avodah zarah*.[12]

3. No Presents

You are not allowed to give free gifts to a stranger who serves *avodah zarah*. However, if you know the person, then you are allowed to give him a present.[113]

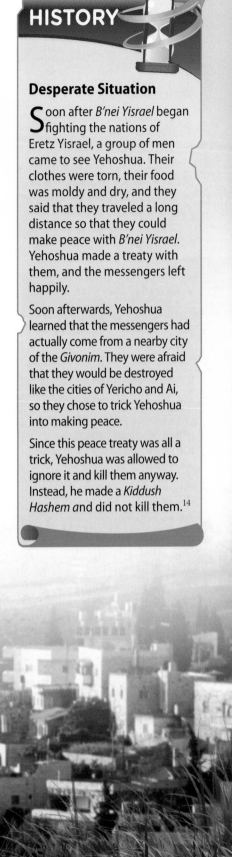

HISTORY

Desperate Situation

Soon after *B'nei Yisrael* began fighting the nations of Eretz Yisrael, a group of men came to see Yehoshua. Their clothes were torn, their food was moldy and dry, and they said that they traveled a long distance so that they could make peace with *B'nei Yisrael*. Yehoshua made a treaty with them, and the messengers left happily.

Soon afterwards, Yehoshua learned that the messengers had actually come from a nearby city of the *Givonim*. They were afraid that they would be destroyed like the cities of Yericho and Ai, so they chose to trick Yehoshua into making peace.

Since this peace treaty was all a trick, Yehoshua was allowed to ignore it and kill them anyway. Instead, he made a *Kiddush Hashem* and did not kill them.[14]

DID YOU KNOW?

Watch and Learn

People pick up habits from the other people they are with. Lot welcomed the *malachim* who visited him in Sedom because he had picked up that *middah* from living in Avraham's house.[15]

OUR SAGES SAY...

Expect No Good Returns

When *Avraham Avinu* made a peace treaty with Avimelech, the king of the *Plishtim*, he sent Avimelech seven lambs.

Hashem told Avraham, "For those seven lambs, the Jews will be in Mitzrayim for seven generations. For those seven lambs, Avimelech's descendants will kill seven *tzaddikim* from your descendants. For those seven lambs, your descendants' seven *Mishkanos* will be destroyed. For those seven lambs, My *Aron Hakodesh* will be in *Pelishti* territory seven months!"[16]

Drive Them Out of the Land

The third mitzvah teaches us that when Jews rule Eretz Yisrael, all non-Jews who serve *avodah zarah* and live in Eretz Yisrael must be driven out. But, if they accept the *Sheva Mitzvos B'nei Noach*, they are allowed to live in Eretz Yisrael.[17]

CHECKPOINT What are forbidden actions that show graciousness to a non-Jew who serves idols?

SELECTED HALACHOS

- Wherever there is a Jewish neighborhood (even outside Eretz Yisrael), there are not allowed to be more than two idol worshippers renting houses. However, one or two idol worshippers are allowed.[18]

- These days, you are allowed to rent houses to non-Jews, since they usually do not serve *avodah zarah*.[19]

- You may compliment how a non-Jew looks, if you want to praise Hashem for His beautiful creations.[20]

- You are allowed to give charity to poor non-Jews, greet them, visit their sick, bury their dead and comfort their mourners, so as not to cause friction.[21]

EXTEND YOUR KNOWLEDGE

Eretz Yisrael for the Jews

The *Chachamim* do not allow us to ask a non-Jew to do something on *Shabbos* which a Jew is not allowed to do. There is one exception to this rule. If a non-Jew in Eretz Yisrael wants to sell his or her house to a Jew, the Jew may ask the non-Jew to write and sign the contract on *Shabbos*, if necessary. Because it is so important to keep all of Eretz Yisrael in Jewish hands, the Rabbis permitted us to ask the non-Jew to write on *Shabbos*![22]

Safed

Tel Aviv Yafo

Jerusalem

Chevron

Be'er Sheva

NEGEV DESERT

Guard Your Eyes

Even though there are not so many people who really serve *avodah zarah* nowadays, there are still many negative influences which you should stay away from, so that you can live a Torah life. These include TV, internet and non-Jewish music. These things mostly talk about or show you things that are not positive and are nothing like our Jewish way of life.

Because they can be so much fun to watch and listen to, it's easy for the *yetzer hara* to convince us that it's not so bad. By staying away from them, we prevent ourselves from copying the dress, manners, and speech of actors and singers who represent the opposite of Jewish values.

BIOGRAPHY

R' Menachem Mendel of Rimanov
תק״ה - תקע״ה (1815 – 1745)

R' Menachem Mendel Turom of Rimanov was one of the top three disciples of R' Elimelech of Lizhensk. He was a great Chasidic leader in Poland. He wrote two seforim: Divrei Menachem and Menachem Tzion. He was known for being strong-minded and firm in his opinions and would not be swayed from doing what was right. He passed away on the 19th of Iyar.

CHECKPOINT Why should you hang around people who have good *middos* and do many mitzvos?

STORY

Non-Jewish Believer

A Polish noblewoman rushed to R' Menachem Mendel of Rimanov to ask him to *daven* for her only son, who was extremely sick. He asked her if she had come to him because she thought he could do magic. "No," she replied, "but I know that you are closer to G-d than most people are, and that is why your prayers are listened to."

"In that case," said the Rebbe, "I shall pray for the child." For three hours, from nine o'clock in the morning until twelve o'clock midday, the *tzaddik* stood, praying so much for the child, that beads of sweat stood out on his face.

The mother went home, and was told that at twelve o'clock, her child had woken up and asked for water. The child grew up to be the famous poet and freedom fighter Count Miechislav Dravski, who enjoyed a warm relationship with the Jews.[23]

UNIT 28

ENDNOTES:

‏16. בראשית רבה נד, ד
‏17. רמב״ם הל׳ ע״ז פ״י ה״ו.
‏18. שו״ע יו״ד סי׳ קנ״א ס״ט. ש״ך ס״ק ט״ו
‏19. רמ״א יו״ד סי׳ קנ״א ס״י
‏20. שו״ע יו״ד סי׳ קנ״א סי״ד
‏21. שו״ע יו״ד סי׳ קנ״א סי״ב
‏22. רמב״ם הל׳ שבת פ״ו הי״א
‏23. סיפורי חסידים פ׳ עקב

‏8. רמב״ם הל׳ ע״ז פ״י ה״א
‏9. שו״ע חו״מ סי׳ תכ״ה באר הגולה אות ש׳
‏10. רמב״ם הל׳ ע״ז פ״י ה״ד
‏11. רמב״ם הל׳ ע״ז פ״י ה״ג
‏12. ע״ז כ, ב. רש״י ד״ה אין משכירין בתים
‏13. שו״ע יו״ד סי׳ קנ״א סי״א
‏14. יהושע פ״ט ואילך
‏15. רש״י בראשית יט, א ד״ה וירא לוט

‏1. ע״ז כא, א
‏2. דברים רבה ה, יד
‏3. מרביצי תורה מעולם החסידות כרך ג׳ ע׳ נז
‏4. יהושע פ״י
‏5. חינוך מצוה צ״ג. וראה שם מצוה תכ״ה
‏6. רמב״ם הל׳ מלכים פ״ו ה״א, וראה מנ״ח מצוה צ״ג אות א׳
‏7. ע״ז כ, א

There are so many people in the world who look different, act differently, and talk differently. **YOU are special**. Don't lower yourself by copying them!

UNIT 29

IN THIS UNIT YOU WILL:

EXPLORE

- Why is being different from non-Jews so important for the survival of our nation?
- Why is the kind of clothing you wear so important?

EXAMINE

- What are you not allowed to copy from the ways of non-Jews?
- When are you allowed to dress like a non-Jew?

EXTRACT

- If you want to show pride in being Jewish, what can you do?
- If you want to keep a strong Jewish identity, what are three things that you can do?

בְּלוֹרִית

חֻקּוֹת הַגּוֹיִם

KEY CONCEPTS

Book: Madda, Section: Idol Worship
סֵפֶר מַדָּע הִלְכוֹת עֲבוֹדָה זָרָה

הֲלִיכָה בְּחֻקּוֹת הַגּוֹיִם
COPYING NON-JEWS

מִצְוָה אַחַת

The Mitzvah

EXAM*I*NE

The unit of *chukos hagoyim* has one mitzvah.

Do not copy the way of life or clothing of the non-Jews.

MITZVAH
57

שֶׁלֹא לָלֶכֶת בְּחוּקוֹת הַגוֹיִם
Not following what non-Jews do

וְלֹא תֵלְכוּ בְּחֻקֹת הַגוֹי אֲשֶׁר אֲנִי מְשַׁלֵּחַ מִפְּנֵיכֶם כִּי אֶת
כָּל אֵלֶּה עָשׂוּ וָאָקֻץ בָּם (ויקרא כ, כג)

Do not follow the customs of the nation that I am driving
out before you, since they did all these perversions and I was
disgusted with them.

**Do not copy non-Jewish actions
or their way of dress.**

ALL PEOPLE   ALL PLACES   ALL TIMES   *MALKUS*

DISCOVERY

Fingerprints

Just like *B'nei Yisrael* has their own identity, there is something that makes each person different.

Every single person has an absolutely unique set of fingerprints that doesn't match anyone else's. Even identical twins do not have the same fingerprints!

Therefore, one way to identify criminals, to protect private information, or to limit access to certain areas, is with fingerprints scanners. For example, a police station has areas where only officers are allowed entry. The officers must press a finger onto a fingerprint scanner to unlock the door.

Mitzvah Messages

EXPLORE

Make a Statement

Have you ever noticed that when you are dressed nicely and neatly, you feel and act differently than when you are in pajamas?

This is because the way you dress changes the way you feel.

We are a unique nation, because we have been chosen from all of the other nations to carry out a special mission. To be successful in our mission, we have to remind ourselves that we are different from everyone else. If we dress like non-Jews or copy what they do, we might forget our special responsibility and privilege of having our special mission.[1]

When you dress in a Jewish way, then you will act in a Jewish way, and you will be able to follow the Torah and do what Hashem wants easily.

CHECKPOINT   Why is it important for a jewish person to look Jewish?

Not Copying Idolaters

You are not allowed to do anything on purpose to look like or act like the non-Jews. This includes many things:[2]

Hair Styles

You may not cut your hair in a style that is clearly a non-Jewish style.[3]

Clothing

You may not wear clothes in the same style as the non-Jews. There are two kinds of clothing which are considered "non-Jewish."

1. If it is **immodest** or **undignified**.

2. If you get **no real benefit** from the clothing and the only reason you are wearing it is to be like the non-Jews. For example, wearing something warm in the summer, when there is obviously no benefit from the clothing.

Clothes and styles that don't fall under either of these two categories may be worn. For example, a coat in the winter is worn for a purpose - to keep you warm - and therefore is not considered copying non-Jews.[4]

Buildings

You are not allowed to build buildings in the same design that non-Jews use for their places of worship.[5] However, buildings used for business or as courthouses may be copied.[6]

 CHECKPOINT   In which three ways are you not allowed to copy the non-Jews?

SELECTED HALACHOS

- You are allowed to wear a uniform for your job, like a white doctor's coat.[7]
- A man is not allowed to grow his hair to show it off,[8] or to grow his hair long, just for fashion.[9]
- Going to the theater or going to stadiums to watch sports games is not considered copying non-Jews, but would be the *aveirah* of *bittul Torah* and might make your *yetzer hara* stronger.[10]
- A Jewish hairdresser may not cut a non-Jew's hair in a style that is specifically non-Jewish.[11]

OUR SAGES SAY...

Clothing Makes the Man

ר׳ יוֹחָנָן קָרֵי לְמָאנֵיהּ מְכַבְּדוֹתַי

R' Yochanan referred to his clothing as "those that honor me."[12]

STORY

Nice Try, But...

Once, the Romans made an evil decree against the Jews. R' Reuven ben Istrobli got his hair cut in the Roman style and approached the Romans to try to trick them into canceling the decree. He almost succeeded, until they realized that he was a Jew and sent him away.

Rabbi Shimon bar Yochai took a different approach; he *davened* for Hashem's help. Hashem answered his *tefillos* and sent a demon to help him. The demon possessed the daughter of the Caesar and drove her insane. She yelled, "Bring Rabbi Shimon bar Yochai! Bring Rabbi Shimon bar Yochai!"

Rabbi Shimon bar Yochai was quickly summoned, and when he arrived, he commanded the demon to leave the body of the princess. Greatly thankful, the Caesar then offered to let him enter his treasury to choose his reward. Rabbi Shimon found the decree in the treasury, and tore it up.[13]

OUR SAGES SAY...

Dare to be Different

Jews must be different from non-Jews in the way they dress and in the way they act, just as they are different in their ideas and what they consider important.[14]

BIOGRAPHY

R' Hillel of Paritch

(1795 – 1864) תקנ"ה – תרכ"ד

R' Hillel Malisov, known as "Reb Hillel of Paritch," was born in Khometz, Russia. When he was young, he was a chossid of R' Mordechai of Chernobyl, and later of R' Dovber of Lubavitch. R' Hillel served as Rav in the towns of Paritch and Babroisk, and wrote "Pelach Harimon," a sefer of chassidic ideas. He guided many Talmidei Chachamim, and was known for always following even the smallest halachah. He passed away in Kherson, Ukraine on א"י מנחם אב.

DID YOU KNOW?

Individualism

When the *B'nei Yisrael* were in *Mitzrayim*, *Chazal* tell us that there were four things that they did not change: their way of dress, their names, their religion, and their language. This kept them obviously apart from the *Mitzrim* and was one of the reasons that they deserved to be taken out of Mitzrayim.[15]

EXTEND YOUR KNOWLEDGE

Historical Developments

Over the years, there were different practices that the non-Jews developed that the *Rabbanim* of those times strictly forbade us to do. Some examples are:

- In non-Jewish houses of worship, the platform is usually in the front of the room. Therefore, many *Rabbanim* ruled that the *bimah* of the *shul* must be in the center of the room, or at least with one row of seats in front of it.

- It was a non-Jewish practice to make the wedding ceremony indoors, usually in their houses of worship. Here too, the *Rabbanim* spoke out strongly against this and ruled that a *chupah* must be held outside, under the stars, or at least in a way that it's opened to the sky.[16]

A STORY

Dress for the Occasion

R' Hillel of Paritch was known for his refusal to change the way he dressed, even when he might have been killed.

He explained that he owned a letter written by R' Pinchas of Koretz. This document said that before the *geulah*, there would be a lot of pressure on the Jews to dress like non-Jews and that they would give in. Only a few individuals would stand strong against the odds and refuse to give up their customary dress. The merit of these strong characters would bring about the *geulah*.

"Therefore," R' Hillel declared, "since I have the paper with this message on it, I will sacrifice anything to follow what it says."[16]

Live the Mitzvah   EXTRACT

Be Proud

You should never be ashamed of who you are. You were chosen by Hashem for a special mission, to bring the light of Hashem's Torah and mitzvos into this world. You were given great responsibilities and privileges, and the way you act and dress should show this.

You should be very careful when you choose your clothing. Are they modest, practical and refined? You should also watch your behavior. Every time you open your mouth, or do any action, you are telling the world that you are proud of who you are and that you are not afraid to be special.

 CHECKPOINT How can the way you show everyone that you are proud to be part of the Jewish nation?

Staying Jewish

There are three things that make us look, act, and feel Jewish, and sets us apart from everyone else:

Jewish Names

According to some, the mitzvah of not copying non-Jews includes not using non-Jewish names.[17]

Jewish Clothing

Tzephania Hanavi gave a *nevuah* about the destruction of the *Beis Hamikdash*: וּפָקַדְתִּי עַל הַשָּׂרִים וְעַל בְּנֵי הַמֶּלֶךְ וְעַל כָּל הַלֹּבְשִׁים מַלְבּוּשׁ נָכְרִי - "And I will deal with the officials, and the king's sons, and all those who wear strange clothing."[18] According to most major *mefarshim*,[19] מַלְבּוּשׁ נָכְרִי (strange clothing) means non-Jewish clothing. Wearing non-Jewish clothing was enough of an *aveirah* for Hashem to punish the Jews by destroying the *Beis Hamikdash*.

Jewish Language

You have to be different than the *goyim* in the way you talk.[20] Whenever possible, you should speak in a Jewish language.[21] Also, your speech should be polite and refined ,and you should remember Hashem and His Torah in your everyday conversation (for example, saying, "I'm well, *Baruch Hashem*").

CHECKPOINT What are the three ways that you can be different than the non-Jews?

DISCOVERY

Identity Theft

One of the fastest growing crimes nowadays is identity theft, which means stealing someone's private information to do a crime in their name.

Identity theft means that a total stranger is going around with a photo ID with your name on it, your credit cards and your bank account information. After the criminal spends a lot of money, who has to pay for it? You!

This crime can make you lose a lot of money, so that no bank will ever lend you money again, and you won't be able to buy a house or a car, all because the banks think that you lost all of your money.

It is extremely important to protect your identity, for your money, and for your *neshamah*!

OUR SAGES SAY...

Children of Kings

כָּל יִשְׂרָאֵל בְּנֵי מְלָכִים הֵן

Every Jew is a child of royalty. You have special responsibilities and privileges that come with being a member of the royal family.[22]

UNIT **29**

ENDNOTES:

1. סה"מ ל"ת ל'

2. רמב"ם הל' ע"ז פי"א ה"א

3. רמב"ם הל' ע"ז פי"א ה"א

4. מהרי"ק סי' פ"ח הובא בכס"מ הל' ע"ז פי"א ה"א ד"ה ולא ילבש. רמ"א יו"ד סי' קע"ח ס"א. וע" אגרות משה יו"ד ח"א סי' פ"א

5. רמב"ם הל' ע"ז פי"א ה"א, כס"מ ד"ה ולא יבנה. וע" ב"ח יו"ד סי' קע"ח ס"ק ה' וט"ז שם ס"ק ג'

6. ש"ך יו"ד סי' קע"ח ס"ק ב'

7. רמ"א יו"ד סי' קע"ח ס"א

8. ב"ח יו"ד סי' קע"ח ס"ק ד'

9. ט"ז יו"ד סי' קע"ח ס"ק א'

10. אגרות משה יו"ד ח"ד סי' י"א

11. רמב"ם הל' ע"ז פי"א ה"ב

16. עי' בשו"ת מנחת יצחק ח"ג סי' ד', וח"ה סי' ל' ובהנסמן שם. ובכ"מ

21. שבת קיג, ב

13. מעילה יז, א-ב, וברש"י שם

14. רמב"ם הל' ע"ז פי"א ה"א

15. זבח פסח להגש"פ פיסקא "מלמד שהיו מצויינים שם"

16. מגדל עוז ע' רלו

17. שו"ת מהר"ם שיק יו"ד סי' קס"ט

18. צפניה א, ח

19. סה"מ ל"ת ל'. רש"י ורד"ק צפניה א, ח

20. סמ"ג לאוין נ'

12. עי' בשו"ת דברי יציב יו"ד סי' נ"ב-נ"ג

22. בבא מציעא קיג, ב

UNIT 30

IN THIS UNIT YOU WILL:

EXPLORE

- Why does doing magic and trying to find out the future show a lack of trust in Hashem?

EXAMINE

- What are the ten *aveiros* of telling the future and doing magic?

EXTRACT

- If you want to say *tefillos* in a time of need, what should you say?

כְּשׁוּף

דֹּרֵשׁ אֶל הַמֵּתִים

KEY CONCEPTS

Book: Madda, Section: Idol Worship

סֵפֶר מַדָּע הִלְכוֹת עֲבוֹדָה זָרָה

הַגָּדַת עֲתִידוֹת

TELLING THE FUTURE AND DOING MAGIC

עֲשָׂרָה מִצְוֹת

Don't panic. Take a deep breath. **Relax.**

The pilot **knows** what he is doing.

PEARLS *of wisdom*

No Need for That Stuff

Hashem says to *B'nei Yisrael*: The non-Jews who have no *nevi'im* and no Torah to guide them use different kinds of magic. However I set *B'nei Yisrael* apart from the non-Jews, and My *Shechinah* rests upon you. You have *nevi'im* and the Torah, so you do not need *Ov* and *Yidoni* to guide you.[1]

HISTORY

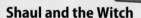

Shaul and the Witch

King Shaul was very nervous about the war he was going to have with the *Plishtim,* so he secretly met with a woman who did *Ov* magic, so that he could find out if he would win.

He asked her to call up *Shmuel Hanavi* from the dead, so that he could ask Shmuel about the future. Shmuel told Shaul that he and his sons would die in battle and the kingship would be passed on to Dovid, because Hashem was angry with Shaul for not listening to the command to kill out *Amalek*.

Shaul accepted what would happen and bravely went to war with his sons against the *Plishtim*. Because he accepted his punishment, his *aveiros* were forgiven and he got a place in *Olam Haba*.[2]

The unit of telling the future and doing magic has ten mitzvos.

1. Do not do anything because of a sign.
2. Do not use the stars to make decisions.
3. Do not do *Ov* magic.
4. Do not do *Yidoni* magic.
5. Do not do anything to tell the future.
6. Do not change anything through magic.
7. Do not say any spells while you are doing an action.
8. Do not ask an *Ov* advice
9. Do not ask a *Yidoni* advice.
10. Do not do anything to communicate with a dead person.

MITZVOS 58-67

אִסּוּרֵי הַגָּדַת עֲתִידוֹת
Not performing any magic or fortune telling

לֹא תֹאכְלוּ עַל הַדָּם לֹא תְנַחֲשׁוּ וְלֹא תְעוֹנֵנוּ
(ויקרא יט, כו)

Do not eat on blood. (58) **Do not act because of omens.** (59) **Do not act on the basis of auspicious times.**

58	שֶׁלֹּא לְנַחֵשׁ **Do not do anything because of a sign.**	MALKUS
59	שֶׁלֹּא לְעוֹנֵן **Do not use astrology to make decisions.**	MALKUS

אַל תִּפְנוּ אֶל הָאֹבֹת וְאֶל הַיִּדְּעֹנִים אַל תְּבַקְשׁוּ לְטָמְאָה בָהֶם אֲנִי ה' אֱלֹקֵיכֶם
(ויקרא יט, לא)

(60) **Do not turn to mediums**, (61) **nor seek out oracles**, to make yourselves impure through them. I am Hashem your G-d.

60	שֶׁלֹּא לַעֲשׂוֹת מַעֲשֵׂה אוֹב Do not do אוֹב magic.		SKILAH
61	שֶׁלֹּא לַעֲשׂוֹת מַעֲשֵׂה יִדְּעֹנִי Do not do יִדְּעֹנִי magic.		SKILAH

לֹא יִמָּצֵא בְךָ מַעֲבִיר בְּנוֹ וּבִתּוֹ בָּאֵשׁ קֹסֵם קְסָמִים מְעוֹנֵן וּמְנַחֵשׁ וּמְכַשֵּׁף. וְחֹבֵר חָבֶר וְשֹׁאֵל אוֹב וְיִדְּעֹנִי וְדֹרֵשׁ אֶל הַמֵּתִים.
(דברים יח, י-יא)

Among you, there shall not be found anyone who passes his son or daughter through fire, (62) **who practices stick divination**, who divines auspicious times, who divines by omens, (63) **who practices witchcraft**, (64) **who uses incantations**, (65) **who consults mediums** (66) **and oracles**, (67) **or who attempts to communicate with the dead.**

62	שֶׁלֹּא לִקְסוֹם Do not do anything to see what will happen in the present or future.		MALKUS
63	שֶׁלֹּא לְכַשֵּׁף Do not change anything through witchcraft.		SKILAH
64	שֶׁלֹּא לַחֲבוֹר חָבֶר Do not say incantations while doing an action.		MALKUS
65	שֶׁלֹּא לִשְׁאוֹל בְּאוֹב Do not ask an *Ov* for advice.		MALKUS
66	שֶׁלֹּא לִשְׁאוֹל בְּיִדְּעֹנִי Do not ask a *Yidoni* for advice.		MALKUS
67	שֶׁלֹּא לִדְרוֹשׁ אֶל הַמֵּתִים Do not do actions in order to talk with a dead person.		MALKUS

ALL OF THESE *AVEIROS* APPLY:
 TO ALL PEOPLE
 IN ALL PLACES
 AT ALL TIMES

HISTORY

Shortsighted

Paraoh's astrologers looked at the stars and saw that the leader of the Jews would die through water, so Paraoh thought that the decree to throw all the baby boys into the river was the best way to get rid of him.

Paraoh did not know that his decree would bring that Jewish leader into his own palace![3]

DID YOU KNOW?

Crystal Ball

Some opinions say that the *Ov* magic was done by using a glass stone.[4]

No-Fuss Exodus

The Jews' faith in Hashem was so strong that they left Mitzrayim without taking any supplies with them, even though they knew that they were going into a huge, empty desert.[5]

DISCOVERY

Thirteen

Some people think that thirteen is an unlucky number. Some people are so scared of it that many tall buildings do not have a 13th floor. People also believe Friday is an unlucky day. Therefore, they get very nervous when Friday falls on the 13th of the month! There is a word for this fear: Paraskevidekatriaphobia.

DID YOU KNOW?

Monster

Although the יְדעׄנִי is usually understood to be a bird, one opinion says that the יְדעׄנִי is not a bird, but a type of beast. It looks like a human being, but is attached to the ground by a cord extending from its stomach. It is very vicious and kills anything within reach. However, you can kill it by shooting arrows at it to cut the cord.[6]

Mitzvah Messages   EXPLORE

Put Your Trust in Hashem

Hashem decides what will happen in the future. You cannot change what He has decided for you. You have to trust that He will lead you in the right direction, and help you do the right thing. Doing any kind of magic to find out what will happen in the future shows that you do not trust Hashem or His plans for you, and that you are trying to be the one in control of your future.[7]

 CHECKPOINT   How does doing magic to know the future show that you do not trust in Hashem?

Details   EXAMINE

אוׄב

Ov magic was done to bring up spirits from the dead to answer questions.

One way to perform *Ov* magic was to burn spices, wave a branch of leaves called myrtle, and say certain words. The person who was asking would hear a voice speaking from underground, answering any question.

Another way to perform *Ov* magic is to take a human skull, burn spices, and say certain words. Then, the person who was asking would hear a voice coming from his or her armpit, answering any question.

The punishment for doing *Ov* magic is *skilah*, if it was done on purpose and there were witnesses there. If it was done unintentionally, the person has to bring a *korban chatas*.

There is also an *aveirah* for following the advice of an *Ov*, not just doing *Ov* magic. The punishment for **following** the advice of the *Ov* is *malkus*. If you did not do the *Ov* magic, but only asked the *Ov*, and did not follow the advice, regular *malkus* is not given, because there was no action, but *makas mardus* **is** given.[8]

יְדעׄנִי

For *Yidoni* magic, the magician would put the bone of a bird in his or her mouth, burn spices, and do certain actions, until he or she fell into a trance. Then, the magician would start telling the future.[9] The punishments for doing *Yidoni* magic, or for asking a *Yidoni* magician, are the same as the punishments for the *Ov*.

מְנַחֵשׁ

A *Menachesh* does actions because of something that happened. Here are some examples:

1. Not going somewhere because your bread or walking stick fell from your hand, which you think means that your trip will not be successful.

2. Making a decision based upon the chirping of the birds, which you think are telling the future.

3. Saying that something must happen first before making a decision to do something.[10] (Like saying, "I will only do _____ if I see three blackbirds in one hour.)

קוֹסֵם

A *kosem* magician does certain actions to go into a trance. Then the magician starts telling the future or giving advice about what a person should do or be careful about.

Kosem magicians do different actions to put themselves into a trance. Some magicians would concentrate on their stick while they hit it on the ground, or they would stare into a mirror while they would whisper certain words. Other magicians would rub sand or pebbles in their hands.[11]

You are not allowed to ask a *kosem* magician for advice.[12] The punishment for **being** a *kosem* is *malkus*, whereas the punishment for **asking** is *makas mardus*.

מְעוֹנֵן

A *me'onen* would look at the stars to predict which days were going to be good, and when certain actions would be successful. Any action that you do because of what you know from the stars is also doing this *aveirah*.[13] You are not allowed to study how to read the stars and understand their messages.

Triumph Over the Dark Arts

A chassid of the *Ba'al Hatanya*, became sick from magic that was done by a mean old Russian couple living next door to his inn. He went to Liadi to ask his Rebbe for help, and made it to the village in time for *Shabbos Parshas Balak*.

The next morning, the Rebbe, who was the *Ba'al Koreh*, asked that this *chassid* be called up to the Torah for the fifth *aliyah*. As the *chassid* stood there, the Rebbe read out the words, "For there is no magic in Ya'akov, nor any future telling among Yisrael" several times with great concentration.

Feeling better, the *chassid* went back home after *Shabbos*, and was greeted with the news that the evil old couple had died suddenly that *Shabbos* morning.[16]

DISCOVERY

Skeptic

Even though Harry Houdini (who was a Jew) was a great magician and escape artist, he spent a great part of his career proving that people who say that they tell the future are really faking.

A *me'onen* magician is also a person who does tricks through fast hand movements, such as turning a rope into a real snake, or throwing a ring in the air and then taking it out of someone's mouth.[17]

Someone who does this would get *malkus*.[18]

חֹבֵר

The *chover* would speak gibberish words because he believed that these words would help stop a person from getting hurt from another person or from a snake, or it would take away the pain from a bite. If you visit a *chover* to be cured or to be helped by the *chover's* "magic spells," you would get *makas mardus*. The *chover* receives *malkus* if he or she does an action while chanting, such as holding something or making hand movements. Otherwise, the *chover* only receives *makas mardus*.[19]

דֹרֵשׁ אֶל הַמֵּתִים

Someone who is *doresh el hameisim* (seeks to communicate with the dead) would do specific actions to convince a dead person to come to them in a dream and answer their questions. These actions include fasting and then sleeping in a cemetery. Other magicians would wear special clothes, chant, burn spices, and sleep alone. The dead person would then appear to them in a dream and answer the questions.[20]

מְכַשֵּׁף

A *mechashef* is a magician who does witchcraft. There are two types of witchcraft:

1. Causing actual changes to something. For example, using witchcraft to harvest a field of cucumbers and then pile the cucumbers up.

2. Using witchcraft to change what people see, hear, touch, smell, and taste. For example, instead of actually harvesting the cucumbers, the מְכַשֵּׁף would make the people see that the cucumbers were harvested, when there was really nothing there.[21]

The first kind of *mechashef* gets *skilah*. The second type of *mechashef* gets *makas mardus* and not regular *malkus*, becasue he didn't actually **do** anything.[22]

CHECKPOINT What are the kinds of telling the future and magic that you are not allowed to do?

EXTEND YOUR KNOWLEDGE

Sometimes it is Okay

When Eliezer went to find a wife for *Yitzchak Avinu*, he *davened* to Hashem and made a sign that if he asks a girl to give him water and she would give him and his camels to drink, it will mean that she is the right one. How was he allowed to do this? Isn't it מְנַחֵשׁ, since Eliezer is doing an action because something else happened?

One answer is that נִחוּשׁ means that you make a sign which has no logical connection to what you want to know. For example, not going somewhere because your bread fell from your hand. There is no connection between the bread falling and not having a good trip.

But in Eliezer's case, he was looking for a special person to be the wife of a *tzaddik*. The signs he made were just a test to see if the girl has good *middos* and would be a good wife for Yitzchak.[23]

Another answer is that נִחוּשׁ is only forbidden when you will **only** do an action if something happens. For example, you are not allowed to say "If this happens, then I will do this action, and if it doesn't happen, then I won't." However, if you have already decided to do something and now you are looking for a sign of encouragement that this is the right thing to do, then it is not a problem.

Eliezer had already decided that Rivkah was going to be Yitzchak's wife. He just wanted a sign from Hashem that he made the right decision.[24]

DID YOU KNOW?

Believe

According to the Ramban,[25] someone who does any of these *aveiros* also goes against the mitzvah of תָּמִים תִּהְיֶה עִם ה' אֱלֹקֶיךָ – you must remain completely faithful to Hashem your G-d.

HISTORY

Wasted Energy

Nevuchadnetzar, king of Bavel, could not decide whether to attack Ammon or Eretz Yisrael. So, he used magic to make his decision. He shot arrows into the air to see whether they would land on his right towards Yerushalayim, or on his left towards Rabba, the capital of Ammon.

He also consulted the *terafim* (images that told the future), and he looked at a liver for hints to the future. In total, he saw the future forty-nine times, and the result was always the same – attack Eretz Yisrael. Therefore, King Nevuchadnetzar sent his troops to Yerushalayim.

In fact, Hashem had already decided to let him conquer the city, because the Jews had done many *aveiros* and needed a warning to to *teshuvah*.[26]

DID YOU KNOW?

Sefer Yetzirah Cow

A *tzaddik* and *Talmid Chacham* are allowed to use the *kabalistic* names of Hashem from *Sefer Yetzirah* to create things, as long as it is for the sake of a mitzvah or *Kiddush Hashem*. This is not actually an act of magic, because it is the power of Hashem in those names that created these things.

R' Chanina and R' Oshiya would learn *Sefer Yetzirah* every Friday, and by using the names of Hashem, they would create a calf and eat it for *Shabbos*.[27]

A person must live a life of purity and holiness to be able to use such powers.[28]

DID YOU KNOW?

G-d-Fearing Nation

The motto "In G-d We Trust" first appeared on the United States two-cent coin in 1864, and is now stamped on every U.S. coin.

- If good things happen to you after you get married, after you have a son, or after you build a house, you are allowed to take that as a sign that you will have success in the future.[29]

- You are allowed to ask a child what *passuk* was learnt that day and view it as a sign as to what will happen in the future. This is considered a minor *nevuah*, not magic.[30]

- You are not allowed to do real magic tricks and even to watch the tricks of a Jewish magician. However, you may watch a non-Jewish magician.[31]

- You are allowed to say magic words if you are being threatened by a dangerous snake or scorpion.[32]

- There is no problem of *doresh el hameisim* if you are *davening* at the grave of a relative or *tzaddik*, since you are not *davening* to the dead person, *chas v'shalom*. Rather you are asking the person buried there to *daven* to Hashem on our behalf. At the graves of *tzaddikim*, we are really *davening* to Hashem, whose *Shechinah* rests at the resting places of *tzaddikim*.[33]

- Some people have a minhag to eat something before visiting a grave, and not to enter the cemetery while fasting, since a *doresh el hameisim* would fast.[34]

Live the Mitzvah

EXTRACT

Hashem Knows Best

You can never know exactly what is going to happen in the future, or if you are making the right decisions. It can be really scary going into the unknown without knowing what will happen to you. But if you have faith that Hashem is looking out for you, and that everything He does is for your own good, you will not be so worried and will be able to have peace in your decisions.

> **CHECKPOINT** What thought can help you so that you won't be worried about the future?

What Else Comes From This?

EXTRACT

Saying *Tehillim*

You are not allowed to say words of Torah if you believe that the words have a magic power to heal a sick person. You are also not allowed to put a *Sefer Torah* or *tefillin* on a baby so that the baby will sleep. The Torah can affect your *neshamah*, not your body.[35]

However, you are allowed to say words of *Tehillim* or learn Torah for a person who needs Hashem's help if you understand that the words themselves do not have the power to heal. Instead, in the **merit** of the learning or *davening*, Hashem will help the person.[36]

UNIT 30

HISTORY

Saved by the Bird

Dovid Hamelech once ran into a giant, Yishbi of Nov, and feared for his life, because the mighty giant wanted revenge for his brother Golias' death at the hands of Dovid. He silently *davened* for someone to help him.

Far away, his general, Avishai ben Tzeruyah, saw a dove flying overhead and flapping its wings in pain. He took it as a sign that the king was in danger, and rushed to help him. Hashem made his path shorter and he was by Dovid's side in an instant. Together, they defeated the giant Yishbi.

After this happened, Dovid's ministers did not let him go out to war by himself, because they could not count on such *nissim* happening all the time.[37]

ENDNOTES:

1. בעל הטורים ויקרא כ, כו
2. שמואל א' פרק כח
3. רש"י שמות א, כב ד"ה לכל עמו
4. רד"ק שמואל א' כח, כד
5. רש"י שמות יב, לט ד"ה וגם צדה
6. ר"ש כלאים פ"ח מ"ה
7. חינוך מצוה רמ"ט
8. רמב"ם הל' ע"ז פי"א הי"ד
9. רמב"ם הל' ע"ז פ"ו ה"ב
10. רמב"ם הל' ע"ז פי"א ה"ד
11. סה"מ ל"ת ל"א. רמב"ם הל' ע"ז פי"א ה"ו
12. רמב"ם הל' ע"ז פי"א ה"ז
13. רמב"ם הל' ע"ז פי"א ה"ח-ט
14. דרשות הר"ן דרוש י"ב

15. חינוך מצוה תק"י
16. סיפורי חסידים פ' בלק
17. סה"מ ל"ת ל"ב
18. רמב"ם הל' ע"ז פי"א ה"ט
19. רמב"ם הל' ע"ז פי"א ה"י
20. רמב"ם הל' ע"ז פי"א ה"יג
21. ב"ח יו"ד סי' קע"ט בביאור דעת הרמב"ם
22. רמב"ם הל' ע"ז פי"א הט"ו
23. ר"ן הובא בכס"מ הל' ע"ז פי"א ה"ה, וכ"ה בדרשות הר"ן דרוש י"ב
24. ע"פ רד"ק שמואל א' יד, ט
25. רמב"ן בהשגותיו בסהמ"צ שכחת העשין מצוה ח'
26. יחזקאל כא, כג-כח וברש"י
27. סנהדרין סז, ב וברש"י ד"ה עסקי

28. ש"ך סי' קע"ט ס"ק י"ח
29. שו"ע יו"ד סי' קע"ט ס"ד ובהגה. ש"ך ס"ק ד'
30. רמ"א יו"ד סי' קע"ט ס"ה, ובט"ז ס"ק ג'
31. פתחי תשובה יו"ד סי' קע"ט ס"ק ז'. וכ"ה בשו"ת יבי"א יו"ד ח"ה סי' י"ה. שו"ת שב"ה ח"ה סי' קכ"ז. וע" בשו"ת אג"מ יו"ד ח"ד סי' י"ג. וע"ע בשו"ת בצ"ה ח"ד סי' י"ג וצ"ע
32. שו"ע יו"ד סי' קע"ט ס"ז
33. זוהר אחרי מות עא, א ב. ב"ח יו"ד ס"ס רי"ז, דרכי תשובה סי' קע"ט ס"ק ק"ו
34. ילקוט אברהם לשו"ע או"ח סי' תקפ"א
35. רמב"ם הל' ע"ז פי"א הי"ב
36. חינוך מצוה תקי"ב
37. סנהדרין צה, א, וברש"י

UNIT 31

IN THIS UNIT YOU WILL:

EXPLORE

- Why does it matter what certain people do?

EXAMINE

- What are the areas of the head and beard that you are not allowed to shave?

EXTRACT

- If you want to train a child to not cut his *peiyos*, what would you do?

תַּעַר

פֵּאוֹת

זָקָן

גִּילּוּחַ

KEY CONCEPTS

Book: Madda, Section: Idol Worship

סֵפֶר מַדָּע הִלְכוֹת עֲבוֹדָה זָרָה

גִּילּוּחַ
SHAVING

שְׁתֵּי מִצְוֹת

If these people do something, that is enough of a reason for you not to do it!

The Mitzvos

EXAMINE

The unit of shaving has two mitzvos.

1. Do not shave the hair on the corners of a male's head.
2. Do not shave any of the five edges of a male's beard.

MITZVOS
68-69

אִיסּוּרֵי גִּילּוּחַ
Not shaving areas that are forbidden to shave

לֹא תַקִּפוּ פְּאַת רֹאשְׁכֶם וְלֹא תַשְׁחִית אֵת פְּאַת זְקָנֶךָ
(ויקרא יט, כז)

(68) **Do not cut off the hair on the edges of your head.**
(69) **Do not shave off the edges of your beard.**

68	שֶׁלֹּא לְהַקִּיף פַּאֲתֵי הָרֹאשׁ Do not shave the hair on the side of a head.	*MALKUS*
69	שֶׁלֹּא לְהַשְׁחִית פְּאַת זָקָן Do not destroy any of the five parts of the beard.	*MALKUS*

MALES · ALL PLACES · ALL TIMES · MALKUS

Mitzvah Messages

EXPLORE

Don't Be Like Them

Some things are wrong to do simply because of the kind of people who usually do them. Leaders who worshipped *avodah zarah* would shave their beards and *peiyos*, so Hashem commands us not to shave our beards and *peiyos* like they do. We will not do anything like someone who is the leader of something as evil as *avodah zarah*![4]

CHECKPOINT Who are you different from when you don't shave your beard?

Details

EXAMINE

Peiyos

Peiyos are the area of hair on the side of your head (near your ear), from your forehead until the bottom of the ear.[5] A male is forbidden to shave this area on himself or on any other male, and a woman is not allowed to shave this area on a male.

The words לֹא תַקִּפוּ – "(they) do not cut off," are in the plural. From this we learn that two people did the *aveirah*. The barber did the *aveirah* of cutting the *peiyos* off a man, and the man did an *aveirah* for having his *peiyos* removed.[6]

Beards

What is Forbidden?

The words לֹא תַשְׁחִית – "do not destroy," teach us that shaving with a razor is forbidden, because it totally destroys the beard. Therefore, a man would only receive *malkus* if the beard was shaved using a razor.[7]

However, there are many different opinions about whether someone is allowed to shave with scissors or something else that doesn't cut as close to the skin as a razor. Some say it is allowed, some say it is forbidden from the *Chachamim*, and some say it is forbidden from the Torah.[8]

Which Parts of the Beard?

There are five "corners" of the face that are considered the beard and not allowed to be destroyed. There are many opinions exactly where these five corners are, and therefore we do not destroy any part of the beard.[9]

Who is Forbidden?

You are not allowed to shave the *peiyos* or beard of **any** male, even a child. Women may shave any hairs that grow in the areas of a beard and *peiyos*, but they are still not allowed to shave any male, including children.[10]

Punishment

Shaving the beard and *peiyos* are forbidden for the person being shaved and the barber. However, the person who is being shaved would only get *malkus* if he turns his head or helps the barber in some way. Otherwise, although they both did an *aveirah*, only the barber is punished and not the person being shaved.[11]

 CHECKPOINT · Which parts of the face are not allowed to be shaved?

OUR SAGES SAY...

Bearded and Beautiful

הַדְרַת פָּנִים - זָקָן

The beauty of the face is the beard.[12]

STORY

Don't Ask Me, Ask Hashem

Someone asked R' Ya'akov Abukra of Tunis, "Rabbi, the Torah says that we may not shave off the beard. Why do we have to do this mitzvah?"

The Rabbi answered, "I was given a prescription by our family doctor for a certain medicine. Now I am going to the pharmacy to find out how this medicine works."

Puzzled, the man asked, "But Rabbi, why ask the pharmacist? It's the doctor who knows about the sickness and its cure, not the pharmacist!"

The Rabbi smiled and said, "That answers your question. Only Hashem knows the real reasons of mitzvos, and no one else!"[13]

Hashem created the world so that there would be differences between all His creations. The beard of a man was to serve as a sign of being different from the woman.

Removing the beard removes that which Hashem put in nature to create divisions. This is similar to the *aveirah* of planting *kilayim*, mixing two different types of plants together.[14]

OUR SAGES SAY...

A Sign of Respect

The Chafetz Chaim writes that someone who has a beard becomes respected and important in the eyes of all people.[15]

HISTORY

Our Pride

Throughout our history, there were periods of great suffering where many people had great *mesiras nefesh* to not shave their beard.

Some of these historical periods include the time when the Communists ruled Russia, and the Holocaust.

SELECTED HALACHOS

- If a woman has a beard, she may shave it.[16]
- Even those *Poskim* who say that you are allowed to shave using scissors,[17] are still careful that the cut is made with the upper blade of the scissors, and not the bottom blade, since the bottom blade cuts too close to the skin.[18]
- The mustache and hair just below the lower lip are not part of the beard and may be shaven with a razor.[19]

EXTEND YOUR KNOWLEDGE

Men Only

The *passuk* says, "Do not cut off the hair on the sides of your head. Do not shave off the edges of your beard."

Since these two *aveiros* are linked to each other in the same *passuk*, we understand that only those who are not allowed to shave their beards are also not allowed to shave the sides of their heads. Since women don't usually grow beards and therefore don't have a mitzvah not to shave them, they also don't have a mitzvah not to shave the sides of their heads.[20]

The halachah is, "Every mitzvah that a woman is not obligated to do, a slave is also not obligated to do."[21] However, because a woman is exempt only because she doesn't actually grow a beard, a slave is still obligated to keep this mitzvah.[22]

Live the Mitzvah

EXTRACT

Not Our Way

Is it actually wrong to wear a nose ring? Or to dye our hair green? Or to use certain words? It's easy to think that since they are not *assur*, it's okay for us to do them.

However, when you look at the people who do these things nowadays, you realize that they're not the kind of people that you really want to be like. Their behavior isn't the greatest, and if you copy the things they wear and the things they do, then your own actions may become like their actions. Therefore, you should avoid doing these things simply because of the kind of people who do them.

Why should you stay away from certain actions even if they are not directly forbidden in the Torah?

Off With His Hair

Many people have a *minhag* not to cut a boy's hair until he is three years old. When he reaches the age of three, we cut his hair, leaving the *peiyos*, and make a big celebration. This ceremony is usually called an "*opsheren*" which in Yiddish means "to cut off."

Some people pay some tuition to the school the child will attend, and some parents take the boy to school on his third birthday to learn the *alef-beis*. The letters of the *alef-beis* are covered with honey, and the child licks the honey off the letters to show the idea that the words of Torah are sweet and pleasant.

Why do we wait until the age of three? One reason is found in the *passuk* "שָׁלֹשׁ שָׁנִים יִהְיֶה לָכֶם עֲרֵלִים לֹא יֵאָכֵל" – Three years you shall not eat the fruits of the tree." People are compared to trees.[23] Just like we cannot eat the fruit of a tree before the tree is three years old, we wait until the age of three, to begin teaching a child Torah and mitzvos.[24]

When we cut his hair, we teach him the importance of the mitzvah of *peiyos* by cutting the hair on his head and leaving the hair in the *peiyos*. Through this mitzvah, we teach the boy that he, as a Jew, is special and different from the non-Jews.[25]

 CHECKPOINT How can a child be trained to leave *peiyos*?

DID YOU KNOW?

Trendsetter

In ancient and medieval times, beards were sometimes in style, so Jews and non-Jews both wore beards. The *Chasam Sofer* explains that the fashion of being clean-shaven is from when there was a Polish king who could not grow a beard. He did not want to stand out, so he decreed that all men had to remove their beards. When this happened, non-Jews outside the kingdom also started doing this.

During this time, many Jewish peddlers in Germany were given permission to shave their beards to protect themselves from the Crusaders who were travelling through the countryside.[26]

PEARLS of wisdom

They Do Count

As we have learned, a child's *peiyos* are not allowed to be cut.

This mitzvah may apply to a child, but do the mitzvos of a child really "count?" Yes! *Chazal*[27] teach us that Hashem says "I am Hashem before you are able to do *aveiros* and after you have done *aveiros*." This means that even the mitzvos that a child does, before he is responsible for his *aveiros*, are special to Hashem.[28]

UNIT 31

ENDNOTES:

22. רמב"ם הל' ע"ז ה"ב. ועיי"ש בנו"כ שמקשים עליו איך למד זה מסוגית הגמרא
23. דברים כ, יט. תענית ז, א. ורש"י ד"ה וכי אדם
24. מדרש תנחומא קדושים, יד
25. שו"ת מהר"ם בריסק ח"ב סי' צ"ח. שו"ת ערוגת הבשם או"ח ח"ב סי' ר"י
26. שו"ת חת"ס או"ח סי' קנ"ט
27. ר"ה יז, ב. ורש"י ד"ה ה' ה'
28. בני יששכר מאמרי חודש אלול מאמר ב'

11. שו"ע יו"ד סי' קפ"א ס"ד
12. שבת קנב, א
13. אור החמה ויקרא ע' קיג
14. רבינו בחיי ויקרא יט, כז
15. חפץ חיים בקונטרס תפארת אדם פ"ה. שם פ"א
16. שו"ע יו"ד סי' קפ"א סי"ב
17. שו"ע יו"ד סי' קפ"א ס"י
18. רמ"א יו"ד סי' קפ"א ס"י
19. רמב"ם הל' ע"ז פי"ב ה"ח. טור יו"ד סי' קפ"א
20. קדושין לה, ב
21. חגיגה ה, א

1. זהר ח"ג קלא, א. שם רפד, א
4. רמב"ם הל' ע"ז פי"ב ה"ז
5. שו"ע יו"ד סי' קפ"א ס"ט
6. מכות כ, א ובברש"י ד"ה דאמר לך מני. וראה תורה תמימה ויקרא יט הערה ריד שפי' זה ברש"י הוא העיקר
7. רש"י מכות כא, א ד"ה ת"ל לא תשחית
8. עי' שו"ת צ"צ יו"ד סי' צ"ג ואורחות חיים להר' קנייבסקי סי' ה. וראה ספר הדרת פנים זקן
9. שו"ע יו"ד סי' קפ"א סי"א
10. השגת הראב"ד הל' ע"ז ה"ז ה"ה, כס"מ שם ה"ה

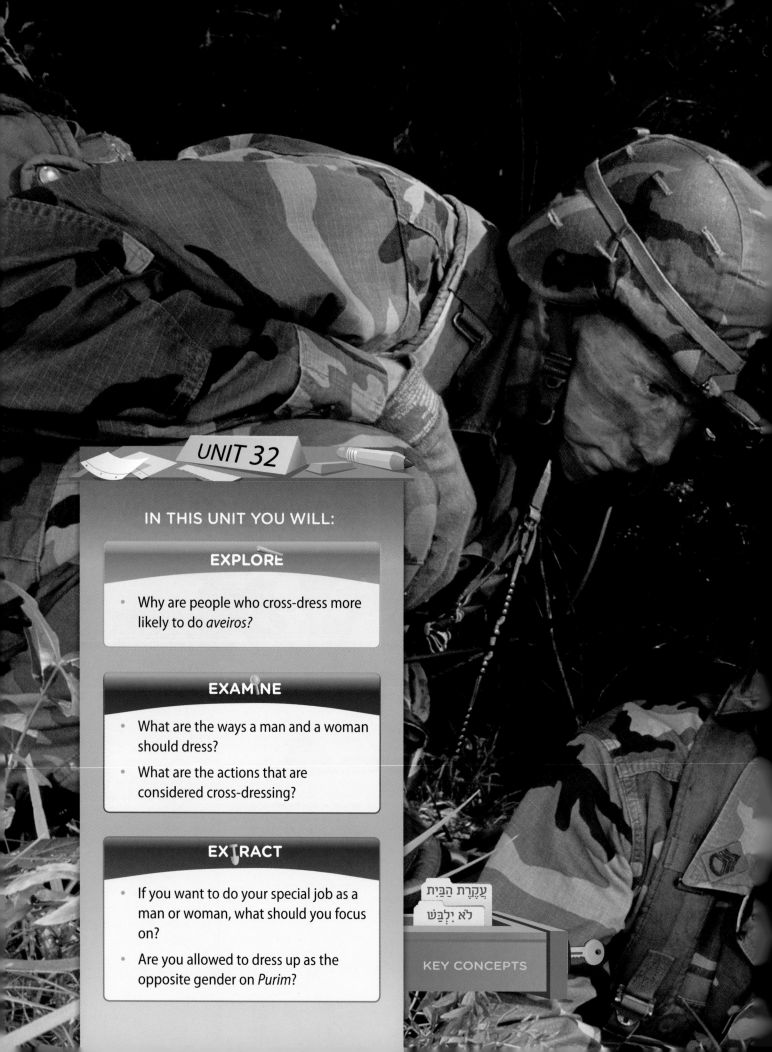

UNIT 32

IN THIS UNIT YOU WILL:

EXPLORE

- Why are people who cross-dress more likely to do *aveiros?*

EXAMINE

- What are the ways a man and a woman should dress?
- What are the actions that are considered cross-dressing?

EXTRACT

- If you want to do your special job as a man or woman, what should you focus on?
- Are you allowed to dress up as the opposite gender on *Purim?*

עֲקֶרֶת הַבַּיִת
לֹא יִלְבַּשׁ

KEY CONCEPTS

Book: Madda, Section: Idol Worship
סֵפֶר מַדָּע הִלְכוֹת עֲבוֹדָה זָרָה

לֹא יִלְבַּשׁ

NOT WEARING CLOTHES OF THE OTHER GENDER

שְׁתֵּי מִצְוֹת

Ever wonder why soldiers wear green or brown uniforms? **These uniforms help them blend in with the trees and bushes so that the enemy can't pick them out.** This is called camouflage. Can you think of other people who might camouflage themselves, and why?

OUR SAGES SAY...

No Mixed Partying

Why does the Torah give us a mitzvah that a woman is not allowed to wear men's clothing and a man is not allowed to wear women's clothing? If this mitzvah is only about wearing the clothing of the opposite gender, then why does the Torah call it an abomination? What's so bad about it?

These mitzvos tell us that a man may not wear women's clothing and mix with women, and a woman may not wear men's clothing and mix with men.[1]

DISCOVERY

Can You See Me?

The leaf insects found in Southeast Asia, mainly Thailand, use camouflage so that they look like a leaf, which they eat and get their nutrients. They do this so perfectly that predators can't tell them apart from the real leaves. To confuse predators even more, when the leaf insect walks, it rocks back and forth, to look like a real leaf being blown by the wind.

The unit of cross-dressing has two mitzvos.

1. A woman is not allowed to wear or do something specifically to look like a man.

2. A man is not allowed to wear or do something specifically to look like a woman.

MITZVAH 70

שֶׁלֹּא תַעֲדֶה אִשָּׁה עֲדִי אִישׁ

A woman must not wear what a man wears

לֹא יִהְיֶה כְלִי גֶבֶר עַל אִשָּׁה וְלֹא יִלְבַּשׁ גֶּבֶר שִׂמְלַת אִשָּׁה כִּי תוֹעֲבַת ה׳ אֱלֹקֶיךָ כָּל עֹשֵׂה אֵלֶּה

(דברים כב, ה)

No male article shall be on a woman, and a man shall not wear a woman's garment. Whoever does such practices is revolting to Hashem your G-d.

Do not wear or do something specifically that looks like a man.

WOMEN   ALL PLACES   ALL TIMES   MALKUS

MITZVAH 71

שֶׁלֹּא יַעֲדֶה הָאִישׁ עֲדִי אִשָּׁה

A man must not wear what a woman wears

לֹא יִהְיֶה כְלִי גֶבֶר עַל אִשָּׁה וְלֹא יִלְבַּשׁ גֶּבֶר שִׂמְלַת אִשָּׁה כִּי תוֹעֲבַת ה׳ אֱלֹקֶיךָ כָּל עֹשֵׂה אֵלֶּה

(דברים כב, ה)

No male article shall be on a woman, **and a man shall not wear a woman's garment.** Whoever does such practices is revolting to Hashem your G-d.

Do not wear or do something specifically that looks like a woman.

MEN   ALL PLACES   ALL TIMES   MALKUS

Mitzvah Messages

EXPLORE

You Are What You Wear

Do you notice that you act differently when you are wearing *Shabbos* clothes and when you are in a bathing suit? What you are wearing changes the way that you act. If you dress like the other gender, you will start behaving more like them, and that makes it easier for you to blend in with them. When you mix with them, you can forget yourself and what you stand for, and you might begin to do *aveiros*. This is why you have a mitzvah to use only the clothing of your own gender.[2]

People Power

This mitzvah also reminds us of the special roles of men and women. Men and women should never feel that they will only find happiness and success in taking on the role of the other gender. If you accept that you each have a special job, and you perform your role the best way that you can, then you will find happiness and success.[3]

 CHECKPOINT How would dressing like the opposite gender help you do more *aveiros*?

Details

EXAMINE

Habits That Are Not Our Own

Men and women may not wear clothing which is worn by the other gender in their culture. They also may not change their appearance in a way that is for the other gender only.[4] Some examples are:

- Men and women may not wear the accessories of the other gender. This includes jewelry or weapons.

- A woman may not shave her head like a man.

- Men may not pluck out or dye white hairs as women do.[5]

- A man may not use a razor to remove the hair from his body, in those countries where only women do so. But he may use scissors.[6] Men may not grow their hair long. Apart from not looking like a woman,[7] another reason for this is to avoid copying the ways of non-Jews.[8]

The Punishment

By wearing the clothing of the other gender, you would be constantly doing this *aveirah*, and you would get *malkus* for each time that you are

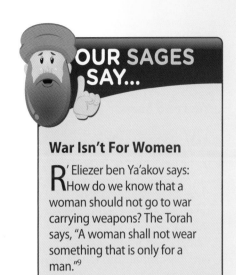

OUR SAGES SAY...

War Isn't For Women

R' Eliezer ben Ya'akov says: How do we know that a woman should not go to war carrying weapons? The Torah says, "A woman shall not wear something that is only for a man."[9]

DID YOU KNOW?

Go for the Natural Look

A man shouldn't use makeup like a woman does.[10]

HISTORY

Yael and Sisra

When Devorah and Barak's army defeated the army of the cruel general Sisra, he ran to the tent of Yael. He thought he would be safe there, because, even though she was Jewish, her family was friendly with the Canaanites. But, this did not stop Yael from killing wicked Sisra. She gave him a drink that made him sleepy, and took a tent peg and hammer and killed him by hammering the tent peg into his head.

Why a tent peg?

The *Midrash* explains that she wanted to avoid doing the *aveirah* of a woman using a man's weapons.[11]

CHECKPOINT What kind of clothing or accessories are you not allowed to wear?

SELECTED HALACHOS

- Even wearing one piece of clothing from the other gender is forbidden. This is even if this does not hide your own gender.[14]

- A man may not take pills that will dye his white hairs back to their original color.[15]

- In times of danger, women may disguise themselves as men. Likewise, boys who have not yet grown their beards may dress as women.[16]

- Clothing that is not specifically designed for a man or a woman, may be worn by either gender. Even wearing them does not make them become designated for a specific gender.[17]

- A man may use an umbrella that was made for women.[18]

STORY

Doesn't Suit Her

R' Zalmele of Vilna once saw his wife take a sword so that she could cut a rope. He immediately told her to find a different tool. "Although you are not doing anything that is specifically forbidden," he said, "it looks wrong for a woman to use a sword."[20]

EXTEND YOUR KNOWLEDGE

Looking in the Mirror

Hundreds of years ago, not everyone had a mirror, and only women used mirrors to help make themselves beautiful, to fix their clothing, put on makeup, and other such uses. Men hardly ever used a mirror. So, a man was not allowed to look into a mirror, as this was an *aveirah* of *lo yilbash* - a man doing something that is specifically for women.

Today, mirrors are much more common, and are not only used for beauty. Many times, you will need to look into a mirror just to check something or other - is this allowed?

Since the situation has changed, the answer is yes: these days, a man may look into a mirror. However, if it is purely for beautification purposes, it may still be *assur*.[19]

BIOGRAPHY

R' Zalmele of Vilna (1755 - 1788) תקט"ו - תקמ"ח

R' Shlomo Zalmen of Volozhin, also known as R' Zalmele of Vilna, was born in the city of Volozhin on כ"ו סיון. He was the brother of the famous R' Chaim of Volozhin. He was one of the great students of the Vilna Gaon, and was well-versed in dikduk and engineering. He passed away at the young age of 32 on ט' אדר ראשון.

Live the Mitzvah

EXTRACT

Take Pride in Who You Are

Men and women have their own special jobs in life. Although they should help each other be successful at their job, each one has their own distinct responsibility: the man learns Torah, works, and provides for the family; the woman's responsibility is to manage the home, while taking care of, nurturing, and educating their children. Each deserve equal credit and support in doing their jobs.

These roles should be guarded and loved. For a man to be special, he does not need to be like a woman, and for a woman to be special, she does not need to be like a man.

CHECKPOINT What are the different jobs of men and women?

What Else Comes From This?

EXTRACT

Clowning Around

There are different opinions about dressing up on *Purim* in clothes of the opposite gender. The *Rama*[21] says that you are allowed to wear clothes of the other gender on *Purim*, since you are only getting dressed up to add to the happiness of *Purim*. However, many *poskim* disagree.[22] You should ask your *Rav* before you wear anything that is questionable.

CHECKPOINT When might you be allowed to dress in clothing of the opposite gender?

DISCOVERY

Can You See Me?

Until the 1900's, armies usually used bright colors and bold, impressive designs for their uniforms. They thought that these uniforms would scare the enemy, make it easier to see who was in the army, and would get new people to join the army. Also, the really bright uniforms helped the armies keep track of who left the army without permission.

Camouflage, on the other hand, is meant to hide its wearer by making it look like the surroundings, making a target harder to spot or hit, or so that you can't tell what it is.

UNIT
32

ENDNOTES:

1. נזיר נט, א

2. סה"מ ל"ת מ'

3. תו"מ תשמ"ה ח"א ע' 128 ואילך

4. רמב"ם הל' ע"ז פי"ב ה"י. ראה שו"ע הרב או"ח סי' ש"א ס"ז

5. רמב"ם הל' ע"ז פי"ב ה"י

6. רמב"ם הל' ע"ז פי"ב ה"ט

7. צפנת פענח פי"א ה"א, ועי' נר מצוה (יהודה בן מנוח) סי' י' אות י"ב ד"ה ואפשר

8. ב"ח יו"ד סי' קע"ח ס"ק ד'

9. נזיר נט, א

10. נזיר נט, א

11. שופטים ה, כו, מדרש משלי לא, יט

12. מנ"ח מצוה תקמ"ב אות ב', תקמ"ג אות ב'

13. רמב"ם הל' ע"ז פי"ב ה"ט

14. רמ"א יו"ד סי' קפ"ב ס"ה

15. אגרות משה יו"ד ח"א סי' פ"ב

16. דרכי תשובה יו"ד סי' קפ"ב ס"ק ח' בשם ספר חסידים

17. דרכי תשובה יו"ד סי' קפ"ב ס"ק י"ג בשם שו"ת אהלי יעקב

18. שו"ת משנה הלכות חלק י"ב סי' ס"ו

19. אגרות משה יו"ד ח"ב סי' מ"א. שו"ת יחוה דעת ח"ו סי' מ"ט

20. תולדות אדם

21. רמ"א או"ח סי' תרצ"ו ס"ח

22. ב"ח יו"ד סי' קפ"ב ס"ק ה' ד"ה ויש וט"ז שם ס"ק ד', הובא במשנ"ב או"ח סי' תרצ"ו ס"ק ל'. ועי' שו"ת יחוה דעת ח"ה סי' נ' ד"ה לאור שמקבץ הרבה דעות שאוסרים

Such a beautiful, special painting! Who is the artist, and could you possibly do such a perfect job?

UNIT 33

IN THIS UNIT YOU WILL:

EXAMINE

- What are the different kinds of damage you are not allowed to do to the body?

EXPLORE

- Are you allowed to do whatever you want with your body?
- Why is it wrong to mourn too much when someone passes away?

EXTRACT

- If you want to thank Hashem for your amazing body, what can you do?
- If we want to stay united as a nation, what should we not do?

כְּתֹבֶת קַעֲקַע
לֹא תִתְגּוֹדְדוּ

KEY CONCEPTS

Book: Madda, Section: Idol Worship

סֵפֶר מַדָּע הִלְכוֹת עֲבוֹדָה זָרָה

קְדוּשַׁת הַגוּף
THE KEDUSHAH OF THE BODY

שָׁלֹשׁ מִצְוֹת

Word Origin

The word tattoo comes from the Polynesian word 'ta,' which means to hit something; and the Tahitian word 'tatau,' which means 'to put a mark on something.'

STORY

Army of Hashem

The *Chafetz Chaim* was asked, "Why must the Jewish people have so many different groups? Some *daven* more, others study more, and still others only want to serve Hashem with joy. Why are we so divided?"

The *Chafetz Chaim* answered, "Look at the Czar's army! He has cannon men, foot soldiers, horseback soldiers, sailors and trumpeters! Does he need them all? Yes – each type of soldier has a special job in fighting the enemy. The cannon men can kill from far away, sailors can attack the enemy at sea, even the trumpeters are important to make the soldiers excited to fight.

So too, the many different groups of Jews can each give their special way of serving Hashem to defeat our common enemy, the *yetzer hara*—together!"[1]

In the unit of keeping your body holy there are three mitzvos.

1. Do not tattoo your skin.

2. Do not cut yourself for *avodah zarah* or because you are sad.

3. Do not pull out your hair because you are sad.

MITZVAH
72

שֶׁלֹּא נִכְתּוֹב בִּבְשָׂרֵנוּ כְּתֹבֶת קַעֲקַע
Not tattooing your skin

וְשֶׂרֶט לָנֶפֶשׁ לֹא תִתְּנוּ בִּבְשַׂרְכֶם וּכְתֹבֶת קַעֲקַע לֹא תִתְּנוּ בָּכֶם אֲנִי ה'
(ויקרא יט, כח)

Do not make gashes in your skin for the dead. **Do not make any tattoo marks on your skin.** I am Hashem.

Do not make a permanent tattoo on your skin.

ALL PEOPLE   ALL PLACES   ALL TIMES   *MALKUS*

MITZVAH
73

שֶׁלֹּא לְהִתְגּוֹדֵד כְּמוֹ עוֹבְדֵי עֲבוֹדָה זָרָה
Not cut tingyourself like thoes who serve *avodah zarah*

בָּנִים אַתֶּם לַה' אֱלֹקֵיכֶם לֹא תִתְגֹּדְדוּ וְלֹא תָשִׂימוּ קָרְחָה בֵּין עֵינֵיכֶם לָמֵת
(דברים יד, א)

You are the children of Hashem your G-d. **Do not mutilate yourselves** and do not make a bald patch in the middle of your head as a sign of mourning.

Do not cut yourself because you are sad that someone died, or for *avodah zarah*.

ALL PEOPLE   ALL PLACES   ALL TIMES   *MALKUS*

MITZVAH 74

שֶׁלֹּא לַעֲשׂוֹת קָרְחָה עַל מֵת

Not making a bald spot on your head to mourn

בָּנִים אַתֶּם לַה' אֱלֹקֵיכֶם לֹא תִתְגֹּדְדוּ וְלֹא תָשִׂימוּ קָרְחָה
בֵּין עֵינֵיכֶם לָמֵת
(דברים יד, א)

You are the children of Hashem your G-d. Do not mutilate yourselves and **do not make a bald patch in the middle of your head as a sign of mourning.**

Do not make a bald spot as a sign of mourning.

| ALL PEOPLE | ALL PLACES | ALL TIMES | *MALKUS* |

Mitzvah Messages

EXPLORE

Masterpiece

Our bodies are amazing works of art. Every tiny detail, down to the thinnest hair, was carefully planned and crafted by the Master Craftsman. To harm such a masterpiece would be very silly and destructive. Not only that, it would be an enormous insult to its Creator because it shows that you think you can improve His work.[2]

Back Home

In ancient times, people would feel so sad after someone they loved died that they would cut themsleves. This made them feel a lot of pain, and they felt like they were mourning the right way. Is this how you should act?

Not at all! The Torah tells us not to mourn too much for someone who dies. It is certainly sad when someone dies, but you must remind yourself that a person's *neshamah*, having finished its mission here in this world, is now back home with Hashem.[3] This is a good reason not to go overboard with your grief.

CHECKPOINT Why are you offending Hashem when you cut your body or harm it in any way?

Mourning Righteousness

Although we must not mourn too much, *Chazal* say that whoever cries for the death of a *tzaddik*, all his sins are forgiven.[4]

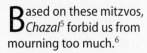

DID YOU KNOW?

Hold Those Tears

Based on these mitzvos, *Chazal*[5] forbid us from mourning too much.[6]

There is no need to hurt yourself out of grief, even when a close relative dies, because you will never lose your Father in Heaven, Hashem. But someone who serves *avodah zarah* is very sad, because he has a "father" of sticks and stones.[7]

PEARLS *of wisdom*

Gam Zu Letovah

Hashem loves you more than a father loves his son. Therefore, everything Hashem does is for your good. Even if, like small children, you do not understand why your Father is doing these things, you must trust that He knows best. This is why you should not mourn too much.[8]

Deserving of Degradation

King Yehoyakim of Yehudah was a cruel person who worshipped all idols and did every *aveirah* possible. His body was covered in tattoos showing pictures of all kinds of idols.

Nevuchadnetzar, king of *Bavel*, was chosen as Hashem's messenger to punish this evil person. When he attacked Yerushalayim, he demanded that the king be brought out to him. King Yehoyakim was brought and tortured, torn to pieces and fed to the dogs. Only his head was left. On it, Hashem wrote the words, "This and more" because the king's punishment was not yet over.

Sure enough, Hashem carried out an unusually harsh and severe punishment for the evil king.[9]

Tattoos

The Procedure

It takes two steps to make a tattoo:[10]

1. Cutting, pricking or making any hole in the skin.

2. Filling the holes with dye or ink or some other color.

You are only *oveir* this *aveirah* if both steps were done, in any order.[11] There is also no minimum size nor are there any specific shapes or letters – any tattoo is forbidden.[12]

The *aveirah* of tattoos applies only to permanent marks on your skin. Therefore, you would not be punished for hand stamps, paint, fake tattoos, or writing with a pen on your hand (like to remember a phone number).[13]

The Punishment

If you are tattooed by another person, you would be given *malkus* only if you helped the tattooist in a way that is like you almost did it.[14]

Damaging Your Body

Making a Wound

You are not allowed to hurt any part of your body for sadness, or as an act of *avodah zarah*.[15]

If you cut your skin from sadness, with your nails or with a tool, you get *malkus*.[16] Even a tiny cut, as long as it bleeds, would make you liable for *malkus*.[17]

If it was for *avodah zarah*, then you would get *malkus* only if you cut yourself with a tool,[18] because that is how the *avodah zarah* is served.[19]

Making a Bald Spot

You would get this *aveirah* if you would make a bald spot the size of a *gris* (about the size of a bean) on your head or by the hair between the eyes, by either pulling out your hair by hand or burning it off with chemicals.[20]

Painstaking Detail

Each and every square inch of the body has about 19,000,000 skin cells!

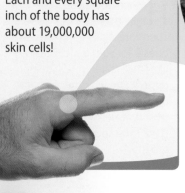

The Punishment

If you make a bald spot for another person, you are *chayav* for *malkus*. If you would help someone make a bald spot on your head, then you would also get *malkus*.[21]

Malkus is given for every cut or bald spot made. For example, if you make **five** wounds to mourn **five** people who died, you would get five sets of *malkus*. The same applies to making **five** wounds or bald spots to mourn **one** person who died, as long as you were warned before you made each wound. Even if all the wounds or bald spots were made at exactly the same time, five sets of malkus are still given.[22]

 CHECKPOINT   What kind of damage are you not allowed to do to your body?

SELECTED HALACHOS

- You are allowed to make a tattoo on a non-Jew.[23]
- You are not allowed to make a tattoo on a child.[24]
- You are allowed to brand (taking a hot piece of metal and pushing it against the skin) a tattoo on an animal so that you know to whom it belongs.[25]
- You are not allowed to do even half of the act of tattooing (for example, just writing or just scratching) even though you wouldn't get *malkus* for it.[26]
- You are allowed to put creams, powders, or even ashes on a cut to help it heal. This is even if it will leave a permanent mark, because other people will know that the "tattoo" was made for the purpose of healing.[27]
- You would not get punished for forced tattooing.[28] An example of forced tattooing would be those Jews who went through the concentration camps during the Holocaust and were cruelly tattood with a number on their arm.
- Someone who has a tattoo may be buried in a Jewish cemetery and participate fully in anything Jewish. Nevertheless, people should still never get a tattoo, since it goes against the Torah.[29]
- You can never cut yourself on purpose, whether or not someone just died.[30]

STORY

Mark of Greatness

After the Holocaust, the *Satmar Rebbe* lived in Eretz Yisrael for one year. In 1946, he moved to the U.S. One of his *chassidim* in Eretz Yisrael asked him, "Rebbe, without you, we have no leader. Who will guide us to follow the Torah"

The Rebbe replied, "When you see a Jew in *shul* wearing *tefillin* on his arm which has numbers tattooed on it, you should turn to this person. This is a person who went through the horrors of the Holocaust, and has the tattooed numbers to prove it. Nevertheless, despite all he has been through, he stands firm in his *emunah* and comes to *shul* to *daven* with his *tefillin*. Such a person's prayers are definitely answered, and therefore, he will be able to help you."[32]

No Two Are the Same

You probably know that no two people have the same fingerprints, but did you know that no two people have the same tongue print?

OUR SAGES SAY...

Two Sides of the Coin

The nations of the world do three things which make Hashem angry, and the Jews use the same three things to make Hashem happy:

1. The nations anger Hashem by (shaving) the hair of their heads (for *avodah zarah*) and the Jewish people make Him happy with the *tefillin* on their heads.

2. The nations anger Hashem with the tattoos on their hands, and the Jewish people make Him happy with the *tefillin* on their hands.

3. The nations anger Hashem with their idols that deny His existence, and the Jewish people make Him happy when they say *Shema* and say that Hashem exists and runs the world.[33]

EXTEND YOUR KNOWLEDGE

Overcome With Grief

The *Gemara*[34] tells us that when R' Eliezer passed away, R' Akiva was so overcome with grief that he hit his body until he bled. At the funeral, he cried out, "Father! Father! Yisrael's chariot and horsemen! I have no one to answer my questions in Torah."

The Ramban[35] explains that what R' Akiva did was allowed, since you are only not allowed to hurt yourself through **cutting**.

The Rosh[36] says that you are not allowed to hurt yourself even through hitting. Yet, R' Akiva was allowed to do this because he was sad about the loss of Torah knowledge, not about R' Eliezer's death itself. The *aveirah* of hurting yourself only applies to sadness over something physical. But if it is for a spiritual sadness, like the loss of a *Rebbe* or *Talmid Chacham*, it is permitted.[37]

Plastic Surgery

Because of this mitzvah that teaches us never to hurt a Jewish body, some *Poskim* do not allow plastic surgery if it is done only for beauty. The body is holy and you have no right to harm it for what you think is "beauty." In fact, the only reason a doctor is allowed to harm a person's body during surgery is because there is a positive mitzvah to "love a fellow Jew" and help him, which pushes away the negative mitzvah. Otherwise, it wouldn't be allowed![38]

Live the Mitzvah

VIP Loan

You are reading this with a pair of eyes that are on loan to you. That hand turning the page is also on loan. Your whole body is a treasure that has been handed over to you for a short time. Take good care of it, keep it clean, feed it with good things, and give it exercise. Count the many blessings you have been given through this one body. Count them in your head when you say the *brachah* of *asher yatzar*, and be thankful.

CHECKPOINT — What can you do to show Hashem that you are thankful for your body?

What Else Comes From This?

Staying United

United in Law

Chazal explain that the words "לֹא תִּתְגֹּדְדוּ - do not cut yourself," also means "לֹא תַעֲשׂוּ אֲגוּדוֹת אֲגוּדוֹת — do not make separate groups." This means that there should not be different groups of Jews in one city.[39] This also means that we should not have two *batei din* in one city who rule on *halachah* differently, since this would lead to arguments.[40]

United in Custom

This rule about different groups in one city also applies to *minhag*, and not just to *halachah*.[41] Therefore, you cannot act differently than the local *minhag*, even if the *minhag* is not as strict with *halachah* as you would like it to be. You may certainly not do this to show that your own *minhag* is the correct one. But you are allowed to be privately more strict if it is not obvious to other people.[42]

CHECKPOINT What should you do if you are in a place that has a different *minhag* than you do?

DID YOU KNOW?

Modeled on Greatness

Hashem created man in His image, therefore, it would be a terrible insult to Hashem to change the body![43]

OUR SAGES SAY...

On Loan

A Jew's body is not his own, but, rather, is Hashem's "property."

Just like when you borrow something, you must be very careful not to damage it, you cannot cause pain to yourself, even by fasting for no reason.[44]

DID YOU KNOW?

Yes, You Too

When Hashem chose the Jews to be His chosen nation at *Har Sinai*, He also chose the physical bodies of the Jews.[45]

UNIT 33

ENDNOTES:

15. חינוך מצוה תס"ז
16. נימוקי יוסף מכות פ"ג במשנה ד"ה והשורט שריטה אחת
17. ערוך לנר מכות כא, א ד"ה וגדיגה א' הוא (ריש העמוד)
18. רמב"ם הל' ע"ז פי"ב הי"ג
19. נימוקי יוסף מכות פ"ג ד"ה על עבודת כוכבים
20. רמב"ם הל' ע"ז פי"ב הט"ו, כס"מ שם ד"ה וחייב על כל הראש
21. רמב"ם הל' ע"ז פי"ב הט"ז
22. רמב"ם הל' ע"ז פי"ב הי"ב וט"ז, מנ"ח מצוה תס"א אות ד' ו'
23. שו"ת נו"ב תניינא אה"ע סי' קל"ה. אבל ע"י מנ"ח מצוה רנ"ג אות ט, ב"י יו"ד סי' קפ"א ס"ה, וברמ"א שם
24. שו"ת יו"ד סי' קפ"א ס"ה ע"פ מנ"ח מצוה רנ"ג אות ט.
25. שו"ת נו"ב תניינא אה"ע סי' קל"ה
26. מנ"ח מצוה רנ"ג אות א'
27. שו"ת יו"ד סי' קפ"ה ה"ג, ש"ך ס"ק ו'
28. שו"ת יו"ד סי' קפ"ה ה"ב
29. פשוט, ואין מפקפק בזה להלכה

30. שו"ע יו"ד סי' ק"פ ס"ו
31. מלכים א' י"ח, כח
32. שדה צופים על מס' סוכה בהקדמה ע' 9
33. אוצר מדרשים אייזנשטיין ע' 247
34. סנהדרין סח, א. וברש"י שם
35. תורת האדם ענין ההספד, הובא בטור וזה כתירוץ הא' בתוס' יבמות יג, ב ד"ה דאמר
36. מו"ק פ"ג סי' צ"ג
37. מנ"ח מצוה תס"ז אות ג'
38. שו"ת ציץ אליעזר חלק י"א א"א מ"א מצוה יד, א
39. יבמות יד, א
40. רמב"ם הל' ע"ז פי"ב הי"ד
41. מג"א סי' תצ"ג ס"ק ו'
42. שו"ע הרב או"ח סי' תצ"ג ס"ז
43. בראשית א, כז
44. שו"ע הרב חו"מ הל' נזקי גוף ונפש ס"ד
45. לקו"א פרק מ"ט

1. חפץ חיים עה"ת ע' רנו
2. רש"י דברים יד, א. ועי' שו"ת ציץ אליעזר חלק י"א סי' מ"א
3. אוה"ח דברים יד, א
4. שבת קה, ב
5. מו"ק כז, ב
6. רמב"ן דברים יד, א
7. דעת זקנים, ספורנו דברים יד, א
8. אבן עזרא דברים יד, א. וראה עד"ז בש"ך עה"ת ויקרא יט, כח
9. סנהדרין קג-קד. ב"ר צד, ט. מו"ק כו, א
10. שו"ע יו"ד סי' ק"פ ס"א
11. ב"ח יו"ד סי' ק"פ ס"ק ב'. ש"ך שם ס"ק א'
12. מנ"ח מצוה רנ"ג אות ז'
13. חינוך מצוה רנ"ג, מנ"ח שם אות א'. ועי' בספר פתשגן הכתב סוף סי' י"ח
14. חינוך מצוה רנ"ג. מנ"ח שם אות ח'. רמב"ם הל' ע"ז פי"ב הט"ז. טושו"ע יו"ד סי' ק"פ ס"ב וסי"א

UNIT 34

IN THIS UNIT YOU WILL:

EXPLORE

- Why does *teshuvah* strengthen your connection with Hashem?

- Why does the idea of *teshuvah* help you serve Hashem?

EXAMINE

- What are the three steps of *teshuvah*?

- What is the test for you to know that your *teshuvah* is sincere?

EXTRACT

- If you want Hashem to forgive you, what can you do?

- If you are looking for help to do *teshuvah*, what can you do?

וִידּוּי

בַּעַל תְּשׁוּבָה

תְּשׁוּבָה

KEY CONCEPTS

Book: Madda, Section: Teshuvah
סֵפֶר מַדָּע הִלְכוֹת תְּשׁוּבָה

תְּשׁוּבָה
TESHUVAH
מִצְוָה אַחַת

You are climbing a very steep mountain. You climb your way up the rocky face, praying that the rope is strong enough to stop you from falling. **You peek at the rope, and to your horror, you see that small strands are starting to pop!** Is the rope going to hold?! Oh, help!

PEARLS of wisdom

Temporary Situation

Most people would translate the word תְּשׁוּבָה as "repenting," which means feeling sorry for what you did. Although *teshuvah* does involve repentance, that's not really what it means. The real meaning of the word *teshuvah* is "returning," from the *shoresh* שב.

"Repentance" means fixing a mistake so that you can start again on a fresh slate. "Returning" means going back to the way things were before, how they should be. Because you are naturally good and naturally close to Hashem, *teshuvah* means going back to the closeness you had with Hashem before you did something wrong.

OUR SAGES SAY...

What Are You Waiting For?

B'nei Yisrael will only be saved through *teshuvah*. The Torah promises that *B'nei Yisrael* will do *teshuvah* towards the end of *galus* and *Mashiach* will come immediately thereafter.[1]

The Mitzvah

The unit of *teshuvah* has one mitzvah.

Confess and regret your *aveiros,* and decide not to do them again.

MITZVAH 75

שֶׁיָּשׁוּב הַחוֹטֵא מֵחֶטְאוֹ לִפְנֵי ה' וְיִתְוַדֶּה

Confessing and regretting your *aveiros* before Hashem and deciding not to do them again

וְהִתְוַדּוּ אֶת חַטָּאתָם אֲשֶׁר עָשׂוּ וְהֵשִׁיב אֶת אֲשָׁמוֹ בְּרֹאשׁוֹ וַחֲמִישִׁתוֹ יֹסֵף עָלָיו וְנָתַן לַאֲשֶׁר אָשַׁם לוֹ

(במדבר ה, ז)

They must confess the sin that they have committed. He must then make a payment to the value of what was lost plus a fifth, and give it to the victim of his crime.

Confess and regret your *aveiros* before Hashem and decide never to go against Hashem again.

ALL PEOPLE · ALL PLACES · ALL TIMES

Unbreakable Connection

Your connection to Hashem is like a rope of 613 strands, one strand for every mitzvah. If you do an *aveirah*, a strand or two might break, but the rope never totally snaps, and you are never totally cut off from Hashem.

By doing *teshuvah*, you are fixing the broken strands of your rope, and making your connection to Hashem stronger than it ever was before. This is just like a rope, which is stronger when it has been broken and then tied back together. When you do *teshuvah*, you are building a stronger connection to Hashem.[2]

Always Determined

Teshuvah also keeps you moving on your way to becoming a better person, even if you sometimes fall. If you could never, ever fix an *aveirah*, you would never even try to be good. You would be extremely sad and might do even more *aveiros, chas v'shalom. Teshuvah* gives you hope and the strength to move away from your *aveiros* and to continue to do good.[3]

 CHECKPOINT What does *teshuvah* teach you about the connection between you and Hashem?

Second Chance

Wisdom was asked: What will happen to someone who does an *aveirah*? Wisdom answered "He will be more evil."

Nevuah was asked: What will happen to someone who does an *aveirah*? *Nevuah* answered: "He should die!"

The **Torah** was asked: What will happen to someone who does an *aveirah*? Torah answered: "He should bring a *korban*, and then he will be forgiven."

Hashem was asked: What will happen to someone who does an *aveirah*? Hashem answered: "He should do *teshuvah*, and he will be forgiven."[5]

A STORY

Literal Minded

Some robbers in R' Meir's neighborhood were causing him a lot of trouble. So, R' Meir *davened* that they should die.

His wife Beruria said to him, "How could you say such a prayer?! The *passuk* says, "Let חֲטָאִים (sins) cease" and **not** "חוֹטְאִים" (sinners)! Instead of *davening* that they should die, *daven* that they should do *teshuvah* and then they won't do the *aveiros* anymore!"

R' Meir listened to the advice of his wise wife, and the men did *teshuvah* and stopped bothering him.[4]

DID YOU KNOW?

True Masters

Teshuvah is so great that *Chazal* say that in the place where someone who did *teshuvah* stands, even the greatest *tzaddikim* cannot stand.[6]

It is so great that when *Mashiach* comes, he will cause even *tzaddikim* to do *teshuvah*.[7]

DID YOU KNOW?

טוֹבֵל וְשֶׁרֶץ בְּיָדוֹ

If you say *viduy*, but don't decide in your heart never to do it again, the *viduy* is useless! The real problem is still there, and you will just do the *aveirah* again.

This is like someone who goes to the *mikvah* while holding a *sheretz* (an insect that makes someone *tamei*). His *tevilah* does not make him pure because he is still holding something that makes him *tamei*.[8]

PEARLS of wisdom

Keep On Trying

*C*hazal say, "If a person says, I will do *aveiros* and then do *teshuvah* later, He is not given the opportunity to do *teshuvah*."

Why is this?

This person did an *aveirah* **because** he thought he could fix it later by doing *teshuvah*. If "*teshuvah*" is what **caused** him to do the *aveirah,* how can it be used now to remove the *aveirah*!?

But does that mean that this person **never** do *teshuvah*?

No! *Chazal* say, "**Nothing** can stand in the way of *teshuvah*."

It will not be made **easy** for the person to do *teshuvah*. It will be very hard for him to do *teshuvah*, and it will need to be a higher level of *teshuvah* than it would have been before.[9]

Details

EXAMINE

How to Do *Teshuvah*

What is תְּשׁוּבָה?

Doing *Teshuvah* is much more than just feeling sorry for doing *aveiros*. There are three steps that you must do to do *teshuvah*:

1. וִידוּי – You must say which *aveirah* you did.

2. חֲרָטָה – You must feel sorry for the *aveirah* that you did.

3. קַבָּלָה – You must accept upon yourself never to go against Hashem's mitzvah again.

You can say that you feel bad for your *aveirah* again and again, but the real test of *teshuvah* is when you have a chance to do the same *aveirah* again, and you take control of your *yetzer hara* and don't do it.

If you can stop yourself from doing the *aveirah* again, this shows that you really meant it when you decided never to do it again.[10]

First Make Amends

Teshuvah may keep you connected to Hashem, but don't think that saying sorry to Hashem is all you need to fix everything. If you hurt someone, you must first ask forgiveness from that person and try to make it up with him, before Hashem will accept your *teshuvah*.[11]

 CHECKPOINT What are the three steps of *teshuvah*?

SELECTED HALACHOS

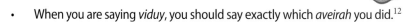

- When you are saying *viduy*, you should say exactly which *aveirah* you did.[12]

- If you hurt another person, and you did not ask for forgiveness before the person passed away, you have to go to that person's grave and ask for forgiveness in front of ten people.[13]

- The ten days between *Rosh Hashanah* and *Yom Kippur* are called עֲשֶׂרֶת יְמֵי תְּשׁוּבָה. During these days Hashem makes Himself especially available for people to do *teshuvah*. Hashem listens to a single person *davening* during these days, as much as He listens to a whole *minyan* during the rest of the year.[14]

EXTEND YOUR KNOWLEDGE

תְּשׁוּבָה or וִידוי?

This mitzvah has three parts. When you do an *aveirah*, you have to verbalize what you have done, feel bad about it, and decide never to do it again. However, the Rambam only counts *viduy* in his list of the 613 mitzvos. Why doesn't he count all three parts?

When there is more than one part to a mitzvah, the Rambam only counts the part that is an action. In this case, saying *viduy* verbally is an action much more than feeling bad or deciding not to do it again. That is why the Rambam lists *viduy* as the mitzvah.

That is also the reason why the Rambam learns the mitzvah from the *passuk* וְהִתְוַדּוּ אֶת חַטָּאתָם and not from the *passuk* וְשַׁבְתָּ עַד ה' אֱלֹקֶיךָ in *Parshas Nitzavim*, because that *passuk* does not mention *viduy*, which according to the Rambam is the main part of the mitzvah.[15]

A STORY

The Door is Never Closed

R' Leib Sarah's convinced a man who had been an *apikores* for many years to go to *shul* on *Yom Kippur*. This was his first time going to *shul* in forty years! The *apikores* had married a wealthy non-Jewish woman and felt that he could never do *teshuvah* for that. R' Leib Sarah's assured the man that he still had a chance to do *teshuvah*. R' Leib Sarah's shared with the man how his own mother married a poor old man, just so that she wouldn't have to marry a wealthy non-Jew who really wanted to marry her.

Throughout the day on *Yom Kippur*, the *apikores* cried bitterly and he begged Hashem to forgive him. At the time of *Ne'ilah*, he went to the *aron kodesh*, hugged the *Sifrei Torah*, and cried out, "Shema Yisrael, Hashem Elokeinu, Hashem Echad." He then screamed the words, "Hashem Hu Ha'Elokim" seven times. After the last time, his *neshamah* left him and he died. As a sign of how *teshuvah* can erase even a great *aveirah*, R' Leib Sarah's remembered this *Ba'al Teshuvah* and he said *kaddish* for his *neshamah* on every *Yom Kippur* after that![16]

OUR SAGES SAY...

Never Again

Viduy is helpful in doing *teshuvah* because when you say the details of what you did, it becomes more 'real' and can help stop you from doing it again.[18]

BIOGRAPHY

R' Leib Sarah's
ת"ץ - תקנ"ו (1730 – 1796)

R' Leib Sarah's (Reb Leib, the son of Sarah) was a talmid of the Ba'al Shem Tov. R' Leib was known as one of the 36 Hidden Tzadikim and he spent his life travelling from place to place, raising funds to get other Jews released from prison and to support other tzadikim. He was born on the 17th of Tammuz and passed away on the 4th of Adar. (According to some, R' Leib Sarah's is the same person who is also known as "The Shpoller Zeide".)

People in some countries apologize a lot more than others. They are more willing to forgive someone when they hear an apology. Because of this *middah*, there are much fewer court cases in those countries than in other places.

STORY

Take Responsibility for Yourself

Elazar ben Durdaya did many *aveiros*. Once, someone told him that he would never, ever be able to do *teshuvah* because his *aveiros* were so terrible.

Elazar was scared and sat among the mountains. He called out to the mountains and the hills, "Mountains and hills! Ask Hashem to have mercy on me!" They answered, "Ask mercy for *you*? We can't help you!" Elazar tried the skies, the earth, the sun, the moon, the stars and the planets, but they all had the same answer.

Finally, he was so miserable and heartbroken that he sat down and cried out, "Hashem! I am the one who has to do *teshuvah*!" and then he died. A voice declared from Above, "Rabbi Elazar ben Durdaya is worthy of *Olam Haba*!"[19]

Live the Mitzvah

EXTRACT

Second Chance

The Gift

When was the last time you wanted to have a second chance at something, only to be told, "No! Sorry, it's too late!" With *teshuvah*, that never happens! Hashem has given us a special gift – the gift of *teshuvah*, which gives you a chance to be a better person. You must use this gift with love and gratitude for His kindness in always giving you the chance to fix all of your mistakes.

Pass It On

You must also pass this gift on to others, by forgiving your friends and giving them another chance. By doing this, you are keeping your friends, and you are showing Hashem that He should judge you favorably and accept your *teshuvah*, just like you have done to your friends.

 CHECKPOINT How can you give someone a second chance?

What Else Comes From This?

EXTRACT

After *Teshuvah*

When a friend does something wrong to you and you forgive him, you might not be as happy and friendly with your friend as you were before you were hurt. But, if your friend would bring you a present and really show you that it will never happen again, you would probably feel the special friendship you had.

Even after you have done proper *teshuvah* and Hashem has forgiven your *aveirah*, you can still do a lot to make Hashem happy by showing Him that you will never do that *aveirah* again.

In earlier generations when people were stronger, they would fast to help them do *teshuvah* more easily and show Hashem that they really mean it. Today, fasting is harder for our bodies, and would make it hard for us to learn, *daven*, and serve Hashem properly. Today, we can accomplish the same thing by giving a lot of *tzedakah*.[20]

Extra Help

Along with the gift of *teshuvah*, Hashem has also given us special tools to help us do *teshuvah*. Some of them are:

1. **The *Shofar*** — The piercing sound of the *shofar* on *Rosh Hashanah* calls to wake you up from your "sleep" and to do *teshuvah*.[21]

2. ***Elul*** — The month of *Elul* is spent preparing for *Rosh Hashanah* and *Yom Kippur*. You should think about how you have behaved in the last year and how you can serve Hashem in a better way. The *shofar* is blown every weekday during *Elul* as a reminder to do *teshuvah*.

3. ***Krias Shema She'al Hamitah*** — In addition to saying *Shema* during *shacharis* and *ma'ariv*, every night before you go to bed, you say *Shema* again. You might also add different *pessukim* such as "*yoshev be'seser elyon*"[22] asking Hashem to protect you from anything bad that might happen during the night.[23]

This is the right time to think about the things you did during the day and see if there was anything that needs to be fixed. If you did any *aveiros*, you should say a short version of "*viduy*" and make a strong descision never to do those things again.[24]

Chazal say that saying *Krias Shema She'al Hamitah* is like holding a sharp, double-edged sword which cuts away the *aveiros* and anything bad that your actions may have caused.[25]

CHECKPOINT What actions and *tefillos* can you do to help you do *teshuvah*?

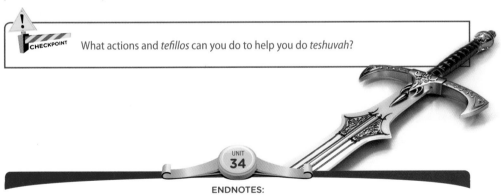

OUR SAGES SAY...

Always Be Prepared

R' Eliezer told his *talmidim* that they should do *teshuvah* one day before they die.

To this, his *talmidim* asked, "But we don't know when we'll die! How would we know when is the right time to do *teshuvah*?"

R' Eliezer explained that because you don't know when you will die, and you want to make sure that you do *teshuvah* before you die, you should be doing *teshuvah* every single day![26]

PEARLS of wisdom

כָּל יָמָיו בִּתְשׁוּבָה

Chazal tell us that we should be doing *teshuvah* all our lives. This is because *teshuvah* is not only for *aveiros*, but also for bad *middos* such as anger, jealousy, and greed. These *middos* can never be fully perfected, so you should spend your whole life working on these *middos*.[27]

Another reason why you should do *teshuvah* your whole life, is because *teshuvah* is about feeling bad about what you have done. As you grow in age and knowledge of Torah and Hashem's greatness, you will realize more and more how silly you were to go against Hashem, and you will feel more and more regret for what you have done.[28]

ENDNOTES:

23. משנ"ב סי' רל"ט ס"ק ט'
24. מג"א סי' רל"ט ס"ק ז'
25. ברכות ה, א, חידושי הצל"ח ברכות ה, א ד"ה אם
26. שבת קנג, א
27. רמב"ם הל' תשובה פ"ז ה"ג
28. ראה פע"ח שער התפילין פ"י ובהגה שם

13. רמב"ם הל' תשובה פ"ב הי"א
14. רמב"ם הל' תשובה פ"ב ה"ו
15. קרית ספר (למבי"ט) על הרמב"ם הל' תשובה פ"א
16. סיפורי חסידים יום הכיפורים
17. רמב"ם הל' תשובה פ"ז ה"ג
18. חינוך מצוה שס"ד
19. ע"ז יז, א
20. שערי תשובה לר' יונה שער ד' אות י"א. ועי' אגה"ת פ"א
21. רמב"ם הל' תשובה פ"ג ה"ד
22. שו"ע או"ח סי' רל"ט ס"א

1. רמב"ם הל' תשובה פ"ז ה"ה
2. אגה"ת פ"ה וט'
3. מורה נבוכים ח"ג פל"ו
4. ברכות י, א
5. פסיקתא דרב כהנא כד, ז
6. ברכות לד, ב
7. ראה זח"ג קנג, ב
8. רמב"ם הל' תשובה פ"ב ה"ג
9. לקו"א פכ"ה
10. רמב"ם הל' תשובה פ"ב ה"א-ב'
11. רמב"ם הל' תשובה פ"ב ה"ט
12. רמב"ם הל' תשובה פ"ב ה"ג

UNIT 35

IN THIS UNIT YOU WILL:

EXPLORE

- Why do you need to say *Shema* so often, and why do you need reminders?

EXAMINE

- What is *Shema*?
- How many times a day do we have to say *Shema* and when?

EXTRACT

- Which other mitzvos are reminders?
- At what other occasions do we say *Shema* besides the times we are obligated to say it?

קְרִיאַת שְׁמַע

KEY CONCEPTS

Book: Ahavah, Section: Reading Shema

סֵפֶר אַהֲבָה הִלְכוֹת קְרִיאַת שְׁמַע

קְרִיאַת שְׁמַע

KRIAS SHEMA

מִצְוָה אַחַת

Reminders, reminders, reminders.

Where would we be without them?

PEARLS
of wisdom

Witness

When the first *passuk* of *Shema* is written in a *Sefer Torah*, *tefillin*, and a *mezuzah*, the last letter of the first word of *shema* "ע" and the last letter of the last word "ד" are written larger than the other letters.

These two letters together spell the word "עֵד" - witness.

When you say *Shema*, you are a witness to the fact that Hashem is the only one G-d, and He has power over all of His creations.[1]

DID YOU KNOW?

Seventy

The *gematria* of the letter "ע," the last letter of the word "שְׁמַע," is 70. There are many connections between the Torah and the number 70:

There are 70 names for the Jewish nation, the Torah has 70 names, and the Torah can be explained in 70 different ways. These special aspects of the Jewish nation are some of the things that set us apart from all the other 70 nations.[2]

The Mitzvah   EXAMINE

The unit of *Krias Shema* has one mitzvah.

Say *Shema* twice every day, once in the morning and once in the evening.

MITZVAH 76

מִצְוַת קְרִיאַת שְׁמַע שַׁחֲרִית וְעַרְבִית
Saying *Shema* in the morning and evening

וְשִׁנַּנְתָּם לְבָנֶיךָ וְדִבַּרְתָּ בָּם בְּשִׁבְתְּךָ בְּבֵיתֶךָ וּבְלֶכְתְּךָ בַדֶּרֶךְ וּבְשָׁכְבְּךָ וּבְקוּמֶךָ
(דברים ו, ז)

Teach them to your children and **speak of them** when you are at home, when travelling on the road, **when you lie down and when you get up.**

Say *Shema* in the morning and evening.

MALES   ALL PLACES   ALL TIMES

Mitzvah Messages   EXPLORE

A Constant Reminder

All the distractions and temptations that you see in the world make it easy for you to forget that you are one of Hashem's children and have a special job to do. Therefore, Hashem has commanded us to announce His Kingship over us twice every day. This reminds you to listen to Hashem and His Torah at all times. Saying *Shema* at night reminds you to watch your behavior at night, and saying it in the morning reminds you to be careful with your actions during the day.[3]

CHECKPOINT How does saying *krias shema* help you keep the Torah and mitzvos?

The *Shema*

What is it?

Shema is made up of three paragraphs, called *parshios*, from the Torah.

1. שְׁמַע - The first *parshah* speaks about accepting Hashem's rulership over us, and some basic mitzvos like *tefillin* and *mezuzah*.

2. וְהָיָה אִם שָׁמוֹעַ - The second *parshah* speaks about doing Hashem's mitzvos.

3. וַיֹּאמֶר - The third *parshah* speaks about *yetzias Mitzrayim* and the mitzvah of *tzitzis*.[4]

When is *Krias Shema* Said?

From the wording of the *passuk* "וּבְשָׁכְבְּךָ וּבְקוּמֶךָ" - "when you go to sleep and when you wake up," we learn that you are supposed to say *Shema* at night, when people go to sleep, and in the morning, when people wake up.[5]

At night, you must say *Shema* anytime from when the stars come out until dawn. The best time to say *Shema* is before midnight, because that is when most people go to sleep, but you are allowed to say it until dawn. Many people fulfill this part of the mitzvah when they daven *Ma'ariv*, and some people fulfill the mitzvah when they say *Shema* before they go to sleep.

During the day, the mitzvah begins from just before sunrise until three hours into the day, since that is the time when most people wake up.[6]

Who Has This Mitzvah?

Any mitzvah which has a specific time of the day or year when it must be done is called a מִצְוַת עֲשֵׂה שֶׁהַזְמַן גְּרָמָה – a positive mitzvah which has to be done at a certain time. Women do not have to do these mitzvos. Since you have to say *Shema* in the morning and at night, it is a *mitzvas asei shehazman gramah* and women do not have to do it.

Brachos Before and After

Ezra Hasofer and his *Beis Din* set three *brachos* to say before and after *Krias Shema*. When you say *Shema* in the morning, you say two *brachos* beforehand, and one afterward. When you say *Shema* in the evening, you say two *brachos* beforehand, and two *brachos* afterwards. These *brachos* are an important part of the mitzvah of saying *Shema* and must not be left out. You are not allowed to change any of the words of the *brachos*.[7]

How Should You Say It?

Shema must be said carefully and with a lot of concentration. You have not done the mitzvah if you did not say the words with concentration and focus.[12] You are not allowed to motion to anyone else with your eyes or lips, or fingers while saying *Shema*, even if it is to do another mitzvah. This would make *Shema* seem "casual," which is wrong.[13]

What is the Right Time and Place?

You must be careful to say *Shema* in a place that is appropriate. There must be no trash, other dirty things, or improperly dressed people near you. You must also be properly dressed in a way that separates your head and heart from the lower half of your body. This means wearing pants, a skirt or other clothing that makes a separation between the top and lower parts of your body.[14]

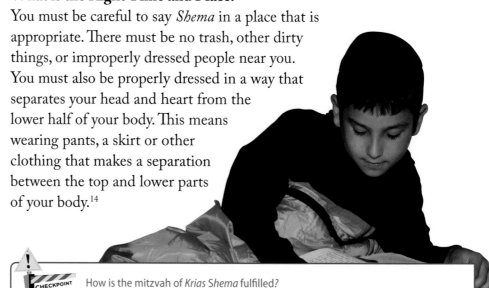

CHECKPOINT How is the mitzvah of *Krias Shema* fulfilled?

A STORY

Just Peanuts

A man wanted to make fun of the Torah, so he said to R' Yitzchak Meir Alter, the first *Gerrer Rebbe*, "Rebbe, I can prove that the Torah is not true. The second paragraph of *Shema* warns of terrible punishments for those who do *aveiros*. For years, I have broken every mitzvah there is, and yet I am blessed with wealth, good health and a happy family."

The Rebbe responded, "Since you are quoting from *Shema*, I assume you have read through the words of *Shema* at least once?"

"Of course I have, Rebbe," replied the man.

"Well then, all those wonderful gifts that Hashem has given you up until now is reward for that one time. Hashem is so forgiving and generous that saying *Shema* even once brings you rewards and happiness beyond your wildest dreams."

Can you imagine how much greater your reward would be if you performed all the mitzvos?[15]

SELECTED HALACHOS

- You are allowed to say *Shema* while you are sitting, standing, lying down on your side, or even while riding an animal.[16]

- You must be very careful to say *Shema* properly, pronouncing each sound correctly, and saying each word clearly and separately.[17]

- Even though you should say *Shema* in *Lashon Hakodesh,* you are allowed to say it in any language.[18]

- You must wash your hands before saying *Shema*.[19]

- *Shema* has 245 words. In order to say 248 words, the same as the amount of *mitzvos asei* and the number of limbs in your body, the last three words ה׳ אֱלֹקֵיכֶם אֱמֶת are repeated by the *chazzan*.[20]

- You must say the *parshios* of *Shema* in order. If the order was changed, you must say it again.[21]

- If you cannot remember whether you said *Shema* or not, you must say it again with the *brachos*.[22]

EXTEND YOUR KNOWLEDGE

שָׁעוֹת זְמַנִיוֹת - Seasonal Hours

The mitzvah of saying *Shema* in the morning must be done during the first three hours of the morning.

An hour in *halachah* is different than a regular hour. You are used to an hour being sixty minutes, no matter the time of the year. In *halachah*, an hour depends on how much daylight there will be that day: You take the total amount of daylight time and divide that by twelve, so that there are twelve even amounts of time during the day. These units are an "hour" - in *halachah* called "Shaos Zemaniyos." This means that in the summer, when there is more daylight, the "hours" are longer than in the winter when there are less daylight hours.

Since there are different amounts of daylight every day of the year and in every place in the world, the deadline to say *Shema* changes every day and in every place!

Punctuality Appreciated

Someone who says *Shema* on time is greater than someone who learns Torah.[25]

Allegiance to the Flag

Every day, hundreds of thousands of school children across the United States say the Pledge of Allegiance at the beginning of the school day. Meetings of Congress and sports games also open with the singing of the National Anthem, as do local government meetings and meetings held by the Royal Rangers, the Boy Scouts of America and other organizations.

Singing these songs is meant to help people focus and remember their loyalty and sacrifice to the country.

OUR SAGES SAY...

Say It Like You Mean It

The Jewish people say to Hashem:

"כִּי עָלֶיךָ הֹרַגְנוּ כָל הַיּוֹם נֶחְשַׁבְנוּ כְּצֹאן טִבְחָה"

"For Your sake we are killed every day; we are considered like sheep for the slaughter."

We are not killed every day - what does this mean?

The passuk means that by saying Shema every day, it is as if we are ready to give up our lives for Hashem right then and there, and Hashem considers it as if we have actually sacrificed our lives for His sake.[26]

Live the Mitzvah

EXTRACT

Remind Me

Have you ever noticed that if you want to remember something, if you don't write a note or repeat it to yourself a few times, you are more likely to forget it? When you say *Shema*, if you don't repeat it often enough and with enough *kavanah*, you might start to forget what this mitzvah teaches us, and you will not be reminded that your purpose in this world is to be loyal to Hashem and do His mitzvos.

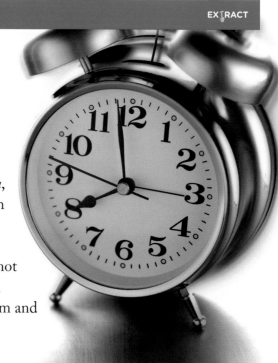

 CHECKPOINT   Why do you need to say *shema* so many times?

What Else Comes From This?

EXTRACT

Famous Last Words

The first six words of *Shema*, "שְׁמַע יִשְׂרָאֵל ה' אֱלֹקֵינוּ ה' אֶחָד" show everyone our strong faith and belief in Hashem. Time and time again, when Jews were given the terrible choice to live by removing Hashem from their lives, or to be killed *al kiddush Hashem*, their decision was that it was better to choose death than to deny Hashem. When being put to death, the last words of a Jew were always "*Shema Yisrael.*"

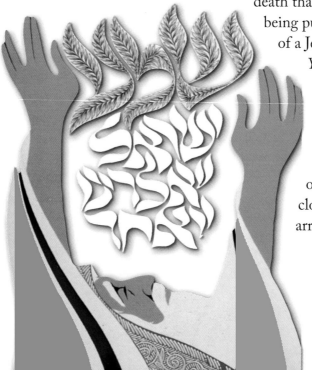

The Finale

Each year, when we daven *Ne'ilah* on *Yom Kippur*, when the gates of *shamayim* are about to close, a powerful moment arrives when we sincerely announce our faith in Hashem. In the passion of the moment, everyone cries out together, "*Shema Yisrael.*" Some *machzorim* note that when you say these words, you should have in mind that you are ready to give up your life *al kiddush Hashem*. If you have this *kavanah* when you say those words, Hashem considers it as if you have actually done so.

 When are special times when the *passuk* of *Shema* is recited?

A STORY

In His Memory

Before his death, Ya'akov wanted to tell his sons what would happen when *Mashiach* comes, and he started to say "...And I will tell you what will happen to you at the end of the days." However, the *Shechinah* left him, and he was not able to tell them. He thought that the *Shechinah* had left him because one of his sons did an *aveirah,* so he asked them "Are any of you not worthy to be near the *Shechinah*?" and they all answered together, "*Shema Yisrael...,*" which meant that they all believed and followed Hashem. Relieved, Ya'akov answered, "*Baruch shem k'vod...*"

Therefore, today we say *Baruch Shem* after *Shema Yisrael.* We say it because we want to honor the fact that Ya'akov said this *passuk.* We say it quietly because it is not written in the Torah as part of the *parshah* of *Shema.*[27]

UNIT 35

Cover Your Eyes

The *Gemara* tells us that R'Yehuda Hanassi would start giving his *shiur* in the morning before the sun would rise. When the sun rose and it was time to say *Shema*, he would cover his eyes and say the first part of *Krias Shema*.[28]

HISTORY

Turn To Hashem

Menachem Mendel Beilis was wrongly arrested on the 21st of July 1911 for the murder of a 13 year old Ukrainian boy, Andrei Yushchinsky.

At the trial, Mr. Gruzenberg, the chief defense lawyer, turned to Beilis in his closing argument and said, "Mendel Beilis! Even if the judges should close their ears, and their hearts should turn from the truth and convict you in the law, do not give up. Turn your *neshamah* over to Hashem. Say *Shema Yisrael!*"[29]

ENDNOTES:

1. בעל הטורים דברים ו, ד
2. בעל הטורים דברים ו, ד
3. חינוך מצוה ת"כ
4. ברכות יג, א. רמב"ם הל' קריאת שמע פ"א ה"ב
5. ברכות י, ב
6. רמב"ם הל' קריאת שמע פ"א ה"ט וי"א
7. רמב"ם הל' קריאת שמע פ"א ה"ה וז'
8. ספרי, הובא במנורת המאור נר ג' כלל ג' ח"א פ"ו (עניני ק"ש). וע" מנחות צט, ב. מדרש תהלים מזמור א, יז
9. רש"י בראשית מו, כט
10. רבינו בחיי דברים ו, ד בתחילתו
11. שבת קיט, ב
12. רמב"ם הל' קריאת שמע פ"ב ה"א
13. שו"ע או"ח סי' ס"א ס"ו
14. שו"ע או"ח סי' ע"ד
15. תורת הפרשה דברים ע' 114
16. רמב"ם הל' קריאת שמע פ"ב ה"ב
17. רמב"ם הל' קריאת שמע פ"ב ה"ח-ט'
18. רמב"ם הל' קריאת שמע פ"ב ה"י
19. רמב"ם הל' קריאת שמע פ"ג ה"א
20. שו"ע או"ח סי' ס"א ס"ג
21. שו"ע או"ח סי' ס"ד ס"א
22. שו"ע או"ח סי' ס"ז
23. מג"א סי' ל"ב ס"ק א'
24. בעל הטורים דברים ו, ד
25. ברכות י, ב
26. זהר-מדרש הנעלם קכד, ב
27. פסחים נו, א. רמב"ם הל' קריאת שמע פ"א ה"ד
28. ברכות יג, ב
29. אג"ק אדמו"ר הריי"צ חי"ג ע' שעא

Most people are proud of their independence, and of the fact that they can do everything without help. But are we really independent? Is being dependent something to be ashamed of?

UNIT 36

IN THIS UNIT YOU WILL:

EXPLORE

- What does *davening* show about your belief in Hashem?
- How does *davening* help you connect with Hashem and reach higher levels in your relationship with Hashem?

EXAMINE

- What are the rules of *tefillah*?
- How often should you *daven* and where?

EXTRACT

- How can you show that you are dependent on Hashem?
- When was the *siddur* made?

תְּפִלָּה

KEY CONCEPTS

Book: Ahavah, Section: Prayer
סֵפֶר אַהֲבָה הִלְכוֹת תְּפִלָּה

תְּפִלָּה
PRAYER

מִצְוָה אַחַת

Declaration of Dependance

...se of human events, it becomes necessary for one people to dissolve the political bands which ha...

...on to which the Laws of Nature and of Nature's God entitle them, a decent respect to the...

...We hold these truths to be self-evident, that all men are...

...rty and the pursuit of Happiness.— That to secure these rig...

...n of Government becomes destructive of these ends...

...ing its powers in such form, as to th...

...for light and transient...

...which th...

OUR SAGES SAY...

Where Does Prayer Come From?

The *Gemara* tells us that our *Avos* established three *tefillos* to say every day.

Avraham Avinu established *Shacharis*, as the Torah says that *Avraham* got up in the morning "to the place where he stood," and "standing" refers to *davening*.

Yitzchak Avinu established *Minchah*, as the Torah says that Yitzchak went out "to speak in the field," and "speaking" also refers to *davening*.

Ya'akov Avinu established *Ma'ariv*, as the Torah says that Ya'akov "reached the place and he slept there;" and "reaching" is also a way to say *davening*.[1]

DID YOU KNOW?

Do As Much As You Want

One of the reasons we don't make a *brachah* on *tefillah* is since there is no limit to how much one should *daven,* and we don't make *brachos* on such mitzvos.[2]

The Mitzvah

EXAMINE

In the unit of *tefillah* there is one mitzvah.

Ask Hashem every day for what you need.

MITZVAH 77

מִצְוַת תְּפִלָּה
Davening to Hashem

וַעֲבַדְתֶּם אֵת ה' אֱלֹקֵיכֶם וּבֵרַךְ אֶת לַחְמְךָ וְאֶת מֵימֶיךָ
וַהֲסִרֹתִי מַחֲלָה מִקִּרְבֶּךָ
(משפטים כג, כה)

You will then serve Hashem your G-d, and He will bless your bread and your water, and will banish sickness from among you.

Ask Hashem for all your needs every day.

ALL PEOPLE   ALL PLACES   ALL TIMES

Mitzvah Messages

EXPLORE

Show Your Dependence

When you *daven,* you want to show that you realize that you need Hashem to survive, and you know that He is the only one who gives you what you need to live.[3]

The first person to realize this was *Adam Harishon*. Hashem had already created the trees, grass, and all other growing plants on the third day of *Ma'aseh Bereishis*, but they stayed inside the ground and did not grow at all. It was only on the **sixth** day, when Adam was created and he *davened* for rain, that Hashem allowed the seeds to sprout and grow.

Hashem waited for Adam to *daven* for rain because he wanted Adam to see for himself that plants need rain to grow, and rain can only come from Hashem. Hashem wanted Adam to see how much he needed Hashem and how much he needed to *daven* to stay alive. Adam understood this, and called all the animals together to praise Hashem for creating them.

We know from Adam that Hashem wants us to *daven* to Him for our needs.[4]

Heartfelt Service

The *passuk* does not say "pray," rather it says "serve" Hashem. From this, the *Midrash* learns that davening is the way we can "serve" Hashem with our heart. More than just saying the words, davening is about **connecting** to Hashem, and pouring out our hearts to Him. It is a time to take a close look at our heart, where its interests really are, and how to dedicate it totally to Hashem.[5]

 CHECKPOINT What does *davening* show about our connection to Hashem?

Details   EXAMINE

The History of *Tefillah*

Thousands of years ago, before the first *Beis Hamikdash* was destroyed, anyone who wanted to *daven* to Hashem could do so in any way. However, after the first *Beis Hamikdash* was destroyed and the Jews were spread out to the other nations, they started speaking new languages and forgot the pure Hebrew that used to be the only language of the Jews.

Because of this, the Jews weren't able to say the right words to *daven* on their own. *Ezra Hasofer* and the *Chachamim* who were with him created a set of eighteen *brachos,* called "שְׁמוֹנָה עֶשְׂרֵה - eighteen," which became the *davening* for all people for all time. This is the main part of *tefillah* today. The rest of the *siddur* was not yet created.

Later, in Rabban Gamliel's time, there were many people who didn't believe in Hashem and His Torah, and they were hurting the faithful Jews terribly. Because

DID YOU KNOW?

Time That Isn't Wasted

If we are judged on *Rosh Hashanah* as to what we will receive for the whole year, then why do we need to *daven* everyday to Hashem to ask Him for things we need, if all that has already been decided?

On *Rosh Hashanah*, we are given a specific amount of goodness that we are to receive, but we still need to pray every day to actually bring down that goodness as quickly as possible.[6]

PEARLS *of wisdom*

Straps and Laces

After winning the war and saving his nephew Lot, Avraham was greeted by the king of Sedom. The king said that Avraham could keep all the spoils that he had won in the war. Avraham did not accept the offer, and said that he wouldn't even take a shoelace or a leather strap since it was not his. As reward for this, his children received the mitzvos of *tefillin* (made of leather) and *tzitzis* (which look like laces).

Avraham instituted *Shacharis*. This is why we wear *tallis* and *tefillin* (with which Avraham was rewarded) during *shacharis* (which Avraham gave us).[7]

DID YOU KNOW?

Two Translations

The word תְּפִילָה has different translations:

1. From the root word of פלל – **to judge**.[9] *Tefillah* is a time for you to judge yourself and think about what you really need from Hashem, and whether you really deserve it, and what you can do to become closer to Hashem.[10]

2. The word *tefillah* also means **attachment**.[28] When you *daven*, you become attached to Hashem. This is a special quality that only a human has; no other being can connect to Hashem like this.[11]

of this, a nineteenth *brachah* was added to the *shemonah esrei* - the *brachah* of וְלַמַלְשִׁינִים, which begged Hashem to get rid of those people who hurt the Jews.

Afterwards, in the times of the *Gemara*, a part of *davening* called *Pessukei D'zimrah* (*pessukim* that praise Hashem) was added to the *davening* with a *brachah* before and after.[12] During this time, *krias shema* and the *brachos* preceding and following it were also added as a set part of the *davening*.[13]

Davening by Numbers

During the week, we *daven* three times a day - *shacharis* in the morning, *minchah* in the afternoon, and *ma'ariv* in the evening. On *Shabbos* and *Yom Tov*, including *Rosh Chodesh*, we add a fourth *tefillah* - *mussaf*. Once a year, on *Yom Kippur*, we add a special fifth *tefillah* - *ne'ilah*, right before the end of the day.

These *tefillos* are instead of the *korbanos* that were given in the *Beis Hamikdash*. *Shacharis* and *minchah* are instead of the *korban tamid* which was brought every day in the morning and afternoon. *Ma'ariv* is instead of the body parts and fats from the day's *korbanos* that would burn through the whole night. On *Shabbos* and *Yom Tov*, we *daven* an extra *tefillah* called *mussaf*, because an extra "*korban mussaf*" was brought.

The only *tefillah* that is not in the place of a *korban* is *ne'ilah* on *Yom Kippur*. We say it just to increase our *davening*.[14]

Be on Time!

Ezra Hasofer and the *Chachamim* with him also taught us the times for *davening*. *Shacharis* is said from sunrise until the fourth hour of the day, and if you missed that time, until midday. *Minchah* is said from half an hour after midday to sunset, and *ma'ariv* is said from nightfall to midnight, and if you missed that time, until the morning. *Mussaf* is said after *shacharis* until the seventh hour of the day, and if you missed that, it can be said throughout the day.

On *Yom Kippur*, *Ne'ilah* is finished just before nightfall.[15]

Anyone who misses these times by accident can make up for it by *davening* the next *tefillah* twice. For example, if

you missed *shacharis*, then you should say the *shemonah esrei* of *minchah* twice – one for *minchah*, and the other for the lost *shacharis*. You can only make up for a missed *tefillah* at the next *tefillah*, and not at any random time of the day. If you missed a *tefillah* on purpose, then you cannot make up for it.[16]

Preparing for *Davening*

There are five things that you must do to prepare for *davening*:[17]

1. Wash your hands. You must wash your hands before you *daven*, even if you already washed *netilas yadayim* in the morning. This time, you can just rinse your hands, and you do not say a *brachah*. If there is no water close by, you must walk very far (up to a *mil* – approximately 2/3 of a mile) in order to find water to wash your hands with before *davening*.[18]

2. Dress appropriately. Any parts of the body which are usually covered, must be covered for *tefillah*. You must be dressed properly, according to the dress code of the time.[19]

3. Find appropriate surroundings. You must make sure that you are not near any garbage, anything that smells bad, or near anything that is very dirty when you *daven*.[20]

4. Go to the restroom. Make sure that you will not have to go to the restroom during *davening*. You should also empty everything in your mouth before *davening*.[21]

5. Think the right thoughts. When you *daven*, you are standing in front of the King of all Kings, Hashem. Therefore, you must clear your mind of any thoughts that might distract you during *davening*. You should *daven* in a way that clearly shows that it is not a burden to *daven*, but a special chance to speak directly to Hashem![22]

Davening Shemonah Esrei

There are seven things that you should be careful of while *davening shemonah esrei*:[28]

1. Stand. You must stand while *davening shemonah esrei* unless you are too sick to stand, or are being forced to sit. Otherwise, if you *davened shemonah esrei* is a non-standing position, you must repeat it.[29] Also, you should not walk around while *davening shemonah esrei* unless in a rare situation when you are traveling and are afraid that you will not have enough time to *daven*.[30]

2. Face Yerushalayim. You should *daven* facing the place where the *Beis Hamikdash* would be. If you are outside of Eretz Yisrael, you should *daven* in the direction that faces Eretz Yisrael (in America and Europe, this direction is east. In other countries, the direction will change depending on where the country is). If you are in Eretz Yisrael, inside any city other than Yerushalayim, you should *daven* in the direction of Yerushalayim. If you are in Yerushalayim itself, you should *daven* facing the *Beis Hamikdash*.[31] If you can't face the right direction, you should imagine that you are standing in front of the *kosel*.[32]

3. Stand in the right way. You should *daven* with your legs together, to look like the angels who have only one leg. You should also bend you head while *davening*. This way you show that you are giving yourself over to Hashem.[33]

4. Be appropriately dressed. Besides being properly covered and wearing respectable clothes, this also includes not holding anything that might distract you during *davening*, like something very valuable.[34]

5. Be in a place that helps you *daven*. This includes: not *davening* on a raised surface so that you don't look haughty before Hashem,[35] and not *davening* in an open place, like a field. The best place to *daven* is in a *shul*. You should have a permanent seat, with space around it so that you will not get distracted.[36]

6. Pronounce the words properly and in a respectful tone. You must be careful not to say the words too loud so that you don't disturb other people who are also *davening*. At the same time, you must be careful to say the words clearly. Otherwise, you must repeat the *davening*.[37]

7. Bow five times. At different times during *shemonah esrei*, you bow down for a total of five times. You should make sure that it doesn't look like the bowing is a hard job, so you should bow quickly and easily.[38]

Strength in Numbers

One important part of *tefillah* is the *minyan* – ten men *davening* together. The *Chachamim* say that whenever ten Jews get together, the *Shechinah* rests with them. Although one is still obligated to *daven* even if there is no *minyan*, one should try to always *daven* with a *minyan*. Hashem never turns down the *tefillos* of a *minyan*.[39]

 CHECKPOINT What are the rules of *davening*?

A STORY

Soldiers and Prayers

R' Akiva Eiger saw the king's doctor as he was passing through town, and asked him to examine a Jew who had a rare disease. When the physician saw the patient, he told R' Akiva Eiger, "There is no cure for this illness." R' Akiva asked, "What if it was the king? Would you have said the same thing?" The physician replied, "Actually, the king did come down with this illness, and the only known cure was a rare bird that lives in a faraway desert. So, the king sent a group of soldiers to search for this bird. After much effort, they were able to catch one, and the king ate it and became well. But how could an ordinary person capture such a bird? That is why I say there is no cure."

R' Akiva Eiger said to himself, "The king has soldiers and we have *tefillah*," and he began to *daven*. He said, "Master of the Universe, the Jewish people are your children. They are kings and the sons of kings. One of Your children needs this bird. Please send it to us!" Sure enough, the bird arrived on his windowsill. It was cooked and served to the sick man, who got better. When the doctor heard about this, he marveled, "Such a thing only the great Rabbi can do!"[40]

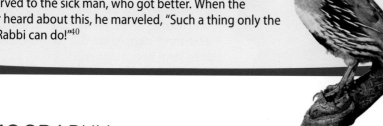

BIOGRAPHY

R' Akiva Eiger (1762 – 1838) תקכ״ב - תקצ״ח

R' Akiva Eiger was born in Eisenstadt, Hungary. He became the Chief Rabbi of Posen, a great Jewish city. He was known as a great posek in halachah, and many well-known Rabbanim and Jewish leaders went to him for his advice. His answers to them are still used today, as well as his short notes printed on the side of the Gemara and Shulchan Aruch. He was known to be especially brilliant, and the questions he asked in Torah learning are very difficult to answer. His great knowledge was also very helpful in stopping people's efforts to change and destroy Yiddishkeit. He passed away on the 3rd of Tishrei. On his matzeivah, which was destroyed by the Nazis ym"sh, was written: "He was a servant of Hashem's servants."

PEARLS of wisdom

Backbone of All the Mitzvos

Originally, there were eighteen *brachos* in *shemonah esrei*. These eighteen *berachos* of *shemonah esrei* are like the eighteen bones in the spine.

The spinal cord is a part of the body that sends the messages from the brain to the other parts of the body. *Davening* is like the spine because it brings life and meaning to all the mitzvos.[41]

DISCOVERY

The Human Spine

One of the major parts of the human body is the spine or the "backbone," which carries the nervous system to your entire body! The spine is made up of many smaller bones called vertebrae. There are 18 vertebrae in what is considered the spine. The 18 *brachos* of *shemonah esrei* correspond to these vertebrae.

There is a tiny growth from the bottom bone, which may correspond to the nineteenth *brachah* of *Velamalshinim*.

You First

Rabah said to Rabah bar Mari, "How do we know that if one person *davens* for his friend, Hashem will help him first?" Rabah bar Mari answered, "As it is written: 'And Hashem changed the fortune of Iyov when he prayed for his friends.'"[42]

DID YOU KNOW?

Davening

Daven is a Yiddish verb meaning "pray."

The origin of this word is uncertain. Some think it comes from the French word *divin* - Divine service. Others suggest that it comes from a Slavic word *davat* meaning "to give."

Others say that it comes from an Aramaic word, דְּאֲבוּהוֹן or דְּאֲבִינַן meaning "of their/our forefathers," since the three *tefillos* were instituted by Avraham, Yitzchak and Ya'akov.

- If you are not sure whether or not you *davened,* you should *daven* again. If the time for that *tefillah* has already passed, you should not *daven* again.[43]

- You should have a set place where you *daven.*[44] Even if you are *davening* in your house, you should set aside a set place at home to *daven.*[45]

- Any group of ten Jews has to either set aside or build a *shul* that they can gather together and *daven* in.[46]

- You should not *daven mussaf* before *shacharis.*[47]

- It is very important to *daven* in the *nusach* of your ancestors.[48]

- If you find yourself in a *shul* that *davens* a different *nusach* than your own, you should *daven* the quiet *shemonah esrei* in your own *nusach,* but participate with the *minyan* in any of the parts that are said out loud in the *nusach* of the shul. This applies even if you are the *chazzan.*[49]

- You must have *kavanah* that you are standing in front of Hashem while you *daven. Davening* without *kavanah* is like a body without a soul, and it's as if you didn't *daven.*[50]

- If you are travelling in a car or plane and cannot stand up for *shemonah esrei,* you should put your feet together and *daven* like that. If possible, you should stand for the beginning and for the "bowings." You should also try to take three steps forward in the beginning and three steps back at the end.[51]

EXTEND YOUR KNOWLEDGE

הֶפְסֵק בַּתְּפִילָה - Interruptions During *Davening*

During *davening*, from the beginning of *pessukei d'zimrah* until the end of *shemonah esrei*, you are not allowed to interrupt your *tefillos* by speaking. If the *minyan* requires you to answer certain things (like *kedushah* or *borchu*), you are usually allowed to interrupt and answer with the right words.

During *shemonah esrei*, you are not allowed to interrupt for anything. Even if a Jewish king would pass by, you may not stop to greet him.[52]

If you are in middle of *shemonah esrei*, you can't even answer to a *minyan*. Instead, you should stop and have in mind to participate with the *minyan*, but not out loud. If you are called up to the Torah, you may not go up.[53]

If a small child is crying, or anyone is bothering your *tefillos*, you are allowed to motion to them to be quiet.[54]

חֲזָרַת הַשַּׁ"ץ - Repetition of the *Chazan*

In the times of the *Gemara*, many people either could not read at all or could barely read the *alef beis*! Because of this, they were not able to *daven* by themselves from a *siddur*. To help them, the *Chachamim* made a rule that a *chazzan* who could read all of the words should repeat the entire *shemonah esrei* out loud, and everyone should say "amen." In this way, even the people who were not able to *daven* themselves would *daven* "through" the *chazzan* and still be considered to have *davened* all of the *tefillos*.

Nowadays the *chazzan* still repeats the *shemonah esrei* even though almost everybody can read from a *siddur*. Whenever there is a *minyan*, everyone listens to the *chazzan* repeat the words and then answers "baruch hu u'varuch shemo" before each *brachah* is finished, and "amen" after each *brachah*.[55]

OUR SAGES SAY...

Know Before Whom You Stand

R' Shimon Hatzaddik said: "He who *davens* should behave as if the *Shechinah* were before him, as it is written, שִׁוִּיתִי ה׳ לְנֶגְדִּי תָמִיד - I have set Hashem before me always."[56]

In fact, many *shuls* have the words of this *passuk* written at the front of the *shul*.

DID YOU KNOW?

Shokeling

Many people sway their bodies back and forth during *tefillah*. There are a lot of *minhagim* about movement during *tefillah*. Some only sway during the beginning parts of *davening*, while others sway for the entire *davening*. Some explain this practice according to *kabbalah*.

Whatever the *minhag* is, the main thing is to focus and concentrate on the *davening*.

A STORY

Cry of the Soul

It was *ne'ilah* on *Yom Kippur* and the *Ba'al Shem Tov* was pale and trembling. Everyone in the *shul* sensed that something was terribly wrong in *shamayim*, so they all cried and *davened* along with the *Ba'al Shem Tov*.

In the *shul* was a young village boy who knew nothing about *davening*, but he wanted to help. So, with all his strength, he thought of the only thing he knew – the crow of a rooster, and screamed it out: "Cock-a-doodle-doo! Hashem, have mercy on us!"

The people in the *shul* were angry at his *chutzpah* and wanted to throw him out. But they were silenced when the *Ba'al Shem Tov*, glowing with joy, announced that this boy's pure cries had broken a terrible decree in *shamayim*.

Live the Mitzvah   EXTRACT

Cry to Hashem

You like to think of yourself as an independent person who can do it all by yourself. But, you aren't! You are like a baby who needs his mother to give him his milk and change his diaper. All he needs to do is open his mouth and cry, and he is answered. As for you, all your needs, all your wants, all your hopes can be answered, if you only open your heart and *daven* to Hashem.

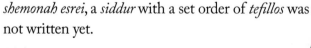

CHECKPOINT   How are you like a baby to Hashem?

What Else Comes From This?   EXTRACT

The *Siddur*

Nowadays it would be nearly impossible to *daven* without a *siddur*. How did the *siddur* first start? One of the other reasons Ezra and the *Chachamim* with him established the *shemonah esrei* was because people were not able to connect with Hashem as much, even though they had the second *Beis Hamikdash*. So many things were different, and the people needed someone to tell them exactly how to talk to Hashem in the right way.

This is why *Ezra Hasofer* decided that Jews should have a book to use as their own mini *Beis Hamikdash* so that they could *daven* from wherever they were, so that they could stay connected with Hashem. Even though Ezra created the *shemonah esrei*, a *siddur* with a set order of *tefillos* was not written yet.

R' Amram Gaon of Sura, Babylon was the one who organized the various *tefillos* and their order, and wrote them down in around the year 850. This became the earliest known *siddur*. About fifty years later, R' Saadia Gaon, also of Sura, wrote another one with the explanations in Arabic.

After this, many more *siddurim* came into being, including those written by the 11th century Shmuel ben Simchah (the *Machzor Vitry*), and the Rambam. After the Rambam, all *siddurim* started to follow the same basic order and use the same *tefillos*. The *Kabbalists* of Tzfas had a great influence on the *siddur*, and they added many *tefillos* that are sung today (especially *Kabbalas Shabbos*) in many shuls.

There are many different kinds of *siddurim* used by Jews worldwide, yet all *siddurim* follow a similar basic structure.

The four **general** *nuscha'os*, of which each one has many *nuscha'os* with various changes, are: *Nusach Ashkenaz, Nusach Sfard, Nusach Sfardi* and *Nusach Ari.*

Siddur Tsarafat, France. 14th-15th century.

Ba'al Shem Tov's *Siddur*

Rhodes *Siddur*

CHECKPOINT — Where does the *siddur* come from?

DID YOU KNOW?

18 Blessings

Shemonah esrei is not the only place where we see the number 18. A *perek* in *Tehillim* that begins with מִזְמוֹר לְדָוִד הָבוּ לַה' בְּנֵי אֵלִים has the name of Hashem written in it eighteen times. The name of Hashem also appears in *krias shema* 18 times.[59]

OUR SAGES SAY...

Our Prayers are Precious

When Jews all over the world *daven* they don't *daven* together, but each *shul davens* at its own time. After all the congregations have finished, the *malach* of *tefillos* gathers them all and makes them into crowns for Hashem."[24]

ENDNOTES:

1. ברכות כו,ב
2. אבודרהם
3. מורה נבוכים ח"ג פמ"ד
4. עי' רש"י ד"ה כי לא המטיר בראשית ב,ה ועי' מו"נ ח"ג פל"ב כעין זה
5. מכילתא דרשב"י שמות כג, כה ע' 350
6. לקו"ת נה,ג ואילך
7. משך חכמה
8. ברכות ח,א וברש"י שם ד"ה כביר לא ימאס
9. ראה מפרשי תהלים קול
10. סידור "אוצר התפילות" (בהתחלת המבוא "מה היא התפלה") מאת המחבר של סדור עבודת לב
11. רש"י בראשית לח,ח ד"ה נפתולי
12. רמב"ם פ"א ה"ד-ה' ופ"ז הי"ד
13. רמב"ם פ"ט ה"א
14. רמב"ם פ"א ה"ח
15. רמב"ם פ"ג ה"א-ז'
16. רמב"ם פ"ג ה"ה ראה כ"ז בשו"ע או"ח סי' ק"ח
17. רמב"ם פ"א ה"א וכל המשך הפרק
18. שו"ע או"ח סי' צ"ב ס"ד-ה
19. שו"ע או"ח סי' צ"א
20. שו"ע או"ח סי' צ' סעי' כ"ו
21. שו"ע או"ח סי' צב' סעי' א-ג

22. שו"ע או"ח סי' צ"ח
23. בשלון חז"ל "עושין רצונו של מקום" שעושין רצון חדש, וע"ד הענין ש"צדיק גוזר והקב"ה מקיים (עי' תענית כג,א "עג עוגה כו'"). וראה פי' הרע"ב אבות פ"ב מ"ד
24. מדרש רבה שמות כ"א
25. ברכות לא,א
26. ברכות ל,ב
27. ברכות לב,א
28. (נפילת אפים) היום היא לאו דוקא חובה (עי' בטור סי' קל"א) ולכן לא נכלל כאן רמב"ם פ"ה והלאה. שם כתוב שמונה דברים, אמנם השמינית
29. שו"ע או"ח סי' צ"ד סעי' ו'-ט'
30. שו"ע או"ח סי' צ"ד סעי' ד'-ה'
31. שו"ע סי' צ"ד סעי' א'-ג'
32. שו"ע או"ח סי' צ"ד סעי' ב' בהג"ה
33. שו"ע או"ח סי' צ"ה
34. שו"ע או"ח סי' צ"ו
35. שו"ע או"ח ריש סי' צ'
36. ראה כל דינים אלו בשו"ע סי' צ'
37. מג"א סי' ק"א סק"ב
38. שו"ע או"ח סי' קי"ג
39. ברכות ח, א
40. אמרות טהורות ע' ק"י

41. לקו"ת פ' בלק דף ע,ד
42. בבא קמא צב,א
43. שו"ע או"ח סי' ק"ז ס"א. ביה"ל סי' ק"ח ד"ה טעה
44. שו"ע או"ח סי' צ"ח ס"ד וסי' צ' סי"ט ע"פ ברכות ו, ב
45. מנ"ב סי' צ' ס"ק נ"ט
46. שו"ע או"ח סי' ק"נ ס"א וברמ"א חו"מ סי' קס"ג ס"א-ב'
47. רמ"א סי' רפ"ו ס"א
48. מנ"ב סי' ס"ח ס"ק ד'
49. שו"ת שאול ומשיב מהדו"ג א', ובשו"ת משיב דבר י"ז
50. שו"ע או"ח סי' צ"ח ס"א
51. מנ"ב סי' צ"ה ס"ק ב וברמ"א סי' צ"ד ס"ז
52. שו"ע או"ח סי' ק"ד ס"א
53. שו"ע או"ח סי' ק"ד ס"ז וברמ"א
54. מנ"ב סי' ק"ד ס"ק א'
55. שו"ע או"ח סי' קכ"ד ס"א-ז'
56. סנהדרין כב, א
57. ברכות י,א
58. של"ה תורה שבכתב פ' ויצא שער השמים פ"ג
59. ברכות כח,ב

UNIT 37

IN THIS UNIT YOU WILL:

EXPLORE

- Why do people bless others?
- Why was the *kohen* chosen to give the *brachos*?

EXAMINE

- How is *Birkas Kohanim* done in our days?
- How was *Birkas Kohanim* done in the *Beis Hamikdash*?

EXTRACT

- How can you give others *brachos* like a *kohen*?
- What should you say during *Birkas Kohanim*?

Why would someone want to give a blessing to someone else?
How do you feel when someone blesses you?

בְּרָכָה
הַמְשׁוּלֶשֶׁת
בִּרְכַּת כֹּהֲנִים

KEY CONCEPTS

Book: Ahavah, Section: Priestly Blessing

סֵפֶר אַהֲבָה הִלְכוֹת נְשִׂיאַת כַּפַּיִם

בִּרְכַּת כֹּהֲנִים
BRACHOS FROM THE KOHANIM

מִצְוָה אַחַת

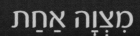

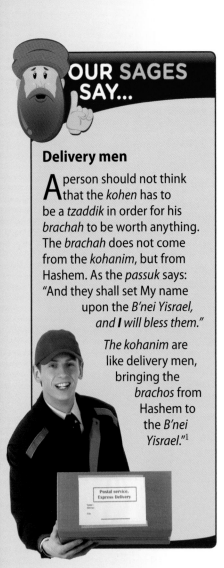
The Mitzvah

The unit of *Birkas Kohanim* has one mitzvah.

The *kohanim* must bless *Bnei Yisrael* every day.

MITZVAH 78

מִצְוַת בִּרְכַּת כֹּהֲנִים בְּכָל יוֹם

The *kohanim* blessing *B'nei Yisrael* every day

דַּבֵּר אֶל אַהֲרֹן וְאֶל בָּנָיו לֵאמֹר כֹּה תְבָרְכוּ אֶת בְּנֵי יִשְׂרָאֵל אָמוֹר לָהֶם

(במדבר ו, כג)

Speak to Aharon and his sons, saying:
This is how you must bless Bnei Yisrael say to them:

The kohanim must bless Bnei Yisrael every day.

KOHANIM | ALL PLACES | ALL TIMES

Mitzvah Messages

Gift from a Loving Heart

Since Hashem loves us so much, He wants only the best for us and selected a special group of holy people to be the delivery men. While Hashem could have chosen any group or specific person to give us His *brachos*, He specially chose the *kohanim* to be His delivery men. This is because the *kohanim* have a higher level of the *middah* of *chessed*, and Hashem wanted the *brachos* to come from a group of people who will give them over in the most loving and wholehearted way. [2]

CHECKPOINT · Why were *kohanim* chosen to give us Hashem's *brachos*?

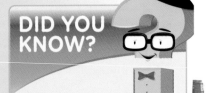

Details

The *Brachah*

The *brachah* that the *kohanim* are commanded to give is made of three *pessukim* from *parshas Nasso*:

‎1. יְבָרֶכְךָ ה׳ וְיִשְׁמְרֶךָ.   2. יָאֵר ה׳ פָּנָיו אֵלֶיךָ, וִיחֻנֶּךָ.   3. יִשָּׂא ה׳ פָּנָיו אֵלֶיךָ, וְיָשֵׂם לְךָ שָׁלוֹם.

The *kohanim* would do this mitzvah in the *Beis Hamikdash* every day, and still do it even today, when we have no *Beis Hamikdash*. There are some differences in the way it is done today and the way it was done in the *Beis Hamikdash*.

Outside Eretz Yisrael

On *Yom Tov*

On *Yom Tov*, even outside of Eretz Yisrael, the *kohanim* themselves say *Birkas Kohanim*. Even though there are many different *minhagim* about how *Birkas Kohanim* is done, the general process is the same.

During the *chazzan's* repetition of *shemonah esrei*, as the *chazzan* approaches the words רְצֵה, all the *kohanim* go up onto the *duchan* - the platform where they will stand when they give the *brachos*. They stand there with their backs to the people, facing the *aron kodesh*. They keep their fingers closed, against their palms, until the *chazzan* finishes saying *modim*.

Before the *kohanim* give the *brachos* to the people, they say a special *brachah* thanking Hashem for giving them the mitzvah to bless the Jews:

בָּרוּךְ אַתָּה ה׳ אֱלֹקֵינוּ מֶלֶךְ הָעוֹלָם אֲשֶׁר קִדְּשָׁנוּ בִּקְדוּשָׁתוֹ שֶׁל אַהֲרֹן וְצִוָּנוּ לְבָרֵךְ אֶת עַמּוֹ יִשְׂרָאֵל בְּאַהֲבָה

"...Who made us holy with the holiness of Aharon, and commanded us to bless His nation *Yisrael* with love."

Then, they turn their faces to the people, spread out their fingers, and lift their hands to shoulder height, with their right hand slightly higher than the left.[3] Now, the *chazzan* says each word of the *brachah* out loud and the *kohanim* repeat it after him. When each of the three *pessukim* are finished, all of the people say "*amen*."

When the *kohanim* finish saying the three *pessukim*, the *chazzan* starts the last *brachah* of the *Shemonah Esrei*. The *kohanim* turn their faces to the *aron*

DID YOU KNOW?

Express Delivery

When Korach fought with Moshe and Aharon, saying that Aharon should not be the *Kohen Gadol*, Hashem caused almonds to miraculously grow on Aharon's staff to show that He had indeed chosen him and his family to be *kohanim*.

Why almonds?

Almonds grow very fast. They show how quickly the *brachos* of *kohanim* can come true.[4]

OUR SAGES SAY...

I'm Here Too

When Hashem gave the *kohanim* the mitzvah of blessing *B'nei Yisrael*, we were disappointed.

"Hashem," they said, "we don't need *the brachos* of the *kohanim*! We only want Your *brachos*!" Hashem answered, "Even though it is the *kohanim* who are saying the words of the *brachos*, I am standing with them and giving you my *brachos*."

That is one of the reasons why the *kohanim* spread out their palms, as if to say, "Hashem stands behind us."[5]

kodesh and close their fingers. They stay standing on the *duchan* until the *chazzan* finishes the *brachah*, and then they go back to their places.[8]

בְּרָכָה הַמְשׁוּלֶשֶׁת - *Brachah* of Three Parts

Outside of Eretz Yisrael, where most people have the *minhag* to say *Birkas Kohanim* only on *Yom Tov*, a small version of the *brachah* is included in the *chazzan's* repetition of *shemonah esrei* in *shacharis* (and also during *minchah* on a fast day). The *chazzan* briefly says the *brachah* and asks Hashem to fulfill it for us, and everyone answers "*amen*." This is called the "בְּרָכָה הַמְשׁוּלֶשֶׁת" – the threefold *brachah*.[9]

In the *Beis Hamikdash*

A similar process for *Birkas Kohanim* took place in the *Beis Hamikdash*, but there were a few differences.

- The *brachah* was said only **once** every single day, after the morning *korban tamid*, even if it was a day on which we would also say *mussaf*.

- The *kohanim's* fingers would be straight and open the whole time they would give the *brachah*.

- The *Kohen Gadol* wouldn't lift his hands above his head (out of respect for the *tzitz* on his head).

- All three *pessukim* would be read together, and the people would say a *passuk* at the end, instead of "*amen*."

- The special and most holy name of Hashem, the שֵׁם הַמְּפוֹרָשׁ, was said in full. This name was only allowed to be said in the *Beis Hamikdash*.[10]

Six Requirements

There are six things that are very important for the mitzvah of *Birkas Kohanim*. Without them, the *brachah* cannot be given:

1. לָשׁוֹן — **language:** the *kohen* must be able to properly pronounce the words.

2. מוּם — **blemishes:** the *kohen* cannot have certain problems with his body.

3. עֲבֵירָה — **sins:** the *kohen* cannot have ever served *avodah zarah*, killed someone, or gone against one of the special mitzvos of a *kohen*.

4. שָׁנִים — **years:** the *kohen* must be old enough to have a full beard.

5. יַיִן — **wine:** the *kohen* cannot drink a *revi'is* of wine, or any amount of any other alcoholic drink before he gives the *brachah*.

6. טוּמְאַת יָדַיִם — **pure hands:** the *kohen* must wash his hands before giving the *brachos*.[11]

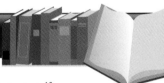

SELECTED HALACHOS

- *Birkas Kohanim* may only be said in *Lashon Hakodesh*.[12]
- The *kohanim* must be standing when they give the *brachah*.[13]
- The *kohanim* and the people in the shul should not look at each other during *Birkas Kohanim*.[14]
- The *kohanim* should not wear shoes during *Birkas Kohanim*.[15]
- Enough time must be given for every word of the *brachah* to be completed before going on to the next word.[16]
- *Birkas Kohanim* is only said with a *minyan*. The *kohanim* are counted as part of the *minyan*.[17]
- Only a male *kohen* over the age of *Bar Mitzvah* can say the *brachah*. However, a *kohen* under the age of *Bar Mitzvah* is allowed to say *Birkas Kohanim* with the other adult *kohanim* for practice and may even say the *brachah*.[18]
  - The people must stand in front of the *kohanim*. Those standing behind the *kohanim* are not included in the *brachah*.[19]
  - There are different *minhagim* about a *kohen* who is an *avel*. Some have the custom not to *duchan* at all the entire twelve months, because *Birkas Kohanim* is a joyous thing and they are not happy.[20]

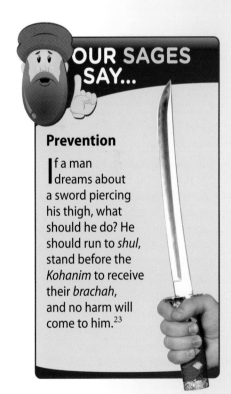

OUR SAGES SAY...

Prevention

If a man dreams about a sword piercing his thigh, what should he do? He should run to *shul*, stand before the Kohanim to receive their *brachah*, and no harm will come to him.[23]

Cover Up

When the *kohanim* give the *brachah* to the people, most people have a *minhag* to cover their faces with a *tallis* so that they won't look at the *Shechinah*. Many have the *minhag* for the children to go under their father's *tallis*.[24]

Chazal say that someone who looks at the *kohanim* in the *Beis Hamikdash* during *Birkas Kohanim* can lose some of their eyesight.[25]

STORY

Best to Leave It

Throughout the generations, great *Rabbanim* have tried to start up the daily *Birkas Kohanim* again, even outside of Eretz Yisrael, but bad things would happen. The *Rabbanim* understood them to be a sign from Hashem that it should not be started again.

The *Ba'al Hatanya* declared, "If I had the strength, I would institute *Birkas Kohanim* every day outside of Eretz Yisrael!"[26]

The Vilna Gaon wanted to have *Birkas Kohanim* said every day in his *Beis Midrash*, but as soon as he decided to start, he was taken into jail.

When R' Chaim Volozhin tried to start up a daily *Birkas Kohanim*, his *Beis Midrash* burned down![27]

EXTEND YOUR KNOWLEDGE

How Often?

A *brachah* must be given with a joyful heart, which is why *kohanim* outside of Eretz Yisrael only give *Birkas Kohanim* on *Yom Tov*, and not the rest of the year when people are worried about making money. Also, the *brachah* is given during *mussaf*, when the people are happily looking forward to going home and celebrating the *Yom Tov seudah* with family and friends.

An exception to this rule is on *Simchas Torah*. On this joyful day, many people make *kiddush* on wine and strong drinks before *mussaf*, and they may become drunk. Since a *kohen* cannot give the *brachos* when he is drunk, we say *Birkas Kohanim* during *shacharis*.

Birkas Kohanim is also given on *Yom Kippur*, which is a joyful day, because we are forgiven by Hashem.

Some *shuls* do not do *Birkas Kohanim* on a *Yom Tov* which falls on *Shabbos*.[28]

Hand Washing Service

Today, the *minhag* is that the *levi'im* wash the hands of the *kohanim* before the *brachah*. Why do the *levi'im* do this?

The *Beis Yosef*[29] writes:

"I heard that this was what they did in Spain, that the *levi'im* would pour out the water on the *kohanim's* hands. I did not know where this *minhag* started, until Hashem graced me and I found it clearly in the holy *Zohar*."[30]

The *Beis Yosef* included this *minhag* in *Shulchan Aruch*.[31] He adds that the *levi* should wash his own hands before pouring water onto the *kohen's* hands. Later, the *Rama* adds that the *minhag* is for the *levi'im* to rely on their own washing before *shacharis* and **not** to wash before pouring water for the *kohanim*.

The *Bach*[32] writes that he found in an old *machzor*, in the name of the *Maharil*, that if there is no *levi* to wash the *kohen's* hands, a *bechor*, a male who is the firstborn of both his father and mother, should do the washing instead.

Live the Mitzvah

EXTRACT

You Can be Like a *Kohen*

Your love to your fellow Jews should bring you to want to bless them.

Even if you are not a *kohen*, you should not think that your *brachos* will not have any effect, because *Chazal* tell us that a sincere *brachah* from even a very simple person can be very, very powerful and should not be treated lightly![33]

Even more so, Hashem calls us a מַמְלֶכֶת כֹּהֲנִים – a nation of *kohanim* – which gives us all the power to give *brachos* like a *kohen* does.[34]

CHECKPOINT   How are you like a *kohen*?

A Hands-on Blessing

The *kohanim* hold their hands in a specific position during *Birkas Kohanim*. There are many *minhagim* as to which position is correct. The *minhag* recorded in *Shulchan Aruch*[35] is to split each hand into two, (spreading the fingers in a "V" shape, apart from the thumb), and then to join them to make five "windows." Many have the *minhag* to engrave the symbol of this hand position on the tombstone of a deceased *kohen*.[36]

Ribono Shel Olam

It is an old *minhag* to use the time when *kohanim* sing the words of the *brachah*, to say a special *tefillah* to heal ourselves of any bad dreams we might have had.[37] Many *siddurim* have a special *tefillah* to be said during *Birkas Kohanim*. When you say this *tefillah*, you should try to finish it together with the *brachos* of the *kohanim*, so that the entire shul can answer "amen" to your request together with the *brachah*.[38]

Singing It in Tune

There are many beautiful tunes sung for the בְּרְכַּת כֹּהֲנִים, and each congregation has their own *minhagim* of which songs to sing.

CHECKPOINT — What do we *daven* for during *Birkas Kohanim*?

DID YOU KNOW?

Kohanim Only

What happens if there are only *kohanim* in the *Shul* and no one else?

If there is only a *minyan* of *kohanim*, then they all say *Birkas Kohanim* together and those who will receive the blessing are their "brothers in the fields" – those who do not come to *shul*.

If there is more than a *minyan*, then only some will go up to say *Birkas Kohanim*, so that there will still be a *minyan* left behind. That *minyan* will be the ones to receive the *brachos*.[39]

OUR SAGES SAY...

Shining Through the Window

The *Midrash* compares the openings between the fingers of the *kohanim* during *Birkas Kohanim* to "windows" through which Hashem's *Shechinah* shines on us.[40]

UNIT 37

ENDNOTES:

1. רמב"ם הל' נשיאת כפים פט"ו ה"ז
2. חינוך מצוה שע"ח. ועי' זח"ג קמה, ב
3. שו"ע או"ח סי' קכ"ח סי"ב
4. לקו"ת סוף פ' קרח. ועי' רש"י במדבר יז, כג ד"ה ויגמל שקדים, ובירמי' א, יב ד"ה היטבת לראות
5. במדבר רבה יא, ב
6. אור החיים בדמבר ו, כד
7. זוהר ח"ג קמז, ב
8. רמב"ם פי"ד ה"ג-ד', י"ב
9. שו"ע ורמ"א סי' קכ"ז ס"ג
10. רמב"ם הל' נשיאת כפים פי"ד ה"ט-י'
11. רמב"ם הל' נשיאת כפים פט"ו ה"א-ה'
12. רמב"ם הל' נשיאת כפים פי"ד הי"א
13. רמב"ם הל' נשיאת כפים פי"ד הי"א
14. רמב"ם הל' נשיאת כפים פי"ד ה"ז
15. רמב"ם הל' נשיאת כפים פי"ד ה"ו
16. רמב"ם הל' נשיאת כפים פי"ד ה"ה
17. מגילה כג, ב, רמב"ם הל' נשיאת כפים פט"ו ה"ט
18. שו"ע או"ח סי' קכ"ח סל"ד, מג"א שם ס"ק מ"ט
19. רמב"ם הל' נשיאת כפים פט"ו ה"ח
20. שו"ע או"ח סי' קכ"ח סמ"ג ובהגה)
21. שיחת אחרון של פסח תשח"י (שיחו"ק ע' רז)
22. מאור ושמש פ' תצוה עה"פ ועשית את מעיל בשם סידור האריז"ל (הובא בס' נטעי גבריאל הל' יו"ט כרך ב' ע' תעז)
23. שיר השירים רבה ג, א [ו]
24. שו"ע סי' קכ"ח סכ"ג, דרכי משה שם ס"ק ט"ו
25. חגיגה טז, א
26. שמועות וסיפורים ח"ב ע' 35
27. שו"ת משיב דבר ח"ב סי' ק"ד ד"ה מש"כ, ערוך השלחן או"ח סי' קכ"ח סס"ד)
28. רמ"א או"ח סי' קכ"ח סמ"ד
29. שו"ע או"ח סי' קכ"ח ס"ק ו-ז'
30. זוהר ח"ג קמו, ב
31. שו"ע או"ח סי' קכ"ח ס"ו
32. ב"ח או"ח סי' קכ"ח ס"ק ג' ד"ה ומצאתי במחזור
33. מגילה ט, א
34. שמות יט, ו
35. שו"ע או"ח סי' קכ"ח סי"ב
36. ס' "הדרת קודש" (שווארץ) ע' ה'
37. ברכות נה, ב
38. ברכות נה, ב. שו"ע או"ח סי' ק"ל
39. רמב"ם הל' נשיאת כפים פט"ו ה"ט
40. במדבר רבה יא, ב

Can you train your brain
to think specific thoughts?

UNIT 38

IN THIS UNIT YOU WILL:

EXPLORE

- How can you control your thoughts
  and feelings?

EXAMINE

- What *tefillin* are made of?
- How and when should you put on
  tefillin?

EXTRACT

- Why do some men wear two sets of
  tefillin?

תְּפִילִין
שֶׁעִבְּבֵד
הַלֵּב וְהַמּוֹחַ

KEY CONCEPTS

Book: Ahavah, Section: Tefillin

סֵפֶר אַהֲבָה הִלְכוֹת תְּפִילִין

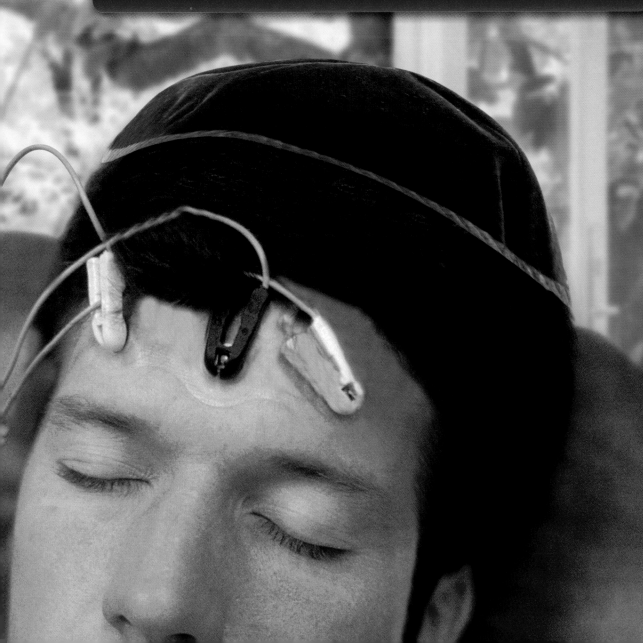

תְּפִילִין
TEFILLIN

שְׁתֵּי מִצְוֹת

OUR SAGES SAY...

Quick Alternative

B'nei Yisrael said to Hashem, "We want to study Torah day and night but we have no time." Hashem answered, "Do the mitzvah of *tefillin* and I will count it as if you had studied Torah day and night."[1]

DID YOU KNOW?

Easier Way In

Someone who puts on *tefillin* even once will be allowed to come into *Gan Eden*.[2]

The unit of *tefillin* has two mitzvos.

1. A man must wear *tefillin* on his head every day.
2. A man must wear *tefillin* on his arm every day.

MITZVAH 79

תְּפִילִין שֶׁל רֹאשׁ

Tefillin of the head

וּקְשַׁרְתָּם לְאוֹת עַל יָדֶךְ וְהָיוּ לְטֹטָפֹת בֵּין עֵינֶיךָ
(דברים ו, ח)

Bind [these words] as a sign on your hand, **and let them be a badge in the center of your head**

Wear *tefillin* on your head.

MALES   ALL PLACES   ALL TIMES

MITZVAH 80

תְּפִילִין שֶׁל יַד

Tefillin of the hand

וּקְשַׁרְתָּם לְאוֹת עַל יָדֶךְ וְהָיוּ לְטֹטָפֹת בֵּין עֵינֶיךָ
(דברים ו, ח)

Bind [these words] as a sign on your hand, and let them be a badge in the center of your head

Tie *tefillin* to your arm.

 MALES   ALL PLACES   ALL TIMES

To Serve Hashem With All Your Being

When you say *Shema*, you are remembering that Hashem is the One creator and ruler of the universe, and that He has taken us out of Mitzrayim so that we can serve Him properly. *Tefillin* also reminds us of this, and help us work on our actions and thoughts so that we can use them to serve Hashem.

How does *tefillin* help us with this? There are two places where *tefillin* are placed - on the arm and on the head. The *tefillin shel yad* is placed on the left arm in a way that it rests just above the **heart**. The *tefillin shel rosh* is placed upon the head, just above the forehead, in a way that it rests upon the front part of the **brain** which controls a person's **thoughts**.

In this way, when you wear *tefillin*, you are reminded to pay attention to your **head** and **heart**, and to use these to serve Hashem. It can also remind you not to be ruled by your heart, since your heart can lead you to do *aveiros*, or to let your thoughts run wild, which can also lead you to do *aveiros*.[3]

CHECKPOINT   What does wearing *tefillin* do to your heart and mind?

The Mitzvah of *Tefillin*

What Are They Made Of?

Tefillin are two black leather boxes worn on the head and arm. These boxes have scrolls of parchment inside of them, which have four different parts of the Torah written on them. Each of these four parts, called *parshios*, mention something about *tefillin*.[4] These four *parshios* are:

קַדֶּשׁ לִי (in *Parshas Bo*), וְהָיָה כִּי יְבִיאֲךָ (also in *Parshas Bo*), שְׁמַע (in *Parshas Va'eschanan*), and וְהָיָה אִם שָׁמֹעַ (in *Parshas Ekev*).

For the *tefillin shel rosh* (the box that is worn on the head) the four *parshios* are written on four separate pieces of parchment and then placed into four

War Dress

וְרָאוּ כָּל עַמֵּי הָאָרֶץ כִּי שֵׁם ה' נִקְרָא עָלֶיךָ וְיָרְאוּ מִמֶּךָ - אֵלּוּ תְּפִילִין שֶׁבָּרֹאשׁ

When the Torah says that, "All of the nations will see that the name of Hashem is on you, and they will be afraid," the Torah is talking about the *tefillin shel rosh*.

This means that because of the mitzvah of *tefillin*, Hashem will make our enemies afraid of us.[5]

DISCOVERY

Handy Reminder

Have you seen anyone tie a knot around their finger to remember to do something? People did this thousands of years ago, and they still do it today. The *Zohar*[6] tells us that R' Chiya and R' Yosi would tie knots to remember things. The *Midrash*[7] says that the butler who was in jail with *Yosef Hatzadik* also tied knots to remind him not to forget about Yosef, who was still sitting in prison after he had been freed. Just like they would tie a string so that they would remember what to do, we tie the *tefillin* around our arm and head to remind us of our mission - Torah and mitzvos.[8]

separate spaces in the box. In the *tefillin shel yad* (the box that is worn on the arm) all the *parshios* are written on one long scroll. The scroll is then rolled up and placed in the box.[10]

What They Look Like

The box of the *tefillin*, where the parchment is put, is called the בַּיִת - "house."[11] Under the *bayis* is a square piece of leather that seals it. This is called the "*titura*" - the "bridge." On the back of the *titura*, there is a little passageway called the "*ma'avarta*," where the leather straps are "passed through" and then tied.[12]

How They Must Be Prepared

There are ten very important rules that have to be followed when *tefillin* are made. If even one of theses rules are broken, the *tefillin* are *passul*, and cannot be used. These rules were taught to *Moshe Rabbeinu* at *Har Sinai* and passed down to us through the *Torah Sheba'al Peh*.

1. The *parshios* written in the scrolls must be written with black ink.

2. The scrolls must be made of parchment from a *kosher* animal.

3. The boxes and their stitches must be perfectly square.

4. The letter *shin* must be raised from the leather on both the right and left sides of the *tefillin shel rosh*.

5. The scrolls must be wrapped in a strip of parchment before they are placed in their compartments.

6. After being wrapped in the cloth, the scrolls should be tied with hair from a *kosher* animal.

7. The stitching of the *tefillin* must be done with the sinew of a kosher animal. These sinews are called *gidim*.

8. A passageway called a מַעֲבַרְתָּא - must be attached to the *bayis* for the straps to pass through.

9. The straps must be black.

10. The straps of the *shel rosh* should be knotted to make a letter *daled* and the straps of the *shel yad* should be knotted to make a letter *yud*.[13]

Wearing *Tefillin*

Where They Are Worn

The *tefillin shel yad* is tied around the upper left arm between the elbow and the shoulder. It should be put on the arm in a way that it is facing towards the heart. After making sure that it is tied to the arm, the straps are then wound around the lower part of the arm and around the middle finger.[14]

The *tefillin shel rosh* is put on the edge of the head, by the hairline, just between the eyes. The knot at the back of the head goes at the base of the skull.[15]

When They Are Worn

Tefillin can be worn anytime during the day, from when it is light enough to recognize a friend in the distance, until sunset.[16] Even though this mitzvah can be done anytime during the day, it is best if it is done during *Shacharis*.[17] *Tefillin* are not worn on *Shabbos* and *Yom Tov*. This is because *tefillin* are considered "signs" of our loyalty to Hashem, and *Shabbos* and *Yom Tov* are also considered "signs" of our loyalty to Hashem, so the extra "sign" of *tefillin* is not needed.[18]

Since the mitzvah only applies during the daytime, and also does not apply on *Shabbos* or *Yom Tov*, it is a *mitzvas asei shehazman gramah*, and women do not have to do this mitzvah.

The *Brachah*

The *brachah* for the *tefillin shel yad* is:

בָּרוּךְ אַתָּה ה' אֱלֹקֵינוּ מֶלֶךְ הָעוֹלָם אֲשֶׁר קִדְּשָׁנוּ בְּמִצְוֹתָיו וְצִוָּנוּ לְהָנִיחַ תְּפִלִּין.

The *brachah* for the *tefillin shel rosh* is:

בָּרוּךְ אַתָּה ה' אֱלֹקֵינוּ מֶלֶךְ הָעוֹלָם אֲשֶׁר קִדְּשָׁנוּ בְּמִצְוֹתָיו וְצִוָּנוּ עַל מִצְוַת תְּפִלִּין.

Some men only make a *brachah* on the *tefillin shel rosh* if they interrupted after the *brachah* on the *tefillin shel yad*.[19]

CHECKPOINT What are *tefillin* and how must they be worn?

EXTEND YOUR KNOWLEDGE

Chol Hamoed

Tefillin are not worn on *Yom Tov*, but what about on *Chol Hamoed*?

Some *Poskim* say that *Chol Hamoed* is like a normal day because you are allowed to do *melachos*, and other *Poskim* say that *Chol Hamoed* is like *Yom Tov*, because we still do the special mitzvos of that *Yom Tov*, like not eating *chametz* or sitting in the *Sukkah*.

Today, there are a few different *minhagim* about wearing *tefillin* on *Chol Hamoed*. Some do not wear *tefillin* at all, some wear the *tefillin* without saying a *brachah* and some wear the *tefillin* with a *brachah*, but say the *brachah* quietly instead of out loud.[20]

STORY

Saved by *Tefillin*

Towards the end of the Second World War, Hershel was travelling on a train to Bucharest. On the way, his precious bag with *tefillin* flew off the train. He decided to leave the train to look for them. His friends begged him not to, but he did not listen and went anyway.

Hershel jumped off and soon found his *tefillin*, but he had to wait a few days to catch the next train to Bucharest.

When he was about to get on the train, someone tapped him, saying, "Hershel, don't go to Bucharest." It was his friend, Srulik, from Bucharest, who told him that the secret police were waiting for him in Bucharest, and his life was in danger.

Relieved, Hershel said, "*Baruch Hashem* my bag fell out of the train! Otherwise I would now be in a jail in Bucharest!"

Srulik was amazed by this story and said, "Hershel, I have not put on *tefillin* today. May I use yours?" Hershel gladly lent him the *tefillin*.

As soon as Srulik put on the *tefillin*, he began to cry. After ten minutes, he was still crying. "I must tell you the truth," Srulik said to Hershel, "When we were saved, the first thing many Jews asked for was a pair of *tefillin* to put on. Others, including myself, asked for food. I never put on *tefillin* again. But from now on, I will never again miss putting on *tefillin*!"

Just before he left, Srulik said to him: "Not only did your *tefillin* save you, but they saved me too."

All in the Mind

While R' Schneur Zalman of Liadi was arrested and was being asked many questions by the cruel officers, the officers brought him his *tallis* and *tefillin*. As the *Rebbe* placed the *tefillin* in its correct place on his head, the officers suddenly became very scared.

Later, R' Schneur Zalman said that this had fulfilled that which the *Gemara* says, "The *passuk*, וְרָאוּ כָּל עַמֵּי הָאָרֶץ כִּי שֵׁם ה' נִקְרָא עָלֶיךָ וְיָרְאוּ מִמֶּךָּ - אֵלּוּ תְּפִילִין שֶׁבְּרֹאשׁ 'All the nations shall see that Hashem's name is upon you, and they shall fear you,' refers to the *tefillin shel rosh*."[21]

Some of his *chassidim* asked "Why doesn't this happen to other people when **they** put on their *tefillin*?

The *Rebbe* replied, "The *Gemara* doesn't say '*tefillin she'al harosh*' – 'on the head,' but, rather, '*tefillin sheberosh*,' - '*tefillin* in the head.'"

A person can't just wear the *tefillin*; he has to wear the *tefillin* and live by their message. Only then will the nations fear you!

DID YOU KNOW?

Major Event

R' Huna fasted forty times when the strap of his *tefillin shel rosh* flipped over.[22]

SELECTED HALACHOS

- The *tefillin shel yad* is put on first since it is mentioned first in the *passuk*.[23]
- You are not allowed to talk starting from when you begin to put on the *tefillin shel yad,* until the *tefillin shel rosh* is in place.[24]
- A person should constantly touch his *tefillin* to remind himself that he is wearing them and that he should not take his mind off them.[25]
- *Tefillin* must be worn with a clean body. Therefore, you are not allowed to sleep in them since you do not have control of you body then.[26]
- *Tefillin* are put on the weaker hand. Therefore, a left-handed person puts *tefillin* on his right hand.[27]
- It a *minhag* to kiss the *tefillin* when putting them on and taking them off.[28]
- *Ashkenazim* stand while putting on *tefillin*. *Sefardim* sit while putting on the *tefillin shel yad* and stand up when they put on the *tefillin shel rosh*.[29]
  - *Tefillin shel yad* and *tefillin shel rosh* are two separate mitzvos, and in certain cases, one mitzvah can be done without the other.[30]
    - It is important to make sure the straps of the *Tefilin* have the black side facing out.[31]

Live the Mitzvah

EXTRACT

Keep it on a Leash

Your heart and mind can get bored and restless very easily and can lead you to do the wrong things. How can you train yourself to act only in the right way and not anything else? Is this even possible?

Of course it is! If you "tie a leash" around your heart, mind, and body, you will be able to show them the right way to think and act. You can show your mind how to think about Torah and Hashem, and you can train your heart and body to not only do all the mitzvos, but love them as well.

The *tefillin* are like the leash that you can use to control and lead your heart and mind.

 CHECKPOINT How can you train yourself to follow Hashem and His Torah?

EXTRACT

Rabbeinu Tam's Tefillin

There are different opinions about the order of the four *parshios* placed inside the *tefillin* compartments.[32]

Rashi says that the order should be like this:

4. וְהָיָה אִם שָׁמֹעַ   3. שְׁמַע   2. וְהָיָה כִּי יְבִיאֲךָ   1. קַדֶּשׁ לִי

Rabbeinu Tam argues and says they should be in this order:

4. שְׁמַע   3. וְהָיָה אִם שָׁמֹעַ   2. וְהָיָה כִּי יְבִיאֲךָ   1. קַדֶּשׁ לִי

Most *poskim* agree with Rashi, and the *tefillin* that are worn today follow his opinion. Some people, out of extra *yiras shamayim*, wear both. These people *daven* normally with the pair of *tefillin* that follow Rashi's order, and then after *davening* put on the pair of *tefillin* that follows *Rabbeinu Tam's* order. They do not repeat the *brachos*, but instead read the words of the these four *parshios* while they are wearing the "Rabbeinu Tam" pair.[33]

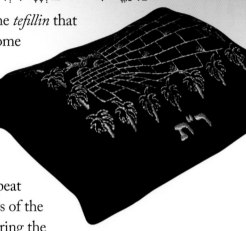

CHECKPOINT   What are two opinions about the order of the *parshios* in the *tefillin*?

UNIT 38

ENDNOTES:

1. מדרש תהלים א, יז
2. ר"ח יז, א, רמב"ם הל' תשובה פ"ג ה"ה
3. שו"ע או"ח סי' כ"ה ס"ה
4. שו"ע או"ח סי' ל"ב ס"א
5. ברכות ו, א
6. זוהר ח"ב קצ, א
7. בראשית רבה פח, ז
8. שמות יג, ט
9. רמב"ם הל' תפילין פ"ג הי"ד
10. שו"ע או"ח סי' ל"ב ס"ב
11. רמב"ם הל' תפילין פ"ג ה"ב, שו"ע או"ח סי' ל"ב סל"ח
12. שו"ע או"ח סי' ל"ב סמ"ד
13. רמב"ם הל' תפילין פ"א ה"ג, פ"ג ה"א

14. שו"ע או"ח סי' כ"ז ס"א וח', ובמג"א שם ס"ק י"ב וי"ג
15. רמב"ם הל' תפילין פ"ד ה"א
16. רמב"ם הל' תפילין פ"ד ה"י. שו"ע או"ח סי' ל' ס"א-ב'
17. רמב"ם הל' תפילין פ"ד הכ"ו
18. מנחות לו, ב
19. שו"ע או"ח סי' כ"ה ס"ה ובהגה
20. שו"ע או"ח סי' ל"א ס"ב ובהגה, ובמג"א וט"ז שם
21. ברכות ו, א
22. מועד קטן כה, א
23. מנחות לו, א. ועי' ט"ו או"ח סי' כ"ה ס"ק ד'

24. שו"ע או"ח סי' כ"ה ס"ט
25. רמב"ם הל' תפילין פ"ד הי"ד
26. רמב"ם הל' תפילין פ"ד הט"ו
27. שו"ע או"ח סי' כ"ז ס"ו
28. אורחות חיים (באכריך) הל' תפילין סי' כ"ח ס"ג
29. רמ"א או"ח סי' כ"ה סי"א. ועי' במג"א שם ס"ק כ'
30. רמב"ם הל' תפילין פ"ד ה"ד
31. שו"ע או"ח סי' ל"ב ס"ג
32. שו"ע או"ח סי' ל"ב ס"א
33. שו"ע או"ח סי' ל"ב ס"ב
34. שבת מט, א
35. ברכות ו, א

UNIT 39

IN THIS UNIT YOU WILL:

EXPLORE

- What does a *mezuzah* show about the people who live there?

EXAMINE

- How is a *mezuzah* made?
- On which doors of the house do you need to put a *mezuzah*?

EXTRACT

- How often do you have to check and make sure that a *mezuzah* is still *kosher*?

שׁוֹמֵר דַּלְתוֹת
יִשְׂרָאֵל
מְזוּזָה

KEY CONCEPTS

Book: Ahavah, Section: Mezuzah

סֵפֶר אַהֲבָה הִלְכוֹת מְזוּזָה

מְזוּזָה
MEZUZAH

מִצְוָה אַחַת

There is no place like home, and everyone should have one. Where is Hashem's home?

So Much for So Little

By doing the mitzvah of attaching a *mezuzah* to your door post, you receive so much reward. You are protected by Hashem and are promised a long life.

Rabbi Abba said, 'See how much kindness Hashem does to His people! He tells them: 'Build a house and write My name (in the *mezuzah*) on the outside. Then, you can sit inside the house and I will stand outside to protect you!"[1]

Based on clear words in the Torah, the *Shulchan Aruch* says that someone who does this mitzvah gets the reward of long life for him and his children.[2]

The Mitzvah

The unit of *mezuzah* has one mitzvah.

Attach a *mezuzah* on each of the door posts of your home.

MITZVAH
81

מִצְוַת מְזוּזָה
The mitzvah of *mezuzah*

וּכְתַבְתָּם עַל מְזֻזוֹת בֵּיתֶךָ וּבִשְׁעָרֶיךָ
(דברים ו, ט)

Write them on the door posts of your houses and gates

Attach a *mezuzah* to the door posts of your home.

ALL PEOPLE • ALL PLACES • ALL TIMES

Mitzvah Messages

The Meaning of the *Mezuzah*

The mitzvos of *Krias Shema* and *tefillin* remind us that Hashem is the One and Only G-d. The *mezuzah* reminds us of this fact as well as the fact that people from Hashem's nation are living in this house.[4]

When an army conquers a piece of land from another country, one of the first things they do is to put their flag in the new land they captured. This means that they now own and control the new land that they fought over and won. The *mezuzah* is like Hashem's "flag" on your home, and shows that you realize that Hashem has total control over your home.[5]

 CHECKPOINT What does having a *mezuzah* on your door show?

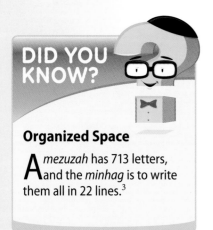

DID YOU KNOW?

Organized Space

A *mezuzah* has 713 letters, and the *minhag* is to write them all in 22 lines.[3]

Details

EXAMINE

Writing a *Mezuzah*

The *mezuzah* is a scroll made from parchment, in which the two *parshios* of שְׁמַע and וְהָיָה אִם שָׁמֹעַ are written.[6] The parchment is similar to the one that is used to make a *Sefer Torah*, and many of the rules of writing the *mezuzah* are the same as the rules of writing a *Sefer Torah*. For example, lines must be scratched on the parchment, a special type of ink must be used, and the letters have to be written in a very specific way.[7]

A *mezuzah* also has some *halachos* which are unique to it.

- The *mezuzah* should be written on **one** piece of parchment, not like a *Sefer Torah* which is made up of many pieces of parchment sewn together.[8]

- The *mezuzah* must have margins on the top, the bottom, and on the side where the writing begins (so that there is room for overlapping after the scroll has been rolled).[9]

- The *mezuzah* must be written כְּסִדְרָן - in the correct order it appears in the Torah (you cannot write the end before the beginning).[10]

Placing the *Mezuzah*

The *mezuzah* is attached to the side of the door which is on the right when you walk into the room. Not all door posts need a *mezuzah*. Since the *passuk* says to put a *mezuzah* "on the door of your house" we learn that it must be considered a "door," and it must be a place which is like "your house."

Therefore, a door post has to meet the following requirements before you put up a *mezuzah*:[14]

1. The doorway leads to a room which is at least 4 cubits by 4 *amos*.

2. The doorway has a piece of wood or other material attached to the door posts, not just two poles or walls.

3. The doorway leads to a regular room, not a holy room like a *shul*.

4. The doorway leads to a place where humans live, not animals.

5. The doorway leads to a clean, dignified room (not a bathroom).

6. The doorway leads to a permanent living place, not a temporary place, like a tent, *sukkah*, or a hotel room.

The *Brachah*

Before attaching the *mezuzah* to the door post, you say this *brachah*:[15]

בָּרוּךְ אַתָּה ה' אֱלֹקֵינוּ מֶלֶךְ הָעוֹלָם אֲשֶׁר קִדְּשָׁנוּ בְּמִצְוֹתָיו וְצִוָּנוּ לִקְבּוֹעַ מְזוּזָה

> **CHECKPOINT** Which kinds of doors need a *mezuzah*?

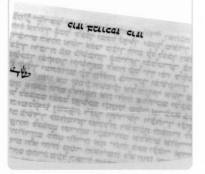
A STORY

Switched Loyalties

When Onkelos became a *ger tzedek*, his uncle, the Roman Emperor Titus, sent his advisors to try to convince him to give up his Judaism. Onkeles argued back so convincingly that he convinced the officers to convert to Judaism too! This repeated itself with a second band of officers as well. Finally, Titus sent soldiers to arrest Onkelos, and instructed them to not even speak to Onkelos, so as not to get convinced by his arguments. As they wordlessly led Onkelos out of his home, he smiled and placed his hand on the *mezuzah*.

The soldiers were so curious that they broke their rule and asked "What was that?" Onkelos smiled calmly and explained. "You see, a human king stays inside his home and has his servants standing outside to guard. Hashem, the King of all Kings, does just the opposite - He stands outside the homes of his servants and protects them. This is what *Dovid Hamelech* says in *Tehillim* 'Hashem will guard your going out and your coming in from now and forever.'"

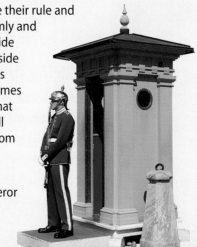

Greatly moved, right then and there, the soldiers decided to convert. When the emperor heard this, he decided to leave his nephew alone and stop trying to bring him back.[16]

SELECTED HALACHOS

- There are different opinions whether the *mezuzah* should be put on the door horizontally or vertically. Therefore, the *mezuzah* is placed on a diagonal slant with the top pointing towards the **inside** of the room.[17]

- The *mezuzah* is put at the bottom of the top third of the door post. If you put it higher, the *mezuzah* is kosher, as long as it's a *tefach* from the top of the door post.[18]

- If you rent a house outside Eretz Yisrael, you have thirty days to put up a *mezuzah*. If you rent **or** buy a house in Eretz Yisrael, or you **buy** outside Eretz Yisrael, you must put up a *mezuzah* right away.[19]

- It is a *minhag* to kiss the *mezuzah* when entering and leaving the room.[20]

- The last words of the *mezuzah*, עַל הָאָרֶץ, must be written on the beginning the last line - they should not be written at the end of the line.[21]

DID YOU KNOW?

So Far So Good

The last words of a *mezuzah* "עַל הָאָרֶץ" are written on a new line. This is to make these words as far apart as possible from the word before them הַשָּׁמַיִם.

The reason for this is to show us that our reward for keeping the mitzvos will be as great as the distance between the heaven and the earth.[22]

STORY

Lapse in Security

A long time ago, in the city of Tzfas, a woman was possessed by an evil spirit. The *Arizal* sent his closest student, R' Chaim Vital, to get rid of the spirit.

R' Chaim Vital managed to do so, and the spirit left the woman. But over the following nights, the spirit was heard outside the woman's bedroom, frightening her at night. She sent a message to inform the *Arizal*. He advised her to check the *mezuzos*.

It turned out that there was no *mezuzah* at all by the bedroom door! That was quickly fixed, and the spirit was never heard from again.[23]

BIOGRAPHY

R' Chaim Vital (1543 – 1620) ה׳ ש״ג - ה׳ ש״פ

R' Chaim Vital was born in Calabria, Italy and later moved to Tzfas in Eretz Yisrael. At first, he studied Kabbalah under R' Moshe Cordovero (known as the Ramak), who was the greatest Kabbalist of that time. However, after the Ramak passed away, R' Chaim became the student of R' Yitzchak Luria, the Arizal. Only two years later, the Arizal passed away. Since the Arizal had never written down his teachings, it was left to R' Chaim to collect his teachings and write them down. Today, these are known as כִּתְבֵי הָאֲרִיזַ״ל – the writings of the Arizal. R' Chaim became a great leader in Kabbalah and was known as a worker of miracles. In 1587, R' Chaim became a Rav in the Beis Din of Yerushalayim but moved back to Tzfas after some years. He then moved on to Damascus, Syria in 1594. At the age of 77 years, he passed away.

The True Master

The *gematria* of the word *mezuzah* is the same as that of Hashem's name – א-ד-נ-י, which is 65. A *mezuzah* shows Hashem's power over our homes and the world.[24]

This is why a Jewish slave, who wishes to stay with his master instead of going free, has his ear pierced by the door post (called the *mezuzah*). He chose to put himself under the power of a human being, and not Hashem. Therefore, his ear is pierced next to the *mezuzah* to remind him of his true Master - the *Ribono Shel Olam*.[25]

65

EXTEND YOUR KNOWLEDGE

Left or Right?

We learned that the *mezuzah* is placed on the right side of the door post, since that is the first direction that a person moves into the room.

But what if the person is left-handed? Shouldn't the person place the *mezuzah* on the left side of the door, if that is the direction the person will first move toward? After all, a left-handed person puts *tefillin* on the other arm, so maybe a left-handed person should move his *mezuzah* to the other side?

The answer is that for a *mezuzah*, there is no difference whether the person is left or right handed, since the *mezuzah* serves as a protection for everyone in the house, not just one specific person. However, *tefillin* is a **personal** mitzvah, and therefore, if the person is left-handed, he puts it on his right hand.[26]

Live the Mitzvah

EXTRACT

A Mini *Mikdash*

You may have thought of your *mezuzah* as something to keep the robbers and evil spirits away. But there is more to it than that. It is a reminder to you to make your home into a home of Torah and *kedushah*: a place that Hashem would be proud to guard and even rest His *Shechinah* within it.

Keep this in mind every time you kiss the *mezuzah*, and soon enough, the time spent living your ordinary life at home will feel more fulfilling and spiritual.

 CHECKPOINT About what should a *mezuzah* remind you?

What Else Comes From This?

Check It Regularly

A *mezuzah* must be checked twice every seven years.[27] A *Yarei Shamayim* should check his *mezuzos* every year during the month of *Elul*.[28] In fact, checking *mezuzos* very often is a *segulah* for long life and proper children.[29] Checking *mezuzos* is actually a great way to solve and fix problems in your household.[30] You do not need to put up another *mezuzah* when you are taking one down to be checked, as long as you are working on getting the *mezuzah* checked, and not just waiting until you remember about it.[31]

Use Its Protective Powers

Throughout the ages, people have believed that the *mezuzah* had the power to protect them, and that it could be used as a magic protection, even when it was not attached to the door. The *Mishnah*[32] mentions people who would attach a *mezuzah* to their walking sticks. Some explain that they did this because they believed they were fulfilling the *mitzvah* and also that it protected them.[33] The *Gemara*[34] tells us stories of how the *mezuzah* protected people from harm. All this shows of the protective power the *mezuzah* has, even when not attached to the door!

CHECKPOINT When should a *mezuzah* be checked?

UNIT 39

ENDNOTES:

1. זוהר ח"ב לו, א

2. שו"ע יו"ד סי' רפ"ה ס"א, ובש"ך שם ס"ק ב'

3. רמב"ם הל' מזוזה פ"ה ה"ה

4. חינוך מצוה תכ"ג

5. אברבנאל דברים פרק כז

6. שו"ע יו"ד סי' רפ"ח ס"א

7. שו"ע יו"ד סי' רפ"ח ס"ז-ח'

8. שו"ע יו"ד סי' רפ"ח ס"ב

9. שו"ע יו"ד סי' רפ"ח ס"א, וי"ד

10. שו"ע יו"ד סי' רפ"ח ס"ג

11. מנחות לג, א

12. רמ"א יו"ד סי רפ"ח סט"ו

13. ראה לדוגמה תיקוני זוהר תקונא עשרין ותרין סח, א-א-ב'

14. רמב"ם הל' מזוזה פ"ו ה"א

15. שו"ע יו"ד סי' רפ"ז ס"א

16. עבודה זרה יא, א. גיטין נו, ב

17. רמ"א יו"ד סי' רפ"ז ס"ו

18. שו"ע יו"ד סי' רפ"ז ס"ב

19. שו"ע יו"ד סי' רפ"ז סכ"ב

20. קצשו"ע סי' י"א סכ"ד

21. שו"ע יו"ד סי' רפ"ח ס"י

22. ט"ז יו"ד סי' רפ"ח ס"ק ה'

23. שבחי האריז"ל ע' 20

24. פי' ניצוצי אורות על הזוהר בא לו, א

25. רבינו בחיי משפטים כא, ו ע"פ פי' "טוב טעם"

26. ב"י יו"ד סי' רפ"ט

27. שו"ע יו"ד סי רצ"א ס"א

28. קשו"ע סי' קכ"ח ס"ג

29. ספר זכירה (סימנר) ענין מזוזה

30. עי' שבחי האריז"ל ע' 20

31. דעת קדושים יו"ד סי' רצ"א ס"ב. ועי' בספר "עלי דשא" (שפירא) סי' ל"ב עלה ט

32. כלים פי"ז מט"ז

33. תיו"ט כלים פי"ז מט"ז

34. ירושלמי פאה פ"א ה"א

35. ספר "עץ חיים" (להאריז"ל) שער הכללים פרק ד'. ועי' פי' הרמ"ז על הזוהר בא לו, א. ועי' בלקוטי לוי"צ ריש פ' בא ע"ג נ

36. טור יו"ד סי' רפ"ה

UNIT 40

IN THIS UNIT YOU WILL:

EXPLORE

- How is a *Sefer Torah* similar to a map?

EXAMINE

- What are the different ways that you can do this *mitzvah*?
- How is a *Sefer Torah* written and who can write one?

EXTRACT

- What are other ways that you can do this mitzvah without actually writing a *Sefer Torah*?
- How can you show respect for a *Sefer Torah*?

קְרִיאַת הַתּוֹרָה

בֵּית מָלֵא סְפָרִים

אוֹת בְּסֵפֶר תּוֹרָה

כְּבוֹד סֵפֶר תּוֹרָה

סִיּוּם סֵפֶר תּוֹרָה

סֵפֶר תּוֹרָה

KEY CONCEPTS

Book: Ahavah Section: Sefer Torah

סֵפֶר אַהֲבָה הִלְכוֹת סֵפֶר תּוֹרָה

סֵפֶר תּוֹרָה
SEFER TORAH

שְׁתֵּי מִצְוֹת

You thought you could manage
your trip without a map, didn't you?
But now you are hopelessly lost!
Do you feel so sure of yourself now?

Continuity

The Torah we use today is written exactly the same way the Torah was written the very first time by Moshe over 3,300 years ago.

PEARLS *of wisdom*

The Last but Not Least

The mitzvah to write a *Sefer Torah* is the last mitzvah written in the Torah. This mitzvah is found right after the Torah warns us that if we do too many *aveiros*, Hashem will turn His face from us and not give us *brachos*.

Even at times when Hashem will hide His face from us, the Torah helps us get through those difficult times.[1]

The Mitzvah

The unit of *Sefer Torah* has two mitzvos.

1. Every man must write a *Sefer Torah*.
2. The king has to write a second *Sefer Torah*.

MITZVAH 82

מִצְוָה לִכְתּוֹב כָּל אֶחָד מִיִּשְׂרָאֵל סֵפֶר תּוֹרָה לְעַצְמוֹ

Each Jewish man must write a *Sefer Torah*

וְעַתָּה כִּתְבוּ לָכֶם אֶת הַשִּׁירָה הַזֹּאת וְלַמְּדָהּ אֶת בְּנֵי יִשְׂרָאֵל,
שִׂימָהּ בְּפִיהֶם לְמַעַן תִּהְיֶה לִי הַשִּׁירָה הַזֹּאת לְעֵד בִּבְנֵי יִשְׂרָאֵל
(דברים לא, יט)

Now write for yourselves this song and teach it to *B'nei Yisrael*. Make them memorize it so that this song will be a witness for *B'nei Yisrael*.

Write a *Sefer Torah* for yourself.

 MEN   ALL PLACES   ALL TIMES

MITZVAH 83

מִצְוָה עַל הַמֶּלֶךְ לִכְתּוֹב סֵפֶר תּוֹרָה אֶחָד יֶתֵ ר
עַל שְׁאָר בְּנֵי יִשְׂרָאֵל

The king must write a second *Sefer Torah* for himself

וְהָיָה כְשִׁבְתּוֹ עַל כִּסֵּא מַמְלַכְתּוֹ וְכָתַב לוֹ אֶת מִשְׁנֵה הַתּוֹרָה הַזֹּאת עַל
סֵפ תֵמִלִּפְנֵי הַכֹּהֲנִים הַלְוִיִּם
(דברים יז, יח)

When the king is established on his royal throne, he must write a copy of this Torah as a scroll edited by the levi'im priests.

Write a second *Sefer Torah* for yourself.

 THE KING   ERETZ YISRAEL   WHEN JEWS RULE ERETZ YISRAEL

Mitzvah Messages

EXPLORE

Your Own Copy

If you have gotten lost in a museum, you know the feeling: *If only I had picked up a map at the front desk, then I wouldn't have to look for a museum worker or someone else who knows the way. It would be so much easier to find my way out if I had my own copy!* That is why Hashem gave us the mitzvah to write our own *Sefer Torah.* Since the *Sefer Torah* is like our map for how to live our life, we each need to have our own copy for our journey in life.[2]

CHECKPOINT How is a *Sefer Torah* like a map?

Details

EXAMINE

Writing a *Sefer Torah*

Every Jew has a mitzvah to write his own *Sefer Torah.* If he cannot do it himself, then he can hire a *sofer* to do it for him. The *sofer* is his messenger to do the mitzvah for him. Another way of fulfilling the mitzvah is to buy a ready-made *Sefer Torah* and fix at least one letter. If he buys the *Sefer Torah* and does not fix anything at all, then he has not done the mitzvah.[3]

Not So Easy

Writing a *Sefer Torah* is a difficult job. It takes a long time, since the *sofer* must make sure that each and every letter is written perfectly and correctly. There is simply no room for mistakes! Not only is the writing a hard job, but preparing the materials that will be used is also quite a task. The *sofer* needs to use special parchment on which to write, and it must come from the skin of a *kosher* animal.[4] Once the parchment is prepared, lines (called *sirtut*) have to be etched

on to the parchment.[8] The writing then goes on these lines. Finally, the *sofer* must use a special ink for the writing.[9]

Each page of the *Sefer Torah* must be organized into *parshios* (similar to paragraphs). There are two types of *parshios*: פְּתוּחָה – an **open** paragraph that ends in the middle of a line, with the next paragraph starting on a new line; and סְתוּמָה – a **closed** paragraph that ends in the middle of the line, with the next paragraph starting on the same line after an empty space of nine letters.[10]

Some exceptions to these rules include *Az Yashir* and *Ha'azinu*, which are written differently.[11]

The People's *Sefer Torah*

Before there were any printed *sefarim*, everyone would have to write their own *Sefer Torah*, because it was the only written source of Torah law. There were no *Chumashim* that you could just buy from a store, or photocopy from a friend! If you wanted to learn Torah, you needed to learn it from a real *Sefer Torah*.

Today, we have *Sifrei Torah* that belong to the community, Torah learning is done with printed books, and the *Torah Sheba'al Peh* was written down a long time ago. Therefore, anyone can do the mitzvah of writing a *Sefer Torah* by writing a regular *Chumash*, *Mishnah*, or *Gemara*.[12]

The King's *Sefer Torah*

A Jewish king has to follow the laws of the Torah even more carefully than everyone else. When he follows the Torah carefully, the people in his kingdom want to follow the Torah even more.

To remind the king how important it is to do every mitzvah exactly, the King has to write his own, second *Sefer Torah*. This Torah must always be with him, when he goes out to war, when he sits down to judge, and even when he eats.

CHECKPOINT How is a *Sefer Torah* written?

DID YOU KNOW?

Stock Up on the Basics

Because we fulfill the mitzvah of writing a *Sefer Torah* today by owning *sefarim*, we might think that we have to buy every single book out there and that they must all be in Hebrew. Not at all! We fulfill the *mitzvah* by buying the basic books of *Tanach*, *Mishnah*, and *Gemara*. Not only that; they don't have to be in Hebrew. They can be in any language we understand![6]

OUR SAGES SAY...

A Letter for Every Jew

The Hebrew word ישראל is an acronym for "יֵשׁ שִׁשִּׁים רִיבּוֹא אוֹתִיּוֹת לַתּוֹרָה - there are 600,000 letters in the Torah."

This shows the special connection that each and every Jew has to the Torah.[7]

SELECTED HALACHOS

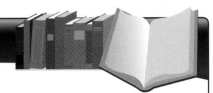

- Even if you have inherited a *Sefer Torah*, you must still write a new one.[13]

- If you own more than one *Sefer Torah*, you may not sell any of them.[14]

- The steps of making a *Sefer Torah* must be done לִשְׁמָהּ - with the specific intention of making a *Sefer Torah*. This includes preparing the parchment as well as the actual writing.[15]

- A *Sefer Torah* must be written with the right hand.[16]

- A *Sefer Torah* is written with margins on the side, to leave room for binding two pages of parchment together.[17]

- A *Sefer Torah* must be written by an adult male.[18]

- Many pieces of parchment are needed for an entire *Sefer Torah*. The separate pieces of parchment are sewn together with a special type of thread, made from the sinews of a *kosher* animal.[19]

EXTEND YOUR KNOWLEDGE

Taking Credit

Why don't we see people writing their own *Sifrei Torah* nowadays? One of the reasons is:

Today, every *shul* has a *Sefer Torah* for the whole community.[20] The community, led by the *Beis Din*, lets everyone in the community "borrow" the *Sefer Torah*.[21] When one is called to the Torah for an *aliyah*, the community considers him to have personally written that *Sefer Torah*, and in this way, he has done the mitzvah.[22]

STORY

A *Sefer Torah* in Jail

In the city of Worms there was an ancient Torah written on parchment made of deerskin. It is said that this scroll was written by R' Meir of Rothenburg, the *Maharam*, while he was in jail.

This Torah was written after R' Meir dreamed that the *malach* Gavriel came to him and announced that he was lending him the thirteenth Torah scroll that Moshe had written before his death, so that he could have a *Sefer Torah* to read from while in jail.

When he woke up, he saw the *Sefer Torah* on the table, and knew it wasn't only a dream. He used this *Sefer Torah* every *Shabbos*, until he finally made the decision to make a copy of it.

He did so, and when the new *Sefer Torah* was completed, the one that appeared in the dream disappeared.[23]

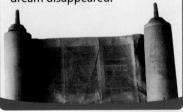

DID YOU KNOW?

One Last *Mitzvah*

Moshe fulfilled this mitzvah by writing (or completing) 13 *Sifrei Torah* on the day he passed away![24]

Live the Mitzvah

EXTRACT

Ways to Fulfill this *Mitzvah*:

בַּיִת מָלֵא סְפָרִים

Buying *sefarim* is one way to do the mitzvah of writing a *Sefer Torah*. Filling a Jewish home with holy *sefarim* brings special holiness into the home. Even small children should own *sefarim*, since it is good training for when they grow older. A Jewish book would therefore make a better birthday gift for your little brother or sister than a computer game!

אוֹת בְּסֵפֶר תּוֹרָה

Buying a letter in a *Sefer Torah* by paying a *sofer* to write a letter for you is another great way to fulfill this mitzvah without having to write your own.[26] Every individual Jew has a unique connection to a specific letter in the Torah.[27] Buying a letter in the Torah brings out that special connection.[28]

CHECKPOINT How can you do this mitzvah without writing your own *Sefer Torah*?

What Else Comes From This?

כְּתַב סְתָּ"ם - The Script Used for *Sefer Torah, Teffilin* and *Mezuzah*

Sifrei Torah, as well as *tefillin*, *mezuzos*, and *megillos* are written in a special script called כְּתַב סְתָּ"ם (which is an acronym of the three words, סֵפֶר תּוֹרָה תְּפִילִין מְזוּזָה) or "*Ksav Ashuri*." This script is so holy that it can only be used for holy purposes. Certain things written in *Ksav Stam*, even not necessarily a *Sefer Torah*, *mezuzah*, or *tefillin*, must be buried.[29]

Honoring a *Sefer Torah*

The *Sefer Torah* is very holy and must be treated with the greatest respect. Here are some examples:

- A special, respectable place is set aside for the *Sefer Torah*.[30]

- Whenever you see a *Sefer Torah*, you should stand up until you can no longer see it, or until it is put in the right place.

- A *Sefer Torah* is respectfully buried when it is no longer *kosher* and not able to be repaired.

- Even the objects associated with a *Sefer Torah* (for example, its cover, the table on which it is read and its jewelry) are to be treated with respect and it is forbidden to throw them away.

- You are not allowed to:

  - Spit or do anything inappropriate in front of a *Sefer Torah*.
  - Turn your back to a *Sefer Torah*.
  - Place anything on top of a *Sefer Torah*, besides for another *Sefer Torah*
  - Throw a *Sefer Torah*.
  - Bring a *Sefer Torah* into a bathroom.[31]

BIOGRAPHY

The Chasam Sofer (1762 – 1840) תקכ"ב - ת"ר

R' Moshe Sofer (or, Schreiber in Yiddish) was born in Frankfurt, Germany. He was known as the Chasam Sofer after his best known sefer, which was a collection of his teshuvos. He wrote many other sefarim including a commentary on the Shulchan Aruch, Gemara and Chumash. He was a great teacher and worked tirelessly against the Haskalah movement that was spreading through Austria, Hungary and Germany. After his first wife passed away, he re-married Sarah, the daughter of R' Akiva Eiger and had ten children. He passed away on the 25th of Tishrei in Pressburg.

DISCOVERY

The First Map

The oldest known world map is the *Imago Mundi* of 6th century BCE Babylonia. This map shows Babylon on the Euphrates, surrounded by a circular area of land showing Assyria, Armenia and several cities. This land mass is shown to be surrounded by a "bitter river" (Oceanus), with seven islands arranged around it, so that it forms a seven-pointed star.

STORY

Share the *Mitzvah*

A *Sefer Torah* was brought before the *Chasam Sofer*. No one knew who had written it and they were not sure if it was written by a proper *sofer*. The *Chasam Sofer* told them to roll it out to the end and they saw that the last lines were not as beautiful and perfect as the rest of the Torah.

It was clear that the *sofer* had followed the *minhag* of honoring the city's people with buying the privilege to write the final letters, which usually come out messy.

The *Chasam Sofer* said that this was enough of a proof that it was a proper *sofer* and was written according to *halachah*.[32]

Honor

The *passuk* זֶה אֵ-לִי וְאַנְוֵהוּ - This is my G-d, and I will glorify Him, means that we must glorify Hashem by doing the mitzvos in a beautiful way. Therefore, we make a beautiful *Sefer Torah*, written by a talented *sofer* with fine ink, a fine pen, and wrap it with beautiful fabric.[33]

The *Chachamim* asked, "Do you have to stand up before a *Sefer Torah*?" R' Chilkiah, R' Simon and R' Elazar said, "If we have to stand up when a *Talmid Chacham*, one who studies the Torah, walks into the room, how much more is it necessary to rise for the *Sefer Torah* itself!"[34]

Siyum Sefer Torah

When a *Sefer Torah* is finished, the whole community celebrates.[35] A few days before the *Sefer Torah* is finished, an announcement is made in *shul*, and everyone is invited to the finishing of the *Sefer Torah*, and the festive meal that follows.[36]

On the day of the event, some people go to the *mikvah* in the morning, and the *shul* is lit up with lights.[37] The last few lines of the new Torah are left empty, allowing those who are there to join in by each writing a letter to complete the Torah.[38] After the *Sefer Torah* is completed, sewn together and wrapped up, it is paraded down the streets under a *chupah*[39] with much singing and dancing.[40] Some have the custom to walk with the Torah holding torches.[41] The honor of holding the *Sefer Torah* is given to those who are there, and each one takes a few steps with the Torah in his arms.

When the people come into the *shul*, the *aron kodesh* is opened, and all the *Sifrei Torah* are taken out, and the people say, "Holy scrolls! Come and greet the new scroll that this person has been able to write and bring here!" The *Sifrei Torah* are then taken out and two lines of people are formed. The new *Sefer Torah* then passes through in the middle.[42]

Many have the *minhag* to recite the *pessukim* of "*atah har'eisah*" like we do on Simchas Torah, and they even do *hakafos* around the *bimah*. To make it clear that these *hakafos* are different than the *hakafos* of *Simchas Torah*, an eighth circle is made.[43] The ceremony is followed by a festive meal.[44]

Krias Hatorah

Another way to do this mitzvah of *Sefer Torah* is by reading the Torah in public.[45] *Moshe Rabbeinu* decreed that three days should not go by without reading the Torah, so he decided that the Torah should be read publicly three times a week: on *Shabbos*, Monday, and Thursday. *Ezra Hasofer* added the *minhag* of reading the Torah on the afternoon of *Shabbos* during *Minchah*.[46]

The Torah is also read on *Yom Tov*, *Rosh Chodesh*, *Chanukah*, *Purim*, and on public fast days.[47] In general, three people are called to the Torah. During *Shabbos Shacharis*, seven people are called to the Torah.[48] On *Yom Tov*, five people are called up. On *Rosh Chodesh* and *Chol Hamo'ed* four people are called up, and on *Yom Kippur* six people are called up. The Torah is read only when there is a *minyan* gathered.[49]

According to the accepted *minhag*, the Torah is completed every year, starting the *Shabbos* after *Simchas Torah* with *Parshas Bereishis* and concluding a year later on *Simchas Torah* with *Parshas V'zos Habrachah*.[50]

CHECKPOINT When do we read from the Torah? Why do we have to read the Torah so often?

UNIT
40

ENDNOTES:

1. ח"ח עה"ת ע' רפא
2. חינוך מצוה תרי"ג
3. שו"ע יו"ד סי' ער"א ס"א ובהגה
4. שו"ע יו"ד סי' רע"א ס"א
5. טור יו"ד סי' ער"ה
6. לקו"ש חכ"ג ע' 25 ובהע' 67
7. הגאון ר' חיים פלאג'י בספרו "נפש כל חי" מערכת ת' אות כ"ו
8. שו"ע יו"ד סי' רע"ה ס"ה
9. שו"ע יו"ד סי' רע"א ס"ו
10. שו"ע יו"ד סי' ער"ה ס"ב
11. שו"ע יו"ד סי' ער"ה ס"ד-ה', ובט"ז שם סק"ז ז'
12. הרא"ש בהל' ס"ת ס"א, הובא בטושו"ע סי' ער"א
13. שו"ע יו"ד סי' ע"ר ס"א
14. שו"ע יו"ד סי' ע"ר ס"א
15. שו"ע יו"ד סי' רע"א ס"א וסי' רע"ד ס"א
16. שו"ע יו"ד סי' רע"א ס"ז
17. שו"ע יו"ד ריש סי' רע"ג
18. שו"ע יו"ד סי' רפ"א ס"א-ד'
19. שו"ע יו"ד סי' רע"ח ס"א
20. שו"ע או"ח סי' ק"נ ס"א
21. "לב ב"ד מתנה עליה" כתובות קו, ב
22. ראה שו"ת קנאת סופרים (למהרש"ק) תשובה ה'
23. ספר המעשיות לר' יחזקאל בן יעקב ע' 314
24. דברים רבה ט, ט

25. עירובין צח, א, ש"ך יו"ד סי' רע"ז ס"ק א' בשם הב"ח
26. ב"י ריש סי' ע"ר בשם הנמוקי יוסף
27. הגאון ר' חיים פלאג'י בספרו "נפש כל חי" מערכת ת' אות כ"ו. ועי' ספר "מדבר קדמות" "מהחיד"א מערכת י' אות ו'
28. תו"מ תשמ"ב ח"א ע' 111-112
29. רמב"ם, רדב"ז, ועוד ראשונים. הובאו כולם בשו"ת רב פעלים ח"ד יו"ד סי' ל"ב
30. שו"ע יו"ד סי' רפ"ב ס"א
31. כל דינים אלו בשו"ע יו"ד סי' רפ"ב, ע"ש בפרטיות
32. שימושה של תורה ע' מ'
33. שבת קלג, ב
34. קידושין לג, ב
35. לכללות הנאמר כאן והמקורות לזה, עי' באורוכה בספר "הנחמדים מפז" לר' פנחס זביחי, בני ברק תשס"ו סי' ג', ובספר "נטעי גבריאל" כרך הכנסת ספר תורה
36. דרשות חתם סופר עמוד רע"ג ד"ה ראשית, אחז"ל מנחות
37. אג"ק לאדמו"ר הריי"ץ ח"ו ע' עג-עד. עי' שו"ת ריב"א חיו"ד סי' קל"ט
38. משנת אברהם סי' א' סכ"ח
39. ענין החופה נזכר בספר "ספר חיים" מהגר"ח פלאג'י סי' מ"ד אות ד'
40. ספר "מטעמים" ע' ספרי תורה וספרים אות ח', ע"ש לכמה מנהגים בזה
41. שו"ת בתי כהונה סי' י"ח

42. אג"ק לאדמו"ר הריי"ץ ח"ו ע' עד-עה. ועי' מנהגים דק"ק וורמייזא אות שט"ו
43. כ"ה מנהג קהלת הולאנד ואיטליה וחסידי רוזין וחב"ד. עי' בספר נטעי גבריאל הנ"ל ע' קעט
44. פמ"ג מש"ז או"ח סי' תמ"ד ס"ק ט
45. ב"י יו"ד סי' ע"ר ס"ב בסופו
46. רמב"ם הל' תפילה פי"ב ה"א. שו"ע או"ח סי' קל"ה ס"א
47. רמב"ם הל' תפילה פי"ב ה"ב
48. שו"ע או"ח סי' קל"ה ס"א, שו"ע או"ח סי' רפ"ב
49. שו"ע או"ח סי' קמ"ג ס"א
50. רמב"ם הל' תפילה פי"ג ה"א
51. תפילין ומזוזות כהלכתן (גרינולד) ע' 149

IN THIS UNIT YOU WILL:

EXPLORE

- Why do people remember some things and forget others?
- Why would someone wear a uniform?

EXAMINE

- What type of clothing needs *tzitzis*?
- How are *tzitzis* made?

EXTRACT

- When is a *tallis* worn?

KEY CONCEPTS

צִיצִית

טַלִּית

טַלִּית קָטָן

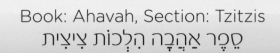

צִיצִת
TZITZIS
מִצְוָה אַחַת

Sometimes you need to add something extra to your clothing or to your body so that you will not forget a specific piece of information.

The *Chilazon*

Techeles is a dye that is mentioned many times in the Torah and is used for many things, such as the clothing of the *kohen gadol*. The *Gemara*[1] tells us that the *techeles* dye comes from the blood of a sea creature known as the *chilazon*. We know that this creature: 1. looks like the sea. 2. looks like a fish. 3. comes up from the bottom of the ocean only once every seventy years. 4. is expensive.

It also says that the *chilazon* is found in the waters between the cliffs of Tzur and Haifa, two cities in Eretz Yisrael.[3]

OUR SAGES SAY...

Strength in Threes

R' Eliezer ben Yaakov said, "Someone who has *tefillin* on his head and on his arm, *tzitzis* on his clothing, and the *mezuzah* on his doorpost, is safe from *aveiros*; as it is written, וְהַחוּט הַמְשֻׁלָּשׁ לֹא בִמְהֵרָה יִנָּתֵק - 'And a cord with three strings does not break easily.'"[4]

The Mitzvah

The unit of *tzitzis* has one mitzvah.

Add strings onto the corners of a piece of clothing that has four corners, and add a *techeles* thread to it.

MITZVAH 84

מִצְוַת צִיצִית
The mitzvah of *tzitzis*

דַּבֵּר אֶל בְּנֵי יִשְׂרָאֵל וְאָמַרְתָּ אֲלֵהֶם וְעָשׂוּ לָהֶם צִיצִת עַל כַּנְפֵי בִגְדֵיהֶם לְדֹרֹתָם וְנָתְנוּ עַל צִיצִת הַכָּנָף פְּתִיל תְּכֵלֶת
(במדבר טו, לח)

Speak to *B'nei Yisrael* and have them **make tassels on the corners of their garments for all generations to come.** They should include a **thread of sky-blue wool in the corner tassels.**

Add strings on the corners of a four-cornered piece of clothing before wearing it, and put a techeles thread on it.

MEN   ALL PLACES   ALL TIMES

Mitzvah Messages

Fixing Forgetfulness

If you didn't do something you were supposed to, you'll probably say, "Oops! I forgot all about it!" It's easy to forget things, so if you are being responsible, you will be careful to write a note, or ask someone to remind you, so that you do not forget, especially if it is important.

This is why Hashem gave us a mitzvah to wear *tzitzis*, to remind us of all Hashem's other mitzvos, since they are so important that you should never say, "But I forgot!"[5]

Dress Up

You can never forget who you are and what you do. Doctors wear white coats, chefs wear aprons, football players wear helmets, and soldiers wear uniforms. Uniforms tell us who people are, what they do, and what is expected of them. People are proud to wear a uniform, and when wearing it, they feel responsible to act properly.

Tzitzis are like your uniform — it gives you a feeling of responsibility to act properly, and to show the world that you are proud to be a Jew.[6]

CHECKPOINT How can *tzitzis* help you serve Hashem?

Details

EXAMINE

The *Tzitzis*

The בֶּגֶד - Garment

If you wear a piece of clothing with at least four corners, you have a mitzvah to tie *tzitzis* to four corners of that piece of clothing.[7] You would only have to wear *tzitzis* if the clothing is at least one *amah* by one *amah* big.[8]

The צִיצִית - Strings

The *tzitzis* are made up of four strings which, when passed through a hole and folded over, are doubled into eight. The strings must be 12 *gudlin*[9] (thumb widths) long and they must be made either from the same material as the clothing, or wool, which is kosher to be used with any material.[10]

The חֻלְיוֹת - Windings

One extra long string called the "shamesh" is then taken and wrapped around the other seven in a special pattern called *chulyos*. When a special, rare dye called *techeles* is available, the *shamesh* string is dyed with *techeles,* and is wrapped with one of the white strings, around the rest of the strings.[11]

Cool Threads

The mitzvah of *tzitzis* is very special to Hashem, and Hashem gives many rewards to someone who is careful with *tzitzis*. Some of them are:

• Someone who is careful to keep the mitzvah of *tzitzis* is worthy to receive the *Shechinah*.[14]

• Someone who is careful to keep the mitzvah of *tzitzis* is rewarded with having enough money to buy nice clothes.[15]

The way that the *shamesh* is wrapped around the rest of the strings is called *chulyos*. There are four sets of *chulyos* which are each separated by two knots. The *shamesh* makes anywhere between seven and thirteen *chulyos* in between each set of two knots.

The most common *minhag* is to have sets of seven, eight, eleven, and thirteen *chulyos*. These numbers add up to 39, which is the *gematria* of ה' אֶחָד.

Some make the number of *chulyos* ten, five, six and five, which is the *gematria* of the letters of Hashem's name י-ה-ו-ה.

The Intention

Preparing the *tzitzis*, including spinning the threads, twisting the threads and dying the *techeles*[18] must all be done with the purpose that it is being done for a mitzvah.[19] This is known as doing it "*lishmah* - for its sake."

Wearing *Tzitzis*

The mitzvah of *tzitzis* only applies during the **day** when you can see the *tzitzis* and they will remind you about Hashem's mitzvos.

Since it is a *mitzvas asei shehazman gramah*, women do not need to keep the mitzvah of *tzitzis*.

The Process

Before you put on *tzitzis*, you should separate and check the strings to make sure they are not tangled together or ripped.[20]

The *brachah* for wearing *tzitzis* is:

בָּרוּךְ אַתָּה ה' אֱלֹקֵינוּ מֶלֶךְ הָעוֹלָם אֲשֶׁר קִדְּשָׁנוּ בְּמִצְוֹתָיו וְצִוָּנוּ עַל מִצְוַת צִיצִית.

You should hold the *tzitzis* in your hands while you make the *brachah*.[22]

DID YOU KNOW?

A Reminder

The *gematria* of צִיצִית is 600. Add to this 8 strings and the 5 knots that are made with the strings of each one of the four corners for a total of 613. The *tzitzis* reminds us of all the *mitzvos* that Hashem has commanded us to keep.[16]

CHECKPOINT How is the mitzvah of *tzitzis* performed?

- On a piece of clothing that has more than four corners, *tzitzis* are placed on the four corners which are furthest away from each other.[23]

- You only have to do the mitzvah of *tzitzis* if you are wearing a piece of clothing that has four corners. If all of your clothing have regular seams and no corners, then you do not have to wear *tzitzis*. Even though we don't have to, we make a special piece of clothing that has four corners and wear it every day just so we can do the mitzvah of *tzitzis*.[24]

- "תַּעֲשֶׂה וְלֹא מִן הָעָשׂוּי" – *Tzitzis* can only be tied into a piece of clothing if the clothing has four corners and needs to have *tzitzis*. If the *tzitzis* were tied to the clothing before it needed to have *tzitzis* (like if the clothing was torn or did not yet have four complete corners) then the *tzitzis* must be retied once the clothing has a full four corners.[25]

- If up to two strings tear on one side of the knots, the *tzitzis* are still *kosher*; however, once three or more tear, it's *passul*.[26]

- If even one string tears off at any point in the *chulyos* or knots, the *tzitzis* are *passul*.[27]

- If your *tzitzis* becomes *passul*, you must take them off. However, if you are in a public place and it will be embarrassing to take them off, you may go home and take them off there.[28]

In the Dark

According to *halachah*, you do not need to wear *tzitzis* at night, but some people have a *minhag* to wear *tzitzis* even at night.

The *passuk* says וּרְאִיתֶם אֹתוֹ[29] - and you should **see** the *tzitzis*. This teaches us that *tzitzis* does not apply at night, because you can't see the *tzitzis* at night, in the dark.[30]

The Rambam explains that you do not need *tzitzis* on any clothing that you wear during the night **time,** even if it is clothing that you usually wear in the day. Any clothing that you wear in the day **time,** even if it is pajamas or any other nighttime clothing, needs *tzitzis*.

The Rosh explains that any **clothing** that would usually be worn at night, like pajamas, does not need *tzitzis*, no matter when you wear it. Any clothing that is usually worn in the daytime, like regular clothes, needs to have *tzitzis*, even if you are wearing it at night.[31]

Therefore, according to the Rosh, you can do this *mitzvah* during the night also, by wearing day-time clothing.

The Arizal instructed to be careful to wear *tzitzis* at night.[32]

He explained that according to *kabbalah*, the rewards and protection that come from wearing *tzitzis* apply at night as well.[33]

According to all opinions, you do not say a *brachah* on *tzitzis* at night.

Not Leaving Without Them

Rabbah was very careful about the mitzvah of *tzitzis*. Once, while going down some stairs, one of the strings of his *tzitzis* tore. He wouldn't move from his spot until new *kosher tzitzis* were tied to his garment.[34]

Shamayim Comes in Thirteen Layers

On each set of *tzitzis* there are anywhere between seven and thirteen *chulyos*. The reason for the numbers seven and thirteen is because there are seven heavens with six atmospheres that separate them (7+6=13).[35]

One Big Mitzvah

The mitzvah of *tzitzis* is equal to all of the mitzvos combined, because wearing them is a reminder to do all of Hashem's mitzvos.[36]

They've Got the Blues

Why are we supposed to use a blue thread for *tzitzis*? *Techeles* looks like the sea, the sea looks like the sky, and the sky will remind you of Hashem's throne.[37]

HISTORY

Who Fish

Many years ago, we lost the secret of exactly what the *chilazon* (from where we get the dye), looks like. In the past few hundred years, many people have tried to find the *chilazon*. R' Gershon Chanoch Henoch Leiner, and Israeli Chief R' Y.I. Herzog both tried very hard to find it.

R' Leiner[38] said that the *chilazon* fish was a kind of squid known as *Sepia Officinalis*, or the cuttlefish, and he made *techeles* from this fish. There is even a factory in Eretz Yisrael that makes this *techeles*.

Rabbi Herzog[39] felt that the *chilazon* was a type of snail called the Janthina.

Another possibility, which is more widely accepted, is that it is the snail *Murex Trunculus*. Rabbi Herzog himself agreed that he liked the *Janthina* snail better, but the *Murex* was the most logical fit for the *chilazon*.

Live the Mitzvah

EXTRACT

Remember the Reminder

We check our *tzitzis* every morning before making the *brachah*, so that we can make sure that there are no torn strings. If there are, then you are not allowed to wear those *tzitzis*. If there is a torn string and you continue to wear the non-*kosher* *tzitzis*, you are doing the *aveirah* of wearing a four-cornered piece of clothing without *tzitzis*.

 CHECKPOINT Why is it important to check your *tzitzis* every day?

What Else Comes From This?

EXTRACT

For the Glory of the People

Men wear a *tallis* specifically to fulfill the mitzvah of *tzitzis*. However, there are many times when men will wear *tallis* just for a *minhag*, not to do the *mitzvah* of *tzitzis*. At these times, the *tallis* is usually borrowed, which means that no *brachah* is said, since the man does not own the *tallis*. When putting on such a *tallis*, the man should keep in mind that he is **not** fulfilling the mitzvah of *tzitzis*.

However, many *shuls* have a "*shul tallis*" that belongs to the *shul*, which is used specifically these times. On such a *tallis*, a man **does** make a *brachah*, since it is like he owns the *tallis*, together with the rest of the *shul*.[40]

Some of the times a man would wear a *tallis* are:

 Aliyah: Many *shuls* have the *minhag* that when a person is called to the Torah, he puts on a *tallis* out of honor for the people in the *shul*.[41]

Birchas kohanim: When the *kohanim* give their *brachah*, it is common in many *shuls* for all the *kohanim* to wear a *tallis*, even those who don't normally wear one.[42]

BIOGRAPHY

R' Gershon Chanoch Henoch Leiner (1839 – 1890) תקצ״ט - תרנ״א

Rabbi Gershon Chanoch Henoch Leiner, was the first Radziner Rebbe. He is referred to by Radziner chassidim as the "Orchos Chaim", the title of his sefer explaining the Tzava'ah - the will - of the Tana R' Eliezer Hagadol. He is also commonly referred to as the Ba'al Hatecheles because he worked so hard to research, produce and influence people to wear techeles on their tzitzis. He passed away on the 4th of Teves, and is buried in Radzin.

Chazzan: In many *shuls*, the *chazzan* wears a *tallis* for the honor of the people in the *shul*.[43]

Yom Kippur: Although a *tallis* is not usually worn during the night *tefillos*, on *Yom Kippur* it is worn throughout *kol nidre* and *ma'ariv*, and on the following afternoon and evening during *ne'ilah* as well.[44]

A bris milah: The *sandek* who holds the baby during the *bris*, and the *mohel*, both wear a *tallis*. Some have the *minhag* that **everyone** who is involved with some honor during the *bris*, like passing the baby, wears a *tallis*.[45]

Drashah: A Rabbi giving a speech to the *shul* wears a *tallis* out of respect for the people in the shul.[46]

Chassan and kallah: Some have the *minhag* that a *chassan* wears a *tallis* either in the morning of his *chupah* or while he is brought to the *chupah*, and it is spread over the *kallah* as well.[47]

Burial: It is customary to bury someone with a *tallis*.[48]

CHECKPOINT When would a man wear a *tallis* without doing the mitzvah of *tzitzis*?

DID YOU KNOW?

Retro Stripes

Have you ever wondered why many *tzitzis* and *talleisim* have stripes on them?

One reason is so that they remind us of the *techeles* which also had a different look than the rest of the strings.[49]

STORY

The *Tzitzis Yid*

R' Yisrael of Ruzhin had the *minhag* to put *tzitzis* on each of his baby sons from the age of thirty days.

Once, one of his infant sons (later known as R' Dovid Moshe of Chortkov) wouldn't stop crying. No matter how hard his mother tried to soothe him, he wouldn't calm down.

She was going to call a doctor, but her husband, R' Yisrael, only laughed.

"It must be that someone forgot to put on the baby's *tzitzis*," he said.

The *Rebbetzin* went to check, and indeed, he was not wearing his *tzitzis*. As soon as she put his *tzitzis* back on, the baby stopped crying.

From that day on, he was called "the *tzitzis Yid*."[50]

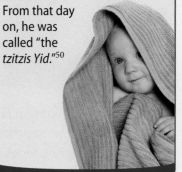

UNIT 41

ENDNOTES:

1. מנחות מד, א
3. שבת כו, א
4. מנחות מג, ב
5. חינוך מצוה שפ"ו
6. עי' מנחות מג, ב ובתוס' ד"ה חותם של טיט. "ואני תפלתי" ע' 101. דרך ה' לרמח"ל חלק רביעי פ"ו ס"ה
7. רמב"ם הל' ציצית פ"ג ה"ג
8. שו"ע פרי הארץ או"ח ח"א סי' א'
9. שו"ע או"ח סי' י"א ס"ד
10. שו"ע או"ח סי' ט' ס"ב-ג'
11. רמב"ם הל' ציצית פ"א ה"ז
12. בראשית רבה מג, ט
13. חסידות בכל דור ודור (אלפסי) ע' 10
14. מנחות מג, ב
15. שבת כג, ב
16. רש"י במדבר טו, לט
17. שו"ע או"ח סי' י"א סי"ד, ובמג"א שם ס"ק כ"ב וט"ז ס"ק ט"ז, ע"ש לחילוקי מנהגים
18. רמב"ם הל' ציצית פ"ב ה"ג

19. רמב"ם הל' ציצית פ"א הי"א. שו"ע או"ח סי' י"א ס"א
20. שו"ע או"ח סי' ח' ס"ז, וט'
21. רמ"א או"ח סי' ח' ס"ו
22. שו"ע הרב או"ח סי' ח' ס"כ
23. רמב"ם הל' ציצית פ"ג ה"ג. שו"ע או"ח סי' י' ס"א
24. רמב"ם הל' ציצית פ"א הי"א. שו"ע או"ח סי' כ"ד ס"א
25. (שו"ת או"ח סי' י' ס"ה)
26. שו"ע או"ח סי' י"ב ס"א ובהגה
27. שו"ע או"ח סי' י"ב ס"א
28. שו"ע הרב או"ח סי' י"ג ס"ד
29. במדבר טו, לט
30. מנחות מג, א
31. שו"ע או"ח סי' י"א ס"א
32. מג"א סי' כ"א ס"ק ב'
33. פרע"ח שער הציצית ספ"א
34. שבת קיח, ב
35. מנחות לט, א

36. מנחות מג, ב, רש"י ד"ה ראיה
37. מנחות מג, ב
38. מאמר שפוני טמוני חול
39. The Royal Purple and the Biblical Blue 1919
40. ראה פרטי הדינים בספר "ציצית הלכה פסוקה" סי' י"ד ס"ג ס"ק ל"ח ואילך
41. מג"א סי' י"ד ס"ק ו'
42. עי' רמ"א סי' קכ"ח סכ"ג
43. מג"א סי' י"ח ס"ק ב'
44. לבוש סי' תרי"ט ס"א
45. ספר "מטעמים" ע' מילה אות נ"ט
46. ערוך השלחן סי' י"ח ס"ז
47. עי' בכ"ז בשו"ת באר משה (שטרן) ח"ו סי' ז. ספר "ציצית הלכה פסוקה" סי' ח' הע' 37 (במקורות להלכה פסוקה)
48. שו"ע יו"ד סי' שנ"א ס"ב
49. פמ"ג אשל אברהם או"ח סי' ט' ס"ק ו'
50. סיפורי חסידים פ' אמור

UNIT 42

IN THIS UNIT YOU WILL:

EXPLORE

- Why is it important for you to know where your food comes from?

EXAMINE

- After eating which foods do you have to say *Birkas Hamazon*?
- What are the *brachos* in *Birkas Hamazon*?

EXTRACT

- Besides for *Birkas Hamazon*, what other *brachos* do you make after eating foods or drinking liquids?

בִּרְכַּת הַמָזוֹן

זִימוּן

כּוֹס שֶׁל בְּרָכָה

KEY CONCEPTS

Book: Ahavah, Section: Blessings

סֵפֶר אַהֲבָה הִלְכוֹת בְּרָכוֹת

בִּרְכַּת הַמָּזוֹן
BIRKAS HAMAZON

מִצְוָה אַחַת

Imagine that you had

no one taking care of you.

How would you ever survive?

A Holy Table

The Torah does not allow us to build a *mizbeiach* made from stones that were cut with any metal materials.[1] This is because we can't use something that usually kills people to try and help people become closer to Hashem and make their lives longer.

Even though we don't have the *Beis Hamikdash* anymore, we still follow this *halachah* on our modern-day *mizbeiach*, a table: When we say *Birkas Hamazon* we make sure to cover or remove any knives that are on the table.

We don't do this on *Shabbos*, because on *Shabbos*, there is no violence and killing.[2]

HISTORY

He Who Sustains Us

When *B'nei Yisrael* were in the *midbar*, they didn't have to worry about food. Every day, Hashem sent *mann* from *shamayim* to feed them. A container of the *mann* was placed in front of the *Aron* to remind us that even when we are busy working to have enough money to live, we should trust in Hashem, the One Who really gives us what we need.[3]

The Mitzvah

There is one mitzvah in the unit of *Birkas Hamazon*.

Say the *brachos* of *Birkas Hamazon* after you have eaten bread.

MITZVAH 85

מִצְוַת בִּרְכַּת הַמָּזוֹן

Saying Birkas Hamazon

וְאָכַלְתָּ וְשָׂבָעְתָּ וּבֵרַכְתָּ אֶת ה׳ אֱלֹקֶיךָ עַל הָאָרֶץ הַטֹּבָה אֲשֶׁר נָתַן לָךְ
(דברים ח, י)

When you eat and are satisfied, you must therefore bless Hashem your G-d for the good land that He has given you.

Bless Hashem after eating bread.

ALL PEOPLE   ALL PLACES   ALL TIMES

Mitzvah Messages

Thank You for Your Kindness

Hashem is so kind that He gives everything in the world what it needs to live, and feeds all of His creatures. If He left us on our own, we would never survive.

To thank Hashem for giving us what we need to live, we say *Birkas Hamazon* after we eat.[4]

 CHECKPOINT What are we saying to Hashem by reciting *Birkas Hamazon*?

Details

EXAMINE

The *Brachos* of *Birkas Hamazon*

There is a *mitzvah* to bless Hashem (known in Yiddish as *bentching*) when you have finished eating bread made from any of the five kinds of grain – wheat, barley, spelt, oats, or rye.[5] According to the Torah, you only have a mitzvah to *bentch* once you are full, but *miderabanan*, you have to *bentch* even after eating only a *kezayis* of bread.[6]

The *Brachos*

There are four *brachos* in *Birkas Hamazon*. The first three are from the Torah, and the fourth was added by the *Chachamim*.[7]

1. הַזָּן אֶת הָעוֹלָם: We thank Hashem for giving us and all of His creations what they need to live, and we ask that we should always have enough food.[8]

2. נוֹדֶה לְּךָ.... בָּרוּךְ אַתָּה ה' עַל הָאָרֶץ וְעַל הַמָּזוֹן: This *brachah* includes two ideas: 1. Praising Eretz Yisrael, and 2. Thanking Hashem for giving us the mitzvos of *milah* and learning Torah.[9]
    During *Chanukah* and *Purim* we add a special *tefillah* called "*Ve'al hanissim*" in this *brachah*. In it, we thank Hashem for the miracles He did for *B'nei Yisrael* in those miraculous times.[10]

3. בּוֹנֶה יְרוּשָׁלַיִם: We ask to Hashem to have mercy on us and to allow us to live with dignity and not have to rely on loans and favors from other people. We end this *brachah* by asking for the rebuilding of the *Beis Hamikdash* in Yerushalayim, and for the return of the Kingdom of *Dovid Hamelech*.[11] On *Shabbos*, we a special *tefillah*, "*Retzeh*," right before we finish the *brachah*. On the *Yamim Noraim*, *Shalosh Regalim* and *Rosh Chodesh*, "*Ya'aleh v'yavo*" is added.[12]

4. בָּרוּךְ אַתָּה ה'... הָאֵ-ל אָבִינוּ... הַטּוֹב וְהַמֵטִיב: We thank Hashem for His goodness, and we also thank our hosts for the meal and our parents. We end with a *tefillah* for the coming of *Mashiach*.[13]

After these four *brachos*, additional sentences are added when you *bentch* on *Shabbos*, *Yom Tov*, *Rosh Chodesh* and for a *bris*. At a wedding and during *sheva brachos*, seven *brachos* are added after *bentching*.[14] Before *bentching*, some chapters of *Tehillim* are said, including "*Al naharos bavel*" on weekdays, and "*Shir hama'alos*" on *Shabbos* and *Yom Tov*.[15]

HISTORY

Origins of the Blessings

The words to say in the different *brachos* in *Birkas Hamazon* were written by Jewish leaders throughout history.[16]

הַזָּן אֶת הָעוֹלָם was instituted by *Moshe Rabbeinu* in the desert when the *mann* fell.

נוֹדֶה לְךָ.... בָּרוּךְ אַתָּה ה' עַל הָאָרֶץ וְעַל הַמָּזוֹן was written by Yehoshua when *B'nei Yisrael* entered Eretz Yisrael.

בּוֹנֶה יְרוּשָׁלַיִם was written by *Dovid Hamelech* and *Shlomo Hamelech*. *Dovid Hamelech* put in the words "עַל יִשְׂרָאֵל עַמֶּךָ וְעַל יְרוּשָׁלַם עִירֶךָ". After building the *Beis Hamikdash*, *Shlomo Hamelech* added "וְעַל הַבַּיִת הַגָּדוֹל וְהַקָדוֹשׁ".

הַטּוֹב וְהַמֵטִיב was written in Yavneh after the Jews were allowed to bury the Jews who were killed in the city of Betar, from the revolt of Bar Kochva. The double words of הַטּוֹב וְהַמֵטִיב refers to the two kindnesses that Hashem did: 1. The Jews were allowed to bury the dead, 2. The bodies of the dead did not rot even after many years![17]

DID YOU KNOW?

He'll Take It Sitting Down

Why do you have to sit down when you *bentch*?

The words of the *passuk* say וְשָׂבַעְתָּ וּבֵרַכְתָּ. We can read these words as שֵׁב עֵת וּבֵרַכְתָּ – "Sit at the time that you *bentch*."[18]

The Story Behind *Hatov Vehametiv*

Bar Kochva, a Jewish leader, led the Jews of the city of Betar in a revolt against Rome after the *Beis Hamikdash* was destroyed. At that time, Beitar was one of the main cities where Jews lived.

For three and a half years, Hadrian, the Roman emperor, was unable to win the battle to conquer Betar.

One day, Bar Kochva made a mistake and thought that the great *tzaddik* R' Elazar of Modi'in was planning to surrender the city to Rome and he killed R' Elazar. At this point, Hashem did not give Betar the same protection and Hadrian was able to break in to Betar, killing thousands of Jews, including Bar Kochva.

Their dead bodies were piled up in a vineyard, and Hadrian cruelly decreed that they could not be buried. They lay there for many years, until Hadrian finally died and the new emperor gave his permission to bury the dead.

Miraculously, after all this time, the bodies had not decayed. The joy and relief the Jews felt at finally being able to bury their dead was expressed in a new *brachah* that was added to the *Birkas Hamazon*.[19]

Saying *Birkas Hamazon*

Birkas Hamazon must be said in the place where you ate. If you are in the same room in which you ate, or if you can see where you sat when you ate, then it is like you are in the exact spot, and you can say *Birkas Hamazon* there.[20]

After finishing the meal, you can say *Birkas Hamazon* as long as you still feel full from your meal. The time frame that the *Chachamim* set for this is the amount of time it takes to walk four *mil*[21] (about 2.5 miles), which is about 72 minutes.[22]

Making a *Zimun*

If three or more men over the age of thirteen are *bentching* together, they must *bentch* with a process called "zimun," an "invited" *brachah*. The leader invites the others to *bentch*, they answer, and then proceed to *bentch*. If there are ten or more people there and most of them are *bentching*, Hashem's name is used in the invitation.[23]

Say it with Wine

The best way to do this mitzvah is to *bentch* over a cup of wine. This cup is called *kos shel brachah*. At the end of *bentching*, the *brachah* of *Hagafen* is made over the wine, and many people have a *minhag* for everyone there to drink from the wine.[24]

 CHECKPOINT How and when do you have to *bentch*?

- You should say *Birkas Hamazon* in Hebrew even if you don't understand Hebrew, but you are allowed to say it in any language that you understand.[25]

- *Birkas Hamazon* should be said out loud, but you would still get the mitzvah if the words were whispered.[26]

- On *Shabbos* and *Yom Tov*, if you forget to say *R'tzeh* or *Ya'aleh v'yavo*, you must say an extra *brachah* before you begin *Hatov v'hametiv*. If you only remembered after you already started to say *Hatov v'hametiv*, then you must go back to the beginning of *bentching* and start again.[27]

- On *Rosh Chodesh*, *Chol Hamoed*, and on *Shabbos* during *seudah shlishis*, if you forgot to say *R'tzeh* or *Ya'aleh v'yavo*, you must say an extra *brachah* before you begin *Hatov v'hametiv*. If you only remembered after beginning *Hatov v'hametiv*, then you should just continue *bentching*.[28]

EXTEND YOUR KNOWLEDGE

Ya'aleh V'yavo on *Yom Kippur*

If a sick person or a child eats on *Yom Kippur*, do they have to say *Ya'aleh ve'yavo* when they *bentch*?

The Rosh[29] says that they would have to say *Ya'aleh ve'yavo*. The Maharam of Rotenberg[30] explains that *Ya'aleh ve'yavo* is added because someone like this is allowed to eat and even has a mitzvah to eat, so, *Yom Kippur* becomes like a regular *Yom Tov*.

The *Shibbolei Haleket*,[31] holds that a sick person or child does not need to say *Ya'aleh ve'yavo*. This opinion comes from his teacher, *R' Avigdor Kohen Tzedek*, who explains that the eating has nothing to do with the day, but is for *pikuach nefesh*. Therefore, it is still like a regular weekday meal.

The *Shulchan Aruch*[32] agrees with the *Rosh*, but the *Taz* strongly argues against it. Therefore, you should ask your Rav for an answer, if this question comes up for you.

BIOGRAPHY

The *Shibbolei Haleket*
Lived approximately ס' ה (1300)

R. Tzidkiyah ben R. Avraham Harofe was born in Rome. When he was young, he studied in Wurzberg, Germany, with students of R' Shimshon Mishantz. During this period, he recorded the local customs and collected halachic rulings of French and German Chachamim. This became the sefer Shibbolei Haleket, which is a commentary mainly on the halachos of Orach Chayim. R' Tzidkiyah also wrote another work, Shibbolei Haleket, part 2, on the halachos of Yoreh Deah.

Live the Mitzvah

EXTRACT

Not by the Strength of My Hand

Since Hashem is the One Who gives you your food, you must not think that it is **your** talent or cleverness in doing business and making money that gets you your food. It is Hashem Who decides whether we earn money or not, and how much. As it says, בִּרְכַּת ה' הִיא תַעֲשִׁיר – **"Hashem's brachos** are what brings wealth."

By thanking Hashem, you are showing that you know that everything comes from Hashem.

> **CHECKPOINT** What does saying *Birkas Hamazon* show about your belief in Hashem?

What Else Comes From This?

EXTRACT

Other After-Blessings

In addition to the *Birkas Hamazon* that we say after we eat bread, the *Rabanan* made other *brachos* that we say after eating different kinds of foods.

מֵעֵין שָׁלֹשׁ

When we eat anything made from the five grains[36] that needs the *brachah* of *mezonos* to be said before eating, a *brachah acharonah,* called "brachah me'ein shalosh" is said.[37] In this *brachah,* we briefly mention the major ideas of the three *brachos* from the regular *Birkas Hamazon.* This *brachah* is therefore known as "me'ein shalosh - like three." This *brachah* is also said for any of the five fruits which Eretz Yisrael is praised for – grapes, figs, pomegranates, olives and dates,[38] as well as after drinking wine.[39]

We begin and end this *brachah* by mentioning the specific food that we ate. For example, after eating one of the *shiv'as haminim,* we end with the words "… for the land and for its **fruits**."[40] On special days such as *Shabbos* or *Yom Tov,* we add a few words to mention the special day.[41]

בּוֹרֵא נְפָשׁוֹת

On all other foods apart from *mezonos*, wine, and the *shiv'as haminim*, we say a short *brachah acharonah* called "*Borei nefashos*." This applies to things such as milk, water, fruit juice, eggs, meat, chicken and fish.[42] If you eat any regular fruit or vegetables, you should also say *Borei nefashos*.

If you eat regular fruit together with the five special fruits of Eretz Yisrael, then you say the after-*brachah* of *me'ein shalosh*. In this case, the *brachah* of *me'ein shalosh* "covers" the regular fruit as well and you do not say *Borei nefashos*.[43]

> **CHECKPOINT** What are the *brachos* you say after eating foods other than bread?

UNIT 42

STORY

Hashem's Agent

Avraham Avinu would tell his guests to *bentch* after they had finished eating and drinking. They would ask, "What should we say?" and he would tell them, "Blessed is the G-d of the Universe of Whose food we have eaten." After this, they were allowed to leave.

If a guest refused to *bentch*, Avraham would demand "Pay me for what you have eaten." When one man asked what he owed, Avraham would say, "One jug of wine costs ten *follera*, a pound of meat costs ten *follera*, a round of bread costs ten *follera*. Who else will give you wine in the desert, who will give you meat in the desert, and who will give you bread in the desert?"

When he heard how expensive everything was, the guest would have no choice but to *bentch*.[44]

ENDNOTES:

1. דברים כז, ה

2. ב"י או"ח סי' ק"פ ס"ק ה'

3. שמות טז, ד-לב. רש"י שם

4. רבינו בחיי דברים ח, י

5. קיצור שו"ע סי' מ"א ס"א

6. שו"ע או"ח סי' קפ"ד ס"ו, מג"א שם ס"ק י"א

7. שו"ע או"ח סי' קפ"ח ס"א

8. ערוך השולחן או"ח סי' קפ"ז ס"ב

9. ברכות מח, ב. שו"ע או"ח סי' קפ"ז ס"ג

10. רמ"א או"ח סי' קפ"ז ס"ד

11. נוסח הברכה

12. שו"ע או"ח סי' קפ"ח ס"ה

13. נוסח הברכה

14. שו"ע אה"ע סי' ס"ב ס"ה

15. מג"א סי' א' ס"ק ה'

16. ב"י או"ח סי' קפ"ז ס"ק א'

17. ברכות מח, ב

18. תוס' ברכות נא, ב ד"ה והלכתא

19. ירושלמי תענית פ"ד ה"ה. בבלי ברכות מח, ב

20. שו"ע או"ח סי' קפ"ד ס"א, מג"א ס"ק א'

21. שו"ע או"ח סי' קפ"ד ס"ה, מג"א ס"ק ט'

22. קצות השולחן סי' מ"ד ס"ק ה'. קשו"ע סי' מ"ד ס"ח

23. שו"ע או"ח סי' קצ"ב ס"א

24. שו"ע או"ח סי' קפ"ב ס"א, ובהגה

25. שו"ע או"ח סי' קפ"א ס"א, משנ"ב שם ס"ק א'

26. שו"ע או"ח סי' קפ"ה ס"ב

27. שו"ע או"ח סי' קפ"ו ס"ו

28. שו"ע או"ח סי' קפ"ה ס"ז-ח'

29. טור או"ח סי' תרי"ח, ט"ז שם ס"ק י'

30. שו"ת מהר"ם מרוטנבורג ח"ד דפוס פראג סי' ע"א

31. שבלי הלקט סי' שי"ב

32. שו"ע סי' תרי"ח ס"י

33. ברכות כ, ב

34. זוהר חדש סח, ב

35. רות רבה ה, טו

36. רש"י ברכות מה, א ד"ה חמשת המינים

37. שו"ע או"ח סי' ר"ח ס"ב

38. שו"ע או"ח סי' ר"ח ס"א

39. שו"ע או"ח סי' ר"ח סי"א

40. ברכות מה, א

41. שו"ע או"ח סי' ר"ח סי"ב

42. שו"ע או"ח סי' ר"ז

43. שו"ע או"ח סי' ר"ח סי"ג

44. בראשית רבה מט, ד

45. שו"ע סי' קפ"ח ס"א

DID YOU KNOW?

Amen

Although we don't usually say *Amen* to our own *brachos*, we do say it after the *brachah* of "*bonei Yerushalayim.*" This is to show the difference between the *brachos* that are from the Torah and the next one, which is from the *Rabbanan*.[45]

PRIVATE
PROPERTY

ASK
BEFORE
USING

UNIT 43

IN THIS UNIT YOU WILL:

EXPLORE

- Why do we make *brachos*?

EXAMINE

- What are the four types of *brachos*?

EXTRACT

- How many *brachos* do you need to say each day?
- How can you show that you know that Hashem really owns everything?

מֵאָה בְּרָכוֹת

בְּרָכוֹת

KEY CONCEPTS

Book: Ahavah, Section: Blessings
סֵפֶר אַהֲבָה הִלְכוֹת בְּרָכוֹת

בְּרָכוֹת
BRACHOS

מִצְוָה אַחַת מִדְרַבָּנָן

Would you pick up something
that is not yours without asking
permission from the owner?

Close Your Hand and Open Your Mouth

R' Chanina bar Papa said: To enjoy this world without first making a *brachah* is like robbing Hashem and *B'nei Yisrael*.[1]

DID YOU KNOW?

No Objection, Your Honor

The *passuk* says to love Hashem with all of your "measures." This can mean giving *brachos* to Hashem for the bad things that happen to us, not just the good things. That is why, when you hear bad news, such as when someone dies, you say the *brachah* בָּרוּךְ דַּיַן הָאֱמֶת - "Blessed is the True Judge."[2]

The Mitzvah

EXAMINE

The unit of *brachos* has one mitzvah from the *Chachamim*.

Thank Hashem by making *brachos* on food, nature, and mitzvos.

MITZVAH DERABANAN
1

מִצְוַת בְּרָכוֹת
The mitzvah to bless Hashem

אָסוּר לוֹ לְאָדָם שֶׁיֵּהָנֶה מִן הָעוֹלָם הַזֶּה בְּלֹא בְּרָכָה
(ברכות לה, א)

A person is not allowed to benefit from this world without a blessing.

Bless Hashem for everything.

ALL PEOPLE   ALL PLACES   ALL TIMES

Mitzvah Messages

EXPLORE

Ask Permission

The whole world and everything in it belongs to Hashem. It would be bad manners to take something without first asking permission, or even just showing that you know that it belongs to Hashem. This is why we make *brachos*, to show Hashem that we have not forgotten that everything belongs to Him, and that we are grateful that we can enjoy His creations.[3]

CHECKPOINT   What are you doing when you say a *brachah*?

The Four Types of Blessings

Making *brachos* is a *mitzvah derabanan*. The *Rabanan* made four types of *brachos*. They are:

1. **בִּרְכוֹת הַנֶּהֱנִין:** *Brachos* that are made on things which give us pleasure, such as food, or sweet-smelling spices.

2. **בִּרְכוֹת הַשֶּׁבַח וְהַהוֹדָאָה:** *Brachos* that praise or thank Hashem for something that is not physical pleasure.

3. **בִּרְכוֹת שֶׁעַל הַמִּצְווֹת:** *Brachos* which are said when you do a mitzvah.

4. **בְּרָכָה אַחֲרוֹנָה:** *Brachos* made after eating foods other than bread.

Here are some examples of each of these:

בִּרְכוֹת הַנֶּהֱנִין

Brachos on Having Pleasure

There are six different *brachos* that can be made on food.

1. "...Who brings out bread from the ground." **בָּרוּךְ אַתָּה ה' אֱלֹקֵינוּ מֶלֶךְ הָעוֹלָם הַמּוֹצִיא לֶחֶם מִן הָאָרֶץ** - This *brachah* is made on all bread that is made from the five grains (wheat, barley, oat, spelt, rye).[4]

2. "...Who creates all kinds of sustenance." **בָּרוּךְ אַתָּה ה' אֱלֹקֵינוּ מֶלֶךְ הָעוֹלָם בּוֹרֵא מִינֵי מְזוֹנוֹת** - This *brachah* is made on any food (other than bread) that is made from the five grains.[5] This includes pasta, cakes, crackers and some kinds of cereals.

3. "...Who creates fruit of the vine." **בָּרוּךְ אַתָּה ה' אֱלֹקֵינוּ מֶלֶךְ הָעוֹלָם בּוֹרֵא פְּרִי הַגָּפֶן** - This *brachah* is made on grape juice or wine.[6]

4. "...Who creates the fruits of the tree." **בָּרוּךְ אַתָּה ה' אֱלֹקֵינוּ מֶלֶךְ הָעוֹלָם בּוֹרֵא פְּרִי הָעֵץ** - This *brachah* is said before eating the fruits of a tree, such as apples or oranges.[7]

5. "...Who creates the fruits of the ground." **בָּרוּךְ אַתָּה ה' אֱלֹקֵינוּ מֶלֶךְ הָעוֹלָם בּוֹרֵא פְּרִי הָאֲדָמָה** - This *brachah* is made on vegetables which grow from the ground, such as carrots or cucumbers.[8]

PEARLS *of wisdom*

G-dly Sparks

All food has a spark of *kedushah* in it. When you say a *brachah* before eating, and you eat in order to have energy to serve Hashem, you are finding that spark and bringing it up so that it can go back to become part of the *Shechinah* again.[10]

OUR SAGES SAY...

Now You Can Have It

R' Levi asks: If we say, 'לַה' הָאָרֶץ וּמְלֹאָהּ - "The earth and everything in it belongs to Hashem," then, how can we also say הַשָּׁמַיִם שָׁמַיִם לַה' וְהָאָרֶץ נָתַן לִבְנֵי אָדָם - "The skies belong to Hashem, and the earth, He has given to the people?"

To whom does the earth really belong, to Hashem or to us?

In truth, there is no contradiction. Before we make a *brachah*, the earth still belongs to Hashem. But after we make a *brachah*, Hashem gives us the earth, and everything that is on it.[11]

6. "...that everything is created through Hashem's word." — בָּרוּךְ אַתָּה ה' אֱלֹקֵינוּ מֶלֶךְ הָעוֹלָם שֶׁהַכֹּל נִהְיָה בִּדְבָרוֹ

This *brachah* is made before eating foods that do not fall into any of the above categories, such as water, meat or fish, eggs, etc.[9]

There are three possible *brachos* you can make before **smelling different spices**. They are:

1. "...Who creates beautiful smelling grasses." — בָּרוּךְ אַתָּה ה' אֱלֹקֵינוּ מֶלֶךְ הָעוֹלָם בּוֹרֵא עִשְׂבֵי בְשָׂמִים This *brachah* is made on beautiful smelling grasses,[14] or flowers that grow out of the ground, such as ground roses.[15]

2. "...Who creates beautiful smelling trees." — בָּרוּךְ אַתָּה ה' אֱלֹקֵינוּ מֶלֶךְ הָעוֹלָם בּוֹרֵא עֲצֵי בְשָׂמִים This *brachah* is made on beautiful smelling trees or other hard plants (like rosemary) and on flowers that grow on a **tree**.[16]

3. "...Who creates different types of smells." — בָּרוּךְ אַתָּה ה' אֱלֹקֵינוּ מֶלֶךְ הָעוֹלָם בּוֹרֵא מִינֵי בְשָׂמִים This *brachah* is made on anything that is not tree nor grass.[17]

When you smell a sweet smelling **fruit**, you say the *brachah* "...Who gives a sweet smell to fruits." — בָּרוּךְ אַתָּה ה' אֱלֹקֵינוּ מֶלֶךְ הָעוֹלָם הַנּוֹתֵן רֵיחַ טוֹב בַּפֵּירוֹת[18]

בִּרְכוֹת הַשֶּׁבַח וְהַהוֹדָאָה
Brachos of Thanking and Praising Hashem

There are many great things that Hashem does, for which you must thank and praise Him. Some of the more common ones are:

1. "...Who has let us live and kept us alive for this moment," and "...Who has done good for me and others." — בָּרוּךְ אַתָּה ה' אֱלֹקֵינוּ מֶלֶךְ הָעוֹלָם שֶׁהֶחֱיָנוּ וְקִיְּמָנוּ וְהִגִּיעָנוּ לִזְמַן הַזֶּה/הַטּוֹב וְהַמֵּטִיב These *brachos* are made when you experience a joyful event that doesn't happen often. If you experience the joy alone, you make a "*shehechiyanu*," and if you share the joy with someone else, you make a "*Hatov Vehametiv*." An example for *shehechiyanu* would be buying a new car, and *Hatov Vehametiv* would be made when a baby is born, since both the father and mother share the joy of the baby.[19]

2. "...Who did a miracle for me at this place." — בָּרוּךְ אַתָּה ה' אֱלֹקֵינוּ מֶלֶךְ הָעוֹלָם שֶׁעָשָׂה לִי נֵס בַּמָּקוֹם הַזֶּה This *brachah* is said when you pass a place where a miracle happened to you.[20]

3. "...Who gives good to the undeserving, for He has given me good." — בָּרוּךְ אַתָּה ה' אֱלֹקֵינוּ מֶלֶךְ הָעוֹלָם הַגּוֹמֵל לְחַיָּבִים טוֹבוֹת שֶׁגְּמָלַנִי (כָּל) טוֹב[21]

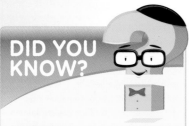

The *Gemara* tells us that this is a special *brachah* of thanks that a person has to make if any of these four things happen:

1. If you safely crossed an ocean.
2. If you safely travel across the wilderness.
3. If you were very sick and then got better.
4. If you were freed from prison.

This *brachah* must be said before a *minyan*, with at least two *Talmidei Chachamim* in the *minyan*. Those in the *minyan* who hear the *brachah* answer מִי שֶׁגְּמָלְךָ (כָּל) טוֹב הוּא יִגְמָלְךָ כָּל טוֹב סֶלָה- "May He Who has bestowed good upon you always bestow good upon you."[22]

4. בָּרוּךְ אַתָּה ה' אֱלֹקֵינוּ מֶלֶךְ הָעוֹלָם עוֹשֶׂה מַעֲשֵׂה בְרֵאשִׁית - "...Who created the wonders of creation." This *brachah* is said when you see something beautiful, such as lightning.[23]

5. בָּרוּךְ אַתָּה ה' אֱלֹקֵינוּ מֶלֶךְ הָעוֹלָם שֶׁכֹּחוֹ וּגְבוּרָתוֹ מָלֵא עוֹלָם - "...His strength and might fill the world." This *brachah* is said when you see or hear something awe-inspiring, like thunder.[24]

בְּרָכוֹת שֶׁעַל הַמִּצְווֹת
Brachos for Mitzvos

These are *brachos* that are said when you do a mitzvah. The *Chachamim* made a rule that before you do a *mitzvas asei*, you must say a *brachah*.[25] This includes many mitzvos such as *tefillin*,[26] *mezuzah*,[27] eating *matzah* on the first night of *Pesach*,[28] *bris milah*,[29] and taking *challah*.[30]

As a general rule; a *brachah* on a mitzvah is always made before performing the mitzvah.[31] This is called עוֹבֵר לַעֲשִׂיָּתָן – "before performing it."

בְּרָכָה אַחֲרוֹנָה
Brachos After Eating

After eating a meal with bread, there is a mitzvah from the Torah to say a *brachah* thanking Hashem for the food. The *Chachamim* added that after **any** food - not just bread - you should thank Hashem.

There are two types of *brachos* added by the *Chachamim* to say after eating:

1. מֵעֵין שָׁלֹשׁ - This *brachah* is made after eating *mezonos*, after eating one of the five fruits for which Eretz Yisrael is known, or after drinking wine.[32]

2. בּוֹרֵא נְפָשׁוֹת - This *brachah* is made after eating any other food.[33]

 CHECKPOINT What are the four kinds of *brachos* from the *Chachamim*?

OUR SAGES SAY...

Amen

R' Yosi says: The one who answers *amen* to a *brachah* is greater than the one who says the *brachah*.

In a battle, the **first** soldiers do hard work, but it's the **last** soldiers who actually win the war.

So too, saying a *brachah* is great because it says that Hashem is in charge of everything. However, the one who answers *amen* agrees with that statement, so he is greater; just like the soldier who **secures** the victory.[34]

PEARLS of wisdom

Made It! Thanks!

The words וְכָל הַ**חַיִּים** יוֹדוּךָ סֶלָה - "And all living things will forever thank You" hints at the four people who have to thank Hashem: 1. **ח**וֹלֶה - someone who was sick and got better, 2. יִסּוּרִין - someone who was freed from prison, 3. יַם Someone who crossed an ocean, 4. מִדְבָּר - and one who travels through the wilderness.[35]

SELECTED HALACHOS

- You don't make a *brachah* when eating spices that are only meant for smelling.[38]

- When you experience an earthquake, you should make the *brachah* עוֹשֶׂה מַעֲשֵׂה בְרֵאשִׁית. You can also make the *brachah* of שֶׁכֹּחוֹ וּגְבוּרָתוֹ מָלֵא עוֹלָם.[39]

- You make a *shehakol* on cornbread, because it is not made from the five grains.[40]

- The correct *brachah* for grapes is *"borei pri ha'etz."* If you accidentally said *"borei pri hagafen,"* you don't have to correct yourself and say *"ha'etz."*[41]

- You should say *brachos* only in Hebrew, even if you don't understand Hebrew. However, if you said it in a language that you understand, you don't need to say it again.[42]

DID YOU KNOW?

True to His Word

When you see a rainbow in the sky, you say,

בָּרוּךְ אַתָּה ה׳ אֱלֹקֵינוּ מֶלֶךְ הָעוֹלָם זוֹכֵר הַבְּרִית וְנֶאֱמָן בִּבְרִיתוֹ וְקַיָם בְּמַאֲמָרוֹ

This means, "He remembers the agreement, stays true to His promise, and keeps His word."[36] After the *mabul*, Hashem told Noach that He would never destroy the world again. As a sign of this promise, He showed Noach the rainbow. When you see a rainbow, you make this *brachah* to remind Hashem of His promise.[37]

EXTEND YOUR KNOWLEDGE

The Order of the *Brachos*

When there are many foods with different *brachos* in front of you, which *brachah* should you make first? There is a specific order of which *brachos* need to be made first. The *Chachamim* learned this from the following *passuk*:

"אֶרֶץ חִטָּה וּשְׂעֹרָה וְגֶפֶן וּתְאֵנָה וְרִמּוֹן אֶרֶץ זֵית שֶׁמֶן וּדְבָשׁ"

"It is a land of wheat, barley, grapes, figs, and pomegranates; a land of olive oil and honey [dates]."

From the order the Torah puts these foods we learn the *"halachic"* order of some of the foods:

1. *Hamotzi* always comes first.

2. Next is *mezonos*, which comes before any of the other fruits and vegetables.

3. After that are *ha'etz* and *ha'adamah*. If you have an option of both fruit and vegetables, the food you like better (either fruit or vegetable) comes first. If you don't have a favorite, then *ha'etz* should go first, and you should pick your favorite fruit first. If some of the fruit is from the *shivas haminim*, those go first.

4. Any food that is *shehakol* comes last.[43]

Live the Mitzvah

הַכָּרַת הַטּוֹב – Recognizing the Good

Be A Thankful Person

Saying *brachos* teaches us that we must be thankful people. Some people expect to get everything they want and think that they deserve it. They do not feel the need to thank the person for giving it to them.

Thankful people know that when someone worked hard for them, they should thank the person and not take it for granted.

Show Appreciation For Hard Work

You know how special your parents are, and how much you love them for everything they have given you. But have you ever really thanked them for all they do for you? Have you ever said, "Mommy, your cooking really keeps me going all day. Thank you!"

Your parents work **very** hard to make sure you have all you need. You must be careful to **show** how thankful you are by saying, "Thank you!"

Mean What You Say

In the same way, you must show your thanks to Hashem. But just thanking is not enough! You have to really show how much you mean it! When you make a *brachah*, you should say it carefully and with feeling, making sure to say each word with proper enthusiasm. What better way to show our thanks to your Father in heaven!

 CHECKPOINT How can you show people that you appreciate what they do for you?

STORY

Worthy of His Riches

R' Chiya bar Abba stayed with a man in Ludkiya for *Shabbos*. This man was very wealthy. When he sat down to eat, his servants brought before him a solid gold table, full of all kinds of delicacies. It needed sixteen men to carry it. Before the man started eating, he said out loud, לַה' הָאָרֶץ וּמְלֹואָהּ.[44]

Even though he was so rich, he knew that the world and everything in it belongs to Hashem!

DID YOU KNOW?

Wonder Bread

The *brachah* that the Jews made on the *mann* that fell from heaven was הַנּוֹתֵן לֶחֶם מִן הַשָּׁמַיִם - "He Who gives forth bread from the heavens."[45]

OUR SAGES SAY...

100, And That's It

Where in the Torah is there a hint to the idea of 100 brachos every day? It says "...and now, what (מָה) to do I ask from you other than to fear Me." Don't read it "מָה" (what), but "מֵאָה" 100.[46] When we make a brachah, Hashem is happy and gives us what we need. This happiness is only complete when 100 brachos are made.[47]

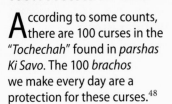

DID YOU KNOW?

100% Protection

According to some counts, there are 100 curses in the "Tochechah" found in parshas Ki Savo. The 100 brachos we make every day are a protection for these curses.[48]

מֵאָה בְּרָכוֹת - A Hundred *Brachos*

In the times of *Dovid Hamelech*, there was a sickness, in which 100 people died every day. *Dovid Hamelech* realized that this was because people weren't doing the mitzvah of making *brachos*. He therefore started the practice of saying 100 *brachos* every day. Later, the *Chachamim* set up the *davening* in a way that everyone could say the 100 *brachos* each day just by saying the daily *tefillos*.

19 *brachos* for each of the three times we *daven Shemonah Esrei.* (19x3=**57**)

2 *brachos* before *krias shema* during *ma'ariv*, and 3 after. (2+3=**5**)

1 for washing before the evening meal, 1 for *hamotzi*, 4 in *Birkas Hamazon*, *hagafen* on the cup of wine over which *Birkas Hamazon* was said, and the *bracha acharonah* on the cup of wine. (1+1+4+1+1=**8**)

The *brachah* of *hamapil* said before going to sleep. (**1**)

The *brachah* you make when washing your hands when you wake up, plus the 17 *brachos* of *birchos hashachar*. (1+17=**18**)

The 3 *brachos* of *birchas hatorah*, the 2 *brachos* said when putting on *tefillin*, and the *brachah* said when putting on *tzitzis*. (3+2+1=**6**)

During *Shacharis* there are the *brachos* of *baruch she'amar*, *yishtabach*, the 2 *brachos* before *krias shema*, and the *brachah* after *krias shema*. (1+1+2+1=**5**)

(57+5+8+1+18+6+5=100) All these bring the total to **100**.[49]

Put it in Writing

Many people write the words לַה' הָאָרֶץ וּמְלוֹאָהּ in the books that they own, to show that they recognize that everything – even their personal belongings – belong to Hashem. They also avoid writing "This book belongs to…" Rather, they simply write their name in the book.[50]

For the same reason, many people have a *minhag* to mention Hashem before writing on any piece of paper, such as a letter or even a note. The best words to write are "בס״ד," which stands for "בְּסִיַּעְתָּא דִשְׁמַיָּא" - with the help of Heaven. This is to show that you recognize that everything comes with Hashem's help.[551]

CHECKPOINT How can you make 100 *brachos* every day?

BIOGRAPHY

The *Tzemach Tzedek* (1789 – 1866) תקמ״ט - תרכ״ו

The third Chabad Rebbe, R' Menachem Mendel Schneersohn of Lubavitch, was born on the 29th of Elul. Orphaned from his mother at age 3, he was raised by his grandfather, Rabbi Schneur Zalman of Liadi, the Ba'al Hatanya. The Tzemach Tzedek set up and supported Jewish farming colonies, giving a source of livelihood to thousands of families. He also was at the forefront of the battle against the Enlightenment (Haskalah) movement, and was arrested or thrown into jail by the Russian authorities no less than 22 times (!) for his efforts. He wrote more than 48,000 pages of Torah writings, and passed away on the 13th day of Nissan.

UNIT 43

ENDNOTES:

1. ברכות לה, ב

2. ברכות נג, א

3. ברכות לה, ב

4. רמב״ם הל׳ ברכות פ״ג ה״א. סמ״ג סי׳ כ״ז ד״ה האוכל פת. קשו״ע סי׳ מ״א ס״א

5. סדר ברה״נ פ״א ה״ג

6. סדר ברה״נ פ״א ה״ב

7. סדר ברה״נ פ״א ה״ב

8. סדר ברה״נ פ״א ה״ב

9. סדר ברה״נ פ״א ה״ב

10. סה״מ ת״ש ע׳ קא

11. ברכות לה, א-ב

12. שו״ע או״ח סי׳ רכ״ט ס״ב

13. שו״ע או״ח סי׳ ר״ו ס״ה, משנ״ב ס״ק י״ח

14. סדר ברה״נ פי״א ה״א

15. סדר ברה״נ פי״א ה״ד

16. סדר ברה״נ פי״א ה״ב

17. סדר ברה״נ פי״א ה״ה

18. שו״ע או״ח סי׳ רט״ו ס״ב, משנ״ב ס״ק ט׳

19. סדר ברה״נ פי״ב ובהמשך הפרק, ע״ש וש״נ

20. שו״ע או״ח סי׳ רי״ח ס״ד

21. שו״ע או״ח סי׳ רי״ט ס״ב

22. שו״ע או״ח סי׳ רי״ט ס״ב

23. ט״ז או״ח סי׳ רכ״ז ס״ק א׳

24. שו״ע או״ח סי׳ רכ״ז ס״א

25. רמב״ם הל׳ ברכות פ״א ה״ג

26. שו״ע או״ח סי׳ כ״ה ס״ה

27. שו״ע יו״ד סי׳ רפ״ט ס״א

28. שו״ע או״ח סי׳ תע״ה ס״א

29. שו״ע יו״ד סי׳ רס״ה ס״א

30. שו״ע יו״ד סי׳ שכ״ש ס״א

31. שו״ע או״ח סי׳ כ״ה ס״ח

32. סדר ברה״נ פ״א הי״ג

33. סדר ברה״נ פ״א ה״ז

34. ברכות נג, ב

35. שו״ע או״ח סי׳ רי״ט ס״א

36. שו״ע או״ח סי׳ רכ״ז ס״א

37. בראשית ט, יב

38. שו״ע או״ח סי׳ ר״ב סט״ז

39. שו״ע או״ח סי׳ רכ״ז ס״א

40. שו״ע או״ח סי׳ ר״ח ס״ח

41. סדר ברה״נ פ״א הט״ז

42. פמ״ג או״ח פתיחה להל׳ ברכות השחר. וע׳ שו״ע הרב או״ח ריש סי׳ קפ״ה. שו״ע סי׳ ר״ו ס״ג. ערוה״ש או״ח סי׳ קפ״ה ס״ד-ז׳

43. עי׳ פרטי הדינים בסדר ברה״נ פ״י

44. שבת קיט, ע׳ ובס׳ "נטעי גבריאל" כרך הכנסת ס״ת ע׳ צח ובה׳ יא שמביא קישור הדברים

45. עשרה מאמרות (להרמ״ע מפאנו) מאמר שבתות ה׳ ו׳

46. מנחות מג, ב, רש״י ד״ה מה ה׳

47. סדר היום בחיוב מאה ברכות בכל יום

48. ספר הרוקח הל׳ ברכות ריש סי׳ ש״כ

49. שו״ע הרב או״ח סי׳ מ״ו ס״א

50. צוואת ר׳ יהודה החסיד אות מ״ז

51. עי׳ שו״ת אג״מ יו״ד ח״ב סי׳ קל״ח

52. רשימות דברים ח״א ע׳ קיא

A *chassan* and *kallah* are like a king and queen on their special day. Would you dare turn up at their wedding looking like you spent the day in a garbage truck?

UNIT 44

IN THIS UNIT YOU WILL:

EXPLORE

- Why do you wash *netilas yadayim* before eating or after waking up?

EXAMINE

- What are the times that you must wash *netilas yadayim*?
- What is the correct way to do *netilas yadayim*?

EXTRACT

- How should you prepare for each new day?
- Why do we wash *mayim acharonim*?

נְטִילַת יָדַיִם

מַיִם אַחֲרוֹנִים

שִׁבְעָה מַשְׁקִין

KEY CONCEPTS

Book: Ahavah, Section: Blessings
סֵפֶר אַהֲבָה הִלְכוֹת בְּרָכוֹת

נְטִילַת יָדַיִם
NETILAS YADAYIM

מִצְוָה אַחַת

DID YOU KNOW?

Why We Wash

Why do you wash *netilas yadayim* in the morning?

There are three main reasons.

1. You can't *daven* if you have touched parts of your body which are usually covered (like your scalp or feet).[1] You wash *netilas yadayim* after waking up because your hands might have touched those parts while you slept.[2]

2. When you sleep at night, your *neshamah* goes up to *shamayim* to get more energy for the next day. When the *neshamah* leaves your body, an impure spirit rests on your body. To remove the *tumah* from your body, you wash your hands in the morning.[3]

3. Just like a *kohen* washes his hands before starting his *avodah* in the *Beis Hamikdash*, you wash your hands when you wake up, before starting a new day of serving Hashem.[4]

The Mitzvah EXAMINE

The unit of *netilas yadayis* has one mitzvah from the *Chachamim*.

Wash your hands after you wake up in the morning and before you eat a meal.

MITZVAH DERABANAN **2**

נְטִילַת יָדַיִם
Washing your hands

וְהִתְקַדִּשְׁתֶּם – אֵלּוּ מַיִם רִאשׁוֹנִים
(ברכות נג, ב)

"And you should make yourselves holy" – this refers to washing the hands before meals.

Wash your hands before eating a meal, and upon getting up in the morning.

ALL PEOPLE   ALL PLACES   ALL TIMES

Mitzvah Messages EXPLORE

Every Day is Special

The *Chachamim* made a rule that you must wash your hands after waking up in the morning, to get ready for the day ahead, a day of serving Hashem. Just

like the the *kohanim* washed their hands every morning in the *Beis Hamikdash* before starting their holy *avodah*, you are getting ready to serve Hashem.[6]

Just like you would want to look your best in honor of a special occasion, you are honoring Hashem by washing off all impurities so that you can "look" your best for Him.

Eating in Purity

In the times of the *Beis Hamikdash*, the *kohanim* would eat *terumah*, gifts of food given to them. The Torah warns the *kohanim* that the *terumah* is holy and cannot be eaten while the *kohen* is *tamei*. Therefore, the *Chachamim* made a rule that before the *kohanim* eat **any** meal, they have to wash their hands to remove all *tumah*. This way, when they eat *terumah*, their hands will certainly be *tahor*. The *Chachamim* made the mitzvah specifically for the hands, because hands are constantly touching things and have the biggest chance of becoming *tamei*.

To protect people even more from eating *terumah* when they are *tamei*, the *Chachamim* made another rule that **all people** - not just *kohanim* - should wash their hands before they eat a meal.[5]

CHECKPOINT Why did the *Chachamim* make a rule that you must wash *netilas yadayim* in the morning and before you eat?

Details

EXAMINE

Netilas Yadayim With a *Brachah*

There are two times when you wash your hands with a *brachah*:

נְטִילַת יָדַיִם שֶׁל שַׁחֲרִית - **Washing Hands in the Morning**

When you wake up, you must wash your hands before you can *daven*.[6] To do this, you take a cup of water in your right hand, and then move it to your left hand.[7] You then wash each hand three times, starting with the right hand, then the left, then the right again, and so on. You need to be careful that the used *tamei* water won't spill onto the floor, so you should wash over another vessel or into a sink.[8]

נְטִילַת יָדַיִם לִסְעוּדָה - **Washing Hands for a Meal**

Before you eat bread, you must wash your hands, just like the *kohanim* did before eating *terumah*. The mitzvah is to pour a *revi'is* (about 4 fl. oz.) of water from a cup or the like, once onto each hand.[9] Although the mitzvah is to wash until your knuckles, you should wash up to the wrist, because the whole hand is *tamei*.[10]

Many people wash each hand more than once, just in case there was some dirt on their hands that would block the water from washing **all** of their hand the first time.[11]

The Hebrew word for bread is לֶחֶם. This word can also be found inside the word מִלְחָמָה - war.

When you eat bread, there is a "war" between the *yetzer hara* and the *yetzer tov*. One wants the bread just to make the hungry body happy, and the other wants to use the bread to be strong enough to serve Hashem.

You must make sure that the *yetzer tov* wins the war![15]

DID YOU KNOW?

Handy Memory Tool

A good hint to remember the seven liquids is י"ד שח"ט ד"ם

1. יַיִן - Wine
2. דְּבַשׁ - Honey
3. שֶׁמֶן - Oil
4. חָלָב - Milk
5. טַל - Dew
6. דָּם - Blood
7. מַיִם - Water

The *Brachah*

When washing in the morning and for a meal, the *brachah* is:

בָּרוּךְ אַתָּה ה' אֱלֹקֵינוּ מֶלֶךְ הָעוֹלָם אֲשֶׁר קִדְּשָׁנוּ בְּמִצְוֹתָיו וְצִוָּנוּ עַל נְטִילַת יָדָיִם.

When to Say it

Usually, a *brachah* is said עוֹבֵר לַעֲשִׂיָּתָן - **before** doing a mitzvah. However, with *netilas yadayim*, you cannot say the *brachah* while your hands are still *tamei*. Therefore, you must wait until your hands are washed before making the *brachah*.

Hashem Commanded Us

This mitzvah is from the *Chachamim*, but the *brachah* still says that **Hashem** commanded it to us. This is because Hashem commanded us to listen to everything the *Chachamim* tell us. Since the *Chachamim* tell us to wash *netilas yadayim*, **Hashem** commands us to listen to them and to wash *netilas yadayim*!

Netilas Yadayim Without a *Brachah*

The *Chachamim* also gave us a *halachah* to wash for foods that have been dipped into liquid, but without a *brachah*. There are seven liquids for which, if used for dipping, you must wash: wine, honey, olive oil, milk, dew, blood and water. Today, since there is no real *tumah* and *taharah* anymore, some people do not have the *minhag* to wash for wet foods.[16]

What to Use for *Netilas Yadayim*

The Vessel

The cup or container that you use for *netilas yadayim* must be big enough to hold a *revi'is* (about 4 fl. oz) of water.[17] It cannot have any holes in it, and there cannot be any spouts or grooves at the top (like you would see on a teapot or water pitcher).[18] If the cup has a spout or holes, it is not kosher for *netilas yadayim*, even if you do not pour from the spout.[19]

The Water

The water must be pure water, without any juices or other liquids mixed into it. The water cannot be colored.[20] If the water was used for work, like washing dishes, watering the garden, or feeding an animal, it is not *kosher* for *netilas yadayim*.[21]

CHECKPOINT   When and how do you wash *netilas yadayim*?

SELECTED HALACHOS

- You should use more than the minimum amount of water (4 fl. oz.) for *netilas yadayim*.[22]

- After washing, you should dry your hands well before eating. Washing without drying your hands afterwards is like eating impure bread.[23]

- The cup that you use must be able to stand by itself. For example, a cup with a pointed bottom would not be *kosher*.[24]

- The water must be poured by a person. Putting your hands under a faucet or a waterfall would not count.[25]

- You should not put your hands in a pail of water and rub them in the water to do the mitzvah. In an emergency, this might be *kosher*.[26]

- You are allowed to dip your hands into a *mikvah* for *netilas yadayim*, if the water is *kosher* for *netilas yadayim*. If you do this, you should say the *brachah* of *al netilas yadayim*.[27]

- Smelly or very bitter water that even a dog wouldn't drink is not *kosher* for *netilas yadayim*.[28]

- If you are travelling and know that you won't find water for at least four *mil* up ahead and one *mil* behind, you may wrap the bread in a cloth before eating it, without washing.[29]

- You should be careful to pay attention the whole time between washing the hands and eating the bread to make sure that your hands don't touch anything which would make them *tamei* again.[30]

EXTEND YOUR KNOWLEDGE

Chatzitzah

To do the mitzvah of *netilas yadayim* properly, the water must touch your **entire** hand. Anything that blocks the water from any part of the hand is called a *chatzitzah*.[31]

Here are a few examples of a *chatzitzah*:

- A band-aid, ring or any object that covers your skin is a *chatzitzah*. This must be taken off before washing.[32]

- Dirt can be a *chatzitah*. If it is just a small amount and you don't care about it, it is not a *chatzitzah*. However, if you do care about it, **any** amount would be a *chatzitzah*.[33]

- Small ink or paint stains that cannot be washed off the hand are not a *chatzitzah*, since they are considered part of the hand.[34]

DISCOVERY

The Black Death

The Black Death was one of the worst plagues in history. It killed around one hundred million people in Europe in the 1300's. This was about 30-60% of the people who lived in Europe.

Since people did not know yet that diseases spread from person to person if germs are passed around, they could not explain why the plague happened. People started accusing the Jews of poisoning the water wells, and Jewish communities were attacked. By the year 1351, 60 major Jewish communities and 150 smaller ones had been destroyed.

One of the reasons the Jews were blamed is because fewer of them were dying than the others.

This was because Jews were the only people at that time who were washing their hands often, and taking a bath at least once a week before *Shabbos*!

OUR SAGES SAY...

Wash or Die

Netilas yadayim is so important that *Chazal* say that if someone does not wash *netilas yadayim*, that person deserves poverty, and it can also lead to early death.[35]

OUR SAGES SAY...

Be Generous

Being generous with water for *netilas yadayim* is a *segulah* for wealth.

As R' Chisda tells us, "I washed *netilas yadayim* with a lot of water, and was blessed with a lot of riches."[36]

STORY

A Sign

A Jewish shopkeeper in the time of King Hadrian would cook and sell both *kosher* and non-*kosher* meat. He did this so no one would know he was a Jew, as many Jews were being killed.

If someone came into the shop to eat, the owner would watch to see if he washed his hands before eating. If he didn't, the owner would assume that he was a non-Jew and would give him the non-*kosher* meat. If he did wash, he was assumed to be a Jew and so would get the *kosher* meat.

One day, a man came in, and did not wash, and the shopkeeper gave him the non-*kosher* meat. When the man came to pay, the shopkeeper told him he had given him the non-*kosher* meat.

The man went pale and said, "But I am a Jew!" The shopkeeper angrily said, "When I saw that you ate without washing your hands, I thought you were a non-Jew!"

From this story, *Chazal* teach that not washing before the meal can lead to terrible *aveiros*![37]

Live the Mitzvah

EXTRACT

Ready, Wash, Go!

Every day is a special day. Every day, you are called upon for the honor and privilege of serving Hashem, the King of kings. Every day is a day for looking and being your best.

So, before you start your day, go through your checklist: are your nails clean? Are your clothes neat and respectful? How about inside your head – are your thoughts clean and positive? Do you feel ready and awake?

Missed a thing or two? Give yourself a good wash, inside and outside. It'll leave you sparkling clean, ready to start your day.

 CHECKPOINT How can this mitzvah help you prepare to serve Hashem?

What Else Comes From This?

EXTRACT

Other Times We Wash

There are some other times that you would wash, but without saying a *brachah*. They are:

- After waking up from a nap in the middle of the day.[38]

- Before you *daven*.[39]

- After cutting your fingernails.

- After taking a bath or shower.

- After touching parts of the body that are normally covered. For example, scratching your scalp.

- After tying your shoes.

- After using the bathroom.

- After visiting a cemetery.[40]

Checklist

מַיִם אַחֲרוֹנִים - Washing After a Meal

The *Chachamim* made another rule that you should wash your hands after a meal, before saying *Birkas Hamazon*.[41] This is called *mayim acharonim*.

One reason for this is to be clean of any impurity before saying *Birkas Hamazon*.[42] The other is to wash off any salt you might get on our hands from the food, just in case it is a type of salt (salt of Sedom) that is extremely dangerous for your eyes.[43] Although this salt is not common today, the *minhag* of washing *mayim acharonim* is still kept, and is very important according to *kabbalah*.[44]

You do not make a *brachah* on *mayim acharonim*, because it is not a mitzvah. It is only a protection against danger.[45] You also do not need to use a full *revi'is* on each hand.[46] You only need to wash the tips of the fingers, until the first joint, and not the whole hand, or even the whole finger. This is because you usually only touch the food with the tips of your fingers.[47]

 CHECKPOINT When are other times we wash our hands?

UNIT 44

ENDNOTES:

1. שו"ע או"ח סי' ד' סי"ח
2. רמב"ם הל' תפילה פ"ד ה"ב
3. זוהר ח"א קפ, ב
4. שו"ת רשב"א ח"א סי' קצ"א
5. חולין קו, א
6. שו"ע או"ח סי' ד' ס"א
7. שו"ע או"ח סי' ד' סי"י
8. שו"ע או"ח סי' ד' ס"ח
9. שו"ע או"ח סי' קס"ב ס"ב
10. שו"ע או"ח סי' קס"ב ס"א ובט"ז שם ס"ק ב'
11. שו"ע או"ח סי' קס"ב ס"ב ובהגה
12. עירובין כא, ב
13. שבת קח, ב. שו"ע או"ח סי' ד' ס"ג. ב"י שם ס"ק ב-ה'
14. שו"ע או"ח סי' ד' ס"ה. משנ"ב שם ס"ק ב' ו"י"ד
15. ראה זוהר ח"ג קפ"ח, ב "נהמא על פום חרבא ייכול"

16. שו"ע הרב או"ח סי' קנ"א ס"ג וד'. ערוה"ש שם ס"ד. ועי' שו"ת שרגא המאיר ח"ד סי' קי"א אות ב'
17. שו"ע או"ח סי' קנ"ט ס"א
18. שו"ע הרב או"ח סי' קנ"ט ס"י
19. שו"ע או"ח סי' קנ"ט ס"א
20. שו"ע או"ח סי' ק' ס"א
21. שו"ע או"ח סי' ק' ס"ה
22. שו"ע או"ח סי' קנ"ח ס"י
23. שו"ע או"ח סי' קנ"ח סי"ב
24. שו"ע או"ח סי' קנ"ט ס"ג
25. שו"ע או"ח סי' קנ"ט ס"ז
26. שו"ע או"ח סי' קנ"ט ס"ח
27. שו"ע או"ח סי' קנ"ט ס"י וכ' ובשו"ע הרב או"ח סי' קנ"ט סכ"ד
28. שו"ע או"ח סי' ק' ס"ט
29. שו"ע או"ח סי' קס"א ס"א
30. שו"ע או"ח סי' קס"ו
31. שו"ע או"ח סי' קס"א ס"א
32. שו"ע או"ח סי' קס"א ס"א וג'

33. שו"ע או"ח סי' קס"א ס"א ובהגה
34. שו"ע הרב או"ח סי' קס"א ס"ה
35. שו"ע או"ח סי' קנ"ט ס"ט
36. שבת סב, ב
37. במדבר רבה כ, כא
38. רמ"א או"ח סי' ד' סט"ו
39. שו"ע או"ח סי' צ"ב ס"ד. סי' רל"ג ס"ב
40. כל זה נרשם בשו"ע או"ח סי' ד' סי"ח
41. שו"ע או"ח סי' קפ"א ס"א
42. רא"ש מס' ברכות פ"ח סי' ו'
43. חולין קה, ב
44. שו"ע או"ח סי' קפ"א ס"י, מג"א ס"ק י'
45. שו"ע או"ח סי' קפ"א ס"ז ובמשנ"ב ס"ק י"ז
46. שו"ע הרב או"ח סי' קפ"א ס"ד
47. שו"ע או"ח סי' קפ"א ס"ה, מג"א שם ס"ק ד'
48. ואני תפלתי ח"א ע' 179
49. ברכות נג, ב

PEARLS of wisdom

Wash Away the Stinginess

There is another reason why you should wash your fingers from the salt of Sedom before *bentching*.

The salt of Sedom is a symbol of meanness and stinginess.

The people of Sedom were so mean that they wouldn't even give their guests salt. The *Chachamim* taught us to wash the salt off our fingers after the meal with *mayim acharonim*, so that we would always remember to be kind to our guests.[48]

OUR SAGES SAY...

Clean and Close to Hashem

וְהִתְקַדִּשְׁתֶּם וִהְיִיתֶם קְדשִׁים כִּי אֲנִי ה' אֱלֹקִיכֶם

And you shall make yourselves holy and you shall be holy, for I am Hashem your G-d.

The *Gemara* explains that the first part of this *passuk* – "you shall make yourselves holy," refers to washing the hands **before** a meal, and the second part – "and you shall be holy," talks of washing the hands **after** the meal.[49]

UNIT 45

IN THIS UNIT YOU WILL:

EXPLORE

- How strong is a Jew's connection to Hashem?

EXAMINE

- What happens when a boy has a *bris milah*?

EXTRACT

- What are the special preparations that are done before a boy has a *bris milah*?

הַטָּפַת דַם
בְּרִית
בְּרִית מִילָה

KEY CONCEPTS

Book: Ahavah, Section: Circumcision

סֵפֶר אַהֲבָה הִלְכוֹת מִילָה

מִילָה
BRIS MILAH

מִצְוָה אַחַת

**How strong is your friendship
with your best friend?**

A Reminder

Moshe was told by Hashem to travel from Midyan to Mitzrayim and help the Jews. He did not want to give his son Eliezer a *bris* before leaving because he was worried that it would be dangerous to travel right after a *bris*. But he didn't want to stay behind and wait until Eliezer healed from his *bris* either. So, he set out on his way without doing the *bris*.

The Torah tells us that along the way to Mitzrayim, Moshe and his family stopped at an inn for the night. While at the inn, a *malach* in the form of a snake appeared and swallowed almost all of Moshe - stopping just before the area where his *bris* was. Moshe's wife Tzipporah immediately understood that Hashem was unhappy that Eliezer had not had a *bris*. Quickly, she took a sharp stone and gave her son Eliezer a *bris milah*. As soon as she did this, the *malach* let go of Moshe.[1]

DID YOU KNOW?

He Waited 99 Years, We Can Wait Eight Days

A baby is only named after his *bris milah* because *Avraham Avinu's* name was changed after his *milah*.[2]

The Mitzvah

The unit of *bris milah* has one mitzvah.

A father must give a *bris milah* to his son.

MITZVAH 86

מִצְוַת מִילָה

The mitzvah of *bris milah*

זֹאת בְּרִיתִי אֲשֶׁר תִּשְׁמְרוּ בֵּינִי וּבֵינֵיכֶם וּבֵין זַרְעֲךָ אַחֲרֶיךָ הִמּוֹל לָכֶם כָּל זָכָר

(בראשית יז, י)

This is My covenant between Me, and between you and your offspring that you must keep: **You must circumcise every male**.

Give your son a *bris milah*.

| MEN | ALL PLACES | ALL TIMES | *KARES* |

Mitzvah Messages

An Everlasting Bond

The word *bris* means "agreement" – a promise between us and Hashem that we will always remain connected no matter what. There are many reasons why Hashem loves us and we love Him. This bond is so deep and strong that it can never be broken. The *bris milah* on a body is a reminder every moment of the special connection that can never be broken.[3]

Connected Beyond Understanding

For most mitzvos, we wait until the child has reached the age of "*chinuch*," the age when he or she is old and mature enough to do the mitzvos and understand what they mean. With *milah*, we don't wait until the child can understand, but we do it on the eighth day after birth, which is the earliest time the baby is healthy enough.[5]

If you decide to do something only because it makes sense to you, you might change your mind the next day, because your reasons will change and now it doesn't make sense to you anymore.

The *bris milah* is called a בְּרִית עוֹלָם - an **agreement forever**, one that comes from Hashem and cannot be changed by a person. Our connection to Hashem is forever, and has nothing to do with what we want, or what we understand. That's why we do the *milah* even before the child understands anything, because the mitzvah has nothing to do with understanding.[6]

When a baby boy is given a *bris milah* and a Jewish name, he becomes part of the Jewish nation.

 CHECKPOINT   Why is a *bris milah* done before a child understands what is happening?

Details

EXAMINE

The Ceremony

When is *Milah* Done?

The mitzvah of *milah* is done on the eighth day from when a baby is born. The day of birth is counted as day one, even if the baby is born towards the end of the day. For example, if a baby is born on a Tuesday, that Tuesday is counted as day one, Wednesday would be day two, until day eight, which would be on the following Tuesday.[7]

The Process

The *bris* must be done during the day,[8] by a Jewish[9] *mohel* who has had a *bris milah* himself.[9] For the *bris* to be *kosher*, blood must come out.[10]

The morning of the *bris*, we make sure to get up early to *daven*, so that the mitzvah can be done as soon as possible (*zerizin makdimin lemitzvos*).[11] During *shacharis*, before we say the *tefillah* of "*Aleinu*," the *bris milah* is done. The *bris* is done specifically then so the boy will be included in the words in *Aleinu* which say that "Hashem has not made **us** like the nations of the world."[12]

The people who bring the baby into the room where the *milah* is done are known as *kvatter/in*.[13] As the baby is brought into the room on a pillow, the *mohel* welcomes him with the call of "*Baruch Habba*."[14] A special chair, called *kisei shel Eliyahu* - the chair of *Eliyahu Hanavi* (who comes to every *bris*) is prepared, and the baby is put on this chair as the *mohel* announces that this is the chair of *Eliyahu Hanavi*.[15]

The baby is then given to the *sandek*, the person who is honored with holding the baby while the *bris milah* is actually done. The *sandek* should be an honorable person who is worthy of having *Eliyahu Hanavi* sit next to him.[22]

Proving Him Wrong

*E*liyahu Hanavi is known as the *malach habris* - the angel of the *bris*, and he comes to every *bris*. The story behind this is that Eliyahu was the *navi* in the time of the evil queen Izevel. Izevel had turned the people away from Hashem, and Eliyahu saw that *B'nei Yisrael* were not doing the mitzvah of *milah*. So, he asked Hashem to stop all the rain. Izevel wanted to kill him for this, so Eliyahu ran and hid in a cave. Hashem asked him what he was doing, and Eliyahu replied that the Jews had forgotten His *bris*.[19] Because he spoke badly about the Jews, and said that they no longer did *bris milah*, Hashem told him that from then on he would have to go to every *bris* to see that the Jews were still keeping Hashem's agreement.[20]

Enter the Soul

*A*ccording to *kabbalah*,[21] the *neshamah* begins to enter the body at the time of the *milah*.

Blessings of the *Bris*

The *mohel* says this *brachah* before doing the *bris*:[23]

"בָּרוּךְ אַתָּה ה' אֱלֹקֵינוּ מֶלֶךְ הָעוֹלָם אֲשֶׁר קִדְּשָׁנוּ בְּמִצְוֹתָיו וְצִוָּנוּ עַל הַמִּילָה" Blessed are You, Hashem, King of the universe, who has made us holy with His mitzvos and gave us the *mitzvah* of *bris milah*.

The father says the following *brachah* while the *mohel* is doing the *milah*:[24]

בָּרוּךְ אַתָּה ה' אֱלֹקֵינוּ מֶלֶךְ הָעוֹלָם אֲשֶׁר קִדְּשָׁנוּ בְּמִצְוֹתָיו וְצִוָּנוּ לְהַכְנִיסוֹ בִּבְרִיתוֹ שֶׁל אַבְרָהָם אָבִינוּ - Blessed are You, Hashem, King of the universe, who has made us holy with His mitzvos and commanded us to bring this boy into the agreement of Avraham our father.

The people who are at the *bris* then say:[25]

כְּשֵׁם שֶׁנִּכְנַס לַבְּרִית כֵּן יִכָּנֵס לַתּוֹרָה וּלְחֻפָּה וּלְמַעֲשִׂים טוֹבִים - "Just as he has been brought into this agreement, so may he enter into Torah, into marriage, and into mitzvos."

The Naming

A *brachah* is then made over a cup of wine. This is followed by the *brachah* אֲשֶׁר קִדֵּשׁ יְדִיד מִבֶּטֶן (Who has made the one He loves holy from the womb). During this *brachah* the child is named. At the words "*bedomayich chayi*" (by your blood you shall live), many people give some wine to the baby with their finger.[26]

The *Seudah*

A festive meal is held after the *bris*. Since the meal is a *seudas mitzvah*, meat should be served.[27] Extra *tefillos* that start with "הָרַחֲמָן" are said during the fourth *brachah* of *Birkas Hamazon* in honor of the *bris*.[28]

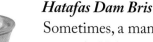

Hatafas Dam Bris

Sometimes, a man had a *bris milah* that was not done properly. When this happens, a ceremony called הַטָּפַת דַּם בְּרִית is done. This is done by drawing a drop of blood from the area where the *bris milah* would normally be. This ceremony is considered a real *milah*. Some of the people who need to have this ceremony are:

- A *ger* who was already circumcised before he became Jewish.[29]

- Someone who had a *bris milah* at night.[30]

- A baby who had a *bris milah* before he was eight days old.[31]

- A child who was born with a *bris*.[32]

The Punishment

Usually, if you don't do a *mitzvas asei*, you would not get a punishment. The mitzvah of *bris milah* is one of the only two *mitzvos asei* which does have a punishment if you don't do it. (The other one is *korban pesach*.) If a man has never had a *bris*, the punishment of *kares* only applies to him, not to his father.[33] This man would only be punished once he has reached *Bar Mitzvah*, when he is old enough to take responsibility to have *milah* done on him.[34]

CHECKPOINT   What is the order of the *bris milah* ceremony?

SELECTED HALACHOS

- *Milah* on the eighth day overrides *Shabbos* and *Yom Tov*. In some cases, like if the *milah* was delayed, *milah* does not override *Shabbos*.[35]

- If the child is unhealthy, we wait until he is completely better, and sometimes, another seven days after that, before doing the *bris milah*.[36]

- If a child is born *bein hashmashos* (between sunset and nightfall), eight days are counted from the following night (which means that the *bris* is on the ninth day) and the *milah* does not override *Shabbos*.[37]

- If two children from the same mother (or father) die from *milah*, the third child is not given a *bris* until he is older and stronger. If two sisters each lost a child after *milah*, any children they or their other sisters may have, must wait until they are older and stronger before having a *bris*.[38]

- Normally, a *mohel* must have a *bris*. However, if a man does not have a *milah* because his older brothers died from it, he is allowed to do the *milah*.[39]

- A woman is considered to be born with a *bris milah* and has a strong connection to Hashem even without a reminder on her body. Therefore, a Jewish woman is allowed to do a *bris milah*, but the *minhag* is for a man to do it.[40]

BIOGRAPHY

R' Shlomo Kluger   (1785-1869) תקמ"ו - תרכ"ט

R' Shlomo Kluger (also known as the Maharshak) was born in Cheshvan 1785 (תקמ"ו). He was the Rav of the great city of Brod in Poland, and the author of about 150 seforim. He is also known for his thousands of responses to halachic questions (תְּשׁוּבוֹת). He passed away in Tammuz 1869 (תרכ"ט).

OUR SAGES SAY...

Hanging By a Thread

The world exists as *sechar* of the mitzvah of *milah*.

The *Midrash* tells us that when Hashem told Avraham to give himself a *bris milah*, He was going to destroy the world if Avraham would not agree.[41]

STORY

Saved By the *Bris*

The baby was taking a long time to arrive to his *bris*, and the *sandek*, R' Shlomo Kluger, asked a family member for the reason.

The family member explained that the baby's father was in the next room, and was very close to death. They were waiting for the father to die so that they could do the *bris* and name the child after his father.

Stunned, Rabbi Kluger asked to be taken to the father. As he came to the deathbed, he said, "Listen, I can't ask the *malach* of healing to heal you, but I **can** ask the *malach* of the *bris* who's coming to heal the child to stop by your room to heal you also."

With that, he called for the *bris* to begin immediately. Three days later, the father of the child was well enough to walk to *shul* on his own two feet.[42]

Hemophilia

Hemophilia is a disease where the person does not have a certain part of their blood called platelets that stops a cut from bleeding. This means that the person would bleed without stopping, even from a tiny cut.

When *halachah* speaks about children dying from *milah*, this is one of the diseases that it refers to.

The first time a doctor officially discovered hemophilia was in 1803, by Dr. John Conrad Otto. However, the disease was already well known to the *Chachamim*[43] over 1400 years before. They even knew that the disease is passed down from mother to son.[44]

Because we have such wonderful medicine today, a baby with hemophilia can have a healthy *bris*.[45]

DID YOU KNOW?

Your Ticket In

Milah saves a person from *Gehinom*. *Avraham Avinu* goes down to *Gehinom* and rescues all the people from there, except for those who cover their *milah* and try to hide that they are Jewish.[46]

EXTEND YOUR KNOWLEDGE

When *Kares* Applies

When would a man get the punishment of *kares* for not doing *milah*?

The Rambam[47] says that the man would only get *kares* if he dies without having a *bris milah*.

The Raavad[48] says that the man deserves *kares* every day after his *Bar Mitzvah* that he has not yet done the *milah*.

The difference between these two opinions is when, during the last years of his life, he was **unable** to be have a *bris milah* for reasons he could not control:

According to the Rambam, the man would not deserve *kares,* since when he died without *milah,* he wasn't **able** to do it, and the Torah does not punish people for something which is beyond their control.

According to the Raavad however, he would still get *kares,* since he was doing the *aveirah* every single day since his *Bar Mitzvah*![49]

The *Shulchan Aruch* rules like the Raavad.[50]

Live the Mitzvah

EXTRACT

Best Friends Forever

If your best friend made you mad one time, would you stop being friends forever? No, you wouldn't – your connection is too strong to be broken over one silly fight. You would want to forgive your friend. In a similar way, your connection with Hashem never breaks, even if you go against Hashem sometimes and do *aveiros.* Just like the *bris* is a permanent sign on your body that never goes away, your connection with Hashem is forever and unbreakable.

This is how we should see all Jews. No matter how far a Jew may be from Torah and mitzvos, he is still forever connected with Hashem. Hashem is always ready to forgive him.

 CHECKPOINT What does *bris milah* show about the connection a Jew has with Hashem?

What Else Comes From This?

Before the *Bris*

Shalom Zachor

Ashkenazim have a *minhag* to make a special meal on the Friday night after a baby boy is born. This is known as a *shalom zachor*. People come to visit the newborn, and sit down to a *seudas mitzvah*.[51] This *minhag* is traced back to the *Midrash* which states that *milah* cannot be performed before a *Shabbos* has passed.[52]

Vachnacht

The night before the *bris* is known by *Ashkenazim* as "*vachnacht*" and by *Sephardim* as "*brit Yitzchak*." Some have the *minhag* to prepare a festive meal.[53] Many have the *minhag* to stay up and learn the entire night, including learning parts of *Zohar* which discuss the *bris milah*, to protect the child from anything that might harm him.[54]

Saying *Shema*

Some have the *minhag* to bring young children on the night before the *bris* to say *krias shema* near the baby. This adds protection for the baby.[55]

CHECKPOINT What are some *minhagim* that people do for a baby boy before the *bris*?

UNIT
45

ENDNOTES:

1. שמות ה, כד, וברש"י
2. זכרון ברית לראשונים ע' 95
3. "אלה המצות" מצוה ב'. וכעי"ז במו"נ ח"ג פמ"ט. ועי' בראשית יז, ז, וברש"י
5. מורה נבוכים ח"ג פמ"ט בסופו
6. לקו"ש חכ"ה ע' 88
7. שו"ע יו"ד סי' רס"ב ס"א
8. שו"ע יו"ד סי' רס"ד ס"א
9. שו"ע יו"ד סי' רס"ד ס"א
10. שו"ת אג"מ יו"ד ח"ב סי' קי"ט
11. שו"ע יו"ד סי' רס"ב ס"א
12. בית א-ל (יעב"ץ) פרפר סי' ב'. ועי' באות חיים ושלום (מונקאטש) יו"ד סי' רס"ה ס"ק ל"ט. אוצר הברית ח"ב ע' רכו
13. ערוך השולחן יו"ד סי' רס"ה סל"ה
14. אבודרהם סדר המילה
15. שו"ע יו"ד סי' רס"ה סי"א
16. תוס' שבת קל, א ד"ה שש אנכי
17. מדרש תנחומא פ' תזריע סי' ז'
18. חינוך מצוה ב'
19. מלכים א' יט, א-י'
20. פרד"א "חורב" פכ"ח בסופו
21. עי' זח"ג צא, ב. מנורת המאור (להר"י אלנקאוה) ח"ד פ' גידול בנים ע' 131. סדר היום (בסוף הספר בפי' המשנה בן

22. קיצור של"ה הל' מילה ע' כז
23. שו"ע יו"ד סי' רס"ה ס"א
24. שו"ע יו"ד סי' רס"ה ס"א
25. ש"ך יו"ד סי' רס"ה ס"ק ג'
26. שו"ע יו"ד סי' רס"ה ס"א. עי' ש"ך שם ס"ק ה'
27. שו"ע יו"ד סי' רס"ה סי"ב ובהגה. מג"א סי' רמ"ט ס"ק ו' בשם רבו של השל"ה. מגדל עוז (יעב"ץ) נחל התשיעי יאור י"ז אות ג'. ברית אבות סי' י"ג אות א'
28. מחזור ויטרי ע' 628
29. שו"ע יו"ד סי' רס"ח ס"א
30. רמ"א יו"ד סי' רס"ב ס"א
31. שו"ע יו"ד סי' רס"ב ס"א. עי' ש"ך שם ס"ק י' וט"ז שם ס"ק ב'
32. שו"ע יו"ד סי' רס"ד
33. חינוך מצוה ב' בסופו
34. שו"ע יו"ד סי' רס"א. פתחי תשובה יו"ד סי' ש"ה ס"ק כ"ה
35. שו"ע יו"ד סי' רס"ב, ו'
36. שו"ע יו"ד סי' רס"ב
37. שו"ע יו"ד סי' רס"ח
38. שו"ע יו"ד סי' רס"ב-ג'
39. שו"ע יו"ד סי' רס"א

ה' למקרא). ועי' בתרגום יונתן בראשית נ, כג. שו"ע הרב (מהדו"ב) סי' ד' ס"ב

40. עבודה זרה כז, א
41. מדרש תנחומא לך לך סי' כ"ד
42. טללי אורות פ' לך לך ע' קסב
43. יבמות סד, ב
44. ט"ז יו"ד סי' רס"ג ס"ק א'
45. נשמת אברהם יו"ד סי' רס"ג ס"ק ה' בשם הגרש"ז אויערבאך זצ"ל
46. עירובין יט, א וברש"י ד"ה ולא מבשקר
47. רמב"ם הל' מילה פ"א ה"ב
48. רמב"ם הל' מילה פ"א ה"ב בהשגות
49. מנ"ח מצוה ב' אות ג'
50. רמ"א יו"ד סי' רס"א ס"א
51. רמ"א יו"ד סי' רס"ה סי"ב
52. ויקרא רבה כז, י. ועי' ט"ז יו"ד סי' רס"ה ס"ק י"ג
53. מחזור ויטרי ע' 627
54. עי' בהנסמן באוצר הברית ח"א פ"ג סי' ז' הערה טו
55. חותם קודש סי' ט' אות ו'
56. היום יום ט' חשון
57. נדה ל, ב
58. דרישה יו"ד סו"ס רס"ד
59. ספר "מטעמים" ע' מילה אות ה'

PEARLS *of wisdom*

What Does He Have that We Haven't Got?

When R' Sholom Dov Ber of Lubavitch was four or five years old, he went to his grandfather, the *Tzemach Tzedek*, on *Shabbos Vayeira*, and began to cry as he asked, "Why did Hashem show Himself to our father Avraham, and not to me?"

The *Tzemach Tzedek* answered him, "When a *tzaddik* decides to give himself a *bris milah* at the age of ninety-nine years old, he certainly deserves that Hashem should appear to him."[56]

DID YOU KNOW?

We Mourn Your Loss

While the child is in his mother's womb, he is taught the entire Torah. When he is born, a *malach* taps him on his mouth and he forgets everything he had learnt.[57] This is one of the reasons for the *shalom zachor* - to comfort the child for the Torah knowledge that he has lost.[58] This is why people serve chickpeas or other foods that are normally served in a mourner's house.[59]

APPENDIX

HOW TO USE THIS BOOK

The **unit number** since the beginning of the curriculum. This helps you keep track of how much you have already learned.

This section has some of the **messages of the** *mitzvos* and how they make us closer to Hashem. You will find this mostly in the orange sections of each unit.

This is the **facts and details** of the mitzvos which you will examine in the blue sections of each unit.

This is the section showing how to **apply the mitzvos** to your life. It also includes **other things which come from the mitzvos in the unit**. These are in the green sections of each unit.

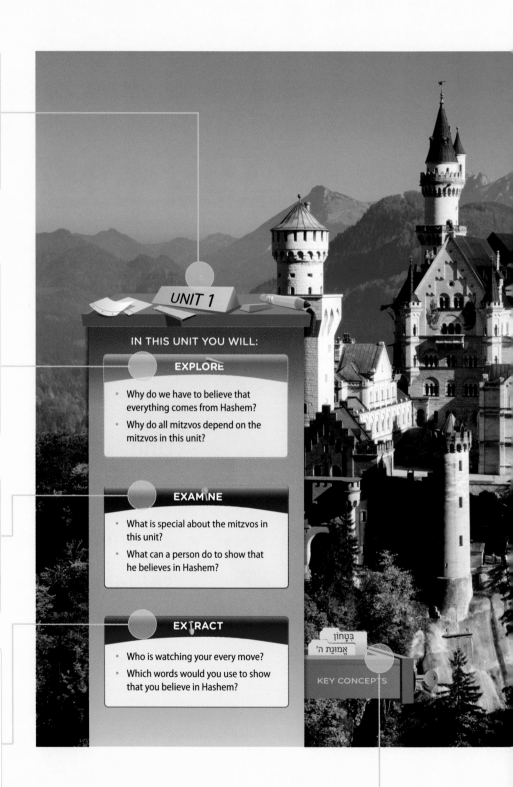

UNIT 1

IN THIS UNIT YOU WILL:

EXPLORE

- Why do we have to believe that everything comes from Hashem?
- Why do all mitzvos depend on the mitzvos in this unit?

EXAMINE

- What is special about the mitzvos in this unit?
- What can a person do to show that he believes in Hashem?

EXTRACT

- Who is watching your every move?
- Which words would you use to show that you believe in Hashem?

בִּטָחוֹן
אֱמוּנַת ה'

KEY CONCEPTS

General topics which you will touch upon in this unit.

SELECTED HALACHOS

When you say *shema*, you must have in mind that Hashem is the only G-d. How can you think about this? Every letter in the word *echad* should be said slowly, with these thoughts:

א: The *gematria* of *aleph* is one, and Hashem in the one ruler over the entire world.

ח: The *gematria* of *ches* is eight, and Hashem is the one G-d over the seven heavens and one earth.

ד: The *gematria* of *daled* is four, and Hashem is the one G-d over everything in the four directions.[9]

Since these thoughts are so important, be careful to say the word *"echad"* slowly. The *aleph* should be said normally, the *ches* a little more slowly, and the *daled* very slowly.[10]

OUR SAGES SAY...

כָּל הַמַּאֲרִיךְ בְּאֶחָד מַאֲרִיכִין
לוֹ יָמָיו וּשְׁנוֹתָיו

Someone who says the word *"echad"* in *shema* slowly and remembers that Hashem is the **only** G-d, will have a long life.[12]

Some **selected halachos** of the mitzvos.

DID YOU KNOW?

Hashem is Here, Hashem is There

The top of the letter וֹ (as written in a *Sefer Torah*) points upwards. This teaches us that the seven heavens and the earth point **up** to Hashem and should help us see how great Hashem is.[13]

A STORY

Looking for G-d

As a small child, *Avraham Avinu* was troubled with the question of who created this wonderful world. He looked at the sun; mighty and powerful in the sky.

"Surely," he thought, "since the sun is so big and powerful, bringing light and warmth to the world, it must be the creator." But at night, the sun set and the moon came out. To Avraham, the moon seemed to be more powerful than the sun. He decided that the moon was the creator and not the sun. Then came morning, and the moon was gone.

Avraham continued his search for a creator, trying many things and giving up on all of them when he realized how limited their power was. Finally, he realized that there was an unseen Creator, Who is always present and Who creates and directs everything in the world we live in. In fact, the sun, moon, and the entire world is not something that exists separately which He must control; they are all Hashem's powers, and the entire world is part of Hashem.[11]

This kind of box contains **a story** relating to the unit. We all love these!

Here you will find a **deeper look** into a specific part of the mitzvah, as a small taste of the beauty and depth of Torah.

OUR SAGES SAY...

It's Just Me in Here

Hashem told *B'nei Yisrael*, "I created everything in this world as a pair. I created heaven and earth, the sun and the moon, a husband and a wife, this world and the World to Come.

But as for Me. I am the only One and there is no other."[14]

PEARLS *of wisdom*

Always Re-creating

The *Ba'al Shem Tov* explained that the *passuk*, לְעוֹלָם ה' דְּבָרְךָ נִצָּב בַּשָּׁמָיִם - "Your words are forever standing in the heavens," means that the words which Hashem used to create the world are being used again and again so that the world can stay in existence.[15]

EXTEND YOUR KNOWLEDGE

Think Good and it Will Be Good

According to the Rambam, it is a mitzvah not to be scared of the enemy when you are going out to war. You must have complete faith that Hashem will save you from the hands of the enemy.[16]

Rabbeinu Yonah explains this even more, and teaches us that we shouldn't ever be afraid when we are in trouble, because Hashem can always save us.[17]

There is one difficulty with this. We know that Hashem punishes us and rewards us based on our actions. What if we do *aveiros* and don't deserve to be saved? Should we be scared then?

Hashem does not only protect us because of our actions. Just by having complete trust in Hashem, we deserve to get the "reward" of being saved!

Live The Mitzvah   EXTRACT

Hashem is Always Here and Watching

When we know that someone is watching us, we are very careful to only do the right thing. We know that Hashem exists and that He sees and knows everything, so of course we are going to be on our best behavior at all times!

Also, when someone is watching us we feel more safe. Since we know that Hashem is always watching us, we also feel safe and know that He will protect us wherever we are.

> CHECKPOINT   How can *emunas Hashem* make us feel safe?

What Else Comes From This?   EXTRACT

Who is in Charge?

We know that Hashem controls everything that happens, since He is the only G-d.

Mentioning Hashem's Control

Since we know that something can only happen with Hashem's help, when we are planning something, we say בְּעֶזְרַת ה' - with Hashem's help, or אִם יִרְצֶה ה' - if Hashem wants. We also make sure to thank Hashem after something happens by saying בָּרוּךְ ה' - Hashem is blessed.[18]

Other things we do, which come from these mitzvos.

How to **apply** the mitzvah and its message to your **daily life.**

בִּטָחוֹן - Trust in Hashem

...e know that everything comes from Hashem, and we know that ...ashem is only good. Therefore, we know that everything that Hashem ...es is for the best. Sometimes, we don't see how something that happens ...n be good, but when we remember that Hashem will only help us, we ...n be calm even if a situation seems terrible.

CHECKPOINT — How can you use your words to show that you know that Hashem controls the world?

A STORY

Never Suffer

A man once came to R' Dovber, the *Maggid of Mezritch*, with a question. "The *Gemara* says that 'A person is supposed to bless Hashem for bad things just as he blesses Him for good things.' How is this humanly possible? How can a person be as grateful for his troubles as he is for his joys?"

R' DovBer replied: "To find an answer to your question, you must go see my student, R' Zusha of Anipoli. Only he can help you in this matter."

He travelled to R' Zusha, who received him warmly, and invited him to make himself at home. The visitor decided to watch R' Zusha for a while to see if he can figure out the answer to his question without explaining why he had come. R' Zusha was extremely poor, there was never enough to eat in his home, and some of his family members were sick. He couldn't think of anyone who suffered more hardship in his life than R' Zusha did. Yet R' Zusha was always cheerful, and constantly thanking Hashem for all His kindness.

But what was his secret? How does he do it? The visitor finally decided to ask his question. He said to his host: "Our Rebbe advised me to come here so that you can help me with an answer."

'What is your question?' asked R' Zusha.

The visitor repeated what he had asked of the *Maggid*; and said that the *Rebbe* had sent him to learn the answer from R' Zusha.

R' Zusha looked at him in surprise, "Why did our *Rebbe* send you to **me**? How would I know? He should have sent you to someone who suffers. I have no suffering in my life…"

The guest understood why the *Maggid* had sent him. R' Zusha accepted everything in his life with such faith in Hashem, that he didn't even feel any suffering! This was the lesson he was to learn.

OUR SAGES SAY...

I'm Getting You Out of This

When someone is *niftar* and they go up to *Shamayim*, Hashem will ask him, "Did you wait eagerly for *Mashiach* to come?" The person might say, "But I didn't know that I had to! Where does it say in the Torah that I have to wait for *Mashiach* to come?"

The Sma"k says, that when Hashem told us *"Anochi Hashem,"* He said, "I am Hashem who took you out of Mitzrayim."

Included in this mitzvah is the mitzvah of knowing that just as Hashem saved us from the *galus* in Mitzrayim, Hashem will save us from any other *galus*, such as the one we are in now.

We have a mitzvah to believe that Hashem will send *Mashiach*, and to wait for him excitedly![19]

> This kind of box contains a **treat from our Chachamim** connected with these *mitzvos*.

UNIT 1

ENDNOTES:

1. בראשית רבה א, י
2. שמות / נ״ז שו שה כח-לכט
3. החינוך בהקדמתו "הערה הַמַּדְּתִּ"
4. חובת הלבבות שער היחוד פ״ז. ראה אוצר המדרשים איינשטיין ע׳ 583
5. חדא״ג מהרש״א מכות כג, ב ד״ה תרי״ג
6. רמב״ם הל׳ סנהדרין פי״ח ה״ב
7. רמב״ם הל׳ תשובה פ״ג ה״ו-ז׳
8. רמב״ם הל׳ מלכים ריש פ״ט
9. ב״י או״ח סי׳ ס״א ד״ה וצריך להאריך
10. מג״א סי׳ ס״א ס״ק ה׳ בשם מגדל עוז על הרמב״ם
11. רמב״ם ריש הל׳ ע״ז
12. ברכות יג, ב
13. שו״ע או״ח סי׳ ס״א ס״ו
14. דברים רבה ב, לא
15. אגרא דכלה בראשית א, כב ד״ה עו יתפרש
16. סה״מ ל״ת נ״ח
17. שערי תשובה שער ג׳ אות ל״ב
18. של״ה שער האותיות אות אמונה
19. סמ״ק מצוה א׳

> These are some sources to *sefarim* which talk about the information in the unit.

ATONEMENT
IN THE TORAH

ATONEMENT • CONTENTS

ATONEMENT IN THE TORAH

INTRODUCTION

Responsibility For Your Actions

Basic Belief

One of the basic beliefs of the Torah is the idea of reward and punishment. Hashem sees all of our actions. Actions that follows the Torah will be rewarded, and actions that go against the Torah and against Hashem will be punished.

There are many types of creatures and animals that live on the earth, yet Hashem created man in a special way. An animal can do whatever it wants, whenever it wants, and Hashem will not punish the animal for anything it does because it has no ability to choose right from wrong.

People, however, are created with the wisdom to make choices. When a person chooses not to make the right choice, they are held responsible for the action and therefore punished. Punishment shows that man is greater than animals.[1]

Deeper Understanding

Opportunity For Atonement

We are Hashem's children. Parents do not take revenge on their children. If their child does something wrong, parents will try to teach the child how to improve, and will help the child to repair any damage caused. Surely Hashem has no desire to take revenge on a person who does an *aveirah*.

Rather, the punishment that the Torah gives a person is an **opportunity** for the person who does an *aveirah*. Doing an *aveirah* makes a stain on a person's *neshamah*. The punishment the Torah gives is a kindness because it cleans the *neshamah* from any stain which the *aveirah* caused.[2]

Fear the Aveirah

It is a basic part of our belief that Hashem sees our actions and will reward and punish us accordingly. However, we should serve Hashem not only for a reward or because we are scared of being punished. Every mitzvah brings us closer to Hashem and every *aveirah* separates us from Him. We should try to serve Hashem because we want to be connected to Him and are afraid of separating ourselves from Him.

This idea can be understood through the following story:

A young boy was told by his father not to walk outside barefoot. "You might step on a thorn!" the father warned. Not following his father's warnings, the boy walked outside without his shoes. Sure enough, a thorn got stuck in his foot. Coming home, the father was worried that the wound might become infected, so he pulled out the thorn. This caused his son extreme pain, more pain than the thorn itself caused. Although it pained the father to see his son in such pain, he knew that this was only for the health of his child.

*The next time the child wanted to go outside barefoot, the father warned him, "Don't go outside without shoes; don't you remember the pain you felt last time when I had to take out the thorn!?" To **this** warning the child listened.*

Silly child! The child should not be afraid of **removing** a thorn! Removing the thorn was for his health! The child should fear getting a thorn stuck in his foot in the first place!

The same is true with *aveiros* and their punishments. We should not fear the punishment, for that is really a **kindness** from Hashem because it removes the damage we caused by doing the *aveirah*. We ought to fear the *aveirah* itself, for that is what separates us from Hashem.[3]

Indicates the Severity of the *Aveirah*

All countries have rules, and punishments for those who break the rules. The size of the punishments is set according to which rule was broken. The more important the rule, the stricter the punishment.

The same applies to the punishments in the Torah. The punishments usually show us how strict the *aveirah* is, and **that** should prevent us from doing it.[4]

General Rules

אוֹנֶס - Not in Control

A person is only punished if he did the *aveirah* willingly. If a person was not in control and did the *aveirah* unwillingly, he is not punished for the actions. For example, if someone said "turn off the light on *Shabbos* or I will kill you!" the person who was then *mechalel Shabbos* will not be punished.

Witnesses And Warning

Beis Din would only give a punishment if there were valid witnesses and the person received a proper warning.

1. עֵדִים - Witnesses

For *Beis Din* to punish someone, there must be two adult male witnesses who testify that they actually **saw** the person perform the *aveirah*. Hearing from someone else who saw, or even standing outside and hearing something happen is not enough. The *eidim* must **see** the *aveirah* being performed.

Before accepting what the *eidim* say, *Beis Din* would ask questions to the *eidim* to make sure they are telling the truth.[5]

2. הַתְרָאָה - Warning

For *Beis Din* to punish someone, they must be certain that the person knew that the action was an *aveirah*. Therefore, the person must be warned right before the *aveirah* is performed, so *Beis Din* knows for sure that it was done on purpose.

To count as a valid *hasra'ah*, the following conditions must be met:

1. The *hasra'ah* must be given less than "*toch k'dei dibbur*" (the time it takes to say "שָׁלוֹם עָלֶיךָ רַבִּי וּמוֹרִי") before the person performs the *aveirah*.

2. The *hasra'ah* must include the punishment which the person will receive for doing the *aveirah*. For example the *eidim* must say, "Don't do this *aveirah*, because if you do it, *Beis Din* will give you *malkus*!"

3. The person doing the *aveirah* must **hear** the *hasra'ah* and willingly go against it.[6]

Admitting To An *Aveirah*

If someone comes before the *Beis Din* and says that he did an *aveirah*, *Beis Din* will not punish the person.[7] The reason for this is that our bodies do not belong to us, rather they are on loan from Hashem. We have no right to cause it any harm by causing ourselves to receive *malkus* or to be killed. Only two valid witnesses can cause *Beis Din* to punish someone.[8]

With regards to monetary laws however, if a person says that he owes money to someone, or that he damaged someone's property, he must pay. This is because our money is ours and we may do with it as we wish.

Even With Good Intentions

Even if the person who did the *aveirah* had good intentions, the punishment is still the same. For example, someone who does magic to help their friend win some much needed money gets the same punishment as someone who did magic to hurt another person. (Unless it was to save a life, in which case it is like an *ones* and no punishment is given.)

Hashem's Judges

A *Beis Din* has the help of Hashem. Every decision that is made according to the process and rules commanded in the Torah is considered to be coming straight from Hashem.[9]

Today

Still Happens

Although there is no *Beis Din* nowadays that gives death punishments, the *Gemara*[10] says that death sentences still happen. Someone who did an *aveirah* that would normally receive *skilah* might fall from a roof or an animal might trample him. Someone who did an *aveirah* that would normally receive *sreifah* might be killed in a fire or by venomous poisons. Hashem still holds each person responsible and gives everyone what they need to erase the *aveirah* from their *neshamah*.

DEATH

Introduction

Not Too Often

Although the Torah gives the death penalty for some *aveiros*, the Torah does not want *Beis Din* to be too harsh. *Beis Din* must look for every possible way to free the person from the death sentence. The *Mishnah*[11] says that a *Beis Din* that carries out a death sentence even once in seventy years is called a destructive *Beis Din*.

Dignified Death

Beis Din always tries to carry out the death sentence in the most respectful way by choosing a death that is as painless and quick as possible. This is because of the mitzvah of "וְאָהַבְתָּ לְרֵעֲךָ כָּמוֹךָ," meaning that we must choose the most respectful death for the person who sinned.[12]

מִיתַת בֵּית דִּין - Death by the *Beis Din*

Rules

Beis Din is given the right to sentence someone to death in one of the four ways described below.[13] In order to give the death sentence, certain conditions have to be met:

- Only a *Beis Din* of at least twenty-three judges can give a death sentence.[14]

- *Beis Din* can only give the death sentence during the times of the *Beis Hamikdash*.[15]

- *Beis Din* can only give the death sentence when the *Sanhedrin* is active in Yerushalayim. When there was an active *Sanhedrin*, other courts of twenty-three were able to give the death sentence even outside of Eretz Yisrael.[16]

- The *Beis Din* must try to find the person innocent.[17]

- There must be two valid *eidim*.[18]

- The *eidim* must have given the person a valid *hasra'ah*.[19]

- The *Beis Din* must scare the *eidim* greatly about the seriousness of killing a person before accepting their testimony.[20]

- There must be a majority of at least two judges who find the person guilty.[21]

- The *Beis Din* must carefully cross-examine the *eidim* to make sure that they are telling the truth.[22]

The *Beis Din* would discuss the case throughout the night, and if all of the above criteria were met, the *Beis Din* would carry out the death penalty the next day.[23]

Four Types

There are four types of death sentences that *Beis Din* would carry out and a total of 36 *aveiros* which deserve a death penalty from *Beis Din*.[24]

1. *Skilah*

Process

The person who did the *aveirah* is brought to the top of a building and pushed off. If he is still alive, stones are thrown on him until he dies.[25]

Who Receives *Skilah*

There are eighteen *aveiros* punishable by *skilah*, including serving *avodah zarah*, being *mechalel Shabbos* and practicing forbidden magic.[26]

In The Torah

Skilah is one of the death sentences mentioned clearly in the Torah.[27] There are actual instances recorded in *Tanach* of stoning, for example the *Mekoshesh Eitzim*.[28]

2. *Sreifah*

Process

The person who did the *aveirah* is held in place while hot melted metal is poured down his throat, burning his insides and killing him almost immediately.[29]

Who Receives *Sreifah*

There are ten *aveiros* punishable by *sreifah*, including many of the forbidden relationships.[30]

In The Torah

Sreifah is one of the death sentences mentioned clearly in the Torah.[31]

3. *Hereg*

Process

The person who did the *aveirah* gets his head cut off with a sword.[32]

Who Receives *Hereg*

There are two *aveiros* punishable by *hereg*; killing someone, and the people of an *ir hanidachas*.[33]

4. Chenek

Process
The person who did an *aveirah* is held still while the two *eidim* wrap a strong cloth around his neck and pull hard, strangling him until he dies.[34]

Who Receives *Chenek*
There are six *aveiros* punishable by *chenek*, including kidnapping and saying a false *nevuah*.[35]

Default Death
It is a *Halachah L'Moshe Misinai*, that whenever the Torah says "he shall die" without stating what type of death, it is referring to *chenek*.[36]

כָּרֵת - Cut Off

Definition

Kareis is a death punishment that Hashem gives directly, without *Beis Din*. The word *kareis* means "cut off," since a person's *neshamah* and body are cut off from this world and *Olam Haba*.[37]

There are different opinions as to what exactly happens to a person who receives *kareis*.[38] Some of them are:

1. Rashi: Dying young and losing, or not having children.[39]

2. Tosafos: Dying before the age of sixty which is considered to be the average age of man.[40]

3. Rambam: Not meriting to enter *Olam Haba*.[41]

4. Ramban: There are three types of *kareis* depending on the severity of the *aveirah* and the status of the person doing the *aveirah*. If the person is generally righteous, he is punished with a shortened life before sixty but enters *Olam Haba*. If he is generally wicked, he is denied his portion in *Olam Haba*. For the most severe *aveiros* of cursing Hashem and serving *avodah zarah*, the person both dies young **and** is denied a portion in *Olam Haba*.[42]

Who Receives *Kareis*
There are forty eight *aveiros* for which a person can receive *kareis*. *Kareis* is given for these *aveiros* only if the person did the *aveirah* on purpose, but did not receive proper *hasra'ah*.

If there was proper *hasra'ah* given by valid *eidim*, these *aveiros* are punishable by other punishments such as *misas Beis Din* or *malkus*.[43]

Definition

This punishment means that the person will die by the hands of Hashem, and is less severe than *kareis* because it has no effect on the person's children. [44]

Who Receives *Misah Bidei Shamayim*

There are twenty two *aveiros* that are punishable with *misah bidei shamayim*, including a *kohen* who is *tamei* and eats *terumah* or serves in the *Beis Hamikdash*.

Erase It Through *Teshuvah*

When the punishment is carried out through *Beis Din*, the person will get punished even if he does *teshuvah* in his heart. [45] This is because a judge can only judge by what he sees, and no one can see inside the heart of another person.

Since Hashem **can** see the truth in everyone's heart, when Hashem carries out the punishment like in the case of *kareis* or *misah bidei shamayim*, a person can do *teshuvah* and the punishment will be erased. [46]

MALKUS

Introduction

Severe Punishment

Malkus is a very serious punishment, and is even considered "half of death." A *Beis Din* that gives *malkus* must have three judges, and they must cross-examine the witnesses as much as they would in a case involving the death sentence. [47]

As with all punishments given by the *Beis Din*, *malkus* is not meant to be overly harsh and the *Beis Din* always tries to give it in the most humane way possible.

Rules

Generally, any *mitzvas lo sa'aseh* (also called a "*lav*") is punishable by *malkus*.

In order for *malkus* to be given, the following criteria must be met:

- There must be a qualified *Beis Din* of three expert judges. [48]
- There must be two valid *eidim*. [49]
- There must have been a valid *hasra'ah*. [50]
- The witnesses are cross-examined. [51]

Process

The person's hands are tied and s/he is whipped with a leather rope while a judge reads *pessukim* from the Torah that talks about punishments.

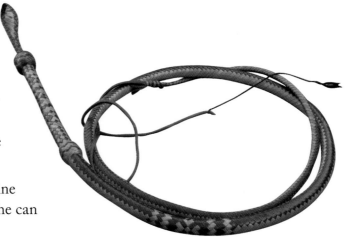

There are many rules for *malkus*, including:

- A maximum of thirty nine lashes are given for one set of *malkus*.[52]

- If the person cannot handle thirty nine lashes, we give him only as many as he can handle.[53]

- A person can receive more than one set of *malkus* at a time for more than one *aveirah*.[54]

Rules and Exceptions

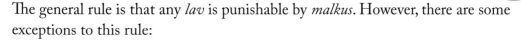

The general rule is that any *lav* is punishable by *malkus*. However, there are some exceptions to this rule:

1. לַאו שֶׁאֵין בּוֹ מַעֲשֶׂה - **a non-action-based** *aveirah*: Any *lav* that does not have to be performed by doing an action, and is transgressed through one's thoughts or even speech (e.g. *lashon hara*).[55]

2. לַאו שֶׁנִּיתָּן לְאַזְהָרַת מִיתַת בֵּית דִּין - **a** *lav* **that is attached to a death sentence**: Any *lav* that can be punished by *misas Beis Din*. (e.g. doing a *melachah* on *Shabbos*). The *lav* in such a case serves only as a warning for the death sentence, not for *malkus*.[56]

3. לַאו שֶׁנִּיתָּן לְתַשְׁלוּמִין - **a** *lav* **that is connected to monetary payments**: Any *lav* that is subject to a fine or other types of payments (e.g. stealing, since the stolen item must be paid back to the original owner).[57]

4. לַאו שֶׁנִּיתֵּק לַעֲשֵׂה - **a** *lav* **that is connected to a positive mitzvah**: Any action that in addition to being a negative mitzvah, has a positive mitzvah as well. (e.g. not taking the young birds from their mother, is connected with the mitzvah to send away the mother bird). If one only transgresses just the *lav*, no *malkus* is given. If one transgresses both the *lav* and the *asei*, *malkus* would be given.[58]

5. לַאו שֶׁבִּכְלָלוּת - **a "general"** *lav*: Any *lav* that includes more than one type of action. For example, when the Torah says "Do not eat on the blood," it includes not eating meat from an animal that has been slaughtered but is still twitching, meat from *korbanos* before their blood is sprinkled, a *Beis*

Din cannot eat on the day they give someone the death sentence as well as other things. If one transgresses any of these, they do not receive *malkus*.[59]

6. **לַאו הַבָּא מִכְּלַל עֲשֵׂה - a *lav* that is learned from a positive mitzvah**: Any *lav* that is learned from a positive mitzvah. (e.g. if someone doesn't listen to a *navi*, he was *oveir* the **positive** mitzvah of "to him you shall listen").[60]

Any *lav* besides any of the six exceptions above is punishable by *malkus*.[61] Altogether, there are 207 *aveiros* punishable by *malkus*.

מַכַּת מַרְדוּת - Malkus For Rebelling

Makas mardus is a *malkus* that *Beis Din* gives as they see fit.

There are two types of *makas mardus*:

1. *Malkus* that the *Chachamim* instituted for their additions to certain mitzvos. For example, the additional things which the *Chachamim* forbid us to do on *Shabbos*.

Being that these *additions* are based on the Torah and serve as a "guard" for the Torah, the rules of these *malkus* are similar to the regular *malkus* and require witnesses, a proper warning etc.

2. In times when a *Beis Din* sees that many people are doing *aveiros,* they can decide to give *malkus* to stop people from doing *aveiros*.

For such a case the rules are not the same as regular *malkus*, and can be given even without a warning.[62]

KORBAN

Introduction

Accidents Need Atonement Too

Someone who did not intend to do the *aveirah* that he did, must bring a *korban*.[63] Although he did not mean to do the *aveirah*, he should have been more careful and is responsible for what he did.[64] Also, the *aveirah* he did damages his *neshamah* even though he didn't mean to do it. He must bring a *korban* to clean his *neshamah*.[65]

How Does A *Korban* Achieve *Teshuvah*?

Why did the Torah command you to kill and bring an animal as a *korban* if it was **you** who did the *aveirah*, not the animal?

Korbanos are a lesson to the person who did an *aveirah*: when you see the limbs being burned and the blood being sprinkled, you should think that really you, who did the *aveirah*, should have **your** limbs burned and **your** blood scattered! Such thoughts would surely bring a person to do *teshuvah*.[67]

Types of *Korbanos*

There are many types of *korbanos* that were brought in the *Beis Hamikdash*, some daily, some weekly, some for individuals, and some for the whole community. Not all of the *korbanos* were brought for *aveiros*; many of them were to thank Hashem or as part of the routine in the *Beis Hamikdash*. Here we will discuss only those *korbanos* that were brought for *aveiros*.

In general, there were four types of such *korbanos*:

1. חַטָּאת

What Is It?

For most *aveiros*, a *Chatas Kavuah* - "set *chatas*" was brought. For some *korbanos*, a rich person must bring a more expensive *korban* and a poor person can bring a less expensive *korban* such as a bird. However, for a *Chatas Kavuah*, **everyone** must bring an **animal.** It is either a female goat or a female sheep.[68]

For Which *Aveiros*?

This *korban* is brought when a person accidentally does any *aveirah* for which one can receive *kareis*.[69]

There are three exceptions to this rule:

1. Cursing Hashem; since it is done with speech and not with an action, there is no *korban* brought.[71]

2. Not doing *milah*; since it is a *mitzvas asei*, there is no *korban*.

3. Not bringing a *korban pesach*; since it is a *mitzvas asei*, there is no *korban*.[72]

Altogether, there are forty three *aveiros* for which one brings a *chatas*.[70]

2. אָשָׁם

An *asham* is a guilt offering. There are two types of *ashamos*; an *asham taluy* - a **dependent** guilt offering, and an *asham vadai* - a **definite** guilt offering.

Asham Taluy

What Is It?

An *asham taluy* is brought when someone is not sure if they have done an *aveirah* or not.

For Which *Aveiros*?

Any *aveirah* that if done by accident a *chatas* would be brought, if one is not sure that the *aveirah* was done, an *asham taluy* must be brought.[73]

Asham Vadai

What Is It?

An *asham vadai* is brought when someone does certain *aveiros* by accident.[74]

For Which *Aveiros*?

An *asham vadai* was brought for five *aveiros*,[75] including stealing, denying it, and then swearing falsely, and when a *nazir* becomes *tamei*.

3. קָרְבָּן עוֹלֶה וְיוֹרֵד

What Is It?

Korban Oleh Ve'yored is a *korban* that is different, depending on the wealth of the person who did the *aveirah*. A rich person must bring a more expensive *korban*, for example a sheep, and a poor person can bring a less expensive *korban*, for example a bird or even a *korban minchah* (flour and oil offering).[76]

For Which *Aveiros*?

There are six *aveiros* for which one brings a *Korban Oleh Ve'yored*,[77] including, swearing falsely, and entering the *Beis Hamikdash* while you are *tamei*.

4. פַּר הֶעְלֵם דָּבָר שֶׁל צִיבּוּר

"The ox of communal error." This *korban* was brought in a very specific scenario: If the *Sanhedrin* made a mistake and permitted something that is really *assur*, and the entire congregation acted on their ruling, the members of the *Sanhedrin* are responsible for this *aveirah* and must bring a *korban*. Even if the *Sanhedrin* didn't act themselves on their own ruling and only the people did, the *Sanhedrin* are still responsible, and the people are not responsible.[78]

If the error was an *avodah zarah* related matter, an ox is brought as an *olah* and a goat is brought as a *chatas* for each one of the twelve *shevatim*, twenty four animals in total.[79] If the error was regarding other *kareis* related matters, only twelve oxen are brought as a *chatas*, one for each *shevet*.[80]

MONETARY ISSUES

Introduction

Don't Cause Another To Lose

A person's money is his own personal property and is his to keep. The Torah forbids anyone to take another person's property or damage it in any way. The Rambam[81] writes very sharply: "The Torah forbids stealing **anything**, even the smallest amount. Even for a joke, and even if you mean to pay it back, everything is forbidden."

If someone did so, they are punished with different fines. There are many types of fines, each one with its own set of rules and details. They can be split into two general groups, those of *nizkei guf* - damages caused by your body; and *nizkei mamon* - damages caused by your possessions.

Rules

קִים לֵיּ בִּדְרַבָּה מִינֵי - Give Him The Bigger One

Sometimes a person can do one action and be *oveir* more than one *aveirah* with more than one punishment. In some of those cases, the Torah says to only give the stricter punishment. For example, if one does an action for which they would receive both the death penalty and a fine, they do not have to pay the fine.

This is also true with *malkus*. If one does an *aveirah* that has both *malkus* and a fine, the person only receives *malkus* and does not have to pay the fine.[82]

Not Any Court

All issues concerning money can be judged by any group of expert rabbis, and in some cases even by a single expert rabbi.

However, all the laws of **knas** (explained below) can only be judged by a *Beis Din* of three expert judges that received *semichah* in Eretz Yisrael.[83]

Nezek

When something that belongs to you damages another person's property, you must pay for the damage.

How much you must pay depends on **how** the damage was caused:

If it was caused in a normal way, for example, if your ox ate someone else's grass, then you must pay נֶזֶק שָׁלֵם - the full damage.

If it was caused in an unusual way, for example, if your ox broke someone's window, then you must only pay חֲצִי נֶזֶק - half of the damage.[84]

קְנַס - Penalty Payment

In addition to paying for the damage caused, in some cases a person must pay a set penalty which is not to pay back damages. This set penalty is called a *knas*.

The general rule is that one must only pay a *knas* if *eidim* testify in *Beis Din* that the person did the *aveirah*. If one admits on their own, they do not have to pay the *knas*.[85]

כֹּפֶר - Atonement

If your animal kills a person, then in addition to the animal being killed, you must also pay a fine called "*kofer*."[86] *Beis Din* works out the amount of this fine based on who was killed.[87]

Returning What You Stole

When someone steals something, if the stolen item is still present, it must be returned. If returning the stolen item would cause an expenses to the thief (for example, returning a stolen beam that was already used to build a building), the thief keeps the item and pays back the **value** of the item. This is to encourage the thief to pay back the loss.[88]

כֶּפֶל - Paying Back Double

If *eidim* testify that someone stole money from another person, the thief must pay **double** the amount that was stolen. This is called "*kefel* - double."[89]

Also, when someone gives an item to a friend to watch, and that friend claims to have lost it, the friend must swear that it was lost and then does not have to pay it back. If it turns out that the friend lied and he really still has it, the friend is like a regular thief and must pay *kefel*.[90]

Paying Back Four Or Five Times

If one steals a sheep or a cow/ox and then sells it or *shechts* it, he is obligated to pay an additional *knas* called אַרְבָּעָה וַחֲמִישָׁה - four or five. One must pay back four times the value of the stolen **sheep**, and five times the value of the stolen **cow**.[91]

חוֹמֶשׁ - Paying Back An Additional Fifth

If someone owes another person money but denies it and swears falsely that nothing is owed, the person must pay back the amount that is owed, as well as an additional *knas* of an extra 25%, called a "*Chomesh*."[92]

In any case when one would have been obligated to pay if they admitted their sin, if they deny and swear falsely about it they must pay a *chomesh*.[93]

Five Kinds Of Damage

One who physically damages (hits, bruises, wounds etc.) another person must pay for five things:[94]

1. נֶזֶק: The damage to the person's value as a servant. For example, if one cut off the hand of another, *Beis Din* evaluates how much the victim would have been worth as a servant with his hand, and how much he is worth now without it. The one who damaged him must pay the difference.

2. צַעַר: How much a person would pay in order to avoid the pain which was caused.

3. רִפּוּי: Any medical expenses required because of the injury.

4. שֶׁבֶת: Money lost because the injured person could not work.

5. בּוֹשֶׁת: The amount a person would pay to avoid the embarrassment of having such an injury.

Each of these five things must be paid whenever they are applicable. If, for example, the person did not have any medical bills, *ripuy* does not need to be paid.[95]

Damaging Property

One who **personally** damages another's property must always pay back the **full** damage. This is different than when someone's **property** damages another person's property (like an ox damaging someone else's property), when there are some cases when only part of the damage must be paid.[96]

Damage That Cannot Be Seen

Some kinds of damage do not change anything **physical** in the object but still ruin its value. For example, if someone who is *tamei* touches another person's *terumah* and makes it *tamei*, the value of the *terumah* is now much lower than it was before. In such cases, the Torah does not require the damage to be repaid.

Nevertheless, the *Chachamim* said that since that the value did go down, the damage should be repaid.[97]

BITTUL MITZVAS ASEI

Severity of *Bittul Mitzvas Asei*

Although there is no punishment mentioned in the Torah for not fulfilling a positive mitzvah, it is a very serious thing.

The Torah[98] says, "Cursed is the one who does not keep the words of this Torah to do them." From the wording "to do them," we see that the Torah punishes and curses the one who does not fulfill the positive mitzvos.[99]

Here are some things that show how severe it is when a person misses out on a *mitzvas asei*.

No Reward In *Olam Haba*

A person's real reward for the mitzvos he does is kept for him to enjoy in *Olam Haba*. All of the many rewards and pleasures that one may experience in this world are like nothing compared to the reward and pleasure the *neshamah* experiences after it passes on into *Gan Eden*.[100] If one does not fulfill a mitzvah, they lose out on this great reward.

No Protection

A mitzvah is like a shield that protects one from evil. When a person passes away, the mitzvos that a person did while he was alive protects him from the fires of *Gehinom*. By not fulfilling the *mitzvos* one loses this protection. This is a terrible punishment.

Blemishing The Body

A limb used to perform a mitzvah becomes holy. For example, when one does a mitzvah with his hand, his hand is made holy by that mitzvah. When he does not do the mitzvah, he blemishes that limb.

Lost Opportunity

In a certain way, not doing a *mitzvas asei* is even more severe than being *oveir* a *mitvzas lo sa'aseh*.

When one does an *aveirah*, it causes spiritual damage, but through *teshuvah*, these damages can be fixed. In contrast, when one does not do a *mitzvas asei*, they did not draw down the *kedushah* they could have. For example, if a person missed out on saying *Shema* yesterday, even if he says it today, the *kedushah* that could have been brought down by saying *Shema* yesterday can never be replaced.

Missing a *mitzvas asei* is a lost opportunity which can never be replaced.[101]

עֲשֵׂה דּוֹחֶה לֹא תַעֲשֶׂה

In light of all of the above we can understand why the *halachah* is that if a person has one action to do which will both fulfill a mitzvah and also be *oveir* an *aveirah* (for example, wearing *tzitzis* made with *sha'atnez*), the general rule is that the *mitzvas asei* pushes away the *mitzvas lo sa'aseh*, and one should perform the mitzvah.[102] This is because missing the *mitzvas asei* can never be fixed.

Also, performing the mitzvah can provide the protection for the damage caused by the *aveirah*.[103]

ATONEMENT ENDNOTES:

1. ס' העיקרים מאמר ד' ריש פכ"ט
2. ראה כוזרי מאמר ב' פמ"ד ועיקרים מאמר ד' פל"ח
3. אור תורה פ' עקב אות ק"ס
4. ראה שו"ת אגרות משה חושן משפט חלק ב סימן ס"ח
5. רמב"ם הל' עדות פ"ג
6. רמב"ם הל' סנהדרין פי"ב
7. סנהדרין ט, ב. רמב"ם הל' עדות פי"ב ה"ב
8. רדב"ז לרמב"ם פי"ח מהל' סנהדרין ה"ו
9. רמב"ן דברים יט, יט
10. סנהדרין לז, ב
11. מכות ז, א
12. סנהדרין נב, ב ובכ"מ
13. סנהדרין מט, ב
14. משנה פ"א דסנהדרין
15. סנהדרין נב, ב
16. משנה מכות ז, א
17. משנה סנהדרין לב, א
18. כתובות פז, ב
19. משנה סנהדרין לב, א
20. משנה סנהדרין לז, א
21. רמב"ם הל' סנהדרין פי"א ה"א
22. משנה סנהדרין לז, א
23. רמב"ם הל' סנהדרין פי"ב ה"ד
24. רמב"ם הל' סנהדרין פט"ו הי"ג
25. משנה סנהדרין מה, א. ומבואר כ"ז ברמב"ם הל' סנהדרין פי"ח מהל' סנהדרין ה"א
26. רמב"ם הל' סנהדרין פט"ו הי"י
27. רמב"ם הל' סנהדרין פי"ד ה"א
28. ויקרא כד, י-כג. יהושע פ"ז. מלכים א' יב, יח. מלכים א' פכ"א. דברי הימים ב' כג, כ-כא.
29. משנה סנהדרין נב, א
30. רמב"ם הל' סנהדרין פט"ו הי"א
31. רמב"ם הל' סנהדרין פי"ד ה"א
32. משנה סנהדרין נב, ב
33. רמב"ם הל' סנהדרין פט"ו הי"ב
34. רמב"ם הל' סנהדרין פט"ו ה"ה
35. רמב"ם הל' סנהדרין פט"ו הי"ג
36. ברייתא סנהדרין נב, ב
37. ראה ריקאנטי בראשית יז, יד ליתר ביאור
38. מו"ק כח, א
39. רש"י ויקרא יז, ט ד"ה ונכרת. ועי' שבת כה, א ד"ה וכרת, חולין לא, א ד"ה טמא ובכ"מ
40. שבת כה, א ד"ה כרת
41. רמב"ם הל' תשובה פ"ח ה"א
42. רמב"ן עה"ת ויקרא יח, כט
43. עי' ספר כללי המצוות שם ערך "כרת"
44. שערי תשובה לר' יונה שער ג'
45. מכות יג, ב "חייבי מיתת ב"ד... אם עשו תשובה אין ב"ד של מטה מוחלין בהן"
46. תוס' כתובות ל, ב ד"ה מיום
47. רמב"ם הל' סנהדרין פט"ז ה"א ע"פ כס"מ שם
48. מכות י, א
49. ספרי שופטים יט, טו "למכות מנין...". רמב"ם ריש פט"ז מהל' סנהדרין
50. סנהדרין מא, א
51. רמב"ם הל' סנהדרין פט"ז ה"ד
52. משנה מכות כב, א
53. משנה מכות כב, א
54. משנה מכות כב, ב
55. מבואר במכות טז, א
56. מכות יג, ב
57. מכות טז, א
58. משנה מכות יז, א
59. סנהדרין סג, א
60. תמורה ה, א
61. רמב"ם הל' סנהדרין פי"ח ה"ב
62. ראה כ"ז בשו"ת רשב"ש סי' תר"י
63. רמב"ם הל' שגגות פ"א ה"א
64. שערי תשובה לר' יונה שער ד'
65. רמב"ן ויקרא ה, ב
67. רמב"ן עה"ת ויקרא א, ט
68. רמב"ם הל' שגגות פ"א ה"ד
69. משנה ריש מס' כריתות
70. רמב"ם הל' שגגות פ"א ה"ד ע"פ לרשימה מפורטת
71. כריתות ז, א
72. כריתות ג, א
73. משנה כריתות כה, א
74. משנה זבחים נג, א
75. משנה זבחים נג, א ומפורט ברמב"ם הל' שגגות פ"ט ה"א
76. משנה כריתות י, א
77. משנה כריתות י, א ומפורט ברמב"ם הל' שגגות פ"י ה"א
78. משנה הוריות ח, א
79. משנה הוריות ט, א
80. משנה הוריות ד, א
81. הל' גניבה פ"א ה"ב
82. סוגיא בכתובות לא-לה
83. רמב"ם הל' סנהדרין פ"ה ה"ח-ט'
84. משנה ב"ק טז, ז ומבואר בגמ' שם טו, ב-טז, ב
85. שבועות מט, א
86. משנה ב"ק מא, א
87. משנה ב"ק מ, א
88. ע"פ מגיד משנה פ"ה מהל' גזילה ואבידה הי"ג "ודע"
89. ב"ק סז, ב
90. משנה ב"ק קח, א
91. ב"ק סז, א
92. ב"ק קג, ב
93. שבועות לו, ב וברמב"ם פ"ז מהל' גזילה ואבידה ה"ב "זה הכלל"
94. משנה ב"ק פג, ב
95. משנה ב"ק פג, ב ובגמ' פה, ב שם. ויתר מבואר ברמב"ם פ"ב מהל' חובל ומזיק
96. משנה ב"ק כו, א
97. משנה גיטין נב, ב
98. דברים כז, כו
99. שערי תשובה לר' יונה שער ג'
100. ראה ריש מס' פאה "אלו דברים שאדם אוכל פירותיהן בעוה"ז והקרן קיימת לו לעוה"ב" הרי מפורש ענין זה
101. תניא פ"א דאגה"ת
102. יבמות ח, א ובכ"מ
103. ראה כ"ז בארוכה ספר "כללי המצוות" ערך "בטל" שמביא כל הדברים הנ"ל, ע"ש

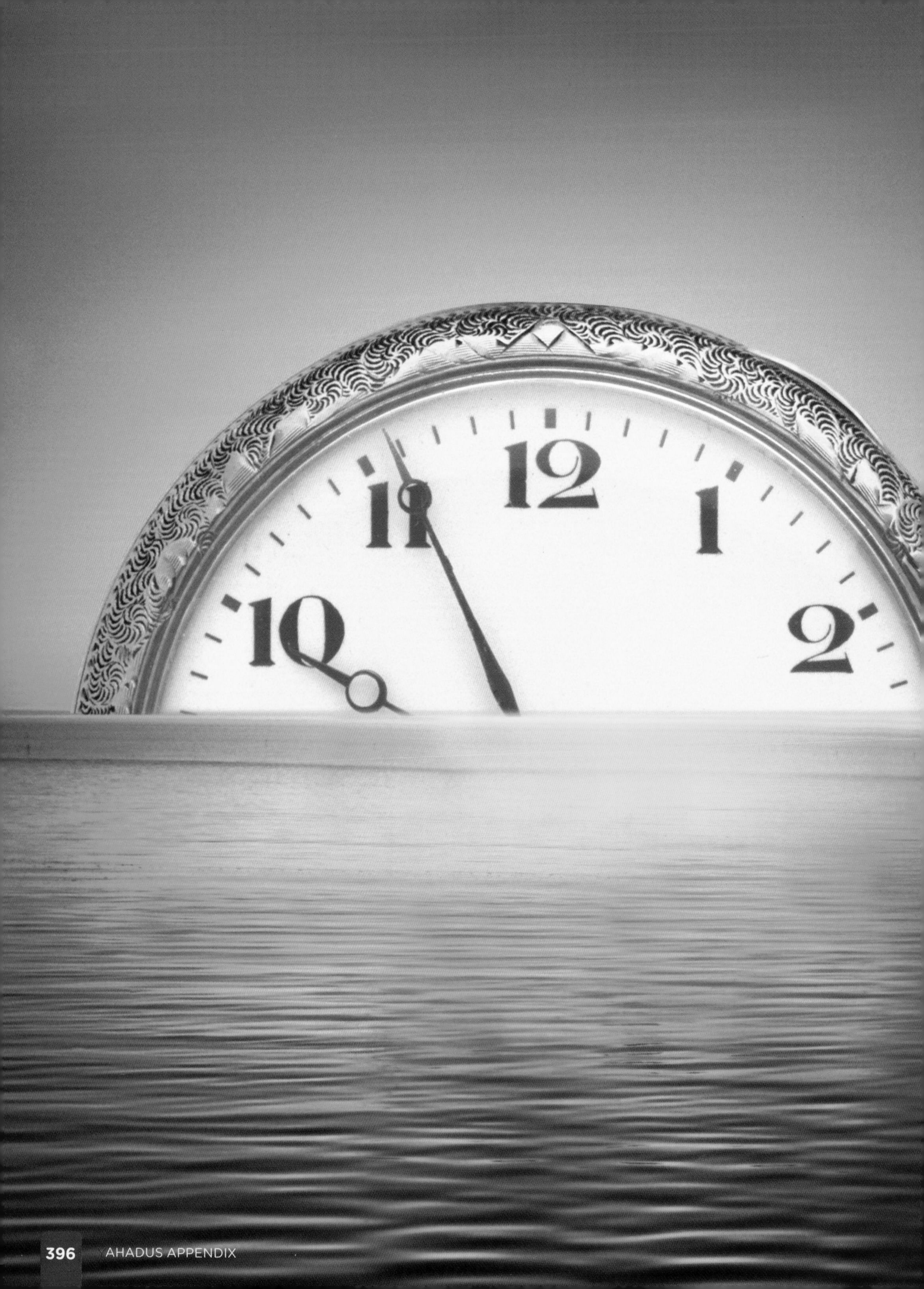

12
1
2
10
11

ZMANIM
TIMES IN HALACHAH

ZMANIM • CONTENTS

ZMANIM - TIMES IN HALACHAH

Many mitzvos must be performed at specific times during the day or night. The calculation of these *halachic* times, known as *zmanim*, depends on many things. Some of these things are: when sunrise and sunset occur, the amount of time between them, and how far north or south the sun is on the eastern horizon before rising.

This appendix will explain the more common *zmanim* and which mitzvos they are connected to.

SEASONAL HOUR

שָׁעָה זְמַנִית - Seasonal Hour

A *sha'ah zmanis* is 1/12 of the daylight hours. That means, if for example, sunrise is at 6:00 a.m. and sunset is at 6:00 p.m., there are 720 minutes of daylight which means that each *sha'ah zmanis* will be exactly 60 minutes (720 ÷ 12 = 60). However, on a long summer day, for example, if sunrise is at 5:00 a.m. and sunset is at 8:00 p.m., there are 900 minutes of daylight. This means that each *sha'ah zmanis* will be 75 minutes (900 ÷ 12 = 75).

Since the length of an hour in *halachah* changes depending on the season of the year, it is called a *sha'ah zmanis* - a seasonal hour.

For most *zmanim*, the time is measured using a *sha'ah zmanis*. When a certain mitzvah must be performed "three hours into the day" for example, this doesn't mean at 3:00 a.m. or three clock-hours after sunrise. It means three *sha'os zmaniyos* into the day.

DAYTIME ZMANIM

עֲלוֹת הַשַּׁחַר - Dawn

Alos hashachar - when the light of the sun starts to be visible - marks the beginning of the day. Any mitzvah that must be performed during the daytime - such as hearing the *shofar*,[1] taking the *lulav* and *esrog*,[2] saying *Shema*,[3] and hearing the *Megillah*[4] - can now be done. Fasts also begin at this time.[5]

For various reasons, however, the *Chachamim* instituted that many of these mitzvos should be delayed until *netz hachamah* or a later *zman* (see further).

According to some opinions, the daylight hours used to calculate *sha'os zmaniyos* begin at *alos hashachar*.[6]

מַשֶּׁיַּכִּיר - When One Can Recognize

The earliest time to put on *tefillin* is "when one can recognize a familiar acquaintance" from a distance of four *amos*.[7] This is approximately one hour before *netz hachamah*.[8] This is also the earliest time one can say *Shema* in the morning.[9]

With regards to *tzitzis*, the time given is "when one can recognize between *techeiles* (a light blue color) and white."[10] Some opinions say that this is a bit earlier than the above time for *tefillin* and *Shema*, and most major *poskim* say that it is the same as the time for *tefillin* and *Shema*.[11]

נֵץ הַחַמָּה - Sunrise

Netz hachamah is about an hour after *alos hashachar*,[12] when the top of the sun is visible over the horizon.[13]

According to many opinions, the daylight hours used to calculate *sha'os zmaniyos* begin at *netz hachamah*.[14]

Those who wish to *daven* "*vasikin*" (a custom of *davening* at the earliest opportunity), start saying *Shemoneh Esrei* at this time.[15]

סוֹף זְמַן קְרִיאַת שְׁמַע - Latest Time For *Shema*

The latest time of the day to fulfill the mitzvah to say the *Shema* in the morning is three *sha'os zmaniyos* into the day.[16] If this time was missed, one should still say *shema* with its *brachos* until *sof zman tefillah*, and without its *brachos* until *chatzos*.

סוֹף זְמַן תְּפִילָה - Latest Time For *Tefillah*

Ideally, the latest time to say the *shemoneh esrei* of *shacharis* is four *sha'os zmaniyos* into the day.[17] If this time was missed, the *Shemoneh Esrei* of *shacharis* may be said until *chatzos*.[18]

This is also the latest time for the *brachos* of *shema*,[19] and the latest time for eating *chametz* on *erev Pesach* (*miderabanan*).[20]

סוֹף זְמַן חָמֵץ - Latest Time For Benefitting From *Chametz* On *Erev Pesach*

Min Hatorah, one can have benefit from *chametz* on *erev Pesach* until *chatzos*. To avoid any mistakes, the *chachamim* made the time earlier by one *sha'ah zmanis*, and said that one may benefit from *chametz* only until five *sha'os zmaniyos* into the day.[21]

חֲצוֹת - Midday

Chatzos is six *sha'os zmaniyos* into the day, which is exactly half way between sunrise and sunset. At *chatzos* the sun is at its highest point in the sky for that day.[22]

Many things in *halachah* are dependent on *chatzos*, such as all the things one is not supposed to do "close to *minchah gedolah*" until one *davens minchah*[23] (e.g. not taking a haircut) start at *chatzos*.[24]

Half-day fasts end at *chatzos*.[25]

מִנְחָה גְדוֹלָה

The earliest time one may *daven minchah* is half an hour after *chatzos*. This is called *minchah gedolah*.[26]

This is also the time when field-workers should stop working on *erev Shabbos*,[27] and when one can start eating *seudah shlishis* on *Shabbos*.[28]

מִנְחָה קְטַנָה

Minchah ketanah is nine and a half *sha'os zmaniyos* hours after sunrise. According to some opinions, it is preferable to wait until this time to *daven minchah*.[29]

This is the time (according to many opinions) about which the *Gemara* says "one who conducts business after *minchah* on *erev Shabbos* will not see blessing."[30]

פְּלַג הַמִּנְחָה

Plag Haminchah is "Half of *minchah*," i.e. half way between *minchah ketanah* and nightfall which is one and a quarter *sha'os zmaniyos* before sunset.

According to R'Yehudah this is the latest time one may *daven minchah*.[31] If one follows this opinion, he must *daven minchah* before *plag haminchah*.[32]

This is also the earliest one may bring in *Shabbos* on Friday afternoon.[34]

זְמַן הַדְלָקַת נֵרוֹת - Candle Lighting Time

The *Gemara*[35] classifies this time as "when the sun dips beneath the trees." The most commonly accepted custom is to light *Shabbos* and *Yom Tov* candles 18 minutes before *shkiah*. Some communities have adopted earlier times for candle lighting time. This is also the time to *daven neilah* on *Yom Kippur*.[36]

שְׁקִיעָה - Sunset

Shkiah is when the last part of the sun dips below the horizon.[37] *Shkiah* is the latest time for *minchah,* and for all mitzvos which need to be performed during the daytime.

If this time was missed, one may still *daven minchah,* and do all "daytime" mitzvos until *tzeis hakochavim* without saying the *brachah* on the mitzvah.[38]

בֵּין הַשְּׁמָשׁוֹת - Between The Days

The exact time of nightfall is unclear. It may be as early as *shkiah*, or as late as *tzeis hakochavim*. The time between *shkiah* and *tzeis hakochavim* is called *bein hashmashos* - between the days, and is sometimes considered as part of the previous day, and sometimes as part of the next day.[39]

NIGHTTIME ZMANIM

צֵאת הַכּוֹכָבִים - When The Stars Come Out

Tzeis hakochavim is the time when three average sized stars are visible in the sky. *Tzeis hakochavim* is the earliest time to fulfill any mitzvah that must be performed during the nighttime, such as saying *Shema* in the evening,[40] and counting the *Omer*.[41] *Tzeis hakochavim* is also the earliest time for *Ma'ariv* according to most opinions.[42]

Fast Ending

There are different opinions about how to calculate when *tzeis hakochavim* takes place. Out of consideration for people's comfort, for the fast days which are *miderabanan*, (all except for *Yom Kippur*,[43]) some people rely on a slightly earlier opinion concerning the end of fast days.[44]

יְצִיאַת הַשַּׁבָּת - The End of *Shabbos*

There are different opinions about how to calculate when *tzeis hakochavim* takes place. A stricter calculation of *tzeis hakochavim* is used to decide when *Shabbos* and *Yom Tov* ends. This ensures that we do not accidentally do *melachah* while it is still *assur*, and that we fulfill the obligation to add time from a weekday onto the *Shabbos* and *Yom Tov*.[45]

חֲצוֹת לַיְלָה - Midnight

Chatzos laylah is the same time as *chatzos*, but in the night. For example if *chatzos* is 12:30 p.m. then *chatzos laylah* is 12:30 a.m.

Preferably, one should say *Shema* at night before *chatzos laylah*,[46] as well as eat the *afikoman* before this time.[47]

SHIURIM
MEASUREMENTS IN HALACHAH

SHIURIM • CONTENTS

INTRODUCTION

There are many different types of measurements in *halachah*. These measurements are very important, as many different *halachos* revolve around them.

From The Torah or From the *Chachamim*?

The *Gemara* discusses whether the *shiurim* are from the Torah or the *Chachamim*, and concludes that they are *Halachah L'Moshe Misinai* - meaning that Hashem told them to *Moshe Rabbeinu* on *Har Sinai*.[48]

Less Than The *Shiur*

One would not be punished if an *aveirah* was performed with less than the required *shiur*. Being that the Torah does not punish for less than a certain amount, does that mean the one is **allowed** to do it?

The *halachah* is that חֲצִי שִׁיעוּר אָסוּר מִדְאוֹרַיְיתָא - half a *shiur* is forbidden from the Torah.

For example, one is not allowed to eat **any** *chametz* on *Pesach*, because less than the *shiur* is also forbidden from the Torah. However one only receives the **punishment** for eating the *shiur* of a *kezayis*.[49]

Less than the *shiur* of an *issur derabanan* is also forbidden, because the *Rabanan* made their rules similar to those of the Torah.[50]

Types of Measurements

In general, there are five different types of *shiurim*:

- **Volume** - for measuring foods and liquids. For example: forbidden foods, *mikvah* and *netilas yadayim*.

- **Distance** - for measuring lengths and distances. For example, the dimensions of a *sukkah*, *techum Shabbos* and distancing plants to avoid *kilayim*.

- **Area** - For measuring spaces. For example, the size of a field for the laws of *peah* and *leket*.

- **Time** - for measuring a length of time. For example, making calculations for *kiddush hachodesh*.

- **Weight/Currency** - for measuring money and spices. For example, sums of money for a *kesubah* and *pidyon haben*, and the weight of the ingredients for the *ketores*.

There are different opinions what each of the *shiurim* are in today's modern measurements. Here the two main opinions are presented; the first (smaller) size is that of R' Avraham Chaim Na'eh, and the second (larger) size is that of R' Avraham Yeshaya Karelitz, commonly known as the "*Chazon Ish*."

All oz., fl. oz. and gallons are **U.S. measurements.**

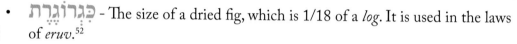

VOLUME

These are the more common *shiurim*.

- קוֹרְטוֹב - 1/64 of a *log*. It is used in the laws of a *mikvah*.[51]
  0.18 fl. oz./5.32 ml. ←→ .32 fl. oz./9.46 ml.

- כְּגְרוֹגֶרֶת - The size of a dried fig, which is 1/18 of a *log*. It is used in the laws of *eruv*.[52]
  0.65 fl. oz./19.2 cm³ ←→ 1.14 fl. oz./33.71 cm³

- כְּזַיִת - The size of an olive, which is 1/12 of a *log*. It is used in many laws, such as the laws of eating (e.g. the amount of "eating" to require *birkas hamazon* is one *kezayis*).[53]
  0.97 fl. oz./28.69 cm³ ←→ 1.68 fl. oz./49.68 cm³

- עוּכְלָא - 1/8 of a *log*, (dry) or half a *revi'is* (liquid). It is used in the laws of honest weights.[54]
  1.46 fl. oz./43.2 ml. ←→ 2.52 fl. oz./74.53 ml.

- כְּבֵיצָה - The size of an egg, which is 1/6 of a *log*. It is used to measure the average "meal" of a person, which is between 6-8 *beitzim*.[55]
  1.95 fl. oz./57.6 cm³ ←→ 3.37 fl. oz./99.66 cm³

- כְּכוֹתֶבֶת - The *shiur* of a *koseves* is the size of a large dried date, and is slightly smaller than a *k'beitzah*.

- רְבִיעִית - *Revi'is* means "a quarter," i.e. 1/4 of a *log*. It is used in many laws such as *netilas yadayim*[56] and *kiddush*.[57]
  2.92 fl. oz./86.4 ml. ←→ 5.3 fl. oz./156.74 ml.

- תּוֹמֶן - 1/2 a *log* (liquid) or 1/8 of a *kav* (dry). It is used in the laws of *eruv*.[58]
  5.84 fl. oz./172.8 ml. ←→ 10.1 fl. oz./298.69 ml.

- לוֹג/רוֹבַע - A *log* is a common liquid measurement which is 6 *beitzim*. *Rova* (quarter) is the same amount of something dry and is a quarter of a *kav*. It is used in the laws of *netilas yadayim*,[59] and in the laws of distancing plants to prevent *kilayim*.[60]

11.68 fl oz./345.6 ml. ←——→ **21.2 fl oz./626.96 ml.**

- קַב - A *kav* is the most basic dry unit from which the other units are derived. It is used in many laws, such as the laws of finding lost objects.[61]

  46.74 fl. oz./1382 cm³ ←——→ **.66 gallons/2389 cm³**

- עוֹמֶר/עִשָּׂרוֹן - 1/10 of an *eiphah*. It is used in the laws of making dough.[62]

  .66 gallons/2488 cm³ ←——→ **1.14 gallons/4300 cm³**

- תַּרְקָב/הִין - *Tarkav* is a dry measurement and comes from *"trei v'kav"* which means "two and a *kav*," i.e. 3 *kav*. *Hin* is the same amount in liquid. It is used in the laws of honest weights.[63]

  1.1 gallons/4.15 L. ←——→ **1.89 gallons/7.15 L.**

- סְאָה - 1/3 of an *eiphah* (or 6 *kav*). It is used in the *shiur* of 40 *se'ah* for a *mikvah*.[64]

  2.19 gallons/8.29L. ←——→ **3.79 gallons/14.34 L.**

- אֵיפָה/בַּת - 1/10 of a *kor* (or 3 *se'ah*). *Eiphah* is the dry measurement, and *Bas* is the same amount in liquid. It is used in the laws of a *kohen* starting his service in the *Beis Hamikdash*.[65]

  6.57 gallons/24.88 L. ←——→ **12 gallons/45.42 L.**

- לֶתֶךְ - 1/2 a *kor*. It is used in the laws of selling property.[66]

  32.87 gallons/124.41 L. ←——→ **60 gallons/227.12 L.**

- כּוֹר - 30 *se'ah*. It is used in the laws of selling property.[67]

  65.73 gallons/248830 cm³ ←——→ **120 gallons/454240 cm³**

The Formula For Dry Measurements

6 *Beitzim* = **1** *Log*	**6** *Kavin* = **1** *Se'ah*	**5** *Eiphos* = **1** *Lesech*
4 *Login* = **1** *Kav*	**3** *Se'in* = **1** *Eiphah*	**2** *Lesachin* = **1** *Kor*

The Formula For Liquid Measurements

12 *Login* = **1** *Hin*   **6** *Hin* = **1** *Bas*

Modern-Day Measurements (Volume)

Measurement*	R. Avraham Chaim Na'eh		Chazon Ish	
Kortov	0.18 oz.	5.32 ml.	.32 oz.	9.46 ml.
Kigrogeres	0.65 oz.	19.22 cm³	1.14 oz.	33.71 cm³
Kezayis	0.97 oz.	28.69 cm³	1.68 oz.	49.68 cm³
Uchlah	1.46 oz.	43.2 ml.	2.52 oz.	74.53 ml.
Kebeitzah	1.95 oz.	57.6 cm³	3.37 oz.	99.66 cm³
Revi'is	2.92 oz.	86.4 ml.	5.3 oz.	156.74 ml.
Tomen	5.84 oz.	172.8 ml.	10.1 oz.	298.69 ml.
Log/Rova	11.68 oz.	345.6 ml.	21.2 oz.	626.96 ml.
Kav	46.74 oz.	1382 cm³	.66 gallons	2389 cm³
Omer/Isaron	.66 gallons	2488 cm³	1.14 gallons	4300 cm³
Tarkav/Hin	1.1 gallons	4.15 L.	1.89 gallons	7.15 L.
Se'ah	2.19 gallons	8.29 L.	3.79 gallons	14.34 L.
Eiphah/Bas	6.75 gallons	24.88 L.	12 gallons	45.42 L.
Lesech	32.87 gallons	124.41 L.	60 gallons	227.12 L.
Kor	65.73 gallons	248,830 cm³	120 gallons	454,240 cm³

*For koseves, consult your Rav

Rules

- Any measurement with regards to eating food is a *kezayis*. This includes *issurim* of eating, such as eating blood, non-kosher food etc. In order to receive the punishment, one must eat at least a *kezayis*.[68] It also applies to **mitzvos** associated with eating, such as eating *matzah*, saying *birkas hamazon*, and eating *korbanos*. In order to fulfill these mitzvos, one must eat at least a *kezayis*.

- There are two exceptions:
  1. Eating on *Yom Kippur*, for which the *shiur* to receive punishment is a *koseves*.

2. For *tamei* food to make other food *tamei* the first food must be at least one *beitzah*.[69]

• There are some things that do not involve eating, and are still measured with a *kezayis*. One example is the mitzvah of burning *chametz*; one need not burn *chametz* less than the size of a *kezayis*.[70]

• For mitzvos and *issurim* that a *shiur* is not specified, many opinions say that the *shiur* is a *kezayis*.[71]

• All mitzvos and *issurim* associated with drinking use the measurement of a *revi'is*.[72]

• Any mitzvah which is measured by a *kezayis*, the measure of the *revi'is* is applied when it comes to drinks. Meaning, if one drinks a *revi'is* of something which requires a *kezayis*, they would receive punishment. For example, drinking a *revi'is* of *chametz* is the same as eating a *kezayis* of *chametz*.[73]

DISTANCE

• אֶצְבַּע - The width of a thumb[74] or 1/4 of a *tefach*.
.79 inches/2 cm ⟷ **.91 inches/2.3 cm**

• טֶפַח - The width of a clenched fist or 1/6 of an *amah*.
3.15 inches/8 cm ⟷ **3.78 inches/9.6 cm**

• זֶרֶת - 1/2 an *amah*.
9.45 inches/24 cm ⟷ **11.34 inches/28.8 cm**

• אַמָה - The length from the elbow to the middle finger or 6 *tefachim*.
18.9 inches/48 cm ⟷ **22.7 inches/57.65 cm**

• רִיס - 2/15 of a *mil* or 1,600 *tefachim*.
140 yards/128 meters ⟷ **168 yards/153.6 meters**

• מִיל - 1/4 of a *parsah* or 2,000 *amos*.
.6 miles/.96 km ⟷ **.71 miles/1.14 km**

- **פַּרְסָה** - 1/10 of a *mehalech yom* or 4 *mil*

  2.39 miles/3.84 km ← → **2.9 miles/4.66 km**

- **מַהֲלַךְ יוֹם** - 10 *parsah* which is "a day's walk," beginning at dawn and ending at nightfall.

  23.86 miles/38.4 km ← → **29 miles/46.6 km**

The Formula For Distance Measurements

4 *Etzba'os* = **1** *Tefach*

6 *Tefachim* = **1** *Amah*

2,000 *Amos* = **1** *Mil*

4 *Mil* = **1** *Parsah*

10 *Parsa'os* = **1** *Mehalech Yom*

Modern-Day Measurements (Distance)

Measurement	R. Avraham Chaim Na'eh		Chazon Ish	
Etzba	.79 inches	2 cm	.91 inches	2.3 cm
Tefach	3.15 inches	8 cm	3.78 inches	9.6 cm
Zeres	9.45 inches	24 cm	11.34 inches	28.8 cm
Amah	18.9 inches	48 cm	22.7 inches	57.65 cm
Ris	140 yards	128 meters	168 yards	153.6 meters
Mil	.6 miles	.96 km	.71 miles	1.14 km
Parsah	2.39 miles	3.84 km	2.9 miles	4.66 km
Mahalach Yom	23.86 miles	38.4 km	29 miles	46.6 km

AREA

- עֲדָשָׁה - The area of a lentil, 1/9 of a *gris*, the area where 2 hairs squared can grow. It is used in the *halachos* of *tzara'as*.

- גְּרִיס - The area of a Cilician bean, the area where 26 hairs grow.[75] Approximately the size of an American dime.

- טֶפַח מְרוּבָּע - A square *tefach*.
  9.92 inches²/64 cm² $\longleftrightarrow$ 14.26 inches²/92 cm²

- אַמָּה מְרוּבָּע - A square *amah*.
  2.48 feet²/.23 meters² $\longleftrightarrow$ 3.5 feet²/.33 meters²

- בֵּית קַב - The area necessary to plant a *kav* of produce, 1/6 of a *beis se'ah*.
  114.8 yards²/96 meters² $\longleftrightarrow$ 165.3 yards²/138.24 meters²

- בֵּית סְאָה - The area necessary to plant a *se'ah* of produce, 50 x 50 *amos*. The area used extensively in the laws of *eruv* is a "*Beis Sa'asyim*," which is the double the area, 100 x 50 *amos*.
  .14 acres/576 meters² $\longleftrightarrow$ .2 acres/829.44 meters²

- בֵּית כּוֹר - The area necessary to plant the amount of one *kor* of produce, which is 30 times a *Beis Se'ah*; see "Volume" above.
  4.27 acres/1.73 hectares $\longleftrightarrow$ 6.13 acres/2.48 hectares

The Formula for Area Measurements

6 *Tefach²* = **1** *Amah Meruba*

8 1/3 *Amah²* = **1** *Beis Kav*

6 *Beis Kav²* = **1** *Beis Se'ah*

30 *Beis Sa'ah²* = **1** *Beis Kor*

Modern-Day Measurements (Area)

Measurement	R. Avraham Chaim Na'eh		Chazon Ish	
Tefach²	9.92 inches²	64 cm²	14.26 inches²	92 cm²
Amah²	2.48 feet²	.23 meters²	3.5 feet²	.33 meters²
Beis Kav	114.8 yards²	96 meters²	165.3 yards²	138.24 meters²
Beis Se'ah	.14 acres	576 meters²	.2 acres	829.44 meters²
Beis Kor	4.27 acres	1.73 hectares	6.13 acres	2.48 hectares

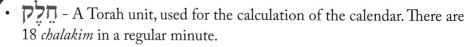

TIME

- חֵלֶק - A Torah unit, used for the calculation of the calendar. There are 18 *chalakim* in a regular minute.

- שָׁעָה - An hour. 1,080 *chalakim*.

- עוֹנָה - A "period" of night-time or day-time. Sometimes it refers to 12 hours, and sometimes it refers to the actual hours of daylight and darkness.

- יוֹם - A day, 24 hours (also referred to as "*Me'es le'es* - from time to time," referring to a full 24 hour period, as opposed to *yom* which can sometimes refer to daylight hours).

- שָׁבוּעַ - A week, 7 days.

- חוֹדֶשׁ - A lunar month on our calendar alternates between 29 and 30 days, since a lunar month is exactly 29 Days + 12 Hours + 793 *chalakim*.

- תְּקוּפָה - A "circuit," a quarter of the solar year.

- שְׁנַת הַלְבָנָה - A regular calendar lunar year (12 months) alternates between 353 - 355 days, and a calendar leap year (13 months) alternates between 383 - 385 days.

- שְׁנַת הַחַמָּה - A solar year, which has 365 ¼ days.

- שְׁמִיטָה - Seven years. A *yovel* is after a cycle of 7 *shemitos*.

- יוֹבֵל - Fifty years.

Other units include:

- הִילוּךְ מִיל - The time it takes to walk a *mil*, see "Length" above.

- כְּדֵי אֲכִילַת פְּרָס - The time it takes to eat half a loaf of bread.

- תּוֹךְ כְּדֵי דִיבּוּר - The time it takes to say שָׁלוֹם עָלֶיךָ רַבִּי וּמוֹרִי.

The Formula for Time Measurements

18 *Chalakim* = **1** *Minute*	**7** *Yamim* = **1** *Shavua*
60 *Minutes* = **1** *Sha'ah*	**4** *Tekufos* = **1** *Shnas Hachamah*
12 *Sha'os* = **1** *Onah*	**7** *Shanim* = **1** *Shemitah*
2 *Onos* = **1** *Yom*	**7** *Shemitos* plus one *shanah* = **1** *Yovel*

WEIGHT/CURRENCY

(The measurements here are according to the Rambam. Rashi has a slightly smaller *shiur*.)

- **פְּרוּטָה** - The weight/value of 1/8 of an *issar* or 0.03 grams of silver.

- **אִיסָר** - The weight/value of 1/2 a *pundyon* or 0.2 grams of silver.

- **פּוּנְדְיוֹן** - The value of 1/2 a *ma'ah* or 0.4 grams of silver.

- **מָעָה/גֵּרָה** - The weight/value of 1/3 of an *istera*, 0.8 grams.

- **אִיסְתְּרָא** - The weight/value of 1/2 a *dinar*, 2.4 grams.

- **דִּינָר/זוּז** - The weight/value of 1/2 a *shekel*, 4.8 grams.

- **שֶׁקֶל** - The weight/value of 1/2 a *selah*, 9.6 grams.

- **סֶלַע/שֶׁקֶל הַקוֹדֶשׁ** - The weight/value of 2 *shekalim*, or 1/25 of a *maneh*, 19.2 grams. This is also referred to as the "*Shekel Hakodesh*," which was used for the mitzvah of *machatzis hashekel*.

- **מָנֶה** - The weight/value of 25 *selaim*, 0.48 kg.

- **כִּכָּר** - The weight of 60 *maneh*, 27kg.

The Formula for Weights/Currency Measurements

8 *Perutos* = **1** *Issar*

2 *Issarin* = **1** *Pundyon*

2 *Pundyonos* = **1** *Ma'ah*

3 *Ma'im* = **1** *Istera*

2 *Istera* = **1** *Dinar*

2 *Dinarim* = **1** *Shekel*

2 *Shekalim* = **1** *Sela*

25 *Selaim* = **1** *Maneh*

60 *Manos* = **1** *Kikar*

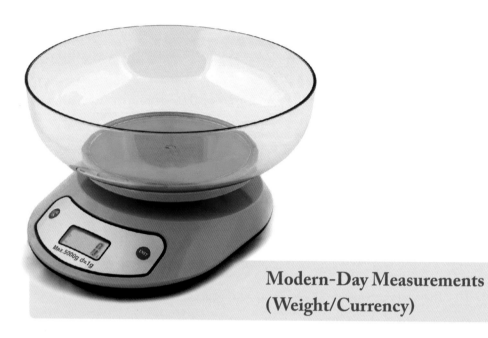

Modern-Day Measurements (Weight/Currency)

Measurement	Equivalent
Kikar	27 kg
Maneh	.48 kg
Sela/Shekel Hakodesh	19.2 grams
Shekel	9.6 grams
Dinar/Zuz	4.8 grams
Istera	2.4 grams
Ma'ah/Gera	.8 grams
Pundyon	Value of .4 grams of silver
Issar	Value of .2 grams of silver
Perutah	Value of .03 grams of silver

ZMANIM AND SHIURIM ENDNOTES:

1. שו"ע או"ח סי' תקפ"ח ס"א
2. שו"ע או"ח סי' תרנ"ב
3. שו"ע או"ח סי' נ"ח ס"א
4. שו"ע או"ח סי' תרפ"ז ס"א
5. שו"ע או"ח סי' תקפ"ד ס"א
6. מג"א סי' נ"ח סק"א
7. שו"ע או"ח סי' ל"ב ס"א
8. כף החיים סי' י"ח סקי"ח
9. שו"ע או"ח סי' נ"ח ס"א
10. שו"ע או"ח סי' י"ח ס"ג
11. עי' בב"י סי' נ"ח ד"ה ומ"ש מצוה מן המובחר השיטות בזה, ובמשנ"ב סי' נ"ח ס"ק ב'
12. שו"ע או"ח סי' נ"ח ס"א וברמ"א
13. ברכות כו, א. משנ"ב בביאור הלכה סי' נ"ח ד"ה כמו שיעור
14. סידור הרב ד"ה זמן ק"ש
15. שו"ע או"ח סי' נ"ח ס"א
16. שו"ע סי' נ"ח ס"א
17. שו"ע סי' פ"ט ס"א
18. שו"ע סי' פ"ט ס"א, ועי' במ"ב סק"ז, ועי' בש"ו הרב סי' פ"ט ס"ב שחולק עליו
19. שו"ע סי' נ"ח ס"ו
20. שו"ע סי' תמ"ג ס"א וברמ"א שם שהוא לפי חשבון שעות זמניות
21. שו"ע סי' תמ"ג ס"א וברמ"א שם שהוא לפי חשבון שעות זמניות
22. יומא כח, ב
23. שו"ע סי' רל"ב ס"ב, ע"ש לרשימה מלאה
24. משנ"ב שם סק"ז
25. עי' שו"ע סי' תקס"ב ס"י

26. שו"ע סי' רל"ג ס"א
27. מג"א סי' רנ"א סק"ד
28. שו"ע סי' רצ"א ס"ב
29. שו"ע סי' רל"ג ס"א
30. פסחים נ, ב ובשו"ע סי' רנ"א ס"א בדעה השני'
31. ברכות כו, ב
32. שו"ע סי' רל"ג ס"א
34. שו"ע סי' רס"ג ס"ב
35. שבת לה, ב
36. שו"ע סי' תרכ"ג ס"ב
37. ירושלמי ריש ברכות "אמר ר' חנינא סוף גלגל חמה לשקוע"
38. שו"ע סי' רל"ג ס"א וברמ"א
39. עי' טור או"ח סי' רס"א ובב"י שם ביאור פרטי ד"בין השמשות"
40. שו"ע סי' רל"ה ס"א
41. שו"ע סי' תפ"ט ס"א
42. ברכות כו, א
43. שו"ע סי' תרכ"ד ס"ב
44. רמ"א סי' תקס"ב ס"א
45. שו"ע סי' רצ"ג ס"ב
46. שו"ע סי' רל"ג ס"ג
47. שו"ע סי' תע"ז ס"ג
48. עירובין ה, ב ובכ"מ
49. ביאור מהרש"ל על הסמ"ג הל' חמץ לכל איסורים
50. שו"ת ריב"ש סי' רפ"ז, ובב"י יו"ד סי' ס"ח לענין דם מבושל
51. שו"ע יו"ד סי' ר"א סכ"ב
52. שו"ע או"ח סי' שס"ח ס"ג

53. שו"ע או"ח סי' קפ"ד ס"ו
54. שו"ע חו"מ סי' רל"א ס"ד ובביאור הגר"א שם סק"ב
55. שו"ע או"ח סי' שס"ח ס"ג
56. שו"ע או"ח סי' ק"ס סי"ג
57. שו"ע או"ח סי' רע"א סי"א
58. שו"ע או"ח סי' שפ"ו ס"ז (שיעור זה הוא לפי שיטת הרשב"ם ב"ב פט, ב.)
59. שו"ע ריש סי' קנ"ח ברמ"א
60. שו"ע יו"ד סי' רצ"ז סט"ז
61. שו"ע חו"מ סי' ר"ס ס"ז
62. שו"ע או"ח ריש סי' תנ"ו, וש"נ השיעור
63. שו"ע חו"מ סי' רל"א ס"ד
64. שו"ע יו"ד ריש סי' ר"א
65. רמב"ם הל' כלי המקדש פ"ה הט"ז, ועי' גם שו"ע הרב או"ח סי' תנ"ו ס"ה
66. שו"ע חו"מ סי' רי"ח סי'
67. שו"ע חו"מ ריש סי' רי"ח
68. עי' בברכות מא, א שנלמד (בדרך אסמכתא) מקרא "ארץ זית שמן ודבש" - "ארץ שרוב שיעוריה כזיתים"
69. כ"ז מבואר בגמ' יומא פ, א, וברמב"ם ריש פי"ד מהל' מאכ"א
70. מג"א סי' תמב ס"ק יב
71. מנ"ח מצוה ח' במותיר פסח ושאר קדשים
72. עי' אנציקלופדיה תלמודית ערך זית סוף פ"א
73. הרא"ה, הובא בר"ן חולין פ' גיד הנשה (לב,ב מדפי הרי"ף)
74. בכל שיעורים אלו של "אמה" "טפח" "אצבע" עי' ברמב"ם הל' ס"ת פ"ט ה"ט
75. נגעים פ"ו מ"א

THE BRACHAH AND HASKAMAH FROM

RAV SHMUEL KAMENETSKY

UPON HIS REVIEW OF BOOK 1 OF THE YAHADUS CURRICULUM

בס״ד.

שמואל קמנצקי
Rabbi S. Kamenetsky

2018 Upland Way
Philadelphia, Pa 19131

Home: 215-473-2798
Study: 215-473-1212

יום ה' פרשת בא שנת תשע"ז

לאנ"ש יחיו הנה מענין דאס ספרים הוו
כללות דניינין שצריכים לדעת
שמרו בהיר ואופן הקלו עליהם.
כדי צורר לרבות שם מבואיין חפצים דברי
סדר כל מינים שמלמדים לעורר הברק הנכון
דברי החינוך.
ונראה דבר שיש חלקים מתוך שילו שלא
ענינים של דורות הנ'. ולנו חיק הקפלה ראוי החינוך
חשובים ולזאת ראוי כפי דברי הטעמאנין ודבר היינו
של בתב שמקולות החיים ואפשר שראוי לחשוב העניין
דיונים שוני דבר פולל התנא שאליגיא לדבר להסביר הענ
נצבנ.
וכבר מתוקי, אף ללית דבר יכול את יודי כופן
פן זאת פעם ובו.

נאום
שמואל קמנצקי

ACKNOWLEDGEMENTS & CREDITS

Director: Rabbi Gershon Eichorn

Editor-in-Chief: Rabbi Zalman Glick

Educational Director: Rabbi S. Binyomin Ginsberg

Rabbinic Advisors: Rabbi Y. Zirkind, Rabbi L. Teitelbaum

Managing Editor: Rabbi Aharon Loschak

RESEARCHERS

Rabbi M. Alevsky

Rabbi R. Andrusier

Rabbi M. Blecher

Rabbi O. Broh

Rabbi L. Groner

Rabbi L. Itkin

Rabbi B. Jurcowicz

Rabbi E. Kazen

Rabbi M. Lipskier

Rabbi Y. Margolin

Rabbi M. Raicez

Rabbi P. Raitman

Rabbi L. Schectman

Rabbi Z. Simon

Rabbi C. M. Telsner

EDUCATIONAL CONSULTANTS

Rabbi M. Greenbaum

Rabbi A. Herman

Mrs. S. Rosenfeld

WRITERS

Mrs. R. Nerenberg

Ms. C. Serebryanski

EDITORS

Rabbi Nisson M. Vaisfiche

Mrs. R. Wechter

Ms. M. Weiss

DESIGN AND LAYOUT

SpotlightDesign.com

Rabbi Gershon Eichorn, *Art Director*

Zalman Friedman

Levi Groner

Levi Blumenfeld

Mrs. I. Wolvovsky

ILLUSTRATIONS

Yanki Gitlin

Zalman Kleinman

Nochum Nodel

Michoel Muchnik

Michel Schwartz

Published by LIVING LESSONS

1375 Coney Island Avenue #207 • Brooklyn, New York 11230

347-709-8660 • www.livinglessons.com